THE
HISTORY
OF
HERODOTUS

VOL. II.

AMS PRESS

NEW YORK

THE HISTORY

OF

HERODOTUS:

Tranſlated from the *Greek.*

By ISAAC LITTLEBURY.

VOL. II.

The THIRD EDITION.

LONDON:

Printed for D. MIDWINTER, A. BETTESWORTH and
C. HITCH, J. and J. PEMBERTON, R. WARE,
C. RIVINGTON, J. BATLEY and J. WOOD, F. CLAY,
A. WARD, J. and P. KNAPTON, T. LONGMAN, and
R. HETT.   M.DCC.XXXVII.

Library of Congress Cataloging in Publication Data

Herodotus.
    The history of Herodotus.

    Reprint of the 1737 3d ed. printed for
D. Midwinter et al., London.
    Includes index.
    1. History, Ancient. 2. Greece—History.
I. Littlebury, Isaac. II. Title.
D58.H4713   1976   930   76-49907
ISBN 0-404-54140-2

Reprinted from the edition of 1737, London
First AMS edition published in 1976
Manufactured in the United States of America

International Standard Book Number:
Complete Set: 0-404-54140-2
Volume II: 0-404-54142-9

AMS PRESS INC.
NEW YORK, N.Y.

THE

Hiſtory of *Herodotus*.

BOOK V.

TERPSICHORE.

 HE Perſians, left in *Europe* under the Orders of *Megabyzus*, ſubdued the Perinthians firſt of all the Helleſpontins, for refuſing to ſubmit to *Darius*, tho' they had before been conſiderably weaken'd by the Pæonians. For the Pæonians, who inhabit upon the River *Strymon*, had been admoniſh'd by an Oracle to invade the Perinthians ; and if they ſhould draw out their Forces, and with Clamours provoke the Pæonians by Name to fight, then to engage ; otherwiſe not. The Pæonians did as they were inſtructed : And the Perinthians marching out, encamp'd before their City. Upon which a Challenge enſued, and three ſingle Combats were fought: The firſt, of two Men ; the fecond, of two Horfes; and the third, of two Dogs. The Perinthians already victorious in two of thefe Duels, were fo full of Joy that they began to fing the Song of Triumph: When the Pæonians recollecting the Anfwer of the Oracle, faid among themfelves, " The " Prediction is now accomplifh'd : Our Work " is next : " And immediately falling upon the Perinthians as they were finging, gave them fo great a Blow, that few efcap'd out of the Field. In this manner the Perinthians were defeated by the Pæonians: But againft *Megabyzus* they behav'd themfelves with the Valour that becomes Men fighting for Liberty ; and were opprefs'd only by the Numbers of the Perfians. After the taking of *Perinthus*, *Megabyzus* advanc'd with his Army, and reduc'd all the Cities and Nations of *Thrace* to the Obedience of the King. For *Darius* had commanded him to fubdue the Thracians. This Nation is the greateft of any among Men, except the Indians : And in my Opinion, if the Thracians were either under the Government of one Perfon, or unanimous in their Counfels, they would be invincible, and the ftrongeft People of the World. But becaufe this is extremely difficult, or rather impoffible, they are of little Strength. They go under feveral Names according to the Places they inhabit; but all obferve the fame Cuftoms, except the Getes, the Traufes, and the Creftoneans, who are feated in the uppermoft Parts. I have already fpoken of the Cuftoms of the Getes relating to Immortality. The Traufes differ in nothing from the reft of the Thracians, except in the Manners obferv'd at the Times of their

3   Nativity

Nativity and Death. When a Child is born, his Relations fitting in a Circle about him, deplore his Condition, on account of the Evils he muſt ſuffer in the Courſe of Life; enumerating the various Calamities incident to Mankind. But when a Man is dead, they inter him with Exultation and Rejoicings, repeating the Miſeries he has exchang'd for a compleat Felicity. Among the Creſtoneans who inhabit the higheſt Part of *Thrace*, every Man has many Wives; and at his Death all theſe Women, ſtrongly ſupported by their ſeveral Friends, contend fiercely, who ſhall be accounted to have been moſt dear to the Husband. In the end, ſhe who is adjudg'd to have merited that Honour, having receiv'd great Commendations both from the Men and Women, is kill'd upon the grave by the neareſt of her Relations, and buried together with the Man: Which is a great Mortification to the reſt, becauſe accounted the utmoſt Diſgrace. The reſt of the Thracians ſell their Children for Tranſportation: and take no care of their Daughters; but ſuffer them to entertain as many Men as they like. Nevertheleſs they keep their Wives under a ſtrict Guard, and purchaſe them of their Relations at a great Rate. To be mark'd on the Forehead is honourable; and a Man without ſuch Marks is accounted ignoble. Idleneſs is eſteem'd decent; Husbandry unbecoming; and to ſubſiſt by War and Rapine is thought glorious. Theſe are the moſt conſiderable Cuſtoms of this Nation. For their Gods, they worſhip only *Mars*, *Bacchus* and *Diana*. But their Kings, beſides the national Deities, adore *Hermes* with great Religion;

ſwearing

swearing by his Name alone, and pretending
to be defcended from him. The Funerals of
eminent Perfons are celebrated in this manner.
They expofe the Corps to publick View du-
ring three Days; and after they have perform'd
their Lamentations, they facrifice all kinds of
Animals, and apply themfelves to feafting.
Then they either burn, or bury the Body in the
Ground: And having thrown up a Mound of
Earth over the Grave, celebrate all manner of
Agoniftical Exercifes round the Place; appointing the greateft Prizes for thofe who fight
fingle Combats. And fuch are their funeral
Rites. Concerning the Northern Parts of this
Region, no Man can certainly affirm by what
People they are poffefs'd. But thofe beyond
the *Danube* are wild and impracticable; inhabited by no other Men, that I have heard of,
but the Sigynes, who wear the Median Habit,
and have Horfes cover'd over with Hair, like
Briftles five Digits long; low of Stature, unable to carry a Rider, and having fhort Nofes
turning upward: Yet they draw a Chariot with
Swiftnefs and the Inhabitants ufe them to that
end. Next adjoining to thefe, are the Henetes,
who dwell in *Adria*, and fay they are a Colony
of the Medes. But by what means that Colony
came thither, I cannot affirm; tho' nothing
be impoffible to happen in length of Time.
The Ligurians, who inhabit beyond *Marfeilles*,
call the Sigynes, Brokers; and the Cyprians
give them the Name of Javelins. The Thracians fay, that the Parts which lie beyond the
Danube are full of Bees, and on that account
impaffable. But I think their Affertion carries
no Appearance of Truth; becaufe that Animal
cannot

cannot endure the Cold; and I am inclin'd to
believe that the excessive Frost of the Northern Climates, are the only Cause why those
Countries are uninhabited. But I have said
enough concerning these Parts: Of which *Megabyzus* reduc'd all the maritim Places to the
Obedience of *Darius.*

NO sooner was *Darius* arriv'd at *Sardis,*
after he had repass'd the *Hellespont,* than remem-
bering the good Offices of *Histiæus* the Milesian,
and the Counsel of *Coes* of *Mitylene,* he sent for
both those Persons, and gave them the Choice
of their Recompence. *Histiæus* being already
Tyrant of *Miletus,* demanded no other Dominion; and only desir'd the Edonian *Myrcinus,* in
order to build a City there. But *Coes,* who was
a private Man, and possess'd of no Government demanded the Dominion of *Mitylene.*
They easily obtain'd all they desir'd, and then
departed to take Possession. About the same
time, by means of a certain Accident, *Darius*
took a Resolution to command *Megabyzus* to
transplant the Pæonians out of *Europe* into *Asia.*
For *Pigres* and *Mastyes,* two Pæonians, being
desirous to become Masters of *Pæonia,* came
to *Sardis* after the Return of *Darius,* accompanied by their Sister, who was a tall and beautiful Person: And observing *Darius* one Day
sitting in the Suburbs of the Lydians, they
dress'd their Sister in the best manner they
could, and sent her down to the River; carrying a Pitcher on her Head, leading a Horse by
a Bridle hanging upon her Arm, and at the
same time spinning a Thred from her Distaff.
Darius looking upon the Maid with Attention
as she pass'd by; because her manner was alto-

A 3
gether

gether different from the Cuftoms, not only of the Perfian and Lydian Women, but of any other in *Afia*, order'd fome of his Guards to obferve what fhe would do with the Horfe. The Guards follow'd her, and found that when fhe came down to the River, fhe water'd the Horfe, and having fill'd her Pitcher, return'd again by the fame way ; carrying the Water on her Head, leading her Horfe, and fpinning, as fhe had done before. *Darius* no lefs furpriz'd with the Account they gave, than with what he himfelf had feen, commanded her to be brought into his Prefence: Where fhe was no fooner intro-duc'd, than her Brothers, who had obferv'd all that pafs'd, appear'd likewife ; and when *Darius* ask'd who fhe was, the young Men made an-fwer, that they were Pæonians, and that the Maid was their Sifter. The King proceeding to enquire, what fort of Men the Pæonians were ; in what Part of the World they liv'd ; and upon what Motive they themfelves came to *Sardis* ; receiv'd for Anfwer, that they came to put themfelves under his Protection ; that *Pæ-onia* is fituate upon the River *Strymon*, not far from the *Hellefpont* ; and that the People are a Colony of Teucrians, from the City of *Troy*. When they had given Account of thefe Particu-lars, *Darius* farther demanded, if all the Wo-men of that Country were as induftrious as their Sifter: And the Pæonians, who had contriv'd the whole Defign to no other End, readily an-wer'd, they were. Upon which a Meffenger was difpatch'd on Horfeback, with Letters from the King to *Megabyzus*, General of his Forces in *Thrace* ; requiring him to compel the Pæonians to leave their Country, and pafs into

Afia

Asia with their Wives and Children. The Courier perform'd his Journey with great Expedition; pass'd the *Hellespont*, and deliver'd the Letters to *Megabyzus*: Who after he had read the Contents, taking Guides in *Thrace*, led his Army towards *Pæonia*. When the Pæonians heard that the Persians were coming to invade them, they drew all their Forces towards the Sea, thinking the Persians would attempt to enter that Way; and prepar'd to dispute their Passage. But *Megabyzus*, understanding that the whole Strength of *Pæonia* was in a readiness to receive him on that Side, took his Way, by the Direction of his Guides, towards the upper Part of the Country: And concealing his March from the Enemy, fell in upon their Cities empty of Men, and easily possess'd himself of all. The Pæonians no sooner heard that their Cities were surpriz'd, than they dispers'd themselves; and every Man returning home, the whole Country submitted to the Persians. And in this Manner all those Pæonians, who were known by the Names of Seiropæonians and Pæoplians together with the People of those Parts that descend towards the Lake of *Prasias*, were expell'd from their antient Seats, and transported into *Asia*. But neither the Inhabitants of Mount *Pangæus*; nor the Doberes, Agrians, or Odomantes; nor those next adjoining to the Lake, were at that time conquer'd by *Megabyzus*. Yet he attempted to subdue a People, who lived upon the Lake in Dwellings contriv'd after this Manner: They drive down long Piles in the Middle of the Lake and cover them with Planks; which being join'd by a narrow Bridge to the Land, is the only Way

A   that

that leads to their Habitations. Thefe Piles
were formerly put down at the common Charge ;
but afterwards they made a Law, to oblige all
Men, for every Wife they fhould marry, to
fix three of them in the Lake, and to cut the
Timber upon Mount *Orbelus.* On thefe Planks
every Man has a Hut, with the Door opening
thro' the Floor, down to the Water. They tie
a String about the Foot of their young Children, left they fhould fall into the Lake ; and
feed their Horfes and other labouring Cattle
with Fifh ; which abound fo much there, that
when they let down an empty Bafket by a
Cord thro' the Aperture of the Door, they
draw it up again in a fhort time, fill'd with two
Sorts of Fifh, call'd *Papraces* and *Tilones.*

AFTER *Megabyzus* had taken the Cities
of the Pæonians, he difpatch'd feven of the
principal Perfians in his Army to *Macedonia,*
with Orders to require *Amyntas* to acknowledge
King *Darius* by a Prefent of Earth and Water.
Macedonia is not far diftant from the Lake of
Prafias. For, paffing by a Mine, which is
near the Lake, and afterwards yielded a Talent of Silver every Day to *Alexander,* Men
afcend the Mountain *Dyforus* ; and on the other
Side, at the Foot of the Hill, enter into the
Territories of *Macedonia.* When the Perfians
were arriv'd, they went to *Amyntas,* and demanded Earth and Water in the name of *Darius. Amyntas* not only gave them what they
requir'd, but receiv'd them for his Guefts ; and
having prepar'd a magnificent Feaft, entertain'd
them with great Humanity. But as the Perfians were beginning to drink after Supper,
" *Macedonian* Friend, faid they, When we

" make

" make a great Feaſt in *Perſia*, our manner is,
" to bring in our Concubines and young Wo-
" men to the Company: And therefore, ſince
" you have receiv'd us ſo affectionately ; treat-
" ed us with ſuch Magnificence ; and own'd
" King *Darius* by the Delivery of Earth and
" Water, we invite you to imitate our Cuſtom."
Amyntas anſwered, " The Manner of our Coun-
" try is quite different ; for we keep our Wo-
" men ſeparated from Men : Nevertheleſs, be-
" cauſe you are our Maſters, and require
" their Attendance, we will do as you deſire."
Having finiſh'd theſe Words, he ſent for the
Women ; who coming in as they were order'd,
plac'd themſelves on the other Side of the Table oppoſite to the Perſians. But when they
ſaw the Women were very beautiful, the Perſians told *Amyntas* that they were not plac'd
with Diſcretion ; and that he would have done
better not to ſend for them at all, than to let
them ſit at that Diſtance, only to offend their
Eyes. Upon this *Amyntas*, compell'd by neceſſity, order'd the Women to ſit down among
the Men : Which when they had done, the Perſians, full of Wine, began to handle their
Breaſts ; and ſome would have proceeded to
Kiſſes. Theſe Actions *Amyntas* ſaw with Indignation ; yet ſeemed unconcern'd, becauſe
he was afraid of the Perſian Power. But his
Son *Alexander*, who was preſent, and obſerv'd
the ſame things, being a young Man and unacquainted with Adverſity, was no longer able
to endure their Inſolence ; and therefore ſaid to
Amyntas : " Father, conſider your Age ; and
" leaving the Company, retire to your Reſt.
" I will ſtay here, and furniſh theſe Strangers
" with

" with all things neceffary." *Amyntas* perceiving
that *Alexander* had fome rafh Defign to put in
Execution ; " Son, faid he, I pretty well dif-
" cern by thy Words, that thou art angry, and
" art refolv'd to attempt fome imprudent Acti-
" on in my Abfence. I charge thee therefore
" to do nothing againft thefe Men that may
" turn to our Difadvantage : But be contented
" to obferve their Actions with Patience ; and
" for my own Part, I will comply, and retire."
When *Amyntas* had given him this Counfel,
and was gone out, *Alexander* fpoke to the Perfians in thefe Terms ; " Friends, faid he, thefe
" Women are at your command : You may lie
" with all, or as many of them as pleafe you
" beft ; and therefore I defire you to declare
" your Intentions with Freedom : For I fee
" you are inclin'd to fleep, and abundantly re-
" plenifh'd with Wine. Only permit them,
" if you think fit, to go out to bathe ; and in
" a little time you may expect their Return."
The Perfians applauded his Propofal, and *Alexander* fending away the Women, order'd them
to their own Apartment : And having drefs'd
a like Number of fmooth young Men in the
Habit of Women, he furnifh'd every one with
a Ponyard, and introducing them to the Perfians, faid : " We have treated you with all
" manner of Variety : We have given you not
" only all we had, but whatever we could pro-
" cure : And, which is more than all the reft,
" we have not denied you our Matrons and
" Daughters to compleat your Entertainment :
" that you may be abundantly perfuaded, we
" have paid you all the Honours you deferve ;
" and at your Return may acquaint the King
" who

" who sent you, that a Grecian Prince of
" *Macedonia*, gave you a good Reception both
" at Table and Bed." Having thus spoken,
Alexander plac'd at the Seat of every Persian
a young Macedonian in the Disguise of a Woman ; who, when the Persians attempted to
caress them, immediately dispatch'd all the
Seven. This was the Fate of these Persians,
and of their Attendants ; who, together with
the Chariots and all the Baggage, presently
disappear'd. After some time, great Search
was made by the Persians for these Men : But
Alexander eluded their Inquiry, by giving a
considerable Sum of Money, and his Sister *Gygea*
to *Bubares* a Persian, one of those who were
sent to enquire after the Generals he had kill'd :
And by his Management the manner of their
Death was conceal'd. This Family is of Grecian Extraction, and descended from *Perdiccas* ;
as not only they themselves affirm, but as I
likewise have been inform'd, and shall relate
hereafter. Nay, the Grecian Judges presiding
in the Olympian Exercises, have determin'd the
Question ; for when *Alexander* came thither
with a Design to enter the Lists, and the An-
tagonists had refus'd to admit him ; alledging,
that those Exercises were instituted for Grecians, and not for Barbarians ; he openly prov'd
himself an Argian ; and on that account being
receiv'd as a Grecian, he ran the Length of
a Stade ; and was the second at the end of the
Race. In this Manner were these things transf-
acted.

MEGABYZUS with the Pæonian Captives,
being advanc'd to the *Hellespont*, imbark'd, and
passing over into *Asia*, arriv'd at *Sardis*. In the
mean

mean time *Hiſtiæus* the Mileſian was employ'd
in building a City on the River *Strymon* in the
Territory of *Myrcinus,* which *Darius* had given
him upon his Requeſt, for the Reward of his
Care in preſerving the Bridge. But *Megabyzus,*
having heard of his Enterprize, no ſooner
arriv'd in *Sardis,* than he ſpoke to *Darius* in
theſe Terms. " O King, ſaid he, what have
" you done, in permitting a bold and ſubtile
" Grecian to found a City in *Thrace ?* A Coun-
" try abounding in Timber for the building
" of Ships; in Numbers of Men fit for the
" Oar; and in Mines of Silver; ſurrounded
" by Multitudes both of Grecians and Bar-
" barians; who, if they once find a Leader,
" will do as he ſhall direct, in all things and
" at all Times. Put a ſtop therefore to the
" Proceedings of this Man, that you may not
" be imbarraſs'd with an inteſtine War. To
" that End, ſend for him by a gentle Meſſage;
" and when he is in your Power, take care
" he may never return to *Greece.*" By theſe
Words of *Megabyzus, Darius* was eaſily perſuaded that he had a clear Foreſight of things;
and ſending for a Meſſenger, diſpatch'd him to
Myrcinus with this Meſſage. " *Hiſtiæus,*
" King *Darius* ſays thus. In all the Compaſs
" of my Thoughts, I have never found a Man
" more affectionate to my Perſon and the Good
" of my Affairs, than thy ſelf; of which Truth
" I have had ample Experience, not by Words,
" but Actions: And on that account having
" great Deſigns to put in execution, I re-
" quire thee to come to me with all Speed, that
" I may conſult with thee concerning them."
Hiſtiæus

Hiſtiæus giving Credit to theſe Words, and highly valuing the Honour of being a Counſellor to the King, went to *Sardis*: Where, upon his Arrival, *Darius* ſaid to him; "*Hiſtiæus*, "I have ſent for thee on this Occaſion. Ever "ſince my Return from *Scythia*, and thy De- "parture from my Sight, I have had no greater "Deſire, than to ſee and converſe with thee "again; perſuaded that a wiſe and affectionate "Friend is the moſt valuable of all Poſſeſſions: "and that both theſe Qualifications concur "in thy Perſon, my own Affairs have given "me ſufficient Proof. Now, becauſe thy Ar- "rival is ſo acceptable to me, I will make thee "an Offer. Think no more of *Miletus*, nor "of the City thou art building in *Thrace*; "but follow me to *Suſa*, and take Part of all I "poſſeſs. Be my Companion and Counſellor."
After this, *Darius* departed for *Suſa*, accompanied by *Hiſtiæus*; having firſt appointed *Artaphernes*, his Brother by the Father, to be Governor of *Sardis*. The Command of the maritime Parts he left to *Otanes*, whoſe Father *Siſamnes* had been one of the Royal Judges; and was put to death by *Cambyſes* for receiving a Sum of Money to pronounce an unjuſt Sentence. By the King's Order his Body was flead, and his whole Skin being cut into Thongs, was extended on the Bench where he us'd to ſit. And when this was done, *Cambyſes* plac'd the Son of *Syſamnes* in the Office of his Father, admoniſhing him to remember on what Tribunal he ſat to adminiſter Juſtice. This *Otanes*, who had perform'd the Office of a Judge on that Seat, now ſucceeding *Megabyzus* in the Command of the Army, ſubdued the Byzan-

tians

tians, and Chalcedonians ; with the Cities cf *Antandrus* and *Lamponium* in *Troas*. He alfo poffefs'd himfelf of *Lemnos* and *Imbrus*, by the Affiftance of the Lesbian Fleet ; both which Places where then inhabited by the Pelafgians. But the Lemnians having fought valiantly, and defended themfelves to Extremity ; fuffer'd much ; and thofe who furviv'd, were compell'd by the Perfians to obey *Lycaretus*, the Brother of *Meandrius* King of *Samos*. This *Lycaretus* en-flav'd the People, and exercis'd all manner of Violence ; charging fome, that they had de-ferted the Army of *Darius* in the Scythian Ex-pedition ; and others, that they had harafs'd his Forces in their Return. Yet he efcap'd not long with Impunity, and was kill'd for thefe Actions in *Lemnos*.

BUT farther Calamities impending over the Ionians, began in *Naxus* and *Miletus*. The firft of thefe was at that time the moft flourifh-ing of all the Iflands : And *Miletus* was then in a State of greater Profperity than ever, and accounted the Ornament of *Ionia* ; tho' that City had before been afflicted with domeftick Diforders during two Generations, till their Differences were compos'd by the Parians ; who, among all the Grecians, had been chofen by the Milefians to that Purpofe, and amended the Government in this manner. Some of their moft eminent Men arriving in *Miletus*, and feeing nothing but Defolation, told the Milefians, they had refolv'd to furvey their whole Country. Which as they were doing, wherefoever they faw in that depopulated Re-gion any Portion of Land well cultivated, they wrote down the Name of the Poffeffor.

After

After they had view'd all the Milesian Territories, and found very few such Possessions ; returning to the City, they called an Assembly, and declar'd that the Government should be put into the Hands of those Persons, whose Lands they had found in good Condition : Not doubting that they would administer the publick Affairs, with the same Care they had taken of their own. They strictly enjoin'd all the rest of the Milesians, who before had been split into Factions, to obey these Magistrates ; and in this manner reform'd the State of *Miletus.* From these two Places the ensuing Evils were deriv'd upon the Ionians. For some rich Men of *Naxus* being banish'd by the People, fled to *Miletus* ; the Administration of which Place was then in the Hands of *Aristagoras* the Son of *Molparogas,* Nephew and Son in Law to *Histiæus* the Son of *Lysagoras,* who was detain'd by *Darius* at *Susa.* For *Histiæus* was Tyrant of *Miletus* ; and during his Detention in *Asia,* the Naxians arriv'd ; and in Confidence of the Engagements they and *Histiæus* were under to a reciprocal Hospitality, desir'd some Assistance of *Aristagoras,* in order to restore them to their Country. *Aristagoras* thinking to get the Dominion of *Naxus,* if these Men were once restor'd by his Power ; took Occasion from their former Hospitality to make them an Offer, in these Terms. " For my own Part, I am " not able to furnish you with a Force sufficiant " ent to re-establish you in *Naxus* against the " Inclinations of those who are in Possession ; " because I hear they have eight thousand " Men arm'd with Shields, and a considerable " rable Number of great Ships. Yet I will

" contrive

" contrive some Way; and use my best Endea-
" vours to assist you on this Occasion. *Arta-*
" *phernes*, the Son of *Hystaspes* and Brother
" of *Darius*, is my Friend.   He commands
" all the maritim Parts of *Asia*, and has a
" numerous Army, with many great Ships.
" This Man, I am persuaded, will do what-
" ever we should ask." The Naxians hearing his
Proposal, desir'd *Aristagoras* to bring about this
Affair in the best manner he could; authorizing
him to promise such Presents as he should think
necessary, and to engage for the Expence of
the Army ; all which, they said, they would
repay ; having great Expectation that their
Countrymen upon their Appearance would do
whatever they should order; and that the rest of
the Islanders should follow their Example.   For
at that time none of the *Cyclades* were under the
Dominion of *Darius*.   Accordingly *Aristagoras*
went to *Sardis*, and acquainted *Artaphernes*,
that *Naxus* was a beautiful and fertile I-
sland, tho' not large, in the Neighbourhood
of *Ionia*, and abounding in Wealth and Servants.   " For these Reasons, said he, I coun-
" sel you to make War upon that Country,
" and re-establish those Persons who have been
" banish'd from thence : Which if you do,
' you shall not only receive a great Sum of
" Money, already lodg'd in my Hands, toge-
" ther with Provisions for the Army (for that
" is no more than just, since the Expedition is
" made on our account); but besides the Ac-
" quisition of *Naxus*, you will put the King
" into Possession of *Paros*. *Andros*, and the rest
" of the dependant Islands that go under the
" Name of the *Cyclades*.   To these, in the next
place

" place, you may without Difficulty add the
" Conquest of *Eubœa*, a great and wealthy
" Island, equal in Extent to *Cyprus*, and very
" easy to be taken. A hundred Ships will be
" sufficient to employ in this Expedition."
" Truly, said *Artaphernes*, you have propos'd
" an Enterprize of great Advantage to the
" King, and prudently advis'd in every thing,
" except the Number of Ships. For instead
" of one hundred, which you demand, two
" hundred shall be ready in the ensuing Spring.
" But the King's Consent must first be obtain-
" ed." With this Answer *Aristagoras* return'd
very well satisfied to *Miletus*.

IN the mean time *Artaphernes* sent to *Susa*,
to acquaint *Darius* with the Enterprize propos'd
by *Aristagoras* ; and after he had obtain'd his
Approbation, made ready two hundred Ships,
and assembled a great Army of Persians and
their Confederates ; appointing for General of
those Forces, *Megabates* a Persian, who was of
the Achemenian Blood, Nephew to himself
and *Darius*, and afterwards married his Daughter to *Pausanias* the Son of *Cleombrotus* a Lacedemonian, who aspir'd to the Dominion of
Greece. When *Artaphernes* had declar'd *Megabates* General, he sent him with the Army to
Aristagoras ; and *Megabates* accompanied by
Aristagoras, with the Ionian Forces, and the
Naxians, departed from *Miletus*, and made a
Feint of sailing to the *Hellespont*. But when
he arriv'd near *Chio*, he anchor'd over against
Mount *Caucasus*, in order to make the Coast of
Naxus by the Favour of a North Wind. But
because the Naxians were not to perish by this
Army, the following Accident happen'd : *Me-*

gabates, visiting the Watches of the Fleet, and finding a Ship of *Myndus* without any Guard, fell into a great Rage, and commanded his Officers to seize the Captain, whose Name was *Scylax,* and after they had bound him, to put his Head thro' one of the Port-holes that were pierc'd for the Oars ; so that his Head appear'd on the Outside of the Vessel, while the rest of his Body remain'd within. *Aristagoras* being inform'd in what manner his Friend *Scylax* of *Myndus* was bound and disgrac'd by *Megabates* went to the Persian ; interceded for him ; and when he found he could obtain nothing, set him at liberty with his own Hands. *Megabates* hearing of this Action, and thinking himself highly affronted, reprimanded him sharply : But *Aristagoras* in answer, said, " What have you to do with these things ? " Has not *Artaphernes* sent you to obey me, " and sail to what Part soever I shall command ? " Why then should you undertake more ?" This Answer was so provoking to *Megabates,* that he dispatch'd certain Persons to *Naxus,* with order to inform the Naxians of the impending Danger. Upon which they, who to that Hour thought of nothing less than of being invaded by those Forces, brought their Wealth with all Diligence into the City, laid up Provisions of Meat and Drink to sustain a Siege, and repair'd their Walls. When they had prepar'd all things, as Men expecting to be attack'd ; the Persians arriving in their Ships, found the Naxians perfectly well provided, and besieg'd them in vain during four Months : So that having consum'd what they brought, together with great Sums furnish'd

by

by *Aristagoras*; and wanting still more to carry on the Siege, they built a Place for the Reception of the *Naxian* Fugitives, and retir'd to the Continent, after they had suffer'd much in the Expedition. *Aristagoras* finding no Way to perform the Promises he had made to *Artáphernes*, and yet remaining charg'd with the Payment of the Army, which was demanded in a peremptory manner; apprehended that upon this ill Success, and the Accusations of *Megabates*, he might be depriv'd of the Dominion of *Miletus*; and on that account began to think of revolting from the King: To which he was solicited by a Message of *Histiæus*, sent to him from *Susa*. For *Histiæus* being desirous to signify his Intentions to *Aristagoras*, and finding no other Way, because all the Passages were guarded, shav'd the Head of one of his Servants, in whose Fidelity he most confided, and having imprinted the Message on his Crown, kept him at *Susa* till his Hair was grown again. When that time was come, he dispatch'd him to *Miletus*, without any other Instructions, than that, upon his Arrival, he should desire *Aristagoras* to take off his Hair, and look upon his Head: On which, as I said before, Characters were impress'd, soliciting him to a Defection. *Histiæus* took this Resolution; because he look'd upon his Residence at *Susa* as a great Misfortune, and entertain'd no small Hope of repassing the Sea, if *Miletus* should revolt: But if nothing new could be attempted there, he concluded he should never return home. And such were the Considerations that prevail'd with *Histiæus* to dispatch this Messenger to *Miletus*.

ALL

ALL thefe things concurring at the fame time, induc'd *Ariftagoras* to confult with thofe of his Faction, and communicate to them his own Opinion, and that of *Hiftiæus*. They all applauded his Sentiment, and encourag'd him to revolt, except *Hecatæus* the Hiftorian ; who at firft diffuaded him from undertaking a War againft the Perfian King ; enumerating the Forces of *Darius*, and all the Nations he com- manded : But finding he could not prevail, he in the next Place advis'd that Care fhould be taken to render the Milefians Mafters of the Sea ; and faid, that being fully convinc'd of the Infufficiency of their Forces, he could fee no more than one Way to effect this. Yet if they would feize the Treafures, which had been dedicated by *Cræfus* the Lydian, in the Temple of *Branchis*, he had great Hope they might acquire the Dominion of the Sea ; and not only convert thofe Riches to their own Ufe, but hinder the Enemy from plundering that Treafure : which indeed was very confidera- ble, as I have already related. However they would not follow his Advice : But at the fame time having taken a Refolution to revolt, they agreed to fend one of the Affembly in a Ship to *Myus* (where the Enemies Forces that came from *Naxus* then were) with Inftructions to endeavour to get into his Hands as many of their Sea-Commanders as he could. *Iatragoras* being charg'd with this Commiffion, circum- vented and feized *Oliatus* of *Mylafa*, the Son of *Ibanolis* ; *Hiftiæus* the Son of *Tymnes*, of *Terme- ra* ; *Cöes* the Son of *Erxandrus*, to whom *Da- rius* had given *Mitylene* *Ariftagoras* of *Cyme*, the Son of *Heraclides*, and many others ; Thus
Ariftagoras

Aristagoras openly revolted against *Darius*, and studied to annoy him by all the means he could invent. In the first place he abolish'd the Tyranny, and establish'd a Commonwealth in *Miletus*; to the end that the Milesians might more readily join with him in his Defection. He effected the same afterwards throughout all *Ionia*; expelling some of their Tyrants by Force; and delivering up all those who were taken from on board the Ships that had been at *Naxus*, into the Hands of the Cities to which they belong'd; in order to gratify the People. The Mityleneans had no sooner receiv'd *Coes*, than they brought him out, and ston'd him to death: The Cymeans banish'd their Tyrant: Many others fled, and the Tyrannies were every where suppress'd. In Conclusion, *Aristagoras* the Milesian having remov'd the Tyrants, and admonish'd each of the Cities to appoint a General, went on an Embassy to *Sparta*, because some powerful Assistance was now become necessary.

ANAXANDRIDES King of *Sparta* was already dead, and his Son *Cleomenes* had at that time Possession of the Kingdom; not on account of his Virtues, but his Blood. *Anaxandrides* had married his Sister's Daughter, and tho' she brought him no Children, yet he lov'd her with great Affection: Which the *Ephori* considering, they sent for him, and said; " If you " neglect your nearest Concernments, we are " not to imitate your Example, and suffer the " Family of *Eurystheus* to be extinguish'd. " Since therefore you have a Wife which bears " no Children, leave her, and marry another; " and so provide for the Security of *Sparta*.

He

He anſwer'd, that he would not do either the one or the other: that, to adviſe him to abandon the Wife he had, and to take another in her place, without any Provocation, was unjuſt ; and therefore he would not obey. Upon this, the *Ephori* and the Senate, after they had conſulted, ſent a Meſſage to *Anaxandrides* in theſe Terms ; " Becauſe we " ſee you are ſo fond of your Wife, be per- " ſuaded to do as we now propoſe, without " Reluctancy ; that the Spartans may not " proceed to a more ſevere Reſolution a- " gainſt you. We require you not to part " with your Wife : Continue to live with her, " as you have done to this time ; but at " leaſt marry another Woman, who is not bar- " ren." To this Propoſal *Anaxandrides* conſenting, married another Wife, and kept two diſtinct Families, contrary to the Cuſtoms of the Spartans. After ſome time, his ſecond Wife was brought to bed of this *Cleomenes*, and became the Mother of one who was to ſucceed in the Kingdom. And now his firſt Wife, who to that time had been barren, found her ſelf with Child : and tho' the thing was really ſo, yet the Relations of his ſecond began to murmur, and ſaid, ſhe only pretended to the Pride of a great Belly, in order to impoſe a ſuppoſititious Child upon the World. While theſe continu'd their Clamour, and the time of her Delivery drew near, the *Ephori* ſuſpecting a Fraud, order'd the Woman to be kept under a ſtrict Guard. Nevertheleſs ſhe had not only *Dorieus*, but after him *Leonidas*, and at a third time *Cleombrotus* ; tho' ſome ſay that *Cleombrotus* and *Leonidas* were Twins. But the Mother

ther

ther of *Cleomenes*, who was the second Wife of *Anaxandrides*, and Daughter to *Perinetades*, the Son of *Demarmenes*, never bore any more Children. *Cleomenes* is reported to have been delirious, and much disorder'd in his Mind: so that *Dorieus*, who surpass'd all the young Men of his Age, conceiv'd great hope of obtaining the Kingdom, on account of his Merit. But after the Death of *Anaxandrides*, when he found that the Lacedemonians had, according to Custom, created his eldest Brother King; full of Discontent and Indignation to be commanded by *Cleomenes*, he demanded a Draught of Men, in order to establish a Colony; and went away without asking the Oracle of *Delphi* to what place he should go, or doing any of those things that are usual on such Occasions; so deeply was he affected with the Indignity. He sail'd to *Libya* under the Conduct of Theban Pilots, and arriving at *Cinype*, settled upon a River, in the most beautiful Part of that Country. But in the third Year of his Establishment, being ejected by the united Force of the Maces, Libyans and Carthaginians, he return'd to *Peloponnesus*; where *Antichares* of *Elionis*, pursuant to the Oracle of *Laius*, admonish'd him to build the City of *Heraclea* in *Sicily*; assuring him that all the Country of *Eryx*, having been conquer'd by *Hercules*, belong'd to his Posterity. When he heard this, he went to inquire of the Oracle at *Delphi*, whether he should possess himself of the Region to which he was sent. The Pythian answer'd he should; and *Dorieus* taking with him the same Army he had in *Libya*, set sail for *Italy*. At that time, as the Sybarites say, they and

their

their King *Telys* were preparing to make War against *Crotona* ; which the Crotonians apprehending, implor'd the Affiftance of *Doricus* ; and having obtain'd their Requeft, march'd in Conjunction with his Forces directly to *Sybaris*, and took the City. This the Sybarites affirm concerning *Dorieus* and thofe who were with him. But the Crotonians deny that any Foreigner took part with them in the War againft *Sybaris*, except only *Callias* of *Elis*, an Augur of Iamidean Defcent, who abandon'd *Telys* King of the Sybarites and deferted to their Side, becaufe he found the Sacrifices inaufpicious which he offer'd for the Succefs of the Crotonian Expedition. Thefe Things they fay : and each Side to confirm their Affertion, bring the following Teftimonies. The Sybarites on their Part fhew a Grove, with a Temple, built at *Cbraftus*, and dedicated, as they fay, to *Minerva*, under the Name of Chraftian, by *Doricus*, after he had taken *Sybaris* : alledging, for a farther and greater Proof, that he was kill'd there, becaufe he had acted contrary to the Admonition of the Oracle. For if he had attempted nothing more than the Enterprize he was fent about, he might have taken and poffefs'd the Country of *Eryx*, and efcap'd that Deftruction which fell upon himfelf and his Army. On the other hand the Crotonians fhew many confiderable Donations, conferr'd upon *Callias* the Elean, in the Territories of *Crotona* ; and now poffefs'd by his Defcendants ; but nothing at all given to *Doricus* and his Pofterity : Whereas doubtlefs, had he affifted them in the War of *Sybaris*, he fhould have been more amply rewarded than *Callias*.

Callias. These are the Testimonies produc'd on both sides; and every Man has the Liberty of adhering to that which he judges more probable. *Dorieus* had for Associates in the Conduct of his Colony, *Theſſalus, Parebates, Chelees* and *Euryleon,* all Spartans; who, after their Arrival with the Army in *Sicily,* were kill'd with him in an unſuccefsful Battle againſt the Phœnicians and Ægeſtans: *Euryleon* alone ſurviv'd this Diſaſter, and having collected the ſhatter'd Remains of their Forces, poſſeſs'd himſelf of *Minoa,* a Colony of the Selinuſians, and deliver'd the Minoans from their Monarch *Pythagoras.* But after he had remov'd him, he ſeiz'd the Tyranny of *Selinus* for himſelf. Yet he continued not long in Poſſeſſion: For the Selinuſians revolting, kill'd him at the Altar of the Forenſian *Jupiter,* where he had taken Sanctuary. *Philippus* of *Crotona,* the Son of *Butacides,* accompanied *Dorieus* in the Time of his Life, and at his Death. He had enter'd into a Contract of Marriage with the Daughter of *Telys* the Sybarite: But being baniſh'd from *Crotona,* and diſappointed of his Wife, he ſail'd to *Cyrene;* from whence he parted to accompany *Dorieus,* with his Ship and Men maintain'd at his own Expence. He had been victorious in the Olympian Exerciſes; and becauſe he was the moſt beautiful of all the Grecians at that time, ſo great Honours were conferr'd upon him, by the Ægeſtans, after his Death, as they had never paid to any other Perſon: For they erected the Monument of a Hero upon his Sepulcher, and adore him with Sacrifices. Such was the End of *Dorieus;* who, if he could have endur'd the Government of

Cleomenes,

Cleomenes, and continued in *Sparta*, had doubt-less been King of the Lacedemonians. For after a short Reign *Cleomenes* died, and left no other Children than one Daughter, whose Name was *Gorgo*.

DURING the Reign of this *Cleomenes*, *Aristagoras* Tyrant of *Miletus* arriv'd in *Sparta*: and going to confer with the King, carried with him, as the Lacedemonians say, a Plate of Brass, on which a Description of the whole Earth, with all the Seas and Rivers, was en-grav'd: And being come into the King's Pre-sence, spoke in these Terms. "Wonder not,
"*Cleomenes*, at the Pains I have taken to come
"hither; the Cause is important: For, to see
"the Posterity of the Ionians depriv'd of
"Liberty, and reduc'd to the Condition of
"Servants, will be extremely grievous and
"shameful, not only to us, but, in the next
"place, to you; because you are the Lea-
"ders of *Greece*. I adjure you therefore by
"the Grecian Gods, rescue the Ionians, and
"deliver your own Blood from Servitude.
"The Enterprize will not be difficult to you,
"who have attain'd to the utmost Height of
"Military Glory. For the Barbarians are
"not valiant, and their Manner in War is
"thus: They use a slight Bow, with short
"Arrows, and engage in Battle, dress'd in a
"long Vest, and wearing a Turban on the
"Head: By which means they become an
"easy Conquest. Besides, those who inha-
"bit that Part of the Continent, possess
"greater Riches in Gold, Silver, Brass, mag-
"nificent Apparel, Horses, and Slaves, than
"all the rest in conjunction. All these things
"you

" you may enjoy if you will, the Countries
" lying contiguous, as I fhall fhew you." Then
pointing to the Defcription of the Earth, which
he brought with him, engrav'd on a Plate:
" Next to thefe Ionians, faid he, the Lydians
" inhabit a fertile Country, abounding in Sil-
" ver: And on the Confines of *Lydia*, thefe
" Phrygians are plac'd to the Eaftward, more
" rich in Cattle, and living in greater Af-
" fluence than any other People I know. Ad-
" joining to thefe are the Cappadocians, by
" us call'd Syrians; and beyond them, the
" Cilicians; whofe Country extends to that
" Sea in which the Ifland of *Cyprus* is fitu-
" ate, and pays an annual Tribute of five
" Hundred Talents to the King. Next to
" the Cilicians, are thefe Armenians, who
" poffefs great Numbers of Cattle; and after
" them the Matienians; beyond whofe Terri-
" tories lies this Province of *Ciffia*, in which *Su-*
" *fa* is built upon the River *Choafpes.* In this
" Place the great King refides, and his vaft
" Treafures are here depofited. If you take this
" City, you may boldly contend with *Jupiter* in
" Wealth. You will not find your Account in
" fighting Battles, to gain a Country of fmall
" Extent, narrow Limits, and indifferent Soil,
" from the Meffenians, who are your Equals
" in War; or from the Arcadians and Ar-
" gians: For none of thefe Nations have ei-
" ther Gold or Silver; the Defire of which in-
" duces fo many Men to hazard their Lives.
" But when an Opportunity is offer'd to con-
" quer all *Afia* with Facility, can you wifh for
" any thing more?" To this Difcourfe of *Ari-*
ftagoras Cleomenes anfwer'd, " Milefian Friend,
" I defer

" I defer to let you know my Refolution till
" three Days are pafs'd." When that Time
was come, and they were both met at the appointed Place, *Cleomenes* ask'd *Ariftagoras*, in
how many Days one might travel from the
Coaft of *Ionia* to the City where the King was.
But tho' *Ariftagoras* was in other things a Man
of Art, and much fuperior in Ability to *Cleomenes* ; yet he made a Slip in this. For defigning to draw the Spartans into *Afia*, he ought
to have abated fomething of the Account :
Whereas he told him plainly, 'twas a Journey
of three Months : Which *Cleomenes* no fooner
heard, than interrupting him from proceeding
in his Difcourfe concerning the Way, he faid,
" Milefian Gueft, depart out of *Sparta* before
" the Setting of the Sun : For you have pro-
" pos'd nothing to the Advantage of the Spar-
" tans, in advifing us to take a March into
" *Afia*, not to be perform'd in lefs than three
" Months after our Landing." When he had
fpoken thefe Words he withdrew ; and *Ariftagoras* taking an Olive-Branch in his Hand,
after the Manner of a Suppliant, went after
Cleomenes, befeeching him to hear ; and at the
fame time defir'd him to fend away his little
Daughter *Gorgo*, who was then with him, being the only Child he had, and about eight or
nine Years of Age. But *Cleomenes* bid him
fay what he wou'd, and not refrain for the
fake of a Child. So *Ariftagoras* began with
the Promife of ten Talents, in cafe *Cleomenes*
would do as he defir'd ; and receiving a Denial, proceeded gradually in his Offers, till he
came to the Sum of fifty Talents ; and then the
Girl cried out, " Father, This Stranger will
" corrupt

" corrupt you, unless you go away presently."
Cleomenes pleas'd with the Admonition of the
Child, retir'd to another Apartment: And
Aristagoras was constrain'd to depart imme-
diately from *Sparta*, without obtaining Leave
to inform him further concerning the Way to
the Place of the King's Residence. But that
Task I shall take upon me.

ALL this Way is furnish'd with Royal
Stations, and magnificent Inns; and is every
where safe, and well inhabited. Twenty of
these Places of Reception are found in *Lydia* and
Phrygia, at the distance of ninety four Parasanges and a half from each other. Out of *Phrygia* Men arrive at the *Alis*, and are oblig'd to
pass that River by the means of certain Sluices
which are built there, with a considerable
Fort. Then entring into *Cappadocia*, and tra-
versing that Country, they find twenty eight
of those publick Stations, within the Space of
one hundred and four Parasanges, before they
arrive on the Borders of *Cilicia*: Where passing
two Gates and two Guards, they cross the
Territories of *Cilicia* by a Way of fifteen Parasanges and a half, and meet with three several Stations. A River call'd *Euphrates*, se-
parates *Cilicia* from *Armenia*; and is not passa-
ble except in Boats. *Armenia* contains fifteen of
these Inns, with one Fort, and fifty six Parasanges and a half in the Way over. Four Rivers
run thro this Country; and Men are necessitated to pass all these in Boats. The first is the
Tigris: The second and third have the same
Name, tho' they are different Rivers, flow-
ing from different Sources. For the first of
these rises in *Armenia*, and the latter in *Matiene*.

tiene. The Fourth is call'd the *Gyndes*, which was formerly cut by *Cyrus* into three hundred and sixty Channels. Next to *Armenia* are the Territories of *Matiene*, containing four Stations: And from thence to *Ciſſia* and the River *Choaſpes*, eleven Stations are found within the Space of forty two Paraſanges and a half. This River alſo is no otherwiſe paſſable than in Boats, and the City of *Suſa* is ſituate on the other Side. All theſe Stations are in number one Hundred and elven: and ſuch are the publick Places of Reception from *Sardis* to *Suſa*. Now if we ſum up the Number of the Paraſanges of this Royal Road, and ſuppoſe every Paraſange equal to thirty Stades, as the Truth is; we ſhall find that the four Hundred and fifty Paraſanges from *Sardis* to the Memnonian Palace, amount to thirteen thouſand five hundred Stades: And he who travels one hundred and fifty Stades every Day, muſt ſpend ninety Days in performing the whole Journey. So that *Ariſtagoras* the Mileſian ſaid right, when he told *Cleomenes* the Lacedemonian, that three Months would be requiſite to arrive at the Place, where the King was. But if any ſhould deſire a more compleat Account, I will ſatisfy him: For adding the Meaſure of the Way from *Epheſus* and *Sardis* to the preceding Computation, the whole Number of Stades from the Grecian Sea to the Memnonian City of *Suſa*, will be fourteen Thouſand and forty Becauſe five Hundred and forty Stades are accounted from *Epheſus* to *Sardis*. And thus three Days Journey are to be added to that of three Months,

ARISTA-

ARISTAGORAS being difmifs'd from *Sparta* went to *Athens*; which City had been deliver'd from their Tyrants in this Manner. After *Ariftogiton* and *Harmodius*, originally defcended from the Gephyræans, had kill'd *Hipparchus* the Son of *Pififtratus* and Brother to *Hippias*, the Athenians during the Space of four Years were no lefs oppref'd by Tyranny than before. *Hipparchus* had feen his own Deftruction manifeftly foretold in a Dream. For in the Night preceding the Panathenian Feftival, a tall and handfome Man feem'd to ftand by him, and pronounce thefe enigmatical Words,

Lyon, with Courage bear the greateft Ill,
For Vengeance always reaches the Unjuft.

At Break of Day he acquainted the Diviners with his Dream; but afterwards, flighting the Event, he celebrated that Solemnity, in which he perifh'd. The Gephyræans, from whom thofe who kill'd *Hipparchus* were defcended, derive their Original from the Eretrians, as they themfelves fay: But I am more certainly inform'd, that they are the Pofterity of thofe Phœnicians, who arriving in *Bæotia* with *Cadmus*, were appointed by Lot to inhabit the Diftrict of *Tanagra*. The Cadmeans were firft expell'd by the Argians; and thefe Gephyræans being afterwards ejected by the Bœotians, betook themfelves to the Athenians; who admitted them into the Number of their Citizens, under certain Conditions and Limitations, which are not neceffary to be mention'd. Thefe Phœnicians who came with *Cadmus*, and the Gephyræans their Descendants, inhabiting this Region, introduc'd many Kinds of Discipline into *Greece*; and particularly Letters, which, as I conceive, were not known among the Grecians before that Time. The first Letters they us'd were entirely Phœnician; but in succeeding Ages they were gradually alter'd both in Sound and Figure; and the Ionians who inhabited the greatest Part of the Country round about, having learnt these Letters from the Phœnicians, made use of them with some small Alteration, and gave out that they ought to go under the Name of Phœnician Letters; as Reason requir'd, because they had been introduc'd by the Phœnicians. Besides, the Ionians, from antient Time, have given the Name of Paper to the Skins of Goats and Sheep, which they then us'd instead of Paper; as many of the Barbarians do to this Day. And I my self have seen in the Temple of Ismenian *Apollo* at *Thebes* in *Bœotia*, some Cadmean Letters engrav'd on certain Tripos's little different from the Ionian Character. One of these Inscriptions runs thus;

Amphytrion *of* Telebois *plac'd me here.*

This was about the Time of *Laius* the Son of *Labdacus*; whose Father *Polydorus* was Son to *Cadmus.* Another Tripos has these words in Hexameter Verses,

   To the Apollo by the conqu'ring Hand
   Of Scæus *offer'd, a rich Gift I stand.*

Scæus was the Son of *Hippoccon*, if he were indeed

deed the Donor of this Tripos; and not a-
nother Person of the same Name, who liv'd a-
bout the Time of *Oedipus* the Son of *Laius*. A
third Tripos is inscrib'd thus, in Hexameters
likewise,

> *To thee, bright* Phœbus, *ever-shining Light,*
> *To thee,* Laodamas *this Off'ring made.*

During the Reign of this Monarch *Laodamas,*
the Cadmeans were expell'd by the Argians;
and retir'd to *Euchelea.* After which the Gephyræans being ejected by the Bœotians, betook themselves to *Athens*; where they erected
their own peculiar Temples, distinct from the
rest of the Athenians, and particularly one to
the Achaian *Ceres,* in which they perform'd the
Orgian Rites. And thus having related the
Dream of *Hipparchus,* with the Original of
the Gephyræans, from whom those who kill'd
him were descended, I shall now resume the
Discourse I began, and shew in what manner
the Athenians were deliver'd from Tyrants.

UNDER the Tyranny of *Hippias,* who
was highly incens'd against the Athenians
for the Death of *Hipparchus,* the Alcmæonides, being of Athenian Extraction, and at
that time banish'd by the Pisistratides, made
great Efforts, in conjunction with other Exiles, to obtain their Return: And tho' their
Endeavours had been unsuccessful; yet still
continuing to apply themselves with Diligence to procure their own Re-establishment,
with the Liberty of *Athens,* they fortified
Lipsydrum in *Pæonia:* And that they might
leave nothing unattempted against the Pi-

sistratides,

fiftratides, undertook by a Contract made
with the Amphictyons, to build the Temple
which now is feen at *Delphi*. Thefe Perfons
being defcended of illuftrious Anceftors, and
very rich, erected a Fabrick, much more magnificent than the Model ; and among other
things, faced the Frontifpiece of the Temple
with Marble of *Paros*, inftead of Stone, which by
their Contract they were to bring from *Parium*.
The Athenians fay, that while the Alcmæonides were at *Delphi*, they prevail'd with the
Pythian by a Sum of Money, to exhort all the
Spartans, who fhould come thither to confult
the Oracle, either on their own account, or
that of the Publick, to deliver *Athens* from Servitude: And that the Lacedemonians finding
this Admonition inceffantly inculcated, fent
Anchimolius the Son of *After*, an eminent Citizen, with an Army to *Athens*, in order to expel
the Pififtratides, tho' they were the chief of their
Allies: So much they preferr'd the Commands
of the God to all human Obligations. Accordingly *Anchimolius* imbark'd ; and arriving
at *Phaleron*, landed with his Army. But the
Pififtratides, who had timely Notice of this
Expedition, demanded Succour of the Theffalians, their Confederates ; which they granted, and unanimoufly refolv'd to fend a Thoufand Horfe to their Affiftance, under the
Conduct of their King *Cineas* of *Coniæa*. Having receiv'd this Reinforcement, the Pififtratides clear'd the Plains of the Phalereans, and
render'd the Country practicable for Horfe :
which when they had done, they order'd the E-
nemy to be attack'd by the Theffalian Cavalry ;
who falling upon the Lacedemonians in their
Camp,

Camp, kill'd great Numbers of them, with their General *Anchimolius*, and forc'd the rest to betake themselves to their Ships. Thus the first Lacedemonian Army was compell'd to retire; and *Anchimolius* was buried at *Alopece* in *Attica*, near the Temple of *Hercules* in *Cynosarges.* But the Lacedemonians sent afterwards a greater Army to *Athens*, by Land, and not by Sea, under the Conduct of their King *Cleomenes* the Son of *Anaxandrides:* Who, when he had enter'd the Territories of *Attica*, was attack'd by the Thessalian Cavalry; which after a short Dispute he put to flight, with the Loss of about forty Men. Upon this Defeat the Thessalians by a precipitate March return'd to their own Country; and *Cleomenes*, accompanied by those Athenians who were desirous to recover their Liberty, march'd directly to the City, and besieg'd the Tyrants in the Pelasgian Fort, to which they had been oblig'd to retire. Yet the Lacedemonians could not by any means have reduc'd the Enemy; both because they themselves were not prepar'd to carry on a long Siege, and the Pisistratides had furnish'd the Place with all kind of Provisions; but must have been necessitated in a few Days to march away to *Sparta*, if an Accident had not happen'd, which was no less pernicious to some, than advantageous to others. For the Sons of the Pisistratides fell into the Hands of the Lacedemonians, as some Persons were endeavouring to convey them privately out of the Country; which broke all their Measures in such a manner, that, to redeem their Children, they yielded to whatever the Athenians would pre-

scribe,

scribe, and oblig'd themselves to depart out of *Attica* in five Days. But soon after, they abandon'd the Country, and retir'd to *Sigeum* upon the River *Scammander*, having possess'd the Dominion of *Athens* six and thirty Years. They came originally from *Pilus* and *Nelea* ; and were of the same Extraction with *Codrus* and *Melanthus*, who, tho' Foreigners, had been formerly Kings of *Athens*. And for this Reason *Hippocrates*, the Father of *Pisistratus* gave that Name to his Son, in Memory of *Pisistratus* the Son of *Nestor*. Thus the Athenians were deliver'd from their Tyrants : And what memorable things they either did or suffer'd, before the Ionians revolted from *Darius*, and *Aristagoras* of *Miletus* came to desire their Assistance, I shall now relate.

THE Power of *Athens* was great before ; but after the Expulsion of their Tyrants, became much greater. Two Men of that City surpass'd all the rest in Authority. One of these was *Clisthenes* who was of the Alcmæonian Blood, and the Person, if we may believe common Fame, who prevail'd with the Pythian to do as I have mention'd. The other was *Isagoras* the Son of *Tisander*, of an illustrious Family ; but from what Original descended, I am not able to discover : Only this I know, that the whole Race offers Sacrifices to *Jupiter* of *Caria*. In their Contests for Superiority, *Clisthenes* finding his Competitor too powerful, studied to become popular, and form'd the Athenians into ten Tribes ; which to that time had been no more than four ; changing the Names they had from *Geleon, Ægicores, Argadeus* and *Opletus*, Sons of *Ion*, into other Appellations deriv'd

riv'd from Heroes who were all Natives of the Country, except *Ajax* only, whose Name he admitted as a near Neighbour and Ally. This he did, as I conjecture, in Imitation of *Clisthenes*, Tyrant of *Sicyon*, his Grandfather by the Mother; who, when he made War against the Argians, silenc'd all the Reciters of Verses, because the People and Country of *Argos* are so much celebrated in those of *Homer*; and having form'd a Design to destroy the Monument of *Adrastus* the Son of *Talaus*, which stands in the Forum of *Sicyon*, because he was an Argian, went to consult the Oracle of *Delphi*, and receiv'd this Answer from the Pythian, " That " *Adrastus* indeed had been King of the Si- " cyonians; whereas he deserv'd to be ston'd." *Clisthenes* finding the God would not yield to his Desires, return'd home, and bent his Thoughts to contrive, how *Adrastus* might of himself become insignificant. When he thought he had found the right way, he sent to the Thebans of *Bœotia*, to acquaint them, that he would bring back the Body of *Melanippus* the Son of *Astacus*; which having done with their Permission, he erected a Temple to him in the strongest Part of the *Prytaneum*. This he did, for I must not omit the true Motive, because *Melanippus* had been the greatest of all the Enemies of *Adrastus*; having kill'd his Brother *Mecistes*, and his Son-in-Law *Tydeus*. After *Clisthenes* had erected this Temple he abolish'd the Sacrifices and Festivals of *Adrastus*; and instituted the same Rites to *Melanippus* as the Sicyonians had been accustom'd to perform in a magnificent manner to the

C 3 other.

other. For *Polybus*, who was Master of *Sicyon*, leaving no Male Line, gave that Country to *Adraſtus* the Son of his Daughter. The Sicyonians, among other Honours paid to him, us'd to celebrate his Misfortunes with tragical Dances ; honouring *Adraſtus*, and not *Bacchus*, to that Time. But *Cliſthenes* transferr'd theſe Dances to the Worſhip of *Bacchus*, and all the other Ceremonies to *Melanippus*. In a Word, he impos'd new Names upon the Dorian Tribes of *Sicyon*, that they might bear no Reſemblance to thoſe of *Argos* ; and by this means made the Sicyonians ridiculous. For he denominated the other Tribes from Words ſignifying Swine and Aſſes, with the Addition of a terminating Syllable : But diſtinguiſh'd his own by a Name deriv'd from his Dominion. So that theſe were call'd Archelaians, while the reſt went under the Names of Swine-herds, Aſs-keepers, and Hogs-herds. The Sicyonian Tribes were call'd by theſe Names in the Time of *Cliſthenes*, and after his Death, during the Space of ſixty Year ; when, by common Conſent they were chang'd into thoſe of Hylleans, Pamphylians, and Dymanates ; and a Fourth Tribe was added, to which they gave the Name of Ægyalean from *Ægyalus* the Son of *Adraſtus*. ¡Theſe things were done by *Cliſthenes* of *Sicyon* : And the Athenian *Cliſthenes*, who was Son to the Daughter of the Sicyonian, and had his Name from him, ſeems to me to have imitated him, from a Contempt of the Ionians ; and that they might not go under the ſame Denomination with the Tribes of *Athens*. For when he had prevail'd with all the Populace to unite and ſide

with

with him, he chang'd the Names of the Tribes, and augmented their Number, from Four to Ten; appointing a Prefident to every one: And thus having gain'd the People, he became much fuperior to his Adverfaries. *Ifagoras* finding his Party broken, form'd a Refolution to apply himfelf for Succour to *Cleomenes* the Lacedemonian; who from the Time he had befieg'd the Pififtratides, was engag'd with him in a Friendfhip of mutual Hofpitality; and befides was fufpected to have made Love to his Wife. In the firft Place therefore, *Cleomenes* fent a Herald to *Athens*, and obtain'd the Expulfion of *Clifthenes*, with many other Athenians; under colour, that they were guilty of an execrable Action. This Crime was laid to their charge by the Advice of *Ifagoras*. For the Alcmæonides, and thofe of their Party, had been the Authors of a Slaughter, in which *Ifagoras* and his Friends were no way concern'd. The Action pafs'd in this manner. *Cylon* an Athenian, having been victorious in the Olympian Exercifes, attempted to make himfelf Tyrant; and to that end, forming a Society of Young Men about his own Age, endeavour'd to feize the *Acropolis:* Which not being able to effect, he fled with his Companions to the Image of the Goddefs. From that Place they were taken by the Naucrarian Magiftracy, who had then the Power in *Athens*, under a Promife, that their Lives fhould be fpar'd. But the Alcmæonides put them all to death. Thefe things were done before the Time of *Pififtratus*. Neverthelefs *Cleomenes*, tho' he had by his Herald ejected *Clifthenes* and his Accomplices, came to *Athens* with a fmall Force,

and

and upon his Arrival expell'd seven Hundred
Athenian Families at the Instigation of *Isagoras.*
When he had done this, he attempted to dissolve the Council, and to put the Power into
the Hands of three hundred Partizans of *Isagoras.* But finding the Council resolv'd to oppose his Design, and not to obey; he and *Isagoras*, with those of his Faction, seiz'd the
Castle: Where they were besieg'd during two
Days by the rest of the Athenians, who adher'd
to the Council. On the third Day they surrender'd, on condition, that all the Lacedemonians in the Place might depart out of the Country. And thus an Admonition which *Cleomenes*
had receiv'd, was ratified by the Event: For
as he came to take Possession of the *Acropolis*,
and was about to enter the Sanctuary of the
Goddess, like one who had some Demand to
make, the Priestess rising from her Seat before he could open the Door, " Lacedemo-
" nian Stranger, said she, return; and come
" not into this sacred Place; for no Dorian
" is permitted to be here." " Woman, replied
" *Cleomenes*, I am not a Dorian, but an Achai-
" an:" And slighting her Admonition, seiz'd
the Fortress: Where the Lacedemonians were
again unsuccessful. The rest were taken by the
Athenians and put to death. Among these
was *Timsitheus*, Brother to *Cleomenes*, of whose
Strength and Enterprizes I could give some
surprizing Instances. After which the Athenians not doubting that they should be necessitated to make War against the Lacedemonians,
recall'd *Clisthenes* with the seven Hundred Families that had been banished by *Cleomenes*;
and sent an Ambassy to *Sardis*, in order to contract

tract a Confederacy with the Perſians. When theſe Ambaſſadors were arriv'd, and had ſpoken according to their Inſtructions, *Artapherenes* the Son of *Hyſtaſpes*, and Governour of *Sardis*, ask'd who the Athenians were, and what Part of the World they inhabited, that they ſhould deſire to make an Alliance with the Perſians. And after he had inform'd himſelf of theſe Particulars, he plainly told the Ambaſſadors, that if they would acknowledge the King by preſenting him with Earth and Water, he was ready to be their Confederate; if not, he commanded them to depart. Upon this Propoſal the Ambaſſadors conſulted together; and being very deſirous to conclude the Alliance, made anſwer, That they would comply: For which they were highly blam'd at their Return. In the mean time *Cleomenes* hearing that the Athenians inſulted him both in their Words and Actions, aſſembled an Army from all Parts of *Peloponneſus*, without diſcovering the Deſign he had to revenge himſelf upon the People of *Athens*, and to put the Power into the Hands of *Iſagoras*, who went with him out of the Fortreſs. Thus having collected great Forces, he march'd into the Territories of *Eleuſis*; while the Bœotians, as had been concerted, poſſeſs'd themſelves of *Oinoe* and *Hyſia* on the Borders of *Attica*; and the Chalcideans ravag'd other Parts of the Country. The Athenians, tho' they were doubtful at firſt to which ſide they ſhould turn their Arms, reſolv'd for the preſent to forbear the Bœotians and Chalcideans; and to bend all their Strength againſt the Peloponneſians, who had invaded *Eleuſis*. When the two Armis were
ready

ready to engage, the Corinthians, who had consulted together, being convinc'd their Cause was unjust, drew off their Forces and march'd away; *Demaratus*, the other Spartan King, and Son of *Ariston*, following their Example. He commanded the Lacedemonians in conjunction with *Cleomenes*, and never before had any Difference with him. But on occasion of this Disunion a Law was made in *Sparta*, that the two Kings should not for the future march out together at the Head of their Armies, as they had done to that Time; and that one of the Tyndarides should remain with the King, who staid at home: For both these also had been formerly accustom'd to accompany the Army, as Inspectors. When the rest of the Confederates perceiv'd that the Lacedemonian Kings could not agree, and that the Corinthians had quitted their Post, they drew off their Forces likewise. And this was the Fourth Expedition the Dorians made into *Attica*. Twice they enter'd, in order to make War; and twice for the good of the Athenian People. In their first Expedition they settled a Colony in *Megara*, during the Reign of *Codrus* King of *Athens*: They arriv'd a second and third time from *Sparta*, with a design to expel the Pisistratides; and a fourth time, when *Cleomenes* at the Head of the Peloponnesians invaded the Country of *Eleusis*. And thus the Dorian Armies had enter'd the Athenian Territories four several times.

AFTER the inglorious Dissipation of this Army, the Athenians desirous to right themselves for the Injuries they had receiv'd, march'd in the first Place against the Chalcideans; and finding

ing the Bœotians arriv'd to their Succour at the
Euripus, refolv'd to attack them firft. Accordingly falling upon the Enemy, the Athenians obtain'd a compleat Victory; kill'd great
Numbers of the Bœotians, and took feven
Hundred Prifoners. Then landing the fame
Day in *Eubœa,* they defeated the Chalcideans;
and left a Colony of four Thoufand Men in
Poffeffion of the Lands belonging to the moft
Wealthy of the Inhabitants, who are call'd by
the Name of the Hippobates. All the Prifoners taken in this Battle, were, together
with the Bœotians, put into Irons, and kept
under a Guard; but afterwards were fet at
liberty by the Athenians in confideration of
a Ranfom of two Mines paid for each Man.
Neverthelefs the Athenians preferv'd the Fetters in the *Acropolis:* Where they remain'd to
my Time, hanging on a Wall; which facing the
Apartment that opens to the Weftward, was
damag'd by Fire in the Median War. The
Tenth Part of this Ranfom they confecrated; and having made a Chariot with Four
Horfes in Front, all of Brafs, they plac'd it in
the Portico of the *Acropolis,* on the Left-fide
of the Entrance, bearing this Infcription,

When the victorious Youth of Athens made
The proud Bœotian and Chalcidean bow
Beneath the Chain, they to Minerva plac'd
This Monument, the Tenth of all the Spoil.

Thus the Affairs of the Athenians flourifh'd.
Yet they are not the only Example of this
Kind. For all Places abound in Inftances of
the Profperity that attends an equal Diftribution
of

of Power. Under their Tyrants indeed they were not inferior in War to any of their Neighbours : But they had no sooner freed themselves from that Servitude, than they far surpass'd all the rest, and became the principal Nation of *Greece :* Which manifestly shews, that as long as they were oppress'd, they acted remissly, and would not exert their Courage to the utmost ; because they knew their Victories could only redound to the Advantage of their Masters ; whereas after they had recover'd their Liberty, every Man contended who should do best, because they fought for themselves. And such was the State of the Athenian Affairs.

AFTER this, the Thebans meditating Revenge against the Athenians, sent to consult the Oracle ; and the Answer of the Pythian was, that they must not expect the Satisfaction they desir'd, from their own Power ; but should go to *Polyphemus,* and ask the Assistance of their nearest Neighbours. With this Answer the Messengers return'd, and when they had reported the Words of the Oracle in a general Assembly, the Thebans said, " Have we not the Ta-
" nagræans, Coronæans and Thespians for our
" nearest Neighbours? Are not these our Com-
" panions in Fight, and always ready to take
" part with us in every War? What need have
" we then to ask their Assistance ? But per-
" haps these Words may contain some other
" Sense." As they were discoursing in this manner, one of the Assembly said, he thought he understood the Meaning of the Oracle.
" For, said he, according to common Fame,
" *Asopus* had two Daughters, *Thebe* and *Ægina.*

I   " Now

" Now becaufe thefe were Sifters, I prefume
" the God admonifhes us to defire the Ægi-
" netes to be our Avengers." The Thebans
approving this Opinion more than any other,
fent to the People of *Ægina*, as their nearest
Friends, to defire Succour according to the
Admonition of the Oracle: And upon their
Request, the Æginetes promis'd to fend the
Æacides to their Affiftance. In conjunction
with thefe, the Thebans attack'd the Athenians;
but being repuls'd with great Lofs, they fent
back the Æacides, and defir'd a farther Supply
of Men. Upon which the People of *Ægina*,
elated with their prefent Felicity, and remembring the antient Differences they had with
the Athenians, invaded the Territories of
Athens at the Defire of the Bœotians, without
any preceding Denuntiation of War. For
while the Athenian Forces were employ'd a-
gainft the Bœotians, they made a Defcent into
Attica, and ravag'd the Country of *Phaleron*,
with many other Places on the Coaft, to the
great Damage of the Athenians. This Enmity of the Æginetes againft the Athenians began thus. The Epidaurians feeing their Country become unfruitful, fent to confult the Oracle
of *Delphi* concerning the Caufe of that Calamity: The Pythian anfwer'd, That if they
would erect the Statues of *Damias* and *Auxefias*,
their Affairs fhould go better. Then the Epidaurians farther demanded, whether thofe
Images fhould be made of Stone or of Brafs:
and the Pythian replied of neither; but of the
Wood of a cultivated Olive. Having receiv'd
this Anfwer, the Epidaurians defired Leave
of the Athenians to cut down an Olive-Tree,

perfuaded

persuaded that those of that Soil were the most sacred: And some say no Olive Trees grew at that Time in any other Country than that of *Athens.* The Athenians told them they were ready to grant their Request provided they would come annually to the City, and offer Sacrifice to *Minerva* and *Erectheus.* This Condition the Epidaurians accepting obtain'd their Desires; and after they had erected the Statues they form'd out of that Wood, their Country became fruitful again, and they perform'd the Promise they had made to the Athenians. In those and the preceding Times, the Æginetes were dependent upon the Epidaurians in all things; and particularly in matters relating to the Distribution of justice, whensoever they were either Appellants or Defendants. But afterwards applying themselves to the building of Ships, they ungratefully revolted from the Epidaurians; and being superior at Sea, among many other Hostilities exercis'd against them, took away the Statues of *Damias* and *Auxesias*; which they carried off, and erected at *Oia* in the midland Part of their own Country, about twenty Stades from their City. When they had done this, to render them propitious, they appointed Sacrifices, accompanied with Dances perform'd by Women in a ludicrous Manner; assigning to each Image ten Men to preside in the Solemnity. On this Occasion these Dancers were permitted to abuse all the Women of that Country with opprobrious Language, but not the Men: Which they did, in Conformity to the former Practice of the Epidaurians; who besides these, had other Religious Ceremonies not

I

fit

fit to be mention'd. When these Statues were taken away, the Epidaurians ceas'd to perform their Contract with the Athenians; and being reminded of their Default, openly infifted that they were under no farther Obligation. For, said they, so long as we had those Images in our Country, so long we complied with our Agreement: But to demand the same Acknowledgment from us since the time they have been taken away, is unjust: The Ægi-netes who are now in Possession, ought to do, as we did before. Upon this the Athenians dispatch'd a Messenger to *Ægina* with Order to demand the Statues; but the Æginetes made answer, that they had no Business with them. The Athenians say, that after this Refusal they fent a Ship with some of their Citizens to *Ægina* by a publick Decree; who upon their Arrival attempted to take off the Statues from the Bases, and to bring them away, because they had been made of Athenian Timber: But finding themselves unable to succeed that way, they threw Cords about the Images and as they endeavour'd to pull them down they were so terrified with Thunder and an Earthquake, that they became outragiously mad, and kill'd one another like Enemies; till no more than one remain'd alive, who escap'd to *Phaleron.* In this manner the Athe-nians relate the Story. But the Æginetes fay they arriv'd with a great Fleet, and not with a single Ship, as is pretended: For they could easily have resifted such a Number as might come in one or a few Ships, tho' they themselves had not been furnish'd with any. Nevertheless they give no certain Account,

whether

whether they left the Athenians to do as they thought fit, out of a Diftruft of their own Naval Strength, or defignedly perform'd the Part they acted; But only fay, that the Athenians meeting with no Oppofition, landed their Men, and march'd directly to the Statues; That after they had in vain endeavour'd to move them from their Pedeftals, they made ufe of Cords to draw them down ; and that the Images upon their Defcent perform'd an Action, which I cannot believe, tho' perhaps fome others may. For, faid they, both thefe Statues fell down on their Knees, and have ever fince continued in that Pofture. Thefe things are related of the Athenians by the People of *Ægina*: And concerning themfelves they fay, that being inform'd the Athenians would not fail to make War againft them, they prevail'd with the Argians to put themfelves into a Readinefs to come to their Affiftance. And accordingly, when the Athenians were landed in *Ægina*, the Argians enter'd the Ifland privately, from *Epidaurus*, and unexpectedly falling upon the Athenians, cut off their Retreat to the Ships: In which Inftant the Thunder and Earthquake happen'd. Thus the Argians and Æginetes relate the Story ; and the Athenians themfelves confefs, that no more than one Man efcap'd out of this Action to *Attica*. But whereas the Argians affirm, that they deftroy'd the Army of *Attica*, one Man only excepted ; the Athenians on the contrary fay, fome Demon interpos'd ; and the furviving Perfon foon perifh'd in this manner: When he return'd to *Athens*, and had given an account of this Difafter, the

Wives

Wives of those who had made the Descent upon *Ægina*, highly incens'd that one Man alone should be left alive of the Whole number, assembled together about him, and asking for their Husbands, kill'd him with the Points of the Pins which fasten'd their Garments. They add, that the Athenians were more disturb'd at this Action, than at their Defeat; and having no other way to punish the Women, compell'd them to alter their Dress, and wear the Ionian Habit. For before that time, the Wives of the Athenians were cloath'd in the Dorian Fashion, little differing from that of *Corinth*. But afterwards they were oblig'd to wear a linen Vest, that needed not to be fasten'd with Pins. Yet if we will speak the Truth, this Garment was originally of *Caria*, and not of *Ionia*. And indeed the ancient Habit of all the Women of *Greece* was the same with that which we now call Dorian. However, from this Event a Custom was introduc'd among the Argians and Æginetes, of making Pins greater by three fourth Parts than before; and of these consisted the principal Offerings that were dedicated in the Temples of the Gods by the Women of *Ægina*: who might not carry to those Places any thing made in the Territories of *Attica*, not even a Pitcher; but were forc'd to drink there in Pots of their own Country. In a word, the Women of *Argos* and *Ægina*, in despite to those of *Athens*, wear at this Day Pins of a greater Size, than they used in antient time. Thus I have related the Original of that Enmity which the Æginetes conceiv'd against the Athenians; and which mov'd them so readily to assist the Bœotians at the Desire of the Thebans;

because

because they had not forgotten the things that had pass'd about the two Images.

WHILE the Forces of *Ægina* were ravaging the maritim Places of *Attica*, and the Athenians prepar'd to march out against them, an Oracle was brought to *Athens* from *Delphi*, exhorting them to defer the Punishment of the Æginetes during thirty Years ; and in the one and thirtieth Year, to build a Temple to *Æacus*, and then to begin the War, with full Assurance of Success : Adding farther, that if they would not be dissuaded from undertaking that Enterprize immediately, they should sustain as great Losses as ther Enemies, and be overcome in the end. When the Athenians heard the Prediction, they built a Temple to *Æacus*, which is now seen standing in the publick Place ; yet would not defer the War for thirty Years upon the Admonition of the Oracle, because they had already suffered by the Hostilities of the Æginetes. But as they were preparing to take their Revenge, the Lacedemonians obstructed their Design. For being inform'd of the Fraud contriv'd between the Alcmæonides and the Pythian, together with all that she had done against the Pisistratides, they perceiv'd they had injur'd themselves doubly ; having expell'd their own Friends and Allies out of *Athens*, and receiving no Thanks from the Athenians for that Kindness. Besides, they were made acquainted with certain Oracles, threatning them with Indignities from the Athenians ; of which they knew nothing till the Return of *Cleomenes* ; who finding them in the *Acropolis*, after they had been in the Possession of the Pisistratides, and left in

that

that Place at their Expulsion, brought them a-way with him to *Sparta.* The Lacedemonians therefore having receiv'd this Informations, and considering the prosperous Condition of the Athenians; with their manifest Unwillingness to acknowledge the Superiority of *Sparta*; were persuaded that if the People of *Attica* should continue in Freedom, they would soon aspire to an Equality; and on the contrary would be weak and humble if they were under a Tyranny: Considering these things, I say, they sent for *Hippias* the Son of *Pisistratus* from *Sigeum* on the *Hellespont*, to which Place the Pisistratides were retir'd; and after his Arrival, having assembled the Deputies of the rest of their Confederates, some of the Spartans spoke to this effect. " Friends and Allies, we are now
" convinc'd of the Error we committed, when
" relying upon deceitful Oracles, we not only
" expell'd from their Country, Men, who
" were our trusty Confederates, and had un-
" dertaken to put *Athens* into our hands;
" but deliver'd the City to an ungrateful Peo-
" ple, who, after they had been set at liberty
" by us, had the insolence to eject our King
" with Loss and Dishonour; and from that
" time have advanc'd both in Pride and Pow-
" er; as their Neighbours the Bœotians and
" Chalcideans have already experienc'd; and
" others may soon feel, if they should hap-
" pen to incur their Displeasure. Since then
" we have been guilty of so great a Fault,
" let us agree to march against them, and en-
" deavour to take Revenge. For to that End
" we have sent for *Hippias*, and summon'd e-
" very one of you; that by common Consent,

" and

" and united Forces, we may reinstate him in
" the Possession of *Athens*, and restore what
" we took away from him." To this effect
the Lacedemonians express'd themselves. But
their Confederates not approving their Proposition, were silent: Only *Soscles* the Corinthian made the following Speech; " Then,
" surely, said he, the Heavens will sink beneath
" the Earth, and the Earth ascend above the
" Air; Men shall live in the Sea, and the
" Fishes possess the Habitations of Men, when-
" soever you, O Lacedemonians, shall dissolve a
" Commonwealth, and endeavour to erect a
" Tyranny; than which nothing can be found
" more unjust, and more pernicious among
" Men! But if a Tyranny appear to you so ex-
" cellent a thing, establish one first in your
" own Country; and then with a better Grace
" you may attempt to set up Tyrants in other
" Places. But would you, who are altogether
" unacquainted with the Exercise of tyrannical
" Power, and have carefully provided to pre-
" vent any such in *Sparta*, condemn your Allies
" to that Shame? I persuade my self, if you
" had been taught by our Experience, you
" would propose better things to us. The
" State of *Corinth* was formerly this: The
" Government being oligarchical was admi-
" nistred by those, who were known by the
" Name of the Bacchiades, and had been ac-
" custom'd to marry only among their own
" Blood. *Amphion*, one of these, had a Daugh-
" ter nam'd *Labda*, who was born lame: And
" because none of the Bacchiades would
" marry her, she was given to *Ction* the Son
" of *Echerates*, of the Tribe of *Petra*, tho'
" originally

" originally of *Lapithe* and *Cenede*. But *Etion*
" having no Children by this Woman, nor by
" any other, went to *Delphi*, on that account;
" and as he enter'd the Temple, the Pythian
" saluted him with the following Lines:

Etion, *less honour'd than thy Merits claim,*
Labda *is pregnant, and a Stone shall bring ;*
To crush the Monarchs, and Corinthus *rule.*

" This Prediction was reported to the Bac-
" chiades, who had not understood a former
" Oracle, concerning *Corinth*, tending to the
" same End with that of *Etion*, and conceiv'd
" in these Terms,

A brooding Eagle on the Rocks should hatch
A Lyon-Whelp, destructive, fierce, and strong.
Consider, Corinth, *and* Pirene *fair,*
What must ensue from this prodigious Birth.

" The Bacchiades, who had never been able
" to comprehend the Meaning of this Oracle,
" no sooner heard that which was deliver'd to
" *Etion*, than they presently understood the o-
" ther ; and perceiving that both these Oracles
" foretold the same Event, they would not pub-
" lish their Suspicions ; but resolv'd to destroy
" whatever should be born to *Etion*. In this
" Resolution, after the Woman was brought to
" bed, they sent ten of their own Number, in-
" to the District where *Etion* liv'd, with Or-
" ders to dispatch the Child : And when those
" Men arriv'd in *Petra*, they went to the House
" of *Etion*, and desir'd to see the Infant: *Labda*

" not

" not at all fufpecting the Caufe of their com-
" ing, and imagining they ask'd that Queftion
" out of Friendfhip to the Father, brought
" the Child and put him into the Hands of
" one of the Ten ; who had made an Agree-
" ment by the way, that whoever fhould
" firft receive the Infant, fhould let him fall
" upon the Floor. But the Child happening
" by ftrange Fortune to fmile upon the Perfon,
" into whofe Hands the Mother had deliver'd
" him, mov'd his Compaffion to fuch a degree,
" that he could not prevail with himfelf to
" perform his Promife. So the firft relenting
" gave him to another, and he to a third ;
" till the Infant had pafs'd thro' the Hands of
" all the Ten : And when none of the Com-
" pany would kill him, they deliver'd him a-
" gain to his Mother, and went out of the
" Houfe. But ftanding ftill before the Door,
" they fell into a warm Debate, mutually
" blaming each other, and efpecially the firft
" who took the Child, for not doing as they
" had determin'd. At laft they all agreed
" to go in again, and that every one fhould
" be equally concern'd in the Death of the
" Infant. But, becaufe the Defolation of *Co-*
" *rinth* was to proceed from the Race of *Etion,*
" *Labda,* who from within had overheard
" all their Difcourfe, fearing they would re-
" turn with a Refolution to kill the Child,
" hid him in a Cypfela of Corn, as the fe-
" cureft Place ; not doubting, if they fhould
" come in again, they would make a moft di-
" ligent Search. Which indeed they did : For
" they return'd, and ftrictly examin'd every Part
" of the Houfe : But not finding the Child,
" they

" they refolv'd to depart, and tell thofe who
" fent them, that they had put their Orders in
" execution. After this, *Etion* brought up his
" Son, and nam'd him *Cypfelus*, from the Mea-
" fure of Corn, in which he lay conceal'd,
" when he efcap'd fo great a Danger. He had
" no fooner attain'd the Age of a Man, than
" he went to confult the Oracle at *Delphi*, and
" in Confidence of an ambiguous Anfwer, at-
" tempted, and fubdued *Corinth*. The Words
" were thefe;

A happy Man is come within my Houfe;
Cypfelus, Etion's Son, and Corinth's King:
He and his Sons: But then no more from him.

" When *Cypfelus* had ufurp'd the Dominion of
" *Corinth*, he behav'd himfelf thus. He ba-
" nifh'd many of the Corinthians, depriv'd
" many of their Eftates, and put a greater
" Number to death. After a Reign of thirty
" Years, attended by conftant Profperity,
" his Son *Periander* fucceeded him in the Ty-
" ranny. He was at firft more mild than
" his Father: But afterwards having by his
" Ambaffadors contracted a Friendfhip with
" *Thrafybulus* Tyrant of *Miletus*, he became far
" more cruel than *Cypfelus*. He fent one to
" ask *Thrafybulus* in his Name, how he might
" manage his Affairs, and govern the Corin-
" thians in the fafeft manner: The Milefian
" conducting this Perfon out of the City, en-
" ter'd with him into a Field of Corn, which
" he travers'd in every Part; and entertain-
" ing him with Queftions frequently repeat-
" ed concerning his Voyage from *Corinth*, cut
D 4   " down

" down and threw away all the tallest Stems
" he found in his Passage; till he had destroy'd
" the best and fairest of the Wheat in that
" manner. When he had done this quite over
" the Piece of Ground, he dismiss'd the Am-
" bassador, without charging him with any
" Message. At his Return, *Periander* was ear-
" nest to know the Answer of *Thrasybulus*,
" but he assur'd him he had receiv'd none; and
" wond'ring he should be sent to such a mad
" Man, who destroy'd his own Goods, related
" what he had seen him do. *Periander* present-
" ly comprehended the Meaning of *Thrasybulus*,
" and understanding that by this Action he
" had counsel'd him to take away the Lives
" of the most eminent Citizens, exercis'd all
" manner of Cruelties in *Corinth*, and by
" Death and Banishment exterminated those
" who had escap'd the Fury of *Cypselus*. Be-
" sides, he stripp'd all the Corinthian Women
" of their Clothes in one Day, on the account
" of his Wife *Melissa*. For when he sent
" Messengers into *Thesprotia* upon the River
" *Acheron*, to consult her after her Death, con-
" cerning a Treasure deposited in her Hands
" by a Friend, *Melissa* appearing, said, she
" would make no Discovery, nor tell in what
" Place it lay, because she was cold and na-
" ked, the Clothes which were buried with
" her proving useless, by reason they had not
" been burn'd. And to confirm the Truth of
" this she added, that *Periander* had put his
" Bread into a cold Oven. When these Words
" were reported to *Periander*, he well under-
" stood the Comparison of *Melissa*, because
" he had indeed lain with her after Death;
" and

" and immediately commanded Proclamation
" to be made, that all the Wives of the Co-
" rinthians fhould appear forthwith in the
" Temple of *Juno.* The Women went thither
" accordingly, richly drefs'd, as their Man-
" ner was on Feftival Days; and were all
" ftripp'd with their Attendants by the Guards
" of *Periander,* which he had privately intro-
" duc'd to that end. Then taking up the Gar-
" ments, he order'd them to be carried and
" burnt on the Grave of *Meliffa,* whilft he per-
" form'd his Devotions there. This done, he
" fent again to enquire concerning the Trea-
" fure of his Friend, and the Phantom of *Me-*
" *liffa* nam'd the Place where fhe had conceal'd
" it. Thefe, O Lacedemonians, thefe are the
" Fruits you will reap by erecting Tyrannies;
" for fuch are the genuine Actions of Tyrants.
" We Corinthians were feized with Admira-
" tion, when we underftood you had fent for
" *Hippias;* but our Amazement is highly aug-
" mented, fince we heard your Propofal. We
" adjure you therefore by the Grecian Gods,
" that you would not eftablifh Tyrannies in
" the Cities of *Greece.* Neverthelefs, if you
" refolve to perfift in your Defign, and againft
" all Right endeavour to reftore *Hippias,* know,
" that the Corinthians will have no Part in
" the Attempt." Thus fpoke *Sofycles,* Ambaffador of *Corinth.* But *Hippias,* after he
had atrefted the fame Gods, told him that
the Corinthians would be the firft of all People to regret the Pififtratides, when the fatal
Time fhould come, that they fhould be opprefs'd by the Athenians: And this he faid, in
Confidence of certain Oracles, which he was
                                        more

more acquainted with than any Man. The rest of the Confederates, who had been silent before, having heard the Speech of *Soficles*, openly declar'd themselves ; and unanimoufly embracing the Sentiments of the Corinthian Ambaffador, adjur'd the Lacedemonians not to introduce any Innovation into a Grecian City. And thus that Defign was defeated.

AFTER the Departure of *Hippias*, *Amyntas* King of *Macedonia*, made him an Offer of *Anthemus*, and the Theffalians another of *Iolcus* ; but accepting neither, he return'd to *Sigeum*, which *Pififtratus* had formerly taken from the Mityleneans, and put into the Hands of his natural Son *Hegefiftratus*, born of an Argian Woman. Yet he was not undifturb'd in his Pcffeffion : For the Mityleneans from *Achilleum*, and the Athenians from *Sigeum*, enter'd into a long War about the City ; the firft demanding Reftitution, and the Athenians rejecting their Claim, and afferting, that the Æolians had no more Right to the Territories of *Ilium*, than they, or any of the Grecians, who affifted *Menelaus* after the Rape of *Helena*. Many remarkable Actions of various kinds happen'd during this War : Among others, one relating to the Poet *Alcæus* ; who being prefent in a Battle, and feeing the Athenians victorious, fled out of the Field and made his efcape : But the Athenians having found his Arms, hung them up in the Temple of *Minerva* at *Sigeum :* And on that Occafion *Alcæus* afterwards compos'd a Poem, which he publifh'd in *Mitylene*, lamenting the Difgrace to his Companion *Melanippus*. In the End, *Periander* the Son of *Cypfelus* being chofen Arbitrator on both

4   fides,

ſices, reconciled the Athenians and Mityleneans, on Condition that each Party ſhould retain what they had. And by this Title the
Athenians poſſeſſ'd *Sigeum.*

AFTER the Return of *Hippias* from *Lacedemon* to *Aſia,* he ſet all his Invention to work
againſt the Athenians ; endeavouring by Aſper-
ſions to render them odious to *Artapbernes,* and
omitting nothing that might tend to reduce
Athens under the Power of *Darius* and himſelf.
Which when the Athenians underſtood, they
ſent Ambaſſadors to *Sardis,* with Inſtructions to
ſollicit the Perſians not to give ear to the Athenian Exiles. But *Artapbernes* haughtily told
them, that if they deſir'd to be ſafe, they muſt
receive *Hippias* again. The Athenians rejected
the Condition, and choſe rather to declare open
Enmity againſt the Perſians. When they had
taken this Reſolution, and were on theſe Terms
with the Perſians ; in that Conjuncture *Ariſtagoras* the Mileſian, who had been commanded
to depart from *Sparta* by *Cleomenes* the Lacedemonian, arriv'd in *Athens* ; which of all the Grecian Cities was the principal in Power. There,
addreſſing himſelf to the popular Aſſembly,
he repeated all that he had ſaid before in *Sparta*
touching the Wealth of *Aſia* : And to encourage them farther to make War upon the Perſians, he aſſur'd them, that having neither
Shield nor Lance, they muſt of neceſſity be
an eaſy Conqueſt. He withall reminded them,
that the Mileſians were a Colony of the
Athenians, and might juſtly expect their Aſſiſtance in this Exigency, ſince they were arriv'd to ſo great Power. In a word, he omitted no kind of Promiſes or Prayers ; till at
length,

length, he obtain'd their Consent. For he
thought a Multitude might with more Facility
be seduc'd than one Man. And thus he, who
had not been able to prevail with *Cleomenes*
the Lacedemonian singly, persuaded thirty
thousand Athenians to do whatever he desir'd.
In this Disposition the Athenians by a publick
Decree determin'd to send twenty Ships to
the Succour of the Ionians, under the Conduct of *Melanthius*, a Man universally esteem'd
in *Athens*. And from this Source the Evils
that afterwards fell upon the Grecians and
Barbarians, were principally deriv'd. *Aristagoras* sail'd before the Departure of this Fleet,
and arriving in *Miletus*, form'd a Design, which
could be of no Advantage to the Ionians ; nor
was contriv'd by him to that End ; but only
to make *Darius* uneasy. He sent a Man into
Phrygia, to the Pæonians, who had been carried
away Prisoners by *Megabyzus* from the River
Strymon, and plac'd in a certain District of
Phrygia ; where they inhabited together. When
this Person arriv'd he made the following
Speech : " Men of *Pæonia*, *Aristagoras* the
" Milesian has sent me hither, to open a Way
" for your Deliverance, if you will take his
" Advice. All *Ionia* has revolted from the
" King, and therefore you may safely return
" to your own Country : For you can meet
" with no Obstruction from hence to the Sea ;
" and the rest shall be our Care." The Pæonians heard the Proposition with exceeding Joy,
and having assembled their Wives and Children, fled away towards the Coast ; a few
only excepted, who fearing the Consequences
staid behind. When they were come to the Sea,
they

they imbark'd; and pass'd over to *Chio*. Where they were no sooner landed, than the Persian Cavalry arriv'd in great Numbers on the Shoar, pursuing the Pæonians; and finding they had made their Escape, sent Orders to *Chio* to command them to return. But the Pæonians slighting the Message, were transported by the Chians to *Lesbos*, and by the Lesbians to *Doriscus*; from whence they march'd by Land into *Pæonia*. In the mean time the Athenians arriv'd with twenty Ships at *Miletus*, accompanied by five more of the Eretrians, who engag'd not in this Expedition on the account of the Athenians; but to requite a preceding Kindness they had receiv'd from the Milesians. For in a former War the Milesians had taken Part with the Eretrians, against the Chalcideans supported by the Samians their Confederates. *Aristagoras*, after the Arrival of this Succour, and the rest of his Allies, resolv'd to attempt *Sardis*. But because he himself design'd to stay at *Miletus*, and not to go with the Army in Person, he appointed his Brother *Charopinus* to command the Milesians and plac'd *Hermophantus* at the Head of the other Forces. The Ionians arriving at *Ephesus*, left their Ships in the Harbour of *Coresus*, belonging to that City; and chusing Ephesians for their Guides, advanc'd with a numerous Army by the Side of the River *Caystrus*; pass'd the Mountain *Tmolus*, and coming before *Sardis*, took the City without Opposition. But *Artaphernes* with a strong Garison kept the Castle from falling into their Hands; and an Accident happening, depriv'd them likewise of the Pillage they expected: For as most of the Houses in *Sardis* were built

with

with Cane; and even those which were built with Brick, were roof'd with Canes, one House being set on fire by a Soldier, spread the Flame throughout the Place. During this Fire, all the Lydians and Persians who were in the City, finding no way open for their Escape, because the Flame had seiz'd the outermost Parts, ran together in great Numbers to the publick Place; thro' the midst of which the River *Pactolus* runs, sweeping down Grains of Gold from the Hills of *Tmolus*, and being afterwards receiv'd by the *Hermus*, passes thro' the same Channel to the Sea. Thus the Lydians and Persians being assembled in great Multitudes upon the Place, and on both sides of the River, were constrain'd to defend themselves: And the Ionians seeing one Part of the Enemy standing in their Defence, and greater Numbers ready to support them, retir'd with Precipitation to the Mountain *Tmolus*, and march'd away by Night to their Ships. In this Conflagration, the Temple of *Cybele*, the Goddess of that Country, was burnt; which afterwards serv'd the Persians for a Pretence to set on fire the Temples of *Greece*. When the Persians who had their Habitations on this side the River *Halys*, were inform'd of these things, they drew together, and march'd to the Succour of the Lydians: But not finding the Ionians at *Sardis*, they followed them with all Diligence to *Ephesus*; where they fought and defeated the Ionian Army with great Slaughter. In this Battle many illustrious Persons were kill'd; and among others, *Eualcides* General of the Eretrians, who on account of his Olympian Victories having
obtain'd

obtain'd divers Crowns, had been highly celebrated by *Simonides* the Cean. Thofe who
efcap'd out of the Field, difpers'd themfelves
into various Places. And fuch was the Succefs
of this Expedition. After which, the Athenians totally abandon'd the Ionians ; and when
they were follicited on their Part by the Ambaffadors of *Ariftagoras* in the moft preffing Terms,
declar'd they would fend them no Affiftance.
But the Ionians, tho' they were depriv'd of
that Succour ; yet becaufe they had done fo
much againft *Darius*, prepar'd themfelves to
carry on the War with no lefs Vigour than
before ; and failing into the *Hellefpont* reduc'd
Byzantium, with all the adjacent Cities under
their Obedience. Then proceeding farther
with their Fleet, they prevail'd with many of
the Carians to become their Confederates ;
for the City of *Caunus*, which before had rejected their Alliance, refolv'd to affift the Ionians
after the burning of *Sardis*. And all the Cyprians, except the Amathufians, readily enter'd
into the fame Confederacy ; having already revolted from *Darius* in this manner : *Onefilus*
the younger Brother of *Gorgus* King of the Salaminians, Son to *Cherfis*, and Grandfon of *Siro-
mus* the Son of *Euelthon*, having formerly foli-
cited his Brother at divers times to revolt a-
gainft the King ; when he heard of the Ionian
Defection, renew'd his Inftances with greater
Earneftnefs than before. But finding he could
not prevail upon *Gorgus*, he waited an Opportunity ; and one Day, when his Brother was
gone out of the City with his Partizans, fhut
the Gates againft him. *Gorgus* being thus excluded, fled to the Medes ; and *Onefilus* having

poffefs'd

possess'd himself of *Salamis*, persuaded the Cyprians to join with him, and besieg'd the Amathusians, who singly refus'd to revolt at his Solicitation. Whilst *Onesilus* was employ'd in the Siege of *Amathus*, *Darius* being inform'd that *Sardis* had been taken and burnt by the Athenians and Ionians, and that *Aristagoras* the Milesian had been the Author of this Confederacy, as well as the Contriver of that Enterprize; was not much concern'd about the Ionians, who, he doubted not, might be easily punish'd for their Rebellion: but demanding what People those Athenians were, he had no sooner receiv'd an Answer to that Question, than taking a Bow into his Hand, he let go an Arrow into the Air, with these Words: " Grant, O *Jupiter*, that I may be reveng'd " of the Athenians!" After he had thus spoken, he commanded one of his Attendants thrice to repeat the ensuing Words, every time he should sit down to eat, " Monarch, re-" member the Athenians." Then calling *Histiæus* the Milesian, whom he had long detain'd with him, *Darius* said ; " I am inform'd, *Histiæus*, that the Governor you appointed to " command in *Miletus* during your Absence, " has executed an injurious Enterprize against " me ; for he has brought Men into *Asia* " from the other Continent, and having per-" suaded the Ionians, who shall not go long " unpunish'd, to join them, has with those " Forces depriv'd me of *Sardis*. Can you " think these Actions commendable ? Or can " any one imagine they were done without " your Advice ? Be careful therefore to avoid " such Faults for the future." To this *Histiæus* " answer'd ;

answer'd, "O King, what have you said?
" That I shou'd advise a thing, which might
" give you the least Occasion of Discontent!
" What Advantage could I propose to myself
" by such an Action? Can I want any thing?
" I who live in the same Splendor with you,
" and am honour'd with the Confidence of
" all your Counsels? If my Lieutenant is guil-
" ty of the Actions you mention, be assur'd,
" he himself has been the Contriver. But
" in the first Place, I cannot persuade my-
" self, that he and the Milesians have attempt-
" ed any thing against your Authority. Yet
" if the Charge should be true, and he has
" indeed done as you have been inform'd, con-
" sider, O King, whether your Affairs are
" not prejudic'd by my Absence from the ma-
" ritim Parts. For the Ionians seem only to have
" waited till I could be withdrawn, to put
" in execution a Design they had conceiv'd
" before; and if I had continued in *Ionia*,
" not one of those Cities would have revolted.
" Dismiss me therefore with Speed, and send
" me back to *Ionia*; that I may restore the
" Affairs of those Countries to their former
" Condition, and deliver the Milesian Deputy
" into your Hands, who has been the Au-
" thor of these Enterprizes. When I have
" perform'd this according to your Desire,
" I swear by the Gods of the King, not to
" change the Garments I wear in my Voy-
" age to *Ionia*, before I render the great Is-
" land of *Sardinia* tributary to *Darius*." *Histiæus* said these Words in order to deceive the
King; and succeeded in his Design. For *Darius* was persuaded to let him go: Only com-

manding him to return to *Sufa*, fo foon as the things he had promis'd fhould be perform'd.

WHEN the News of *Sardis* was brought to the King, and he fhot an Arrow into the Air; whilft he conferr'd with *Hiftiæus*, and *Hiftiæus* was on his Journey to the Sea; in all this Time the following Actions pafs'd. *Onefi-lus* the Salaminian, who was employed in the Siege of *Amathus*, having receiv'd Information, that a great Army under the Conduct of *Arty-bius* a Perfian, was fuddenly expected to land in *Cyprus*, fent Heralds to demand the Affiftance of the Ionians: who without much hefitation affembled a confiderable Fleet, and fail'd to *Cyprus*. The Perfians on their Part landing their Men from *Cilicia*, march'd up to *Salamis*; while the Phœnicians kept cruifing with their Ships about the Promontory which is called the Key of the Ifland. In the mean Time the Cyprian Princes fummon'd the Ionian Captains together, and fpoke to them in thefe Terms; " Men of *Ionia*, we give you the Choice ei-" ther to fight againft the Perfians or Phœni-" cians. If you chufe to engage the Perfians " in a land Battle, 'tis time to bring ycur " Forces afhoar, that we may go on board " your Ships, and fight the Phœnicians: But " if you are more willing to make an Experi-" ment of your Strength againft the Phœnici-" ans do as you think convenient; that whe-" ther you determine one way or the other, " we may endeavour with all our Power to " preferve the Liberty of *Cpyrus* and *Ionia*." To this Difcourfe the Ionians anfwer'd, " We " are fent by the general Council of *Ionia* to " defend the Sea; and not to deliver our Ships

" to

" to the Cyprians, in order to fight the Perſi-
" ans by Land. We ſhall endeavour to do
" our Duty in the beſt manner we can, accord-
" ing to the Inſtructions we have receiv'd. On
" your part, the Remembrance of the Evils
" you ſuffer'd under the Tyranny of the Medes,
" ought to incite you to exert the utmoſt
" of your Courage and Virtue." Soon after
this anſwer made by the Ionians, the Perſians
were ſeen advancing into the Plains of *Salamis*; upon which the Kings of *Cyprus* drawing
up their Forces in order of Battle, plac'd the
beſt of the Salaminians and Solians againſt the
Front of the Perſians, and all the reſt of the
Cyprians againſt the Enemy's Auxiliaries. *Oneſilus* voluntarily plac'd himſelf directly againſt
Artybius the Perſian General, who was mounted on a manag'd Horſe accuſtom'd to riſe a-
gainſt an arm'd Enemy. Of this *Oneſilus* had
been already inform'd; and having with him
an Officer well skill'd in Military Affairs, and
of great Boldneſs, he ſaid to him; "*Artybius*
" is mounted on a Horſe, taught to ſtand up-
" right, and with his Feet and Teeth to kill
" the Man he is puſh'd againſt; Chuſe there-
" fore immediately, whether thou wilt under-
" take to deal with *Artybius* or his Horſe. I
" am ready anſwer'd the Officer, to do both,
" or either, or any other thing you ſhall com-
" mand; but I ſhall take liberty to propoſe
" that which I think moſt conducing to your
" Honour. He who is a King and a General,
" ſhould never decline to engage againſt one
" who is of the ſame Condition. For if you
" kill him, your Glory is great; and if he
" kills you, which the Gods avert, you are

" only

" only unfortunate in part, because you fall
" by a noble Hand. In the mean time we
" Subjects will fight against those who are
" our Equals: And as to the Horse, you have
" nothing to fear; for I take upon me, to
" prevent him from falling upon any Man,
" for the time to come." Soon after these
Words, the Armies engag'd both by Sea and
Land. All the Ionians fought vigorously, and
defeated the Phœnicians at Sea: But the Samians surpass'd the rest in Valour that Day.
By Land when the Armies met, and the Battle was begun, *Artybius* push'd his Horse towards *Onesilus*, and *Onesilus* struck *Artybius*, as
he had concerted before with his Officer. The
Officer on his part, seeing the Horse raising
his Feet to the Shield of *Onesilus*, struck him
with a Scythe, and cut them both off: So
that *Artybius* the Persian General, fell with
his Horse to the Ground at one Blow. But
as the Dispute grew hot on both sides, *Stesenor*
Tyrant of *Curium*, which is said to be a Colony of *Argos*, revolted to the Enemy with
a considerable Number of Forces under his
Command; and presently after this Treachery
of the Curians, the Chariots of War belonging
to *Salamis* follow'd their Example: By which
means the Persians obtain'd the Victory, and
the Cyprians were put to flight with great
Slaughter. Among others *Onesilus* the Son
of *Cherfis*, who had persuaded the Cyprians
to revolt, was kill'd in this Battle; together with *Aristocyprus* King of the Solians,
the Son of that *Philocyprus*, who of all the
Princes of his Time is most commended in the
Verses of *Solon* the Athenian, which he made
during

during his Stay at *Cyprus*. The Amathufians cut off the Head of *Onefilus*, becaufe he had befieg'd their City, and plac'd it over the Gates of *Amathus*: Where, after fome time when the Head was become empty, a fwarm of Bees enter'd and fill'd the Skull with Honey. Upon which the Amathufians confulting the Oracle, were admonifh'd, that if they would interr the Head, and facrifice annually to *Onefilus*, as to a Hero, their Affairs fhould profper. The Amathufians did accordingly, and continued thofe Sacrifices to my Time. The Ionians, who had fought by Sea on the Coaft of *Cyprus*, hearing the Difafter of *Onefilus*, and that the reft of the Cyprian Cities were befieg'd, except *Salamis*, which the Salaminians had reftor'd to their former King *Gorgus*, fail'd away to *Ionia*. Of all the Cities of *Cyprus*, *Soli* fuftain'd the longeft Siege: But in the fifth Month the Place was taken by the Perfians; after they had undermin'd the Walls. And thus the Cyprians having been a free People during one Year, were again reduc'd into Servitude.

DAURISES, *Hymees*, and *Otanes*, whofe Wives were Daughters to *Darius*, having together with other Perfian Generals, purfued thofe Ionians who made War againft *Sardis* to their Ships, and afterwards defeated them in the Field, feparated themfelves, in order to deftroy the Cities. *Daurifes* directing his March towards thofe of the *Hellespont*, took *Dardanus*, *Abydus*, *Percote*, *Lampfacus*, and *Pefus*; employing no more than one Day in the Reduction of each. But advancing from *Pefus* towards *Parium*, he receiv'd a Meffage, importing, that the Carians

E 3   entertaining

entertaining a Correspondence with the Ionians, had likewise revolted from the Persians. Upon this Advice he abandon'd the *Hellespont*, and led his Army against the Carians ; who being inform'd of his March, before his Arrival in their Territories, assembled their Forces at a Place call'd the *White Columns*, upon the River *Marsya*, which passes thro' the Country of *Hydrias*, and falls into the *Meander*. Divers Propositions were made in this Camp ; but none, in my Opinion, so good as that of *Pixodarus* the Son of *Mausolus*, a Cyndian, who had married the Daughter of *Syennesis* King of *Cilicia*. He advis'd, that the Carians would pass the *Meander*, and fight the Persians on the other side ; that having the River in their Rear, and no Way left to retreat, they might be necessitated to keep their Ground, and surpass the common Valour of Men. But the Carians rejecting his Proposition, resolv'd to let the Persians pass the *Meander* ; to the end that if they should be beaten, the River might be in the Way, and cut off their Retreat. So the Persians advancing pass'd the *Meander* ; and the Carians expecting the Enemy on the Banks of the River *Marsya*, fought a long and bloody Battle, till at last, oppress'd with Numbers, they were totally defeated. In this Action two Thousand Persians and ten Thousand Carians were kill'd. The rest of the Carians who escap'd out of the Fight, fled to *Labranda*, and betook themselves to a vast Grove, sacred to the military *Jupiter*, and fill'd with Plane-trees. They are the only People we know, who sacrifice to that Deity, under the Name of the God of Armies. When they had taken sanctuary

ary

ary in that Place, willing to make the beſt Proviſion they could for their own Safety, they conſulted together, whether they ſhould ſurrender themſelves to the Perſians, or entirely abandon *Aſia*: And while they deliberated about this Affair, the Mileſians with their Confederates came to their Aſſiſtance: Which ſo encourag'd the Carians, that they immediately chang'd their Deſign, and reſolv'd to try the Fortune of War again. Accordingly they met the Perſians and fought another Battle with more Obſtinacy than the former; but in the end were put to flight, with great Slaughter; in which the Mileſians ſuffer'd moſt. Yet after this Blow the Carians continued to carry on the War; and hearing that the Perſians deſign'd to invade their Cities, plac'd an Ambuſcade on the Way to *Daſus*; into which the Perſians falling by Night, were cut in Pieces, with their Generals *Dauriſes*, *Amorges* and *Siſamaces*. *Myrſes* the Son of *Gyges* was likewiſe involv'd in this Slaughter: And ſuch was the End of theſe Perſians. *Heraclides* the Son of *Ibaxolis*, a Myleſian, was the Author of this Enterprize.

HYMEES, another of thoſe who purſu'd the Ionians after the Expedition of *Sardis*, bending his March towards the *Propontis*, took the City of *Cius* in *Myſia*. But hearing that *Dauriſes* had quitted the *Helleſpont*, and was advancing againſt the Carians, he abandon'd the *Propontis*; and being arriv'd with his Army on the *Helleſpont*, ſubdued all the Æolians of the Ilian Coaſt, together with the Gergithes, who were the only remaining People of the ancient Teucrians: And after the Conqueſt of theſe Nations died at *Troas*. In the mean time *Artapbernes*,

Gover-

Governor of *Sardis*, and *Otanes*, who was one of the three Generals, being appointed to invade *Ionia*, with the confining Territories of the Æolians, possess'd themselves of *Clazomene*, belonging to the Ionians, and took *Cyme* from the Æolians. The News of which Disasters so discompos'd the Mind of *Aristagoras* the Milesian, who knew he had been the Disturber of *Ionia*, and Author of these great Confusions, that he began to consider how to make his Escape; since he evidently saw he could do nothing effectually against *Darius*. To that end he summon'd those of his Faction together; and having told them their common Safety requir'd, that Care should be taken to secure a Place of Refuge, in case they should be expell'd from *Miletus*; he ask'd, whether he ought to conduct a Colony to *Sardinia*, or to the City of *Myrcinus*, built by *Histiæus* in the Country of *Edone*, which he receiv'd from *Darius*. But *Hecatæus* the Historian, Son to *Hegesander*, declar'd his Opinion against both these Propositions, and said, that if they should be compel'd to relinquish *Miletus*, they ought to build a City in the Island *Lerus*, and there continue quiet, 'till they could safely return back again. This was the Counsel of *Hecatæus*. Nevertheless *Aristagoras* chusing rather to go to *Myrcinus*, left the Government of *Miletus* in the Hands of *Pythagoras* an eminent Citizen; and together with all those who were willing to accompany him, sail'd into *Thrace* and took Possession of the Region to which he was bound. But as he was besieging a Place situate beyond those Limits, he perish'd with his Army by the Hands of certain Thracians, who before had offer'd to surrender upon Terms. THE

THE

History of *Herodotus*.

BOOK VI.

ERATO.

THUS died *Aristagoras*, who induc'd the Ionians to revolt: And *Histiæus* Tyrant of *Miletus*, having obtain'd Leave of *Darius*, went to *Sardis*, where when he arriv'd from *Susa*, *Artaphernes*, Governour of *Sardis*, ask'd his Opinion concerning the Cause of the Ionian Defection. *Histiæus* said, He could not imagine: And pretending to be ignorant of all that had pass'd, seem'd extremely surpriz'd at the Account he heard. But *Artaphernes* perceiving his Dissimulation, and being fully inform'd of the true Reason of the Revolt, reply'd, " *Histiæus*, this " Affair stands thus ; Thou wast the Maker of " that Shoe, which *Aristagoras* put upon his " Foot." By which Words *Histiæus* collecting that *Artaphernes* was well inform'd ; and fearing the Consequences, went away the following Night towards the Sea, and deceiv'd *Darius*: For instead of reducing the great Island of *Sardinia*, according to his Promise, he took upon himself the Conduct of the Ionian War against the King. At his landing in *Chio* he was seiz'd by the Chians, upon Suspicion that he had some Design to execute there in favour of *Darius*. But when they understood the whole

Truth,

Truth, and found he was an Enemy to the King they set him at liberty again. During his Stay in that Place, being question'd by they Ionians to what end he had so earnestly press'd *Aristagoras* by Messages to revolt from *Darius*, and brought such Disasters upon *Ionia*; he conceal'd the true Reason, and told them, that the King had resolv'd to bring the Phœnicians into *Ionia* and to transport the Ionians into *Phænicia*. This, he said, was the Cause of his Message to *Aristagoras*: and thus he alarm'd the Ionians; tho' indeed *Darius* had never form'd any such Design. After these things, he gain'd one *Hermippus* an Atarnian, and sent him to *Sardis* with Letters to certain Persians he had discours'd with before concerning a Revolt. But *Hermippus* not delivering the Letters to the Persons to whom they were address'd, put them into the Hands of *Artaphernes*; who by this means perceiving what was doing, commanded the Messenger to deliver the Letters of *Histiæus* according to his Instructions, and bring to him the Answers he should receive from the Persians. Thus *Artaphernes* having made a full Discovery, put many of the Persians to death, and caus'd a great Disorder in *Sardis*. *Histiæus* disappointed of these Hopes, was conducted back to *Miletus* by the Chians at his own Request: But, the Milesians being pleas'd with their Deliverance from *Aristagoras*, and the Liberty they enjoy'd, would by no means receive another Tyrant into their Country. Upon which, endeavouring to enter the City by Night with an arm'd Force, he was wounded in the Shoulder by a Milesian, and after that Repulse return'd to *Chio*. But finding he could not persuade the
Chians

Chians to entrust him with their Fleet, he pass'd over to *Mitylene* and prevail'd with the Lesbians to furnish him with eight Ships ; which they fitted out, and accompanied him to *Byzantium*. In this Station they took all the Ships that came out of the *Euxin*, except such as were willing to take part with *Histiæus*.

DURING the Course of these Actions done by *Histiæus* and the Mityleneans, the Enemy prepared to attack *Miletus* with a formidable Army, and a numerous Fleet. For the Persian Generals slighting the other Places had drawn all their Troops together in order to that Attempt. Their maritim Forces consisted of the Phœnicians, Cilicians and Ægyptians, with the Cyprians, who had been lately subdued: But of all these, the Phœnicians shew'd the greatest Zeal to forward the Enterprize. When the Ionians heard of the Enemy's Preparations against *Miletus* and the rest of *Ionia*, they sent the principal Persons of their several Councils to the General Assembly ; where being arriv'd, and consulting together, they unanimously resolv'd, that they would not bring together any Land Forces to oppose the Persians ; but whilst the Milesians should defend the City to the utmost of their Power, would arm and fit out all the Ships they had ; and then repairing with all Expedition to *Lade*, a little Island near *Miletus*, engage the Enemy in a Sea Battle within View of the Milesians. In this Resolution the Ionians mann'd their Ships, and appearing at the Rendezvous in Conjunction with those Æolians who inhabit *Æolia*, drew their Fleet into the following Order. The Milesians with 80 Ships were

rang'd

rang'd at the Head of the Line, ſtretching to
the Eaſtward; and next to theſe the Prienians
with twelve Ships, and the Myuſians with
three, followed by ſeventeen of the Teians,
and a hundred Sail of Chians. The Centre
was compos'd of the Erythræans in eight, the
Phocæans in three, and the Lesbians in ſeventy
Ships. The Samians alone with ſixty Sail were
plac'd in the Rear to the Weſtward. So that
the whole Ionian Fleet conſiſted of three
hundred fifty three Ships. And though three
Barbarians arriv'd on the Mileſian Coaſt with
ſix hundred Ships, and all their Land Forces;
yet the Perſian Generals hearing the Number
of the Ionian Fleet, began to fear they ſhould
not obtain the Victory, nor be able to take
Miletus, unleſs they could be Maſters at Sea:
And apprehendiug the Diſpleaſure of *Darius*,
if the Event ſhould prove unſucceſsful, ſum-
mon'd together the Tyrants of *Ionia*, who having been expell'd by *Ariſtagoras* out of their
Dominions, had fled to the Medes, and at that
time accompanied the Enemy in the Expedition
againſt the Mileſians. To theſe Men, when
they were met together, the Perſians ſpoke in
the following Terms; "If any among you, O
" Ionians, are deſirous to ſhow your Affection
" to the King's Service, this is the Time.
" Let every one of you endeavour to divide
" his own Subjects from the reſt of the Con-
" federacy; promiſing, in order to that End,
" that none ſhall ſuffer on account of their
" Rebellion; that we will neither burn the
" Temples, nor their own private Houſes; and
" that they ſhall be as favourably treated as be-
" fore. But if they refuſe this Offer, and re-

4 " ſolve

" folve to determine the Dispute by the Sword,
" acquaint them with the Evils which will in-
" evitably ensue upon their Obstinacy : That,
" after we have conquer'd, they shall be re-
" duc'd to the Condition of Slaves: That we
" will make Eunuchs of their Youth ; transport
" all their Virgins to *Bactria*, and give their
" Country to another People." When the
Persians had expres'd themselves in this manner, and Night was come, every one of the
Ionian Tyrants dispatch'd a Messenger to those
he had formerly commanded, with Instructions
to let them know what they were to expect.
But the Ionians, upon the Reception of these
Messages, despis'd their Menaces, and would
not be guilty of so great Treachery : For each
Nation was of opinion, that they alone were
solicited by the Enemy. Such were the Actions of the Persians immediately after their Arrival before *Miletus*.

THE Ionians having assembled their Fleet
near *Lade*, call'd a Council of War ; in which,
after divers Propositions had been made, *Dionysius* General of the Phocæans spoke to this effect.
" Our Affairs, O Ionians, are upon a Needle's
" Point ; we must either vindicate our Liberty
" now, or be totally enslav'd and punish'd as
" Fugitives. If you would submit to some
" Hardships at this time, you may indeed be
" uneasy for the present : But those Toils will
" enable you to preserve your Freedom, and
" overcome your Enemies. Whereas if you
" abandon your selves to Effeminacy and Dis-
" order, I despair to see you escape with Im-
" punity out of the Hands of the King. Yet
" could I persuade you to follow my Advice,

" and

" and to permit me to regulate your Conduct,
" I would undertake, unless the Gods inter-
" pose, either that our Enemies will not fight
" us at all, or if they do, that they shall be
" beaten." When the Ionians heard this, they
consented to put themselves under the Discipline of *Dionysius*; who every day drawing the
Fleet into Order of Battle, commanded the
Squadrons frequently to change their Stations,
that he might accustom the Rowers to the Labour of the Oar; and oblig'd all the Soldiers
to wear their Armour. When they had perform'd his Orders, they lay at Anchor the remaining Part of the Day: And thus he exercis'd the Ionians in the Fatigues of War. Seven Days they continued to obey the Commands
of *Dionysius*: But being unacquainted with such
Hardships, and exhausted by daily Labour, and
the scorching Heat of the Sun, they began to
complain one to another in such Terms as these;
" What Demon have we neglected, and now
" pay so dear for our Contempt? Senseless
" and depriv'd of Understanding, we have
" surrender'd our selves into the Hands of an
" insolent Phocæan; who, though he brought
" in no more than three Ships to the common
" Defence, destroys us by intolerable Hard-
" ships. Great Numbers of us are already
" fallen into Distempers; and we may reason-
" ably expect many more will soon be in the
" same Condition. 'Twere better for us to suf-
" fer any other thing, than the Pressures we
" now lie under: Better, to expect a future Ser-
" vitude, of what sort soever, than to draw
" upon our own Heads the Addition of these
" present Calamities. Let us take Courage then,

" and

" and no longer submit to his Commands."
This Discourse was so universal, that they unanimously refus'd to obey the Orders of *Dionysius,*
and forming a Camp in the Island, sat under
the Shade of their Tents, and would not return to perform their Exercise on board. The
Generals of the Samians observing these things,
and seeing great Disorders among the Ionians,
accepted the Proposal they had receiv'd on
the Part of the Persians, by a Message from
Æaces the Son of *Syloson,* exhorting them to
abandon the Confederacy : And being persuaded that the Ionians could not possibly prevail
against the King, because they knew, if that
Fleet of *Darius* should be destroy'd, he would
send another five times as powerful ; they embrac'd the Occasion ; and perceiving the Ionians would not acquit themselves like Men,
thought they should be Gainers, if they could
preserve their Temples and private Houses from
Destruction. This *Æaces,* who prevail'd with
the Samians, was the Son of *Syloson,* the
Son of another *Æaces;* and being Tyrant of
Samos, had been depriv'd of his Dominions
by *Aristagoras* the Milesian, as the rest of the
Ionian Tyrants were. In this Disposition of
things, the Phœnicians advanc'd with their
Ships, and the Ionians came on likewise in
Order of Battle : But I cannot affirm with
certainty, who among the Ionians behav'd
themselves well or ill, after the two Fleets
were engag'd ; because they mutually accuse
one another. Yet they say, that the Samians, in pursuance of their Agreement with
Æaces, immediately hoisting Sail went out of
the Line, and return'd to *Samos,* eleven Ships
only

2

only excepted, the Captains of which ftaid and fought, in difobedience to their Leaders ; and for this Action were rewarded at their Return by the Community of *Samos*, with an Infcription on a Pillar, declaring their Names and Families, in order to tranfmit their Memory to Pofterity with Honour ; which Monument is ftill feen in the publick Place. When the Lefbians, who were in the next Station, faw that the Samians had betaken themfelves to Flight, they follow'd their Example ; and moft of the Ionians did the fame. But among thofe who perfifted in the Battle, the Chians, as they fuffer'd the greateft Lofs, fo they gave the moft fignal Proofs of their Valour, and defended themfelves to Extremity. They brought, as I faid before, one Hundred Ships, each of which had forty chofen Citizens on board ; and tho' they faw that the greateft Part of the Confederates had abandon'd the common Caufe, they would not be perfuaded to imitate their Treachery : But chufing rather to remain with the few, they advanc'd and engag'd the Enemy : till at laft, after they had taken many Ships, and loft more of their own, they fled away homewards with the reft. Thofe Chians, who had their Ships difabled in the Fight, being purfued by the Enemy, made the beft of their Way to *Mycale* ; and having run their Ships a-ground on that Shoar, march'd by Land into the Country of *Ephefus*, and arriv'd near the City by Night, at a Time when the Women were celebrating the Rites of *Ceres*. The Ephefians altogether ignorant of what had befall'n the Chians, and feeing an arm'd Multitude within their Territo-

ries,

ries, thought they could be no other than Robbers, who had a Design upon the Women; and in that Opinion sallying out with the whole Force of the City, kill'd them all on the Spot: And this was the Fate of those Chians. In the mean time *Dionysius* the Phocæan, when he saw the Ionians totally defeated, abandon'd the Fight, and sail'd away with three Ships he had taken from the Enemy. But not at all doubting that *Phocæa* would be subdued with the rest of *Ionia*, instead of returning home, he went directly to *Phœnicia*; and after he had made Booty of many trading Ships on that Coast, sail'd away with immense Riches to *Sicily:* From whence he committed great Depredations upon the Carthaginians and Tuscans; yet always sparing the Grecians. The Persians on their part, having obtain'd this Victory over the Ionians, besieg'd *Miletus* both by Sea and Land; and after they had undermin'd the Walls, and employ'd all manner of military Engines in the *Siege*, took and destroy'd the City in the sixth Year after the Revolt of *Aristagoras*, and reduc'd the Inhabitants to Servitude, as the Oracle had foretold. For when the Argians consulted the Pythian touching the Fortune of their City, they receiv'd a double Answer; partly concerning themselves, and partly respecting the Milesians. That which was address'd to the Argians, we shall repeat in a proper Place; the other Part relating to the Milesians, was comprehended in the following Lines.

Miletus, *Source of Ill, thy Stores shall serve*
To feast, and to enrich a Multitude.

*Men with long Hair shall sit and see their Feet
Wash'd by the Virgins* ; Didyma *shall see
Her Altars to another Place transferr'd.*

These things fell upon the Milesians at that
Time : For the greater Part of the Men were
kill'd by the Persians, who wear long Hair ;
their Women and Children were made Slaves,
and the Temple in *Didyma*, with the Grove
and Oracle, were reduc'd to Ashes. The
great Riches deposited in this Place, we have
already mention'd on divers Occasions. All
the Milesian Prisoners were conducted to *Susa* :
From whence *Darius*, without any other ill
Usage, sent them to inhabit the City of *Am-
pe*, situate near the Mouth of the *Tigris*, not
far from the Place where that River falls into the Red-Sea. The Persians reserv'd to
themselves the Lands that lie about *Miletus*,
with all the level Country, and gave the Carians of *Pedieis* Possession of the Hills. In this
Desolation, the Sybarites, who after their Expulsion, went to inhabit the Cities of *Laos*
and *Scydrus*, requited not the former Kindness
of the Milesians. For after the Crotonians
had taken *Sybaris*, the Milesians shav'd the
Heads of all their Youth, and gave publick
Demonstrations of their Sorrow ; because these
two Cities had been more strictly united in
Friendship than any other. But the Athenians
behav'd themselves in another manner, and
many ways manifested the Sense they had of
the Calamities of the Milesians ; particularly
when *Phrynicus* had compos'd a Dramatic Poem
concerning the Destruction of *Miletus*, the whole
Theatre burst into Tears at the Representation ;
fin'd

fin'd him a thousand Drachma's for renewing
the Memory of a Misfortune they took to be
their own; and gave order that the Piece
should never more appear in publick. In this
manner the Milesians were ejected.

BUT the Samians who were of any Consideration, not approving what their Generals
had done in favour of the Medes, assembled
a Council after the Event of the Battle at
Sea, and took a Resolution to relinquish their
Country before the Arrival of their Tyrant
Æaces; left by continuing in *Samos*, they
should become Slaves to him and the Medes.
In that Conjuncture the Zanclæans, a People
of *Sicily*, being desirous to have a City inhabited by the Ionians, sent Messengers to *Ionia*,
with Orders to solicit them to settle a Colony in that Part which faces the Tyrrhenian
Sea, and is called the beautiful Coast. Upon
this Invitation the Samians, and such Milesians has had escap'd by Flight, were the only
Ionians who went thither. During their Voyage, and at the time of their landing in the
Country of the Epizephyrian Locrians, the
Zanclæans, with *Scythes* their King, were employ'd in the Siege of a Sicilian City; which *A-
naxilaus*, Tyrant of *Rhegium* and an Enemy of
the Zanclæans, understanding, he insinuated to the
Samians, that it would be more advantageous for
them to seize the City of *Zancle* in the Absence
of the Inhabitants, than to settle on the Coast
design'd for their Establishment. The Samians
soon persuaded to do as he advis'd, possess'd
themselves of *Zancle* accordingly; which the
Zanclæans hearing, hasten'd to recover their
City, and call'd to their Assistance *Hippocrates*,

Tyrant

Tyrant of *Gela* their Ally. But *Hippocrates* arriving with his Army, caus'd *Scythes* King of *Zancle* to be seiz'd for abandoning the City, and banish'd him with his Brother *Pythogenes* to *Inycum:* After which, by an Agreement made with the Samians, and confirm'd on both sides with an Oath, he betray'd the rest of the Zanclæans, on Condition to have one half of the Slaves and Plunder of the City, besides all that should be found in the Country. Under colour of this Contract, *Hippocrates* took the greater Part of the Zanclæans, and treated them as Slaves, delivering three hundred of the principal Citizens to be put to death by the Samians; but they would not commit so cruel an Action. In conclusion, *Scythes* King of the Zanclæans made his Escape from *Inycum* to *Hymera*, and there imbarking, pass'd over into *Asia* to *Darius*, who thought him the most sincere of all the Grecians he had seen in his Court. For *Scythes*, after he had made a Voyage to *Sicily* with the King's Leave, return'd back again, and died among the Persians, very old and very rich. Thus the Samians at once escap'd the Yoke of the Medes, and without Pains made themselves Masters of *Zancle*, a great and beautiful City.

AFTER the Battle which was fought by Sea for the Possession of *Miletus*, the Phœnicians by Order of the Persians, conducted *Æaces* the Son of *Syloson* to *Samos*, in recompence of his Merits and Service. This was the only City of all those that revolted from *Darius*, which escap'd with its Houses and Temples undestroy'd; because the Samians had abandon'd their Allies in the Engagement at Sea. The Persians after the

Reduction

Reduction of *Miletus*, foon poffefs'd themfelves of *Caria* ; partly by a voluntary Submiffion of the Inhabitants, and partly by Force.

WHILE *Hiftiæus* the Milefian continued about *Byzantium*, intercepting the trading Ships of the Ionians in their Paffage from the *Euxin*, he receiv'd an Account of all that had pafs'd at *Miletus* ; and leaving the Care of his Affairs on the *Hellefpont* to *Bifaltes* of *Abydus*, the Son of *Apollophanes*, he took the Lesbians with him, and fail'd to *Chio :* Where meeting with Oppofition from a Guard which was pofted in a deep and narrow Pafs, he kill'd great Numbers on the Spot : And afterwards marching with the Lesbians from a fmall Town of the Ifland, fubdued the Reft of the Chians, confiderably weaken'd by the preceding Fight at Sea. But becaufe the great Defolations which are about to fall upon any City or Nation, feldom happen without fome previous Signs, the Chians had divers very remarkable. For of one hundred Young Men they fent to *Delphi*, two only return'd home, after they had loft ninety-eight of their Companions by the Plague. And a little before the Battle at Sea, a Houfe in the City falling upon the Heads of one hundred and twenty Boys, as they were learning to read, kill'd all that Number, except one. After thefe divine Admonitions, the Difafter of their Fleet enfued ; which brought the City upon her Knees : And the Invafion of *Hiftiæus* with the Lesbians following upon this, and furprizing the Chians in that low Condition, finifh'd the Cataftrophe of the Ifland. From thence *Hiftiæus* with a numerous Army of Ionians and Æolians went to *Thafus*, and while he

was

was besieging that Place, receiv'd Information, that the Phœnicians had left *Miletus*, with a Design to invade the rest of *Ionia.* Upon which, breaking up from *Thasus*, he pass'd over to *Lesbos* with all his Forces; and from thence, because he found his Army under a Consternation, he sail'd again to *Atarneus*, under pretence of collecting Provisions in that Country, and on the Plains of *Caicus* in *Myfia.* But *Harpagus*, a Persian General, being in those Parts with a considerable Army, fell upon him soon after his Landing, kill'd most of his Men upon the Place, and took *Hiftiæus* Prisoner in the following manner. Whilst the Grecians made a long and vigorous Resistance against the Persians at *Malene* in the Country of *Atarneus*, the Enemy's Cavalry came pouring in upon them with such Fury, that they were forc'd to abandon the Field: Which *Hiftiæus* perceiving, and hoping the King would not put him to death for his Offence, he suffer'd himself to be taken Prisoner; too much desiring to preserve his Life. For as he fled, and was ready to fall into the Hands of a Persian, who had a Sword drawn to kill him, he in the Persian Language discover'd himself to be *Hiftiæus* the Milesian. And I am of opinion, that if he had been conducted alive to *Sufa*, *Darius* would have pardon'd his Fault, and giv'n him his Liberty. But lest that should happen, and *Hiftiæus* escaping, should again insinuate himself into the King's Favour, *Artaphernes* Governour of *Sardis*, and *Harpagus*, whose Prisoner he was, order'd him to be crucify'd at his Arrival in that City, and sent his Head embalm'd to *Darius* at *Sufa.* When the King was

inform'd

inform'd of this Action, he exprefs'd his Difcontent againft the Authors, becaufe they had
not brought *Hiftiæus* alive to his Prefence, and
commanded his Head to be wafh'd, and de-
cently interr'd; as the Remains of a Man, who
had highly merited of himfelf and the Perfians.
Thus died *Hiftiæus.*

THE Perfian Fleet, which winter'd at *Miletus*, eafily fubdued, in the following Year,
Chio, *Lesbos* and *Tenedos*, Iflands lying near the
Continent; and in every one of thefe, when
the Barbarians had poffefs'd themfelves of the
Place, they hunted the Inhabitants into a fort
of Net. For taking one another by the Hand,
and forming a Line from the North to the
South Side, they march'd over the Ifland, and
drove all the People before them. They took
the Ionian Cities on the Continent by the
fame Fleet, but attempted not to inclofe the
Inhabitants in the fame manner; becaufe that
was impoffible. And after they had done this,
the Perfian Generals made good the menacing
Meffages they had fent to the Ionians, when
the two Armies were in View. For upon
the Reduction of the Ionian Cities, they made
Eunuchs of the handfomeft of the Youth; fent
the moft beautiful Virgins to the King, and
burnt the private Houfes and Temples. Thus
the Ionians were the third time conquer'd;
once by the Lydians, and twice afterwards
by the Perfians. This done, the Perfian Fleet
having already reduc'd the Places fituate on
the Right-hand of thofe who fail into the
Hellefpont, departed from *Ionia*, and fubdued
all the Countries that lie on the Left, and belong to *Europe.* Of this Number were the Helle-

ſpontin *Cherſoneſus*, containing many Cities,
Perinthus, Selybris, Byzantium, and divers wall'd
Towns of *Thrace.* The Byzantians, with the
Chalcedonians, who are ſituate beyond them,
would not wait the coming of the Phœnician
Fleet; but leaving their Habitations, and flying to the *Euxin*, built the City of *Meſambria*,
on that Sea. In the mean time the Phœnicians
burnt the Places I have mention'd, and ſailing
to *Proconneſus* and *Artace*, ſet fire to theſe likewiſe: After which they return'd to *Cherſoneſus*,
in order to deſtroy all thoſe Cities they had
not ruin'd at their firſt landing. As for *Cyzicus*,
they had not touch'd there; becauſe the Cyzice-
nians were under the Obedience of the King
before the Phœnician Expedition, having already capitulated with *Oebares* the Son of *Megabyzus*, Prefect of *Daſcylium.* The reſt of the
Cherſoneſian Cities were ſubdu'd by the Phœnicians, except *Cardia*, which was then under
the Dominion of *Miltiades* the Son of *Cimon*,
and Grandſon to *Steſagoras*, and had been formerly acquir'd by *Miltiades* the Son of *Cypſelus*
in the following manner. The Thracian Do-
lonces, antient Inhabitants of that Part of *Cherſoneſus*, having ſuffer'd much in a War a-
gainſt the Abſynthians, ſent their Kings to
enquire of the Delphian Oracle concerning
the Event; and were admoniſhed by the Pythian, to deſire the firſt Man, who after their
Departure from the Temple ſhould invite
them to lodge in his Houſe, to lead a Colony into their Country. Accordingly the
Dolonces paſſing by the *Sacred Way* thro' the
Territories of the Phocæans and Bœotians, and
receiving no Offer of Entertainment, turn'd
into

into the Road of *Athens*. In that time *Pififtra-tus* had indeed the supreme Power; but *Milti-ades* the Son of *Cypfelus* was not without Au-thority in *Athens*; being of an illuftrious Fami-ly, antiently defcended from *Æacus* and *Ægina*, and afterwards eftablifh'd among the Atheni-ans by *Philæus* the Son of *Ajax*, the firft of that Blood that fettled there. This *Miltiades* fitting before his Gates, and feeing the Dolon-ces pafling by, cloth'd and arm'd in a different manner from the Athenians, call'd out to them and upon their coming to him, defir'd they would be his Guefts, and accept the Entertain-ment of his Houfe. They accepted his Invi-tation; and after they had been hofpitably en-tertain'd acquainted him with the Oracle, and reqefted him to act in conformity to the Admonition of the God. *Miltiades* hearken'd to their Propofition; and complied with more readinefs, becaufe he grew impatient of the Government of *Pififtratus*, and defir'd an Op-portunity to withdraw. In thefe Sentiments he went to *Delphi* to confult the Oracle, whe-ther he fhould yield to the Requeft of the Do-lonces; and receiv'd an incouraging Anfwer from the Pythian. Upon which *Miltiades* the Son of *Cypfelus*, who had formerly been victo-rious in the Olympian Chariot-race, taking with him all fuch Athenians as were willing to join in his Expedition, fet fail with the Do-lonces: and arriving in their Country, was invefted with the foveregin Power. The firft thing he did was, to build a Wall upon the Ifth-mus of *Cherfonefus*, from the City of *Cardia* to that of *Pactya*, in order to prevent the Ab-fynthians from infefting the Country for the future

future with their Incursions. This Isthmus is thirty-six Stades in Breadth; and the whole Length of *Chersonesus*, beginning in that Place is four hundred and twenty Stades. When *Miltiades* had built this Wall on the Neck of *Chersonesus*, and by that means excluded the Absynthians, he in the next place made War upon the Lampsacenians; and falling into an Ambuscade, was taken alive by the Enemy. But *Crœsus* the Lydian, having a great Esteem for him, and hearing this Event, dispatch'd a Messenger to *Lampsacus*, with Orders to demand the Liberty of *Miltiades*, and to threaten, if they refused to comply, that he would use them as Pines. The Lampsacenians differing in Opinion about the Meaning of the Menace sent by *Crœsus*, *That he would use them as Pines*, were not a little perplex'd at his Message. But so soon as one of their Senators, understanding the Sense of those Words, had acquainted them, that the Pine alone of all Trees perishes entirely upon cutting, without emitting any after-Shoots; the Lampsacenians dreading the Power of *Crœsus*, deliver'd *Miltiades*, and sent him home. Thus having escap'd by the means of *Crœsus*, and afterwards dying without Children, he left his Dominion and Riches to *Stesagoras* the Son of *Cimon*, his Brother by the same Mother. The Chersonesians honour him with Sacrifices, as the Founder of their City, in the accustomed manner, having instituted Gymnastic and Equestrian Exercises on that Occasion, in which no Lampsacenian is permitted to contend for the Prize. During the War, which still continued against the People of *Lampsacus*, *Stesagoras* likewise died
without

without Children; being kill'd by the Blow of
an Ax, he receiv'd on the Head from the
Hand of one, who pretending to be a Deserter,
was indeed a most cruel Enemy: After whose
Death the Pisistratides sent *Miltiades*, the Son
of *Cimon* and Brother of *Stesagoras*, to *Chersonesus* with one Ship, to take upon him the Government; having been already favourable to
him in *Athens*, as if they had not had any
Part in the Murder of his Father *Cimon*; which
I shall relate in another Place. Arriving in
Chersonesus, he kept himself retir'd under Colour of honouring the Memory of his Brother
Stesagoras; which the Chersonesians hearing,
the principal Persons of every City assembled
together; and coming to his House with Intentions to condole with him, were all seized
and imprison'd. By this means *Miltiades* made
himself Master of *Chersonesus*; entertained five
hundred Auxiliaries for his Guard, and married *Hegesipyla*, Daughter to *Olorus* King of
Thrace. But he had not been long in Possession before he met with greater Difficulties
than he had yet experienc'd. For in the third
Year of his Government he fled out of the
Country, not daring to wait the coming of the
Scythian Nomades, who having been irritated
by the Expedition of *Darius*, had assembled
their Forces, and advanc'd to the Frontier of
Chersonesus. Nevertheless, upon the Departure
of the Scythians, he was again restored by
the Dolonces: And in the third Year after this
hearing that the Phœnicians were at *Tenedus*,
he put all his Riches on board five Ships, and
sail'd for *Athens*. But when he had pass'd the
Coast of *Chersonesus*, in his Voyage from *Cardia*,
and

and was failing thro' the Bay of *Melane*, the Phœnician Fleet fell in with his Ships, and took one of the five, commanded by *Metiochus*, his eldeſt Son, tho' born of another Woman, and not of the Daughter of *Olorus* King of *Thrace*; whilſt he with the other four eſcap'd to *Imbrus*. The Phœnicians underſtanding that the Captain of the Ship they had taken, was the Son of *Miltiades* conducted him to the King, in hope of meriting his Favour in a peculiar manner; becauſe *Miltiades* had formerly endeavour'd to perſuade the Ionian Generals to comply with the Scythians, when they were deſir'd to break the Bridge and return home. But *Darius*, after the Phœnicians had put *Metiochus* the Son of *Miltiades* into his Hands, was ſo far from doing him any hurt, that on the contrary he conferr'd great Benefits upon him. For he preſented him with a Houſe and Lands, and gave him a Perſian Wife, by whom he had Children of honourable Eſteem among the Perſians. In the mean time *Miltiades* arriv'd at *Athens* from *Imbrus*, and during that Year the Perſians attempted nothing more againſt the Ionians: On the contrary, one thing was done very much to their Advantage. For *Artaphernes* Governour of *Sardis*, having oblig'd the Enemies to ſend Deputies to him, compell'd the Ionians to enter into an Agreement to be mutually anſwerable for all future Injuries, and to deſiſt from commiting Depredations one upon another. After which he meaſur'd their Lands by Paraſanges, (each containing thirty Stades) and ſettle the Tribute they ſhould pay in proportion to the Extent of their Territories. This Regulation eſtabliſh'd by *Artaphernes*, being

little

little different from that which they were under before, continued to be observ'd by the Inhabitants in our Time. And thus the Differences of the Ionians were compos'd.

I N the beginning of the next Spring, after the King had recall'd his Generals, *Mardonius* the Son of *Gobryas*, a young Man, who had newly married *Artozostra* the Daughter of *Darius*, march'd down to the Coast, with numerous Forces to be employ'd both by Land and by Sea ; and embarking in *Cilicia*, set sail with the Fleet, while the other Generals led the Land Army to the *Hellespont*. When he had pass'd the Coast of *Asia*, and was arriv'd in *Ionia*, he did an Action which will seem incredible to those Grecians, who cannot believe that *Otanes* endeavour'd to persuade the seven Persians to establish a Democracy in *Persia*, as most advantageous to the Nation. For *Mardonius* depos'd all the Ionian Tyrants, and settled a popular Government in every City. After which he departed to the *Hellespont* ; and having there assembled a great Army, with a numerous Fleet, pass'd over that Sea into *Europe*, and turn'd his march towards *Eretria* and *Athens*. The Reduction of these Places was indeed the Pretext of their Enterprize : but they really intended no less than to subdue all the Grecian Cities they could. For with their Fleet they reduc'd the Thasians without Resistance, and with their Land Forces added *Macedonia* to their former Conquests ; which they had carried to the Borders of that Country before this Expedition. From *Thasus* their Fleet stood over to the Continent, and coasted along the Shoar to *Acanthus* : But as they were

endeavour-

endeavouring to double the Cape of Mount *Athos*, they were surpriz'd in a Storm of Wind blowing from the North with such insupportable Violence, that more than one half of their Ships were driven ashoar against the Mountain. The general Report is that they lost by this Disaster three hundred Ships, and upwards of twenty thousand Men: Many of these being devour'd by monstrous marine Animals which abound in that Sea, many dash'd in pieces on the Rocks: while some, who could not swim, perish'd in the Water, and others died with Cold. In the mean time *Mardonius* incamping with his Army in *Macedonia*, was attack'd in the Night by the Bryges, a People of *Thrace*, who kill'd great Numbers of his Men, and wounded the General himself. Nevertheless they could not preserve themselves from falling under the Power of the Persians; but were subdued by *Mardonius* before he quitted those Parts: And then, considering the Loss he had received from the Bryges, and the greater Disaster of his Fleet at mount *Athos*, he thought fit to retire, and accordingly repass'd into *Asia* with his Forces, after an unsuccessful Expedition.

IN the following Year, *Darius* being inform'd by the Neighbours of the Thasians, that they design'd to revolt, dispatch'd a Messenger to command them to demolish their Walls, and to send away their Ships to *Abdera*. For the Thasians, who had been besieged by *Histiæus* the Milesian, and wanted not considerable Revenues, applied their Riches to the Building of Ships, and fortifying their City with a stronger Wall. Their Revenues arose partly from the Continent,

nent, and partly from their Mines: those of *Scapte*, which were of Gold, producing to the Value of eighty Talents yearly; and those of *Thasus* something less; yet in such a Quantity, that having their Lands free, the Thasians usually receiv'd in all two hundred Talents yearly from the Continent and from the Mines; and sometimes, in the best Years, three hundred. I myself have seen all these Mines: Of which the most memorable are those found by the Phœnicians, who accompanied *Thasus*, when he settled in this Island, and gave his Name to the Country. These Phœnician Mines are situate between the Enyrians and Cenyrians of *Thasus*; where a great Mountain, which fronted *Samothracia*, has been overthrown by the Miners in Search of the Oar.

THE Thasians in obedience to the King demolish'd their Walls, and sent away all their Ships to *Abdera*. After which *Darius* resolving to try whether the Grecians would submit, or make War against him, sent his Heralds into divers Parts of *Greece*, to demand Earth and Water in his Name: And when he had done this dispatch'd other Messengers to the tributary Cities on the Coast, with Orders to build large Ships, and Vessels of Transportation for Horse. Whilst these Preparations were carried on, many People of the Continent made their Submission to the Persian in the Manner requir'd by his Heralds: And all the Islanders in general complying with their Demand, deliver'd the usual Present of Earth and Water in Testimony of Obedience. When the Athenians heard these things, and that the People of *Ægina* had done like the rest, they suspected these last had willingly

4 　　　　　　　　　lingly

lingly embrac'd this Occasion of joining with
the Persians; in order to make War against
Athens; and readily taking the Opportunity,
sent to *Sparta*, and accus'd the Æginetes, as
the Betrayers of *Greece*. Upon this Complaint
Cleomenes the Son of *Anaxandrides*, at that time
King of *Sparta*, pass'd over to Ægina, with
intention to seize the principal Persons concern'd in that Action; and endeavouring to
put his Design in execution, met with Opposition from many of the Æginetes; but chiefly from *Crius* the Son of *Polycritus*, who told
him plainly, that he should not carry off any
one of the Inhabitants with Impunity; that
he came to make this Attempt without the Consent of the Spartans, corrupted by Athenian
Money; and that if things had not been so,
the other King of *Sparta* would have accompanied him on this Occasion. Which Words
were spoken by *Crius* upon a private Message
he had receiv'd from *Demaratus*. When *Cleome-*
nes was ready to depart, he ask'd *Crius* his Name,
and after *Crius* had informed him,
said, " *Crius*, you would do well
" to point your Horns with Brass;
" for you have a formidable E-
" nemy to encounter." *Demaratus* the Son of
Ariston was likewise King of *Sparta* at the same
time with *Cleomenes*; and staying at home, as-
pers'd the Conduct of his Collegue. He was
indeed of the younger Branch; but as they were
both descended from the same Stock, their No-
bility was equal; except only that the Family of *Eurysthenes*, being the elder, was more
respected. The Lacedemonians differing from
all the Poets, affirm, That they were not con-

* This Word
in the Greek
signifies a Ram.

ducted

ducted into the Region they now poſſeſs, by
the Sons of *Ariſtodemus* ; but by their King
Ariſtodemus himſelf, who was the Son of *Ariſto-
machus*, Grandſon of *Cleodæus*, and Great-grand-
ſon to *Hyllus* : That in a little time after their
arrival, *Argiva* the Wife of *Ariſtodemus*, and
Daughter, as they ſay, to *Auteſion* the Son of
Tiſamenes, whoſe Father was *Therſander* the
Son of *Polynices*, brought him two Male Children at a Birth ; whom he had no ſooner ſeen
than he died by Sickneſs : That the Lacedemonians, according to the Cuſtom they obſerv'd in
that Age, determining to receive the eldeſt for
their King, and not knowing which to chuſe,
becauſe they were in every thing alike, went
to examine the Mother touching the Birth of
the Children : That ſhe, either really ignorant,
or, which is more probable, diſſembling the
Knowledge ſhe had, out of a great Deſire to
ſee both her Sons created Kings, denied ſhe
knew any thing of the Primogeniture : That
the Lacedemonians continuing ſtill in doubt,
ſent to inquire of the Oracle at *Delphi*, what
Reſolution they ſhould take ; and that the
Pythian exhorted them to receive both for
their Kings, but to pay the greateſt Honours
to the eldeſt : That after this Anſwer they
were in no leſs Perplexity than before ; till
one *Panites* a Meſſenian advis'd the Lacedemonians to obſerve which of the two Children
the Mother would firſt waſh and feed ; aſſuring
them, that if ſhe was conſtant to the ſame Method, they might be certain of the thing
they ſo much deſir'd to know ; but if ſhe ſhould
vary in her manner, and apply her Care in-
differently to both, they ought to believe ſhe

knew nothing of the Matter in queſtion, and endeavour to find out ſome other Expedient: That the Spartans, in purſuance of his Advice, having diligently obſerv'd the Mother, who had no Suſpicion of their Deſign; and imagining they perceiv'd her to give the Priority to one of the Sons of *Ariſtodemus,* rather than to the other, they took him as the Eldeſt; educated him at the Expence of the Publick; nam'd him *Euryſthenes,* and gave the Name of *Procles* to the Younger: That theſe two Brothers, after they had attain'd the Age of Men, could never agree during all the time of their Lives; and that this Animoſity became hereditary in their Deſcendants. The Lacedemonians are the only People of *Greece* who report theſe things: But I muſt not omit to mention what the reſt of the Grecians ſay on this Subject. They affirm then, That all the Dorian Kings from *Perſeus* the Son of *Jupiter* by *Danae,* are rightly computed by the Grecians, and were accounted Grecians in thoſe Times. I ſay, from *Perſeus,* and go no higher; becauſe he had no Sirname deriv'd from a mortal Father, as *Hercules* had from *Amphytrion:* And therefore I may with reaſon forbear to look backward farther than *Perſeus.* But if we trace the Genealogy of *Danae* the Daughter of *Acriſius,* and enumerate their Anceſtors of the Male Line, we ſhall find that the Leaders of the Dorians were originally Natives of *Egypt:* And this is the Account given by the Grecians. Nevertheleſs, the receiv'd Opinion among the Perſians is, that *Perſeus,* being an Aſſyrian by Birth, became a Grecian by ſettling in *Greece,* which none of his Anceſtors had ever done. For

z   the

the Ancestors of *Acrisius* were no way related to *Perseus*, but were Ægyptians, as the Grecians themselves own. And this I think sufficient to say concerning these things; forbearing to mention in what manner they who were Ægyptians, accepted the Offer of the Dorian Kingdom; because others have related that Transaction; and contenting myself with giving an Account of such Particulars as I find to have been omitted by them. The Spartans conferr'd these Honours upon their Kings. In the first place, That they should enjoy the Priesthood, both of the Lacedemonian and the Olympian *Jupiter:* That they might make War in any Region at their pleasure; and that no Spartan should hinder them from so doing, under Penalty of incurring the Guilt of Impiety: That in all Expeditions they should lead the Van, and bring up the Rear in their Return: That in the Field they should have a hundred chosen Men for their Guard: That they might sacrifice what kind of Cattle they should think fit before they began their March, and that the Skins with the Chine should belong to them. These Advantages they have in times of War; and in peaceable times those that follow. In the Celebration of all publick Sacrifices, the Kings sit first down to the Feast, are first serv'd, and receive a double Allowance of whatever is given to the rest of the Company. They have the first Potion at the Libation, and the Skins of the Victims. Every New Moon, and Seventh Day of every Month, a whole Victim is presented to each of them in the Temple of *Apollo* at the publick Charge; accompanied with a Measure of Flour, and the

fourth

fourth Part of a Laconian Veſſel of Wine.
They have the principal Places at all publick
Spectacles; and may appoint ſuch Citizens as
they pleaſe, to receive and entertain Strangers.
Each of theſe Kings have the Privilege of e-
lecting two Pythians; who are to be ſent upon
occaſion to conſult the Oracle of *Delphi*, and
have their Proviſion with the Kings at the
publick Charge. When the Kings are not preſent at Supper, two Meaſures of Flour, with
a Flaggon of Wine, are ſent home to each:
But when they are preſent, they receive a
double Portion of every thing. And if they
are invited to eat with private Perſons, they are
treated with the ſame Honours. They have
the keeping of all Prophecies, which they are
oblig'd to communicate to the Pythians. But
the Kings alone have the Direction of the following Affairs. They have the Power of determining who ought to marry thoſe Heireſſes,
who have not been contracted during the Lives
of their Fathers. They have the Care of the
publick Highways: And if any Man deſires to
adopt a Son, he is oblig'd to perform that Act
before the Kings. They may be preſent, whenever they pleaſe, in the Aſſembly of the Senate,
which conſiſts of twenty eight Senators: And
if they are abſent, two of thoſe Senators who
are moſt truſted by the Kings, enjoy their Privileges, and have two Ballots beſides their
own. Theſe Advantages are conferr'd by the
Republick of *Sparta*, upon their Kings while
they live; thoſe which follow, when they are
dead. Horſemen are diſpatch'd thro' all *Laconia*
to notify their Death: Women are appointed to
march thro' every Part of the City, beating upon
Kettles;

Kettle; during which time one Man and one
Woman, both free-born, are oblig'd under great
Penalties, to appear out of every House with
all the Marks of Mourning and Lamentation.
To be short, the Lacedemonians celebrate the
Funerals of their Kings in the same Manner as
is practised by the Barbarians of *Asia*; who
for the most part, vary nothing from the Spartans in the Performance of these Ceremonies.
For upon the Death of a Lacedemonian K ing
certain Numbers of the Inhabitans of the
Country are oblig'd to attend the Funeral with
open Breasts, those of the City being singly
exempted: And when many Thousands of these
are met together, with the Helotes, and even
Spartans both Men and Women, they cou-
rageously cut themselves on the Forehead, and
with incessant Howlings cry out, that the
last King was the best they ever had.   If
one of their Kings die in War, his Effigy is
prepar'd and expos'd to puclick View, plac'd
on a Bed of State.   When they bury him,
all Business ceases for ten Days; the Courts are
not assembled, and the Mourning continues during that time.   Their Customs are farther
conformable to those of the Persians; in that,
when a King dies, and the Successor enters
upon the Administration, he remits whatever
Debts may be due from any Spartan to the
King or the Publick; as the King of *Persia* at his Accession to the Throne dischar-
ges all the Cities from the Arrears of Tribute due to his Predecessor.   In other things
the Lacedemonians resemble the Ægyptians in their Manners.   For every Herald, Mu-
sician, and Cook, takes upon him the Pro-

feffion

feffion of his Father: So that a Mufician begets a Mufician; one Cook begets another,
and the Son of a Herald is always of the fame
Profeffion, no Man endeavouring to fupplant
him by fhewing he has a clearer Voice; but
on the contrary every one continues to exer-
cife his Father's Art.   And fuch is the Account
of thefe things.

WHILST *Cleomenes* continued at *Ægina*,
endeavouring to promote the common Caufe of
Greece, *Demaratus* accus'd him at home; not fo
much out of Kindnefs to the *Æginetes*, as
from motives of Envy and Hatred.   But *Cleomenes*, upon his Return, confulting in what
manner he might deprive *Demaratus* of the
Kingdom, took this Pretext to colour his Defign.   When *Arifton* reign'd in *Sparta*, he married two Wives, and had no Child by either;
but not acknowledging any Defect in himfelf,
he married a third in this manner.   He had a
Friend, who was a Spartan, and more entrufted
by him than any other Citizen.   The Wife of
this Man was the moft beautiful Woman of
all *Sparta*, tho' fhe had formerly been exceedingly deform'd.   But her Nurfe perceiving
her Deformity, and knowing her to be the
Daughter of eminent Perfons, and that her
Parents were fenfibly afflicted with the Misfortune, determined to carry her every day
to the Temple of *Helena*, which is built in
Therapne, above the Temple of *Apollo*.   Hither
fhe daily brought the Child, and ftanding before the Image of the Goddefs, pray'd fhe might
no longer continue in that Deformity.   The
common Report is, that as the Nurfe was one
day going out of the Temple, a Woman appear'd

pear'd to her, and ask'd what she had in her
Arms: that the Nurse answer'd she carried an
Infant; which when the Woman desir'd to see,
the Nurse refus'd to comply, because the Parents had commanded her to shew the Child to
none: that upon this Refusal the Woman ex-
pressing a greater Desire to see the Infant,
prevail'd at last upon the Nurse to grant her Request; and stroaking the Head of the Child
with her Hands, said she should become the
most beautiful Woman of *Sparta*; and from that
Day her Deformity began to diminish. When
she had attain'd to a convenient Age, she was
married to *Agetus* the Son of *Alcides*, and Confident of *Ariston*. Pleas'd with the Beauty of
this Woman, *Ariston* contriv'd the following
Design. He acquainted *Agetus*, who was her
Husband and his familiar Friend, that he
would make him a Present of any one thing
he should chuse out of all his Possessions, on
Condition he would oblige himself to do the
like to him. *Agetus* not suspecting any Design
upon his Wife, because he knew *Ariston* had
one already, accepted the Proposal; and an
Oath for mutual Performance was sworn on
both sides. Accordingly *Ariston* gave him the
thing he chose out of all his Treasures; and
then pretending to the same Compliance from
Agetus, demanded his Wife. *Agetus* acknow-
ledg'd all other things to have been included
in the Agreement, but thought that his Wife
had been excepted. Nevertheless finding himself under the Obligation of an Oath, and
deceiv'd by the Artifice of the King, he permitted him to take her away. In this manner
Ariston married a third Wife, and at the same

G 4 time

time divorc'd his second. But before the usual Term was expir'd, and the ten Months elaps'd *Demaratus* was born of this Woman: And when one of his Servants came to tell him as he sat with the Ephori, that he brought him the News of a Son; *Ariston* not forgetting the time of his Marriage, but counting the Months upon his Fingers, said with an Oath in presence of the Ephori, *This Child is not mine.* The Ephori seem'd at that time to make no account of those Words: But when the Boy grew up, *Ariston* repented of what he had said, being then fully persuaded that *Demaratus* was his Son. He give him the Name of *Demaratus*, because before his Birth the Spartans had made publick Supplications, that *Ariston*, whom they esteem'd the most illustrious of all the Kings they ever had, might have a Son. After some time *Ariston* died, and *Demaratus* obtain'd the Kingdom. But the Fates seem'd to have determin'd that the Words of the Father should deprive the Son of his Authority: and therefore as he had formerly been accus'd by *Cleomenes* for leading away the Army from *Eleusis*; so he was now again for procuring *Cleomenes* to be recall'd from his Expedition against the Ægi-netes, who were in the Interest of the Medes. When *Cleomenes* had thus begun to take his Revenge, he enter'd into an Agreement with *Leutychides* the Son of *Menaris* and Grandson of *Agis*, a Person of the same Family with *Demaratus*; under this Condition, that if he should make him King in the Place of *Demaratus*, *Leutychides* should accompany him in an Expedition against the Æginetes. *Leutychides* was an Enemy of *Demaratus*, chiefly for this Reason. He

had

had been upon the point of marrying *Percalum*,
the Daughter of *Chilon* the Son of *Demarmenes*;
when *Demaratus* by an infidious Contrivance
difappointed him of his Bride, and having poffefs'd himfelf of the Woman by Violence, retain'd her for his Wife. On this account *Leutychides* became his Enemy, and at the Inftigation of *Cleomenes*, fwore *Demaratus* had no
Right to be King of *Sparta*, becaufe he was
not the Son of *Ariston*; confirming his Affeve-
ration with the Words fpoken by *Ariston*, when
upon the Meffage he receiv'd concerning the
Birth of his Son, and the Computation he made
of the time elaps'd after his Marriage, he affirm'd with an Oath, that the Child was not
his. Infifting upon the Authority of thefe
Words, *Leutychides* openly maintain'd that *Demaratus* was neither the Son of *Ariston*, nor
rightful King of *Sparta*; and for the Truth of
his Affertion appeal'd to the Ephori, who then
fat by the King, and heard him pronounce
the Words in Queftion. Thus the Matter being drawn into Difpute, the Spartans determin'd to enquire of the Oracle at *Delphi*, whether *Demaratus* were the Son of *Ariston* or not.
But before this Refolution was divulg'd, *Cleomenes* with a timely Forefight took care to pre-
engage one *Cobon* the Son of *Aristophantus*; who
being a Perfon of great Authority in *Delphi*, prevail'd with *Perialla* the Arch-Prieftefs to give
fuch an Anfwer as *Cleomenes* defir'd. So that
when the Spartans came to confult the Oracle, the Pythian pronounc'd *Demaratus* not to
be the Son of *Ariston*: Which Collufion being
afterwards difcover'd, *Cobon* fled from *Delphi*,
and *Perialla* was depriv'd of her Dignity. By
this

this means *Demaratus* was depos'd; and in conclusion betook himself to the Medes on account of an Affront he receiv'd. For after his Deposition, being chosen into the Magistracy, as he was one Day present at the Gymnastick Exercises of the Youth, *Leutychides* who had been appointed King in his room, sent a Messenger to ask him in Derision, " What he thought of being an in-" ferior Magistrate after he had been a King." *Demaratus* disturb'd with the Insolence of his Message, answer'd, " That he indeed had ex-" perienc'd both, but *Leutychides* had not ; " and added, That this Question should be " the Cause either of innumerable Calamities, " or great Prosperity to the Lacedemonians." When he had said these Words, and cover'd his Face, he went out of the Theatre to his House, where he sacrific'd an Ox to *Jupiter*; and sending for his Mother to the Oblation, put the Entrails of the Victim into her Hands, and spoke to her in these pathetick Terms : " Mother, I adjure you by all the Gods, and " by *Jupiter*, the Deity of our House, to tell me " the Truth, and let me know plainly who was " my Father. For in these late Contests *Leuty-* " *chides* affirm'd that you were with Child by " your former Husband before you became the " Wife of *Ariston :* Others with more Impu-" dence say, you had the Company of one " who kept the Asses, and that I am the Son of " that Wretch : I adjure you therefore by the " Gods to inform me of the Truth. For if you " have done as they say, you are not sin-" gly guilty ; others have done the like. Be-" fides, many of the Spartans are persua-
" ded

" ded that *Ariston* was incapable of begetting
" Children : Otherwise, they say, his for-
" mer Wives had not been unfruitful." When
Demaratus had thus spoken, his Mother answer'd him in this manner : " Son, because
" you so earnestly desire me to speak the
" Truth, I shall conceal nothing from you.
" The third Night after *Ariston* had conducted
" me home to his House, a Phantom entire-
" ly like him in Shape, enter'd my Chamber,
" and having lain with me, put a Crown on
" my Head, and went out again. *Ariston*
" himself soon after came in, and seeing the
" Crown on my Head, ask'd, Who had made
" me that Present. I answer'd, He himself :
" But perceiving he would not own the thing,
" I added an Oath to my Assertion, and told
" him he did not well to deny what he had
" done, having been so lately in my Cham-
" ber, and giving me the Crown after he had
" lain with me. When *Ariston* heard me swear
" with such Assurance, he presently concluded
" that something divine had been with me.
" And indeed, not only the Crown was found
" to have been taken from the Monument of
" the Hero *Astrobacus*, which stands by the
" Gates of the Palace, but the Prophets like-
" wise affirm'd, That the Hero himself had
" brought it. This, my Son, is the whole
" Truth, which you so much desir'd to know :
" And therefore either the Hero *Astrobacus*, or
" else *Ariston* was your Father; for I conceiv'd
" you in that Night. And as to that Reproach
" which your Enemies endeavour chiefly to
" fasten upon you, by affirming that *Ariston*
" himself, when he receiv'd the News of your
                                    " Birth,

" Birth, faid in the prefence of many Perfons,
" that you could not be his Son ; thofe Words
" were thrown out by him for want of fuffi-
" cient Information concerning fuch matters.
" For Women are not always accuftom'd to
" bear their Children ten Months : But fome
" are deliver'd in nine, and others even in fe-
" ven. You, my Son, was born within the
" Space of feven Months ; and *Arifton* himfelf
" was in a little time convinc'd, that thofe
" Words were the Effect of his Ignorance.
" Believe nothing therefore in Derogation of
" your Birth ; for I have told you all the Truth
" with Sincerity. And if *Leutychides* or any
" other has calumniated us with the Fable of
" the Keeper of our Affes, may their Wives
" bring them Children fo begotten." *Demara-*
tus having thus fatisfied himfelf concerning the
matter he defir'd to know, prepared all things
neceffary for his Voyage, and departed to *Elis* ;
pretending he defign'd to go to *Delphi*, in order to confult the Oracle. But the Lacedemonians fufpecting that he intended to make
his Efcape, follow'd him to *Elis* ; and finding
he had already pafs'd over to *Zacynthus*, they
purfued him thither, and feiz'd him with his
Attendants. Yet they could not obtain their
Ends ; becaufe the Zacynthians refus'd to deliver him up ; and by that means he made his E-
fcape into *Afia*, where *Darius* receiv'd him honourably, and prefented him with Lands and Cities. Thus *Demaratus* went away to *Afia*, unfor-
tunately difgrac'd, after he had been famous a-
mong the Spartans both in Counfel and Action,
and crown'd at the Olympian Exercifes, for
the Victory he obtain'd in the Chariot-Race ;
which

which had never happen'd before to any King
of *Sparta*. *Leutychides* the Son of *Menaris*, created King in the place of *Demaratus*, had a Son
named *Zeuxidamus*, who by some of the Spartans is call'd *Cyniscus*. This *Zeuxidamus* was
never King of *Sparta*; for he died before his
Father, leaving behind him a Son named *Ar-
chidamus*. *Leutychides*, after the Death of his
Son, took for his second Wife *Eurydame* the
Sister of *Menius*, and Daughter to *Diactoris*,
who brought him no Male Child, and only one
Daughter nam'd *Lampito*, whom he gave in
Marriage to *Archidamus* the Son of *Zeuxidamus*.
Nevertheless, *Leutychides* could not continue in
Sparta to the end of his Life; but by his own
Crime made some kind of Reparation to *De-
maratus*. For while he was making war in
Thessaly at the Head of the Lacedemonian Ar-
my, and might easily have conquer'd all the
Country, he suffer'd himself to be corrupted
with Money; and was surpriz'd in the very
Act of carrying away Silver in both his hands.
On this account being summon'd to appear
in the Court of Justice, he fled from *Sparta*;
his House was demolish'd, and having made
his Escape to *Tegea*, he ended his Life in that
City.

C L E O M E N E S having successfully accomplish'd his Design against *Demaratus*, and being
highly incens'd against the Æginetes for the
Affront he had receiv'd, oblig'd *Leutychides* to
accompany him in his Expedition to *Ægina*;
and finding no Opposition from the Æginetes,
who would not resist both the Kings united
against them, they took ten of the most eminent Citizens in Birth, Riches and Dignity,

(among

(among them *Crius* the Son of *Polycritus*, and *Casambus* the Son of *Aristocrates*, who had the principal Authority) carried them away Prisoners to *Attica*, and put them into the Hands of the Athenians their greatest Enemies. After this Expedition, *Cleomenes* growing jealous of the Spartans because they had discover'd his fraudulent Practices against *Demaratus*, fled away privately to *Thessaly*; and from thence passing into *Arcadia*, began to form new Designs, soliciting the Arcadians to make War upon *Sparta*, and engaging them by an Oath to follow him to what Part soever he would lead them. He likewise endeavour'd to persuade the principal Inhabitants to accompany him to *Nonacris*, a City of *Arcadia*, not far from *Pheneos*, in order to swear by the Stygian Waters, which, the Arcadians say are found in that Place. And indeed there is a Spring distilling slowly from a Rock into a Bason inclos'd with a Wall. When the Lacedemonians were inform'd of these Intrigues of *Cleomenes*, they fear'd the Event, and recalling him to *Sparta*, restor'd him to his former Dignity. But he was no sooner return'd, than he fell into a Frenzy, of which he had felt some Attacks before; striking the Spartans without Distinction, when they came near him, with his Sceptre, on the Face. His Relations seeing these outragious Actions, and perceiving him to be depriv'd of his Understanding, resolv'd to fetter him. But when he found himself treated in this manner, and saw only one of his Keepers with him, he demanded his Sword. The Keeper at first refused to obey; yet after *Cleomenes* had threaten'd to punish him for his Disobedience, dreading the effect of his

Menaces,

Menaces, becaufe he was one of his Helots, he gave him his Sword : Which *Cleomenes* taking into his Hand, began to cut his Flefh from the Ancle upward, and made long Incifions reaching to his Thigh : Then proceeding by the Hip and Groin, he arriv'd at his Belly, which he ripp'd up, and died in this manner. Moft of the Grecians fay, he was thus punifh'd for fuborning the Pythian to frame the Anfwer fhe gave concerning *Demaratus :* The Athenians alone pretend, that his Invafion of *Eleufis,* where he pillag'd the Temples of the Gods, drew thefe Difafters upon him : and the Argians affirm that he came to this miferable End becaufe he had violated the Temple of *Argos,* by cutting in pieces thefe Argians who took Sanctuary there after the Battle ; and burnt down the facred Grove in Contempt. For when *Cleomenes* confulted the Oracle of *Delphi,* the Anfwer he receiv'd was, that he fhould take *Argos.* Upon this Affurance marching at the Head of the Spartans he arriv'd at the River *Erafinus,* which, as they fay, beginnings at the Stymphalian Lake, and paffing thro' a fubterraneous Cavity of the Earth, rifes again in *Argos,* and on that account by the Argians is called *Erafinus. Cleomenes* upon his Arrival facrific'd to the God of the River : But finding the Entrails of the Victim without any Marks of a fuccefsful Paffage, he faid, that tho' he could not be difpleas'd with *Erafinus* becaufe he would not betray his own People, yet the Argians fhould have no caufe to rejoice. Decamping therefore with his Army, he march'd to *Thyrea ;* where, after he had facrific'd a Bull to the Sea, he imbark'd, and tranfported all his

Forces

Forces to the Country about *Tiryns* and *Nauplia*.
The Argians hearing of their Arrival, march'd
out towards the Sea, and being advanc'd near
the City of *Tiryns*, to a Place call'd *Sipea*, they
incamp'd in view of the Lacedemonians, leaving only a small Interval between the two
Armies. They were not afraid of coming to a
fair Battle, but of being surpriz'd by Fraud and
Stratagem; because the Oracle, they and the
Milesians had jointly receiv'd from the Pythian,
seem'd to predict such an Event. The Words
were these:

> *When in the Streets of* Argos *Female Pride*
> *Shall be exalted, and the Male expel;*
> *Then shall be Argian Dames so sadly mourn,*
> *That every one who passes by may say,*
> *Kill'd by a Spear the deadly Serpent lies.*

All these things happening together, struck the
Argians with great Terror; so that they resolv'd to govern their Actions by the Signals of
the Enemy; and accordingly when any thing
was signified to the Lacedemonians, they took
the same for a Signal to themselves. *Cleomenes*
being inform'd that the Argians regulated their
Actions by the Signals they heard from his
Camp, gave order to the Spartans, that instead
of going to Dinner upon the usual Signal, they
should betake themselves to their Arms, and
march out against the Argians. The Lacedemonians executed his Order, and falling upon the
Argians at the time of their Dinner, kill'd
many on the Spot; and having driven a far
greater Number into the Grove, surrounded
them there. After which *Cleomenes* having receiv'd

ceiv'd full Information by Deferters concerning
their Perfons, fent a Herald to fummon by
Name all the Argians who had taken Sanctuary
in the facred Ground, to come out and pay
their Ranfom; which in *Peloponnefus* is fix'd at
two Mines of Silver for every Man. Upon
this Summons fifty of the Argians coming out
one after another, *Cleomenes* caus'd them to be
put to death whilft thofe who ftill continued
within, could not fee the Slaughter, by reafon
of the Thicknefs of the Grove: till at laft one
of the befieg'd getting up into a Tree, difcover'd the Treachery, and prevented the reft
from obeying his Summons. *Cleomenes* feeing
this, commanded all the Helots to furround
the Grove with combuftible Materials; and
after they had executed his Orders, he fet fire
to the place. When all was in a Flame, he ask'd
one of the Fugitives, to what God that Grove
was confecrated; and being told to *Argos,*
Cleomenes, with a deep Sigh, faid, " O *Apollo!*
" O Prophet! how haft thou deluded me, by
" promifing that I fhould take *Argos?* Now I
" know thy Prophecy is accomplifh'd." After
fome time *Cleomenes* fent home the greater
Part of his Army to *Sparta,* and retaining a
thoufand chofen Men with him, went to
the Temple of *Juno,* in order to facrifice on
her Altar. But the Prieft forbidding him
to proceed, told him that no Stranger might
facrifice in that Temple: Which Refufal *Cleo-*
menes taking in Difdain, commanded his Helots to drag the Prieft from the Altar and
beat him. In the mean time he himfelf facrific'd; and when he had perform'd his Devotions, went away to *Sparta.* At his Return

he was summon'd to appear before the Ephori
by his Enemies, who accus'd him of Corruption; and affirm'd that in Consideration of Money receiv'd, he had neglected the Conquest
of *Argos,* which he might easily have accomplish'd. I know not whether the Answer of
Cleomenes were true or false: But however his
Answer was, that he thought the Oracle ful-
fill'd when he had taken the Temple of *Argos,*
and therefore resolv'd not to attempt the City,
before he had inquir'd whether Heaven would
favour or obstruct his Enterprize; and that
whilst he was sacrificing in the Temple of *Juno,*
he saw a Flame issuing from the Breast of the
Image; which he understood to be a Sign that
he should not take the City of *Argos:* For said
he, if the fire had proceeded from the Head,
I should have thought the place might have
been taken by attacking the Castle; but perceiving it issuing out of the Breast, I concluded
that the Goddess would not permit more to be
done. These Reasons seem'd probable to the
Spartans, and *Cleomenes* was accquitted by a
great Majority. In the mean time *Argos* was
so exausted of Men by the Defeat of the Argians, that their Servants took upon them the
Administration of Affairs, and exercis'd all
the Magistracies; but when the Sons of those,
who had been kill'd, grew up, they asserted
their Right, and ejected them out of the City.
These Servants after their Expulsion took *Tiryns* by Assault, and continued there in peaceable Possession, till they were persuaded by
one *Cleander,* an Arcadian Prophet of Phigasean
Extraction, to attack their Masters; and entering into a long War, were at last sub-

dued

dued by the Argians, tho' not without great
Difficulty.

TO the Guilt of these Actions the Argians
attribute the Madness and Death of *Cleomenes.*
But the Spartans deny that he was punish'd
with Distraction by any superior Power; and
affirm that his Folly proceeded only from an
intemperate abuse of Wine, which he had
learnt by conversing with the Scythians. For
the Nomades of *Scythia,* whose Country *Darius* had invaded, being desirous to revenge
that Injury, sent Ambassadors to conclude an
Alliance with the Spartans on these Terms:
That the Scythians should endeavour to make
an Irruption into *Media* by the River *Phasis.*
That the Spartans should enter the Persian Dominions by the way of *Ephesus;* and that both
Armies should meet and join together at a
certain place appointed to that end. They say
that by conversing too much with these Scythians *Cleomenes* contracted an habit of Intem-
perance; that his Madness was deriv'd from
this Cause, and that the Phrase of playing the
Scythian, by which Men understand drinking
Wine too liberally, was introduc'd on this occasion. These things are said by the Spartans
concerning *Cleomenes:* But I am of opinion
that he punish'd himself for the Wrong he had
done to *Demaratus.*

WHEN the Æginetes were inform'd of the
Death of *Cleomenes,* they sent Ambassadors to
Sparta with loud Complaints against *Leutychides*
on account of the Hostages detain'd at *Athens:*
And the Lacedemonians having summon'd an
Assembly to deliberate concerning the matter,
resolv'd that the Æginetes had been treated

with Indignity by *Leutychides,* and therefore determin'd that he should be deliver'd into their hands, and carried Prisoner to *Ægina* in the place of those who were detain'd by the *Athenians.* But when they were ready to carry him away, *Theasides* the Son of *Leoprepes,* an eminent Spartan, spoke to them in these Terms: "Men of *Ægina,* said he, what are you about to do? Are you resolv'd to take away the King of *Sparta* because he is deliver'd into your hands? Consider whether the Spartans, when you shall have executed the Order they have now given in Anger, will not bring all the Evils and Desolation of War into your Country on this Occasion." The *Æginetes* having consider'd these Words were contented to desist; on condition nevertheless that *Leutychides* would accompany them to *Athens,* and procure the Restitution of the Hostages. Accordingly *Leutychides* went to *Athens,* and after he had demanded the Persons in question, the *Athenians* seeking by an artificial Evasion to elude his Instances, told him that having receiv'd the Hostages from two Kings in Person, they could not justly restore them to one in the absence of the other. *Leutychides* finding the *Athenians* resolv'd upon a Denial, said, "Do that, O *Athenians,* which pleases you best. If you restore the Hostages, you will do an Action of Justice: If not, the contrary. Yet I will tell you what happen'd formerly concerning a thing deposited in *Sparta.* We Spartans say, that about three Ages have pass'd, since one *Glaucus* the Son of *Epicydides* liv'd in *Lacedæmon;* a Man singularly eminent in all manner of "Virtues,

" Virtues, and more esteem'd for his Justice
" than any other Person among the Lacede-
" monians. In his time a certain Milesian
" came to *Sparta*, and being desirous to be
" acquainted with him spoke to him in these
" Terms; *Glaucus*, said he, I am a Milesian,
" and now come to enjoy the Benefit of thy
" Justice, which is so highly celebrated thro'
" all *Greece*, and principally among the Io-
" nians. I have consider'd that *Ionia* is al-
" ways expos'd to great Dangers; and that
" on the contrary, *Peloponnesus* is perpetually
" secure, because the Inhabitants are known
" to have no Riches. Upon this Reflection
" I have determin'd to deposit with thee one
" half of my Estate, which I have reduc'd in-
" to Money; being fully assur'd it will be
" safe in thy hands. Take then this Silver,
" with this Token, and deliver the Money
" to no other than the Person who shall bring
" the like Mark. When the Milesian had said
" these Words, *Glaucus* receiv'd the Treasure,
" with a Promise to do as he desir'd. After
" a long time the Sons of this Man coming
" to *Sparta*, address'd themselves to *Glaucus*,
" and having shew'd him the Token, demand-
" ed the Money which had been deposited in
" his hands. *Glaucus* in a passion told the Men
" he remembred nothing of the matter, and
" neither knew, nor cared to know what they
" meant. Yet, said he, if I can recover the Me-
" mory of this thing, I will do my Duty; because
" if I have been intrusted, common Justice ob-
" liges me to Restitution. But if on the con-
" trary I have receiv'd nothing, I shall seek that
" Satisfaction which the Laws of *Greece* allow:

H 3 " And

" And therefore I affign you the term of four
" Months to return hither in order to finifh
" this Affair. The Milefians thinking they
" had been defrauded of their Money, departed
" from *Sparta.* But *Glaucus* having afterwards
" inquired of the Oracle at *Delphi,* whether
" he fhould retain thefe Riches by Perjury,
" receiv'd this Anfwer from the Pythian in
" Verfe:

Perfidious Oaths, and violated Faith,
Are oft attended by a prefent Gain:
Swear boldly then ; becaufe the honeft Man
Muft die as furely as the vileft Slave.
But know, that fpeedy Vengance fhall o'ertake
The perjur'd Criminal ; his Son difgrac'd,
Abject, and fcorn'd, fhall the whole Houfe deftroy:
Then fhall the Offspring of the Juft rejoice.

" When *Glaucus* heard this, he pray'd the God
" to pardon the Words he had faid. But the
" Pythian told him, that to tempt the God, or
" commit the Crime, was the fame thing. So
" *Glaucus* fent for the Milefians and reftor'd the
" Money. Now I fhall inform you, O Atheni-
" ans, with what Defign I have related this
" Event. The Pofterity of *Glaucus* is utterly
" extinguifh'd ; we know not where his Houfe
" ftood, but both he and his are totally extir-
" pated: By which you may fee that you ought
" to entertain no other Thought concerning a
" thing depofited, than to make Reftitution to
" the Owner." *Leutychides* having finifh'd thefe
Words, and finding he could not prevail with
the Athenians, departed from *Attica.*

BUT

BUT before the Æginetes receiv'd the Punishment they deserv'd for the Injuries they had done to the Athenians in favour of the Thebans, they executed the following Enterprize. Being incens'd against the Athenians, and thinking themselves injur'd, they prepar'd to take their Revenge; and to that end, knowing that the Athenian Galley, which they us'd to send annually to *Delphi*, was then at *Sunium*; they intercepted the Vessel, and bound many principal Athenians who were found on board. From the time of that Disaster the Athenians resolv'd to omit nothing they could imagine, in order to distress the Æginetes. *Nicodromus*, the Son of *Cnæthus*, an eminent Person of *Ægina*, had formerly retir'd out of the Island in Discontent; and now hearing that the Athenians were determin'd to attack the Æginetes, he enter'd into an Agreement with them to deliver the City into their Hands on a certain Day, if they would be ready to assist him in his Enterprize at the time appointed. In pursuance of this Engagement, *Nicodromus* seiz'd that part of the Place which is call'd the Old-Town, for the Athenians: But they fail'd to arrive at the Day prefix'd; because they had not a sufficient Number of Ships to fight the Æginetes: and while they were in Treaty with the Corinthians for Succour, the Opportunity was lost. Nevertheless the Corinthians, who were then great Friends to the Athenians, assisted them at their Request, with twenty Ships; but took five Drachma's for each; because by their Laws they were forbidden to let them go without Reward. When the Athenians had receiv'd this Succour, and made

H 4   ready

ready their own Fleet, they fail'd to *Ægina*
with feventy Ships in all, and arriv'd one day
too late. For *Nicodromus* finding himfelf difappointed by this Delay, had already made
his Efcape by Sea with divers of his Accomplices; who were all receiv'd by the Athenians, and permitted to fettle in *Sunium*; from
whence they afterwards infefted the Æginetes,
and committed many Depredations on the
Ifland. In the mean time the moft wealthy Citizens of *Ægina* having overpower'd the Plebeians of the Party of *Nicodromus*, put as many of
them to death as fell into their Hands; and in
their Rage incurr'd the Guilt of a facrilegious
Crime, which they could never expiate; but
were ejected out of the Ifland before they had
appeas'd the Anger of the Goddefs. For as
they led to Execution feven hundred of the
People they had taken Prifoners, one of them
getting loofe, fled to the Temple of *Ceres* the
Legiflatrefs, and entering the Portico, laid hold
upon the Hinges of the Gate: But they purfuing him clofe, and having in vain endeavour'd to drag him from the Place, cut off
both his Hands, which they left faften'd to the
Gate, and forc'd him away in that Condition. After the Æginetes had done thefe things,
they fought a Battle by Sea againft the Athenians with feventy Ships; and being defeated,
fent again to the Argians to defire their Affiftance. But the Argians refufing to fuccour them,
alledg'd in their Juftification, that the Ship-
ping of *Ægina* had been made ufe of by *Cleomenes* againft the Territories of *Argos*, and that
the Æginetes had landed their Forces with
the Lacedemonians; as fome of the Sicyonians
had

had likewife done in the fame Expedition ; with
this difference, that when the Argians had fen-
tenc'd both Nations to the Payment of one
thoufand Talents for their Offence, the Sicyonians acknowledging their Fault, agreed with
the Argians for one hundred Talents : But the
Æginetes were fo arrogant, that they would
not condefcend to own themfelves in the wrong.
For thefe Reafons none of the Argians were
authoriz'd by the Publick to affift the Æginetes:
Only about a thoufand Voluntiers under the
Conduct of *Eurybates*, who had been victorious
in all the five Olympian Exercifes, march'd to
their Succour.   But the greater part of thefe
perifh'd in the War againft the Athenians, and
never return'd home from *Ægina. Eurybates*
himfelf after he had kill'd three feveral Anta-
gonifts in fingle Combat, died by the Hand of
Sophanes the Son of *Deceles*, who was the fourth
he encounter'd.   Neverthelefs, the Æginetes
having found an Opportunity of attacking the
Athenians when they were in Diforder, obtain'd
a Victory, and took four Ships with all the
Men that were on Board.

WHILST the Athenians were thus en-
gag'd in a War againft *Ægina, Darius* was not
remifs in his Affairs ; but being continually
put in mind by his Servant to remember the
Athenians, and inceffantly furrounded by the
Pififtratides who were their Enemies, he refolv'd to fubdue all thofe Parts of *Greece*,
which had denied him Earth and Water.   To
this End he remov'd *Mardonius* from his
Command, becaufe he had not fucceeded in
his Expedition by Sea ; and fent *Datis* a Native of *Media*, and *Artaphernes* the Son of his
Brother

Brother *Artaphernes*, to make War upon *Eretria* and *Athens*, with Orders to destroy those Cities, and bring all the Prisoners to him. After these Generals had been declar'd and had taken leave of the King, they advanc'd at the Head of a numerous and well provided Army into a Plain of *Cilicia*, situate near the Sea, and encamp'd there. In the mean time the Fleet arriv'd with Vessels for the Transportation of Horses ; which *Darius* in the preceding Year had commanded the tributary Provinces to furnish : And when the Men and Horses were all imbark'd, they sail'd for the Coast of *Ionia*, with six hundred Galleys. In this Voyage they would not shape a direct Course by the Continent of *Thrace* and the *Hellespont* ; but departing from *Samos* made an oblique Passage thro' the Icarian Sea among the *Cyclades* ; chiefly, as I conjecture, dreading to double the Cape of Mount *Athos*, where they had sustain'd so great a Loss in the former Year ; and partly in order to attack the Island of *Naxus*, which they had not yet reduc'd. Accordingly, when the Fleet arriv'd at *Naxus*, the Persians desir'd to make their first attempt upon that Place. But the Naxians remembring what had pass'd before, abandon'd their Habitations and fled to the Mountains : Upon which the Persians took as many Prisoners as they could seize ; and after they had burnt the City with the Temples, departed to the rest of the Islands. During this Enterprize, the Delians left their Islands, and transported themselves to *Tenus* : But when the Fleet arriv'd at the Height of *Delos*, *Datis*, who had the Van, not permitting the Ships to anchor in that Harbour, proceeded to *Rhenea* ; and be-

ing

ing there inform'd where the Delians were, he sent a Herald to them with this Message: " Sacred Men, upon what Motive have you " relinquish'd your Habitations, and by your " Flight discover'd the ill Opinion you have of " me? I am not your Enemy in Inclination ; " and besides I have receiv'd a Command from " the King, that in the Region, where two " Gods are born, I should commit no Violence " either against the Inhabitants or the Place. " Return therefore to your Houses, and resume " the Possession of your Island. " After he had sent this Message to the Delians, and burnt the Weight of three hundred Talents in Frankincense upon the Altar, he sail'd with the whole Fleet towards *Eretria*, accompanied by the Ionians and Æolians. The Delians say, that upon his Departure the Island of *Delos* was shaken by an Earthquake, the first and last ever felt in that place to our time ; and that the God thereby foretold the Calamities impending over the Men of that Age. For under the Reigns of *Darius* the Son of *Hystaspes*, of *Xerxes* the Son of *Darius*, and of *Artaxerxes* the Son of *Xerxes* ; I say, during the time of these three Kings, more disasters fell upon *Greece* than in twenty Generations before ; partly brought upon us by the Persians, and partly by the principal Powers of the Country contending for Superiority. So that the Island of *Delos*, tho' unmov'd before, might probably be shaken at that time, as a former Oracle had predicted in these Words :

I'll Delos *shake, however yet unmov'd.*

And

And certainly the Names of these three Kings are rightly explain'd by the Grecians: For in our Language *Darius* signifies a violent Master; *Xerxes* a martial Man; and *Artaxerxes*, a mighty Warriour.

AFTER the Barbarians had left *Delos*, they went to the other Islands, where they recruited their Army with Men, and took the Sons of the Inhabitants for Hostages. Then advancing farther among the Islands, they arriv'd at *Carystus*, the People of which refus'd either to put Hostages into their hands, or to fight against their Neighbours of *Athens* and *Eretria*. For this cause the Carystians were besieg'd by the Persians, and their Territories ravag'd, till at last they surrender'd at discretion. By this time the Eretrians being inform'd that the Persians were coming to invade them with their Fleet, implor'd the Assistance of the Athenians; who, at their request, order'd those four thousand Men that were in Possession of the Lands formerly belonging to the Chalcidean Cavalry, to march to their Succour. But the Counsels of the Eretrians were corrupted and unsteddy; and tho' they had desir'd the Aid of the Athenians, they could not come to any settled Resolution. For some among them propos'd to abandon the City, and to retire into the Mountains of *Eubœa*; whilst others were ready to betray their Country to the Persians, in Expectation of private Advantages to themselves. So that *Æschines* the Son of *Nothon*, a Man of principal Authority in the City, being perfectly inform'd of these Divisions, communicated the present State of their Affairs to the Athenian Forces, and advis'd

vis'd them to return home, that they might not be involv'd in the common Ruin. The Athenians follow'd his Counsel, and by a timely Retreat to *Oropus*, sav'd themselves from Destruction.

IN the mean time the Persians arriving on the Coast of *Eretria*, brought their Fleet to an Anchor at *Chærea, Ægilia*, and the Temple; and having possess'd themselves of those Places, landed their Horses with diligence, and prepar'd all things in order to a Battle. But the Eretrians having been oblig'd by a Plurality of Voices not to abandon the City, apply'd themselves wholly in making provision for the Defence of their Walls, and would not march out to offer Battle to the Enemy: Which when the Persians perceiv'd they began to attack the Place; and after six Days had pass'd with various Success, and great Slaughter on both sides, *Euphorbus* the Son of *Alcimachus*, and *Philagrus* the Son of *Cyneus*, Men of considerable Figure among the Eretrians, betray'd the City to the Persians. In this manner the Persians became Masters of *Eretria*; where, after they had pillag'd and set fire to the Temples, in revenge for those which had been burnt at *Sardis*, they enslav'd the Inhabitants, pursuant to the Orders of *Darius*. When they had taken this City, and rested a few days. they sail'd to *Attica*, and ravag'd the Country, supposing the Athenians would act no otherwise than the Eretrians had done. *Marathon* is a Region of *Attica*, more commodious for Horse than any other of that Country, and situate near *Eretria*. To this Place therefore *Hippias* the Son of *Pisistratus* con-

4

ducted

ducted the Persians upon their landing ; Which
when the Athenians heard, they sent their
Forces thither also under ten Captains ; and one
of these was *Miltiades*, whose Father *Cimon*, the
Son of *Stesagoras*, had been formerly oblig'd to
fly from *Athens* in the time of *Pisistratus* the Son
of *Hippocrates*. During his Exile he obtain'd
the Olympian Prize in the Quadrijugal Chariot-race, and transferr'd the Honour to *Miltiades* his Mother's Son. In the next Olympian
he obtain'd a second Victory with the same
Horses, and permitted *Pisistratus* to be proclaim'd Victor ; by which Concession he had
Liberty to return home upon his Honour. At
last having had the same Glory a third time, he
was assassinated in the Night by the Treachery
of the Sons of *Pisistratus*, after the Death of
their Father. For they suborn'd certain Persons
to that purpose, who kill'd him in the *Prytaneum*. He lies interr'd without the City, beyond
the Highway of *Diacæle* ; and his Mares which
had won him three Olympian Prizes, are buried
over against his Monument. Indeed *Evagoras*
the Lacedemonian had a set of Mares, that had
done the same before ; but besides these, none
ever arriv'd to that Excellence. *Stesagoras*, the
eldest Son of *Cimon*, was educated in *Cherfonefus* under the Care of his Uncle *Miltiades* ;
but the younger, in *Athens* with his Father,
and had the Name of *Miltiades* from his Ances-
tor, the Founder of *Cherfonesus*. This *Miltiades* returning at that time from *Cherfonesus*,
was made Captain of the Athenians, after he
had twice escap'd Death ; once, when the
Phœnicians pursu'd him to *Imbrus*, exceedingly desirous to take a Man of that Importance,
in

in order to prefent him to the King; and a fecond time, when, after he had efcap'd the Phœnicians, and was return'd home, where he
thought himfelf in Safety, his Enemies accus'd
him to the Magiftrates of ufurping the Tyranny
of *Cherfonefus*. But he was clear'd of this Accufation, and elected Captain of the Athenians
by the Suffrages of the People.

WHILST thefe Generals were yet in the
City, they fent a Meffage to *Sparta* by one *Phidippides* an Athenian, who was a Meffenger by
Profeffion. To this Man, as he himfelf faid,
and affirm'd to the Athenians, *Pan* appear'd
about Mount *Parthenius* beyond *Tegea*, calling
him loudly by his Name, and commanding him
to ask the Athenians, why they made fo little
account of him, who had always been inclin'd
to favour them, and had already often deferv'd
well of their State, as he refolv'd to do for
the future. The Athenians being then in a
profperous Condition, gave credit to this Report, built a Temple to *Pan* at the Foot of
the *Acropolis*, and from that time honour'd him
with annual Sacrifices and a burning Lamp.
This *Phidippides*, who faid he had feen *Pan*
in his way, arriving in *Sparta* on the fecond
Day after his Departure from *Athens*, fpoke to
the Senate in thefe Terms: " Men of *Lace-
" demon*, faid he, the Athenians defire you
" to affift them, and not to fuffer the moft an-
" tient of all the Grecian Cities to be en-
" flav'd by Barbarians: *Eretria* is already de-
" ftroy'd, and *Greece* already weaken'd by the
" Lofs of fo confiderable a Place." The Lacedemonians having heard the Meffage deliver'd
by *Phidippides*, in purfuance of his Inftructions,
confented

confented to fuccour the Athenians, but could not do it immediately, without violating one of their Laws. For being then at the ninth Day of the Moon, they faid they might not march into the Field before the Moon was full, and therefore would wait that Conjuncture. In the mean time *Hippias* the Son of *Pififtratus*, having introduc'd the Barbarians into the Plain of *Marathon*, dreamt one night that he lay with his Mother; and from thence concluded, that he fhould certainly recover the Dominion of *Athens*, and die an aged Man in his own Houfe. But whilft he was employ'd in tranf-porting the Booty of *Eretria* to *Ægilia*, an Ifland belonging to the Styrians; in ranging the Ships of the Perfian Fleet in the Port of *Marathon*, and in drawing up the Barbarians in order of Battle, he happen'd to cough and fneeze with fuch Violence, that moft of his Teeth were fhaken in his Head, and one falling out into the Sand, could not be found, tho' all poffible Search was made for it. Upon which Acci-dent, with a deep Sigh *Hippias* faid to thofe who were prefent, " This Country neither " belongs to us, nor will ever be fubdued by " us: And I fhall have no other Part here " than that where my Tooth lies." Thus he thought his Dream was accomplifh'd.

WHEN the Athenians had drawn their Forces together at the Temple of *Hercules*, the Platæans came in to their Affiftance with all the Men they could raife. They were already under the Pro-tection of *Athens* and the Athenians had gone thro' many Dangers in their Defence. For when the Platæans faw themfelves opprefs'd by the Thebans, they firft offer'd their Submiffion

to

to *Cleomenes* the Son of *Anaxandrides*, and to the
Lacedemonians.   But they rejected the Offer in
these Terms, "We are plac'd, said they, at such
" a Distance from you, that in time of Neces-
" sity our Succours will prove ineffectual.   For
" your Country may be frequently ravag'd be-
" fore we can be inform'd of your Danger.   We
" advise you therefore to put your selves under
" the Protection of the Athenians, who are
" your Neighbours, and sufficiently able to de-
" fend you."   This Counsel the Lacedemonians
gave not out of any good Will to the Platæans;
but because they were desirous to see the Athenians weaken'd by a War against the Bœotians.
However, the Platæans approving their Advice,
went to *Athens*; and arriving there when the
Athenians were met to sacrifice to the twelve
Gods, they sat down by the Altar in the pos-
ture of Suppliants, and made their Submission in
that place.   Which when the Thebans heard,
they sent an Army against *Platæa*; and at the
same time the Athenians march'd to assist the
Platæans.   But as they were ready to engage in
Battle, the Corinthians apprehending the Consequences, interpos'd their Offices to reconcile
the contending Parties, and with the Consent
of both sides determin'd the Dispute on this
Agreement;   " That the Thebans should per-
" mit all those Bœotians, who would no
" longer be counted Members of *Bæotia*, to
" do as they thought most convenient for
" themselves."   After this Reconciliation the
Corinthians return'd home, and as the Athenians
were retiring likewise, the Bœotians fell upon
them in their March, but were repuls'd with
Loss.   Upon which Success the Athenians en-

larg'd the Frontier of the Platæans, and instead of that appointed by the Corinthians, fix'd the Limits of the Thebans at *Asopus* and *Hyssa.* In this manner the Platæans came under the Protection of the Athenians, and join'd their Forces at *Marathon.* When the Army was assembled, a Division arose among the Athenian Captains; some delivering their Opinion against fighting, because they were far inferior in Number to the Medes; and others as vehemently pressing to come to a Battle: Among the last was *Miltiades,* who finding they could not agree, and that the worst Opinion would probably prevail, went to *Callimachus* of *Aphidna,* at that time Polemarch in the Army, and elected to that Office by the Athenians with the Privilege of an eleventh Voice. For in former times the Athenians made the Polemarch equal to the Captains in the Decision of all Matters in debate. To this Person therefore *Miltiades* apply'd himself in these Words: " You alone, " O *Callimachus,* must now determine, either " to see the Athenians reduc'd to the Condition of Slaves, or by preserving the Liberty of your Country, leave an eternal Monument of your Fame, surpassing the Glory of *Harmodius* and *Aristogiton.* For the " Athenians were never in so great Danger " from the time they were first a people. " If they fall under the Power of the Medes, " one may easily imagine what Usage they " must expect from *Hippias:* But if they " conquer, *Athens* will be the principal City " of *Greece.* To let you know then by " what means these things may be effected " and from what Cause the Fate of *Athens* is " now

" ~~now in your Hands I shall acquaint you~~
" ~~that we are at this Instant divided in Opi-~~
" nion touching a Battle, some of us proposing
" to fight, and others advising the contrary.
" If we decline a Battle, I foresee some great
" Dissention will shake the Fidelity of the
" Army, and induce them to a Compliance
" with the Medes. But if we fight before
" the Corruption slides into the Hearts of the
" Athenians, we may hope from the Equity
" of the Gods to obtain the Victory. All
" these things are in your Power, and en-
" tirely depend upon the Resolution you shall
" take. For if you would support my Opi-
" nion with the Accession of your Vote, you
" will see your Country free, and *Athens* the
" most illustrious City of *Grece:* But if you
" join with those who would dissuade us from
" a Battle you can expect no other Consequen-
" ces than such as are most contrary to these
" Hopes." *Callimachus,* convinc'd by the force
of these Reasons, gave his Opinion with
those who were for fighting; and by that
means a Resolution was taken to engage the
Enemy. All those Captains, who in the Council of War had press'd for a Battle, whenever their Turn came to command the Army,
yielded that Honour to *Miltiades :* But tho' he
accepted the Power, yet he would not hazard
an Engagement before his own Day. When
therefore that Day was come, the Athenians
were drawn up in this Order of Battle. *Callimachus* plac'd himself at the Head of the right
Wing ; because the Laws of *Athens* assign'd
that post to the Polemarch. Then the Tribes,
rang'd in a Line, follow'd in order ; and last of

all

all the Platæans were posted on the Left: From which time, in the Solemnity of the Quinquennial Sacrifices, the Athenian Orator is oblig'd to pray for the Welfare of the Platæans, as well as for the Prosperity of *Athens.* The Athenian Forces drawn up in this manner, were equal in Front to the Medes. But because they had not a sufficient Number of Men in the Centre, that Part was extremely weak, and the main Strength of the Army consisted in the two Wings. When all things were thus dispos'd and the Sacrifice rightly perform'd, the Athenians ran with speed towards the Enemy, tho' the Interval between the two Armies was no less than eight Stades in Length. The Persians seeing the Athenians advancing with such Precipitation, prepar'd themselves to sustain the Attack, imputing their Haste to Folly and Desperation; because they were not only few in Number, but wholly destitute both of Horse and Lancers. But the Athenians coming up with the Barbarians, fell on with such Valour, that their Actions deserve ever to be remembred with Honour. For they were the first of all the Grecians, who had the Courage to look upon the Median Habit without Fear, and to stand before the Men who wore that Dress; whereas in former time the bare Name of the Medes was a word of Terror in every Part of *Greece.* After a long and obstinate Fight, that Part of the Barbarian Army, in which were the Persians and the Saces, broke the Center of the Athenians, and pursued them thro' the Plain. But the Athenians and the Platæans, who were in the right and left Wings, defeated the Barbarians on both sides;

and

and having suffer'd them to fly out of the Field, clos'd the two Points, and fell upon those who had broken their Centre. When they had defeated these, they pursued the broken Enemy with great Slaughter to the Sea, and set fire to their Fleet. In this Battle *Callimachus* the Polemarch, after he had given signal Proof of his Valour, was kill'd, with *Stasileus* the Son of *Thrasylus*, one of the Commanders in chief: and *Cynegyrus*, the Son of *Euphorion*, having laid hold on the Prow of one of the Enemy's Ships, had his Hand struck off with an Ax, and died of his Wound. Many other Persons of considerable Name were slain in this Action; and after seven Ships of the Enemy had been taken by the Athenians, the Barbarians imbark'd in the rest; and having put the Booty of *Eretria* on board, sail'd by the Promontory of *Sunium*, with a Design to surprize *Athens* before the Return of the Army. The Athenians say this Enterprize was undertaken at the Solicitation of the Alcmæonides, and that they held up a Shield for a Signal to the Persian Fleet. However, whilst they were doubling the Cape of *Sunium*, the Athenians decamping from the Temple of *Hercules* in *Marathon*, march'd with all possible diligence to the Succour of their City; and before the Barbarians could arrive, came and encamp'd at another Temple of *Hercules* in *Cynosargis*. Upon which the Barbarians having already pass'd the Harbour of *Phaleron* belonging to the Athenians, assembled their Fleet, and set sail, in order to return to *Asia*. In this Battle of *Marathon*, were kill'd about six thousand three hundred of the Barbarians, and one hundred and ninety two Athenians

But

But here I muſt not omit a moſt ſurpriſing thing
which happen'd during that Action. One E-
pizelus the Son of Cuphagoras, an Athenian,
fighting in the Rank with a becoming Valour,
loſt his ſight on a ſudden without receiving either Wound or Blow in any Part of his Body ;
and from that time continued blind to the end
of his Life. I have heard him, relating the manner of his Misfortune, affirm, that he thought
he ſaw a Man of uncommon Height ſtanding
before him in compleat Armour, holding a
Shield cover'd by the Length of his Beard ;
and that this Phantom afterwards paſſing by
him, kill'd the Perſon who ſtood next in the
Rank.

DATIS, in his return to *Aſia*, arriving at *My-*
conus, dreamt he ſaw a Viſion ; and tho' he would
not publiſh the Particulars, yet upon the firſt
Appearance of Day he order'd all the Fleet to
be ſearch'd ; and having found a gilded Image
of *Apollo* in one of the Phœnician Ships, enquir'd
from what Temple they had taken it. When he
was inform'd where they had the Statue, he
ſail'd in his own Ship to *Delos*, and finding the
Inhabitants return'd thither, he depoſited the
Image in one of their Temples, commanding
the Delians to tranſport it to *Delium*, a City of
Thebes, built on the Sea-coaſt over againſt *Chal-*
cis ; and after he had given this order put to
Sea again. Nevertheleſs, becauſe the Delians
fail'd to execute his Command, the Thebans
themſelves ſending to *Delos* upon the Admonition of the Oracle, brought away the Statue
twenty Years after. In the mean time *Datis*
and *Artaphernes* arriving in *Aſia*, conducted the
Eretrian Captives to *Suſa* : And tho' *Darius* had
                                        expreſs'd

express'd great Indignation against the Eretrians before the Reduction of that Place, and charg'd them with the Guilt of beginning the War; yet finding they were now his Prisoners, and entirely in his Power, he did them no other hurt, than to send them to inhabit a Station belonging to himself in the Region of *Cissia*, and going by the Name of *Anderica*, distant from *Susa* two hundred and ten Stades; and forty Stades from a Well which yields Brimstone, Salt and Oil, in this manner: They let down a Bucket, fasten'd to a Crane, into the Well; and having drawn it up again, put the Liquor into a Cistern: Then they pour off the same Liquor a second time into a Vessel prepar'd for that purpose, and the Separation is presently made. For the Brimstone and Salt subside by different ways; and the Oil, which is black, of a strong Scent, and by the Persians call'd Radinace, is skimm'd off and put into Jarrs. In this Country *Darius* plac'd the Eretrians, who still continue to inhabit the same Region, and have preserv'd their antient Language to our Time. Thus I have finish'd what I had to say concerning the Affairs of the Eretrians.

AFTER the full Moon, two thousand Lacedemonians arriv'd in *Athens*, with so great a desire of finding the Enemy, that they had spent but three Days in their March from *Sparta* to *Attica*: And tho' they came too late to be present at the Battle, yet being violently bent upon seeing the Medes, they proceed to *Marathon*; and when they had satisfied their Curiosity, commended the Athenians for their Valour, and return'd home. But I am amaz'd, and can

         never

never comprehend that the Alcmæonides should in concert with the Enemy hold up a Shield for a Signal to the Persians; as if they would have been contented to see the Athenians subject to the Barbarians, and to *Hippias*; they who had ever shewn as much Hatred to Tyrants, or more, than *Callias* the son of *Phænippus*, and Father of *Hipponicus*; tho' *Callias* was the only Man among the Athenians, who, besides many other Actions of the utmost Enmity, had the Courage to purchase the Goods of *Pisistratus*, when after his Expulsion they were publickly sold by a Decree of the People. *Callias* indeed deserves always to be remembred with Honour, as well for the eminent Part he had in restoring the Liberty of his Country, as for the Actions he perform'd at the Olympian Exercises. He won the Race with a single Horse, and was second in the Quadrijugal Course. He had been before victorious in the Pythian Solemnities, and distinguish'd himself by his Magnificence in the View of all the Grecians. He was so indulgent to his three Daughters, that when they had attain'd to marriageable Years, he presented them with immense Riches and permitted them to chuse their Husbands out of all the Families in *Athens*. But since nothing is more evident, than that the Alcmæonides were no less Haters of Tyrants than *Callias*, my Wonder is the greater; and I can never believe that they made a Signal to the Persians; they, I say, who in all time had avoided to live under Tyranny, and had actually by their Contrivance expell'd the Family of *Pisistratus*; acquiring by that Action a better Title, in my Opinion, to be call'd the Deliverers

of

of *Athens*, than *Harmodius* and *Ariftogiton*. For thefe Men by killing *Hipparchus*, only exafperated thofe who furviv'd; but could not prevent them from continuing the Tyranny. Whereas the Alcmæonides manifeftly reftor'd the Freedom of *Athens*, if we may believe that they induc'd the Pythian to admonifh the Lacedemonians to refcue the Athenians from Servitude, as I mention'd before. Perhaps fome may pretend, that finding themfelves afterwards upon the fame Level with the People, they grew difcontented, and were willing to betray their Country: On the contrary, no Men were ever in greater Efteem among the Athenians, or had a greater Share in the publick Honours; and therefore Reafon forbids us to think that they held up the Shield on that account. That a Shield was feen, cannot be denied; for the thing is true: But who the Perfon was that held it up, is altogether unknown to me. The Alcmæonian Family had ever been confiderable in *Athens*, and receiv'd an additional Luftre from *Alcmæon* and *Megacles*. For when the Lydians were fent by *Cræfus* to confult the Oracle of *Delphi*, *Alcmæon* the Son of *Megacles* was their Confident, and entertain'd them hofpitably: Which *Cræfus* underftanding, at their Return, he fent for him to *Sardis*, and after his Arrival gave him as much Gold as he could carry about his Body at once. *Alcmæon* having confider'd how to improve the Liberality of *Cræfus* to the beft Advantage, put on a Coat of a vaft Compafs, with Bafkins proportionably wide, and in that Drefs being conducted to the Treafury, he plac'd himfelf upon a great Heap of Gold; and after he had

cramm'd

cramm'd as much into his Buskins as they could contain, fill'd his Garments on all sides, loaded his Hair with Ingots, and put many Pieces into his Mouth; he went out of the Treasury, hardly able to drag his Buskins after him, and resembling any thing rather than a Man. When *Crœsus* saw him in this Condition, with his Mouth full, and every other Part loaded with Gold, he broke into a Fit of Laughter, and gave him all he had brought out, with many other Presents of no less Value. Thus *Alcmæon* having enrich'd his Family, was enabled to breed Horses, with which he won the Quadrijugal Prize at the Olympian Exercises. But in the second Generation after him, *Clisthenes* Tyrant of *Sicyon*, rais'd this House to a higher Degree of Glory than ever they had attain'd before. This *Clisthenes*, who was the Son of *Aristomymus*, and Grandson to *Myron* the Son of *Andreas*, had a Daughter nam'd *Agarista*, which he purpos'd to marry to the Man he should judge most worthy among all the Grecians. To that end, during the Olympian Solemnity, in which *Clisthenes* obtain'd the Victory in the Quadrijugal Race, he caus'd open Proclamation to be made, that whoever of the Grecians thought himself worthy to be Son-in-Law to *Clisthenes* should come to *Sicyon* before the Expiration of sixty days; because he had determin'd to marry his Daughter within the Compass of a Year after that time. Upon which Notification all such Grecians as thought highly of themselves and their Country, went to *Sicyon*; where *Clisthenes* had made Preparations for Races and Wrestling. From *Italy*, arriv'd *Smindyrides* the Son of *Hippocrates,*

crates, a Man plung'd in Voluptuousness beyond most Examples, and born at *Sybaris*,
which was then at the Height of its Prosperity; with *Damas* of *Siris*, the Son of *Sa-
myris* sirnamed the Wise. From the *Gulph* of *Ionia* came *Amphimnestus* the Son of *Epistrophus* of
Epidamnus; and from *Æolia*, *Males* the Brother of *Titormus*, who surpass'd all the Grecians
in Strength, and had retir'd to the Extremities
of *Æolia*. From *Peloponnesus*, arriv'd *Leocides*
the Son of *Phidon* Tyrant of *Argos*: of that
Phidon, I say, who prescrib'd Measures to the
Peloponnesians; and exceeding all the Grecians
in Arrogance, remov'd the Elian Judges, and
assum'd to himself the Power of appointing the
Olympian Exercises: *Amiantus* an Arcadian
of *Trapezus* and Son to *Lycurgus*; with *Lapha-
nes* the Azanian of *Pæus*, Son of that *Euphorion*,
who, according to a common Report, entertain'd *Castor* and *Pollux* in his House, and from
that time receiv'd all Strangers with great Hospitality: These, with *Onomastus* of *Elis*, the
Son of *Agæus*, came from *Peloponnesus*. From
Athens came *Megacles* the Son of that *Alcmæon*
who visited *Cræsus*; and *Hippoclides* the Son of
Tisander, in Riches and Beauty surpassing all
the Athenians of his time. From *Eubæa*, *Lisa-
nius* alone, a Native of *Eretria*, which was then
in a flourishing Condition. From *Thessaly*, *Di-
actorides* of *Cranon*; and from the Molossians,
Alcon. All these were Pretenders to the Daughter of *Clisthenes*, and arriv'd in *Sicyon* 'fore the
sixty Days were expir'd. *Clisthenes*, in pursuance of his Design, first examin'd every one
touching his Country and Descent: After which
he detain'd them a whole Year, in order to in-

form himself fully of their Fortitude, Tempe-
rance, Inftitution, and Manners; converfing
with them frequently apart, and together, and
conducting the Youngeft to the Gymnaftic Exercifes. Above all he endeavour'd to difcover
their Inclinations when he entertain'd them
with Feafting; for he tried all Experiments,
and treated them with great Magnificence
during the whole time they ftaid with him.
But among the feveral Candidates he principally favour'd the Athenians; efpecially *Hippoclides* the Son of *Tifander*; becaufe he was e-
fteem'd for his Courage, and deriv'd his Defcent
from the Corinthian *Cypfelides.* When the Day
was come, which *Clifthenes* had appointed for
naming the Perfon he fhould chufe; he facrific'd a Hecatomb, and invited the Pretenders,
with all the Sicyonians, to the Feaft. After
Supper they enter'd into a Difpute concerning
Mufick, and other things that occafionally fell
into Difcourfe at that time: And as the Wine
went warmly about, *Hippoclides* with an affuming Air commanded the Mufician to play a
Tune call'd *Emmelia*; in which being readily o-
bey'd, he danc'd with much Satisfaction to himfelf; tho' *Clifthenes* obferving all that pafs'd, began to fufpect the Event. When *Hippoclides* had
finifh'd his Dance, and refted fome time, he
commanded a Table to be brought in; which
was no fooner done, than mounting upon it, he
firft imitated the Laconian Meafures, then
danc'd after the Athenian manner; and laft of
all fetting his Head upon the Table, and erecting his Feet, he mov'd his Legs in fuch Pof-
tures, as he had already practis'd with his
Hands. Tho' the firft and fecond of thefe

Dances

Dances had sufficiently diffuaded *Cliftbenes* from chufing a Son-in-Law of fo much profligate Impudence; yet he contain'd himfelf, and would not break out into an open Paffion. But when he faw him endeavouring with his Legs to imitate the Actions of his Hands, he loft all Patience, and cried out, " O Son of *Tifander* " thou haft danc'd away thy Marriage." The other anfwer'd, " That is not the care of *Hip-* " *poclides.*" Which Saying afterwards obtain'd the Authority of a Proverb. Then *Cliftbenes* having commanded Silence, fpoke to thofe who pretended to his Daughter, in thefe Words: " I commend you all, and am willing to gratify " you all, if I could; without diftinguifhing " any one in particular, to the Difadvantage " of the reft. But becaufe I have no more " than one Daughter, and confequently can- " not comply with the Defires of fo many " Perfons, I give a Talent of Silver to every " one of thofe who fhall be excluded; as well " in acknowledgment of your Readinefs to en- " ter into my Family by this Match, as of the " time you have fpent in a long Abfence from " your Habitations; and I give my Daughter " *Agarifta* to *Megacles* the Son of *Alcmæon*, to be " his Wife under the Conditions and Ufages of " the Athenians." *Megacles* immediately de- clar'd his Confent, and the Nuptials were cele- brated in the Houfe of *Cliftbenes.* Thus the Dif- pute fo long depending between thefe Rivals was determin'd, and the Alcmæonides became famous in *Greece.* Of this Marriage was born a Son nam'd *Cliftbenes* from the Father of his Mother. He divided the Athenians into Tribes and eftablifh'd the Democratical Government.

Megacles

Megacles had also another Son nam'd *Hippocrates* who was the Father of another *Megacles*, and of another *Agarista*, so call'd from the Daughter of *Clisthenes*. This *Agarista* being afterwards married to *Xanthippus* the Son of *Ariphron*, and big with Child, dreamt she had brought forth a Lyon, and within few Days was deliver'd of *Pericles*.

MILTIADES having by his Success at *Marathon* acquir'd a much greater Reputation in *Athens* than he had before, demanded seventy Ships of the Athenians, with Men and Money proportionable ; in order to undertake an Expedition, which he kept private ; and only told them, that if they would follow him, he would put them into possession of great Riches ; and lead them into a Country, from whence they should bring home Gold in abundance without Difficulty. The Athenians accepting the Proposition with Joy, prepar'd the Ships accordingly : And when *Miltiades* had receiv'd all things necessary to his Enterprize, he set sail for *Paros* ; under Colour that the Parians had assisted the Persians with their Ships in the Expedition to *Marathon*. But the Truth is, he was incens'd against the Parians because *Lysagoras* the Son of *Tiseus*, a Man of Parian Extraction, had spoken ill of him to *Hydarnes* the Persian. When *Miltiades* arriv'd at *Paros*, he besieg'd the City, and sending in his Heralds, demanded a hundred Talents of the Parians ; threatning, in case of Refusal, not to draw off his Army before he had taken the Place. But the Parians refusing to deliberate whether they should give Money to *Miltiades*, applied themselves wholly to contrive by what means they might defend the

4

City ;

City; repairing their Fortifications in divers
Places, and working in the Night, till they had
made their Walls doubly higher than before
in that Part where they were least defensible.
Thus far all the Grecians agree in their Report: The rest, as the Parians say, pass'd in
this manner.   When *Miltiades* saw all his Measures broken, one *Timo*, a Woman of *Paros*,
Subpriestess of the National Gods, and then his
Prisoner, came to him and counsel'd him, if
he valued the taking of *Paros*, to do as she
should advise. *Miltiades* having heard her Proposal, went directly to the Inclosure of the
Temple dedicated to *Ceres* the Legislatress,
without the City; and after he had endeavour'd in vain to open the Gate, he mounted
the Wall, and leap'd down, with a Design to
enter the sacred Place, in order to do something, or to move something, which ought
not to have been mov'd.   But while he stood
before the Doors, he was seiz'd with a sudden Horrour; and resolving to return, leap'd
back again from the same Place, and broke his
Thigh, tho' some say he fell upon his Knee.
Thus *Miltiades* having neither obtain'd the
Money he demanded, nor taken *Paros*, return'd to *Athens* with Disgrace, after he had
ravag'd the Country, and besieg'd the City
twenty six Days.   When the Siege was rais'd,
the Parians being inform'd of the Counsel
which *Timo* had given to *Miltiades*, and desiring to bring her to Justice, sent Deputies to
inquire of the Oracle at *Delphi*, whether
they should punish her with Death, for endeavouring to betray the City to the Enemy, and
discovering the sacred Mysteries to *Miltiades*,
which

which ought not to be reveal'd to any Man. But the Pythian not permitting them to do as they desir'd, affirm'd that *Timo* was not the Author of that Advice; and that the Gods having determin'd the Destruction of *Miltiades*, had only made her the Instrument of his Death. This Answer the Pythian gave to the Parians.

WHEN *Miltiades* was return'd to *Athens*, many of the Athenians were incens'd against him, and none more than *Xanthippus* the Son of *Ariphron*, who accus'd him to the People for deceiving the Athenians, and desir'd he might be punish'd with Death. *Miltiades* could not be present to defend himself, because his Thigh beginning to mortify, render'd him unable to move from his Bed. But his Friends appearing for him, alledg'd in his Favour the Actions he perform'd at *Marathon*; together with the Acquisition of *Lemnos*; which *Miltiades* reduc'd under the Dominion of *Athens*, after he had expell'd the Pelasgians for the Injuries they had done to the Athenians. These Allegations prevail'd so far with the People, that they would not sentence him to Death; but fin'd him fifty Talents for his Crime. Soon after which, *Miltiades* ended his Life by the Putrefaction and Mortification of his Thigh; and his Son *Cymon* paid his Fine. As for *Lemnos*, *Miltiades* took possession of that Island, on the following Occasion. The Pelasgians had been already driven out of *Attica* by the Athenians; whether justly or unjustly I shall not determine; having nothing more to say than what is reported on both sides. *Hecataeus*, the Son of *Hegesander*, affirms they were unjustly expell'd. For, says he, when the Athe-

nians
3

nians faw that the Lands about *Hymeſſus*, which they had given to the Pelaſgians in Payment for the Wall they had built about the *Acropolis*, were improv'd from a barren and unprofitable Soil, into a fertil and well cultivated Region, they grew envious of their Proſperity; and coveting to reſume the Country, drove out the Pelaſgians without any other Pretence whatever. On the other hand the Athenians affirm, that they were juſtly ejected on account of the Injuries they had done. For they faw that while the Pelaſgians continued to inhabit under Mount *Hymeſſus*, they frequently left their Habitations, and in Contempt of the Athenians offer'd Violence to their Sons and Daughters who were ſent for Water to the place call'd the *Nine Fountains*; becauſe in thoſe times neither they nor any other People of *Greece* were furniſh'd with Slaves: That the Pelaſgians not contented with theſe Attempts, were at laſt manifeſtly detected to have form'd a Deſign againſt *Athens*; and that the Athenians, to ſhew themſelves as generous as the others had been baſe, when they had the Power of puniſhing theſe Offenders for their manifeſt Treachery, choſe rather to command them only to depart the Country: Which the Pelaſgians obeying poſſeſs'd themſelves of *Lemnos*, and other Places. Thus *Hecatæus* relates this Occurrence in one manner, and the Athenians in another. But thoſe Pelaſgians who inhabited *Lemnos*, deſiring to be reveng'd, and knowing all the Feſtival Days of the Athenians, fitted out ſome Gallies of fifty Oars each; and having laid an Ambuſcade for their Wives as they celebrated the Feaſt of *Diana* in *Brauron*,

they furpriz'd a great Number; carried them
away to *Lemnos*, and kept them for Concubines.
These Women abounding in Children, taught
their Sons the Language of *Attica*, and Manners of the Athenians: By which means they
not only refus'd to converse with the Sons of
the Pelafgian Women; but if any one of their
Number was attack'd, they all immediately
ran to his Affiftance, and reveng'd the Injury.
Thus thinking themfelves worthy to command
the Sons of the Pelafgians, they eafily became
their Mafters. When the Pelafgians were inform'd of thefe things, they confulted together; and judging fuch Arrogance infupportable, drew this Confequence: If, faid they,
at thefe Years they have learn'd to defend one
another, and conftantly endeavour'd to ufurp
a Superiority over the Children of our legi-
timate Wives; what will they not do, when
they attain the Age of Men? Which Thought
made fo deep an Impreffion in the Minds of
the Pelafgians, that they refolv'd to murder the
Children they had by the Women of *Attica*;
and, to compleat their Cruelty, difpatch'd the
Mothers after them. From this atrocious
Crime, and that which was perpetrated before
by thofe Women, who with the Affiftance of
Thoas kill'd their Hufbands, all enormous Actions pafs among the Grecians under the Name
of Lemnian. But the Pelafgians, after the
Murder of thefe Children with their Mothers,
perceiving their Lands to become barren, their
Wives unfruitful, and their Flocks not to yield
the ufual Increafe; tormented with Famine,
and deftitute of Children, fent to *Delphi*, in
order to be inform'd by what means they might
be

be deliver'd from thefe Calamities ; And being admonifh'd by the Pythian to give Satisfaction to the Athenians in the manner they fhould
defire, they went to *Athens*, and profefs'd themfelves ready to fuffer any Punifhment they fhould
think fit to impofe on account of the Irjuries
they had receiv'd. The Athenians having
heard their Offer, prepar'd a magnificent Feaft
in the *Prytaneum* ; and when they faw the table
furnifh'd with all kind of Provifions, they commanded the Pelafgians to furrender their Country, in as good a Condition. To which they
anfwer'd, " That they would obey, when the
" North Wind fhould carry a Ship in one Day
" from the Territories of the Athenians to
" their Ifland :" Well knowing the thing to be
impoffible, becaufe *Attica* is fituate much more
to the Southward than *Lemnos*. But many
Years after they had given this Anfwer, when
the Hellefpontin *Cherfonefus* became fubject to
the Athenians, *Miltiades* the Son of *Cymon* having imbark'd at *Eleus*, a City on the *Hellefpont*
was carried by a ftrong Etefian Wind in one
Day to *Lemnos* ; and immediately commanding
the Pelafgians to depart out of the Ifland, reminded them of their folemn Promife, which
they hop'd never to fee accomplifh'd. The
Hephæftians obey'd the Order of *Miltiades* :
But the Myrinæans, not acknowledging *Cherfonefus* to belong to *Attica*, fuftain'd a Siege, till
they were compell'd to furrender. And in this
manner *Lemnos* was reduc'd by *Miltiades* under the Power of the Athenians.

THE

THE

History of *Herodotus.*

BOOK VII.

POLYMNIA.

WHEN *Darius* the Son of *Hystaspes* had receiv'd the News of the Battle fought at *Marathon*, he became much more incens'd against the Athenians, than he had been before for the Invasion of *Sardis*, and much more diligent in his Preparations to carry on the War against *Greece*. He dispatch'd Messages to the several Cities of his Dominions, enjoining every one in particular to raise a greater Number of Forces than ever, sufficiently furnish'd with Horses, Ships, and all manner of Provisions. These Commands of the King put all *Asia* into a Ferment during the Space of three Years. But in the fourth Year, when the best of his Forces were assembled, in order to invade *Greece*; the Ægyptians, who had been subdued by *Cambyses*, revolted from the Persians. So that *Darius* being irritated at once against the Grecians and Ægyptians, resolv'd to make War against both. But when he had prepar'd all things for his Expedition to *Greece* and Ægypt, a great Contest arose between his Sons concerning the Succession of the kingdom: For by the Customs of *Persia* the King is oblig'd to nominate his Successor,

K 3

before he departs to put himself at the Head of the Army. *Darius* had three Sons by the Daughter of *Gobryas*, his first Wife; all born before he was King: And after his Succession to the Throne, he had four more by *Atossa* the Daughter of *Cyrus*. Of the first, *Artabazanes* was the eldest: Of the latter, *Xerxes*: And these two being born of different Mothers, were Competitors for the Succession. *Artabazanes* urg'd that he was the eldest of all the Sons of *Darius*, and that by the Customs of all Nations the eldest Son had a Right to the Kingdom: On the other hand, *Xerxes* alledg'd, that he was the Son of *Atossa* the Daughter of *Cyrus*, who had delivered the Persians from Servitude. *Darius* had not yet declar'd himself in favour of either, when *Demaratus* the Son of *Ariston*, who had been depriv'd of the Kingdom of *Sparta*, and arriv'd at *Susa* about that time, hearing of this Dispute between the Sons of *Darius*, went to *Xerxes*, as I am inform'd, and counsell'd him to add these Reasons to his Defence: That he was born after *Darius* had obtain'd the Kingdom, with all the Dominions of *Persia*; whereas *Artabazanes* was only Son of *Darius* a private Man; and consequently, to let another enjoy the Advantages that belong'd to him would be contrary to the Rules of Equity and Justice; and that by the Laws of *Sparta*, all Children born before their Father was invested with the Royal Dignity, were excluded from the Succession, if he had any Son to succeed him, born after that time. These Reasons having been produc'd by *Xerxes* at the Suggestion of *Demaratus*, appear'd so just to *Darius*, that he declar'd him King. But I am inclin'd to

x

believe,

believe, that without this Advice, *Xerxes* would have been King ; becaufe the Authority of *Atoffa* was too great to be refifted. When *Darius* had nominated *Xerxes* to fucceed him and firmly refolv'd to purfue his intended Enterprizes, he died, in the fecond Year of the Revolt of *Ægypt*, after he had reign'd thirty fix Years ; and had not the Satisfaction of executing his Defigns either againft the Ægyptians or Athenians.

XERXES the Son of *Darius* fucceeding him in the Kingdom, fhew'd little Difpofition at firft to make War againft *Greece*, and bent his Thoughts wholly upon the Reduction of *Ægypt*. But *Mardonius* the Son of *Gobryas* by the Sifter of *Darius*, and confequently Coufin German to *Xerxes*, in confidence of the Authority he had with the King, fpoke to him on that Subject to this Effect : " S I R, if you " fuffer the Athenians to go unpunifh'd, after " all the Mifchiefs they have done to the Perfi- " ans, we fhall be difhonour'd. However, at " prefent finifh the Enterprize you have begun ; " and when you fhall fee the Infolence of the " Ægyptians humbled, lead your Army againft " *Athens* ; that all Men may fpeak of you with " Honour, and no Nation for the future may " dare to attack any of your Dominions." To this Difcourfe, hitherto tending only to Revenge, he added, That *Europe* was a beautiful Country ; abounding in delicious Fruits, and Men of invincible Courage : In a word, too excellent to be poffefs'd by any other than the greateft of Kings. Now, tho' his own youthful Ambition, and a violent Defire to fee himfelf made Governour of *Greece*,

were

were the principal Motives he had to give this Counsel; yet he at last prevail'd with *Xerxes* to do as he advis'd; and was not a little assisted in his Design by a favourable Conjuncture. For about that time the Aleuadian Kings of *Thessaly* sent Ambassadors to *Xerxes*, with Orders to solicit him to invade *Greece*, and to promise him all manner of Assistance on their Part. The Pisistratides likewise, then in Exile at *Susa*, us'd the same Persuasions; and in order to compass their Design, produc'd a certain Athenian nam'd *Onomacritus*, who, they said, could interpret Oracles, and explain the Divinations of *Musæus*. This Man was reconcil'd to them before their Arrival in *Persia*, but had been formerly their Enemy. For he was first banish'd from *Athens* by *Hipparchus* the Son of *Pisistratus*, upon the Discovery of *Lasus* the Son of *Hermion*, who surpriz'd him in the very Fact of inserting a supposititious Oracle among those of *Musæus*, importing, that the Islands about *Lemnos* should be swallow'd up by the Sea: and on that account *Hipparchus* expell'd him out of *Athens*, after he had us'd his Conversation with great Familiarity. This *Onomacritus* having accompanied the Pisistratides to *Susa*, was recommended by them to the King as an extraordinary Person; and being introduc'd into his Presence, recited some of his Oracles; always remembring to suppress those that foretold any Disaster to the Barbarians, and producing only such as were favourable to their Affairs. Among those of the last Sort, he repeated one, which foretold that a Bridge should be laid over the *Hellespont* by a Persian; and descended to all the Circumstances belonging to that Enterprize.

Thus

Thus *Xerxes*, partly on the Hopes he conceiv'd from these illusory Oracles, and partly at the Instigation of the Pisistratides and Aleuadians, determined to make War against *Greece.* Nevertheless, in the first place, and in the second Year after the Death of *Darius*, having assembled an Army, in order to punish the revolted Ægyptians, he reduc'd all *Ægypt* to a worse Condition of Servitude than they had felt under his Father, and gave the Government of that Country to his Brother *Achæmenes* the Son of *Darius*; who was afterwards kill'd by *Inarus* the Son of *Pfammitichus*, a Lybian. When *Xerxes* had thus recover'd *Ægypt*, and was about to prepare all things for his Expedition against *Athens*, he summon'd a Council of the principal Persians, as well to hear their Opinions, as to declare his own; and after they were all assembled, spoke to this effect: " I will not, O Per- " sians, be the Author of new Institutions, " but shall act in Conformity to those I have " receiv'd. For I am instructed by Men of " elder Years, that from the time we wrested " the Power out of the hands of the Medes, " and *Cyrus* dethron'd *Astyages*, we never liv'd " an inglorious, unactive Life; but by follow- " ing the Hand of God, which was our Guide, " we have attain'd to a great measure of Pros- " perity. The Actions perform'd by *Cyrus*, " by *Cambyses*, and by my Father *Darius*, to- " gether with the Nations they conquer'd, " are too well known to you to need a Re- " petition. As for me, since I took Posses- " sion of the Throne, my principal Care has " been not to fall short of my Predecessors in " Glory, and to acquire as great a Proportion
" of

" of Power to the Perſians. Revolving theſe
" Thoughts in my Mind, I am perſuaded,
" we may at once obtain a glorious Name,
" with the Conqueſt of a Country not infe-
" rior to that we now poſſeſs, but rather
" more abounding in all things; and at the
" ſame time revenge the Injuries we have re-
" ceiv'd. To this end therefore I have called
" you together, and ſhall acquaint you with
" the Enterprize I have form'd. I deſign to
" lay a Bridge over the *Helleſpont*, and to
" tranſport an Army by the way of *Europe* in-
" to *Greece*, that I may puniſh the Athenians
" for the Injuries they have done to the Per-
" ſians and to my Father. You know *Darius*
" had determin'd to make War againſt thoſe
" Men, but Death prevented him from execu-
" ting his Deſign. I reſolve therefore to do Juſ-
" tice to my Father and the Perſians, and not to
" lay down my Arms, till I have taken and
" burnt *Athens*, whoſe Citizens were the firſt
" Aggreſſors in this War againſt me and my Fa-
" ther. For before any Violence had been done
" on either ſide, they invaded *Sardis*, in con-
" junction with *Ariſtagoras* the Mileſian, our
" Servant; and burnt down the Sacred Groves
" with the Temples. And how they treated
" you, when you made a Deſcent into their
" Territories under the Conduct of *Datis* and
" *Artaphernes*, is ſufficiently known to you all.
" Theſe things have excited in me an ardent
" deſire to invade their Country with Fire and
" Sword: being aſſur'd, and not without good
" reaſon, that if we can ſubdue the Athe-
" nians, with their Neighbours, who inhabit
" the Counttry of *Pelops* the Phrygian, the Per-

" ſian

" fian Dominions will be bounded by no o-
" ther Limits than the Heavens ; and the Sun
" fhall not behold any Region diftinguifh'd
" from us, or exempted from our Obedience.
" For I intend, with your Concurrence, to
" march thro' all the Parts of *Europe*, and
" to reduce the whole Earth into one Empire ;
" being well inform'd, that no City or Nation
" of the World will dare refift my Arms, af-
" ter the Reduction of thofe I have men-
" tion'd. And thus, not only the Guilty, but
" likewife thofe who have not at all offended
" us, muft equally fubmit to the Yoke of Servi-
" tude. If then you will gratify my Defires,
" prepare all things neceffary for this Expedi-
" tion, that you may be ready to attend me at
" the time I fhall appoint. And I now pro-
" mife, that he who fhall appear at the head of
" the beft Troops, fhall be rewarded by me,
" in the manner he fhall judge moft honou-
" rable. But left I fhould feem to impofe my
" own Sentiments upon you, I defire you to
" debate the matter, and deliver your Opini-
" ons with Freedom." After *Xerxes* had finifh'd thefe Words, *Mardonius* rofe up, and
faid : " SIR, You are not only the moft excel-
" lent of all the Perfians that have liv'd before
" your Time, but likewife of all that fhall
" be born in future Ages. And as in other
" things you have fpoken moft judicioufly and
" truly ; fo you have rightly determin'd, no
" longer to fuffer the European Ionians to infult
" the Perfians, who ought not to be the Ob-
" jects of their Contempt. For what greater
" Indignity can be imagin'd, than if, after we
" have conquer'd the Saces, Indians, Æthiopi-

" ans and Assyrians, with many other power-
" ful Nations, which never offer'd to do us
" any Wrong, in order only to enlarge our Do-
" minions, we should suffer the Grecians to
" go unpunish'd, who have first provok'd us
" by their injurious Attempts? Of what are
" we afraid? What Forces, what Treasures
" have they? We know their Manner of fight-
" ing; and we are no less inform'd of the
" Paucity of their Numbers. Besides, we have
" already subdued their Descendants the Ioni-
" nians, Æolians and Dorians, who inhabit
" within our Territories. I learnt by Expe-
" rience what they are, when I was command-
" ed by your Father to make War against
" them. I penetrated into *Macedonia*, and ad-
" vanc'd almost to *Athens*; yet no Man had
" the Courage to oppose my Passage. The Gre-
" cians, as I am inform'd, are accustomed to
" take up Arms rashly, and manage their Wars
" without Art or Knowledge. For when they
" have declar'd War against one another, they
" march into the most open Plain they can find,
" and fight a Battle; in which the Conquerors
" never go away without great Loss; and the
" Conquer'd, to say all at once, are cut in
" pieces. Whereas being of the same Lan-
" guage, they ought rather to adjust their Dif-
" ferences by Ambassadors, and try all ways
" of Accommodation, before they have Re-
" course to Arms: Or if these Means prove
" ineffectual, they ought at least to post them-
" selves in Places of difficult Access, not easily
" penetrable on either side. Yet these very
" Men, tho' accustom'd to this ill Method,
" never ventur'd to entertain a Thought of
" fighting

" fighting during all the time I continued in
" *Macedonia.* How then shall they dare to resist
" you, attended by all the Forces and Ships of
" *Asia?* For my own part, I cannot imagine
" that the Grecians will ever proceed to such a
" Degree of Audaciousness. But if I should
" happen to be deceiv'd, and they should be so
" ill advis'd to appear in Arms against us, they
" must learn by a dear-bought Experience, that
" we know more of military Affairs than all
" other Men of the World. However, let us
" try the Experiment: For nothing moves with-
" out a Cause, but all things are accomplish'd
" by Labour and Industry." When *Mardonius*
had thus flatter'd the Inclinations of *Xerxes* by a
courtly Assentation, and the rest of the Persians
continued silent, because they would not venture
to propose a contrary Opinion, *Artabanus* the
Son of *Hystaspes,* and Uncle to *Xerxes,* in confidence of his Dignity, deliver'd his Sentiments
in the following Terms: "SIR, said he, un-
" less Men will hear different Opinions, they
" can never chuse the most advantageous, but lie
" under a Necessity of following that which is
" first propos'd. Whereas when various and
" contrary Opinions have been heard, Men are
" enabled to discern the best Counsels; as they
" distinguish the purest Gold, by Comparison
" with that which contains a greater Quantity
" of Allay. I endeavour'd to dissuade *Darius*
" your Father and my Brother, from making
" War against *Scythia,* a Country destitute of
" Cities in any Part: But he hoping to conquer
" the Scythians, rejected my Advice, undertook
" that Expedition; and after he had lost the best
" of his Forces, was compell'd to retire with
" the

" the reſt. You are now diſpoſing all things to
" attack a much braver Nation than the Scy-
" thians ; Men, who have diſtinguiſh'd them-
" ſelves with Glory both by Sea and Land : and
" therefore I think my ſelf oblig'd to inform you
" of the Dangers that attend your Enterprize.
" You ſay, you have reſolv'd to lay a Bridge o-
" ver the *Helleſpont*, in order to tranſport your
" Army into *Europe*, and to march directly to
" *Greece*. But this Deſign will bring you under
" a Neceſſity of beating the Grecians either by
" Land or by Sea ; perhaps in both : Yet, as
" I am inform'd, they are a warlike People, and
" that they will not be an eaſy Conqueſt, one
" may conjecture from this Example : The A-
" thenians alone defeated and ruin'd that nu-
" merous Army which invaded *Attica*, under
" the Conduct of *Datis* and *Artaphernes*. But
" if they ſhould try their Fortune by Sea, and
" obtain the Victory ; if upon that Succeſs
" they ſhould ſail to the *Helleſpont*, and deſtroy
" your Bridge ; What could be imagin'd more
" terrible ? I ſhall not pretend that theſe
" Thoughts are the Reſult of my own Wiſdom :
" On the contrary, they are only the Effects of
" former Experience. How near were we to
" utter Deſtruction, when your Father had
" paſs'd into *Scythia* by the Bridges he laid
" over the Thracian *Boſphorus*, and over the
" *Iſter?* For the Scythians arriving on the
" Banks of that River, moſt earneſtly deſir'd
" the Ionians left there for a Guard, to break
" the Bridge : And if *Hiſtiæus*, Tyrant of
" *Miletus*, had aſſented to the Opinion of the
" reſt, and had not vigorouſly oppos'd that
" fatal Deſign, the Deſtruction of the Perſian
" Name

" Name was inevitable. I tremble to think,
" that the King, with all he poffefs'd, lay then
" at the mercy of one Man. Let me perfuade
" you therefore, not to expofe your felf to fo
" great Dangers without neceffity: Diffolve
" this Affembly; and after a more deliberate
" Reflection upon thefe things, declare your In-
" tentions, and take fuch Meafures as you
" fhall judge moft advantageous. I have ever
" found, that to form a Defign upon the beft
" Counfels, is in all Events moft ufeful: For
" if the expected Succefs fhould not follow;
" yet he who has taken the moft rational
" Meafure, has always the Satisfaction of
" having done his Part, tho' Fortune happen to
" be fuperior to Wifdom. But if he who
" rafhly undertakes an imprudent Enterprize,
" fhould chance to profper, he indeed accom-
" plifhes his Defign, and yet deferves no lefs
" Blame than if he had fail'd of Succefs. You
" fee the greateft Animals are moft frequently
" ftruck with the Thunder of *Jupiter*, and not
" long permitted to continue their Ravages,
" while the moft inconfiderable are fpar'd. You
" fee thofe Bolts ever lanc'd againft the ftate-
" lieft Edifices, and moft lofty Trees. For the
" God takes a pleafure in depreffing whatever
" is too highly exalted. Hence great Armies
" are often defeated by fmall Numbers of Men;
" when ftruck by the jealous God with a pa-
" nick Fear, or terrified by the Noife of his
" Thunder, they become deftitute both of Vi-
" gour and Courage: becaufe God will not
" fuffer any Mortal to think magnificently of
" himfelf. In all Actions Precipitation produces
" Errors, which for the moft part are attended
" with

" with pernicious Confequences. Bu: many
" Advantages flow from deliberate Coun-
" fels ; perhaps not prefently apparent, yet
" moft certainly enfuing afterwards. This, O
" King, is the Advice I would perfuade you
" to purfue: And as for thee, *Mardonius*, thou
" Son of *Gobryas*, ceafe to talk impertinently
" of the Grecians ; becaufe they are no way
" fit to be contemn'd. By unjuft Detraction
" you endeavour to engage the King to make
" War againft them ; and, in my Opinion,
" have ftrenuoufly exerted your Efforts that
" way. But I hope fuch Methods fhall not
" prevail. For Calumny is a deteftable thing,
" as it is a Combination of two againft one :
" Becaufe he who calumniates another, does him
" an Injury in his Abfence: And he who be-
" lieves the Calumny, is no lefs unjuft, in gi-
" ving his Affent to the Accufation, before he
" is duly inform'd. In a word, the abfent
" Perfon receives a double Injury ; being falfly
" accus'd by one, and unjuftly condemn'd by
" the other. But, *Mardonius*, if nothing can
" diffuade you from making War againft the
" Grecians, let the King continue in *Perfia*
" and our Children be depofited in his hands :
" Then go on with your Expedition, accom-
" panied by the beft Forces you can chufe,
" and in what Numbers you think fit : And
" if things fucceed in the manner you have
" fuggefted to the King, I will be content-
" ed to forfeit my own Life, and the Lives
" of my Children. But if, on the contrary,
" the Event be fuch as I have foretold, then
" let your Children fuffer Death, and you al-
" fo if ever you return. If you refufe to ac-

4   " cept

" cept these Conditions, and obstinately re-
" solve to lead an Army into *Greece*, I venture
" to affirm, that some of those you shall leave
" in this Place, will certainly hear, that *Mar*
" *donius* having brought some fatal Disaster up-
" on the Persians, was devour'd by Dogs and
" Birds in the Territories of *Athens* or *Lacedæ-*
" *mon* ; or perhaps in his March thither ; con-
" vinc'd by too late Experience that the Gre-
" cians are another Sort of Men than he had
" represented them to the King." When *Ar-*
tabanus, had thus spoken, *Xerxes* with Indignation replied : " *Artabanus*, said he, you
" are my Father's Brother ; and that Quality
" alone exempts you from receiving the just Re-
" compence of your foolish Discourse. Yet I
" will set a Mark of Dishonour upon you ;
" and since you have shewn so much Cowardice
" and unworthy Fear, you shall not accompany
" me in my Expedition against *Greece*; but
" shall stay behind among the Women, whilst
" I accomplish my Designs without you. I
" should not be the Son of *Darius* who deriv'd
" his Blood from *Hystaspes, Arsames, Ariaram-*
" *nes, Teispes, Cyrus, Cambyses,* and *Achæmenes,*
" unless I can be aveng'd upon the Athenians.
" I know too well that if we continue quiet,
" they will find themselves Employment, and
" enter our Territories with an Army. We
" ought to judge of their future Enterprizes
" by those that are pass'd. They have al-
" ready burnt *Sardis,* and made Excursions
" into *Asia.* Thus both Parties have advanc'd
" too far to retreat, and must resolve either
" to conquer or serve. All these Domini-
" ons must fall under the Power of the Gre-

L " cians,

" cians, or their Country be an Accession
" to this Empire. For no Way can be found
" to extinguish our mutual Enmity. They
" have been the first Aggressors; and we can-
" not omit to take our Revenge, unless we de-
" termine to sacrifice our Glory. Besides, I
" would be inform'd upon the Place, what Mis-
" chiefs those Men can bring upon me, who
" were so entirely conquer'd by *Pelops* the
" Phrygian, a Servant of my Ancestors; that
" both the Inhabitants and the Country they
" possess, are call'd by his Name." With
these Words *Xerxes* ended his Speech. But
when Night came, reflecting on the Opinion
of *Artabanus*, he fell into great Perplexity;
and, as that time frequently suggests the best
Counsels, concluded at last, that a War against
Greece would not terminate to his Advantage.
Having thus alter'd his Resolution, he fell
asleep, and, according to the Report of the
Persians, saw in a Dream a Man of uncommon
Stature and Beauty standing by him, and utter-
ing these Words. " Have you then chang'd
" the Design you had form'd to lead an Army in-
" to *Greece*, after having given positive Orders
" to the Persians to assemble their Forces?
" You have not done well to alter your Re-
" solution; neither will you find any Man
" of your Opinion. Resume therefore with-
" out Delay the Enterprize you determin'd
" by Day to undertake." The Phantom having pronounc'd these Words disappear'd:
And the next Morning *Xerxes* neglecting his
Dream, summon'd the same Persons together again, and said; " Pardon me, O Per-
" sians, if I now deliver an Opinion contrary
" to

" to that I declar'd yesterday : For I have not
" yet attain'd to a consummate Prudence in the
" Conduct of my Affairs: Neither shall those
" ever be absent from my Presence, who dis-
" suade me from this Enterprize. When I heard
" the Opinion of *Artabanus*, I broke out into
" a sudden Passion, so incident to Youth ; and
" threw out such Language against him, as
" was neither fit for me to use, nor for a Per-
" son of his Gravity to hear. But now ac-
" knowledging my Error, I resolve to follow
" his Advice : and therefore since I have laid
" aside my Design of invading *Greece*, you
" may enjoy the Advantages of Peace at
" home." When the Persians heard this
they were transported with Joy, and prostra-
ted themselves before the King. But in the
following Night the same Phantom appear'd
again to *Xerxes* as he slept, and pronounc'd
these Words : " Son of *Darius*, you seem to
" have abandon'd the Thoughts of your in-
" tended Expedition, and to make no more
" account of my Admonition, than if I had
" not spoken to you at all. Know then that
" unless you instantly undertake this En-
" terprize, you shall become mean and con-
" temptible, in as little time as you have been
" rais'd to Greatness and Power." Terrified
with this Dream *Xerxes* hastily left his Bed ;
sent for *Artabanus*, and when he came, spoke
thus to him: " *Artabanus*, I confess my Indis-
" cretion, when I revil'd you with ill Lan-
" guage for the good Counsel you gave me. But
" soon repenting of my Rashness, I deter-
" min'd to follow your Advice. Nevertheless
" whatever Inclination I have to do so, I find

" the

" the Execution impossible. For I had no
" sooner alter'd my Resolution, acknow-
" ledg'd my Error, than I was admonish'd in
" a Dream that I could not desist from my
" design'd Expedition without Shame: And
" just now the Phantom appear'd again, pres-
" sing me to the same Effect, and threatning the
" greatest Calamities if I should fail. If God
" be the Author of this Dream, and would
" have our Expedition to *Greece* go forward,
" you will see the same Vision I have had,
" and receive the same Command. To this
" end I think convenient that you should sit
" in the Throne, cloth'd in all my Royal
" Robes and afterwards sleep in my Bed."
Artabanus at first pray'd to be excus'd, as not
deserving the Honour of sitting on the King's
Throne: But when he saw he could not prevail, he did as *Xerxes* desir'd, after he had deliver'd his Sentiments in this manner. "For
" my part, said he, I have the same Esteem for
" one who knows how to assent to the best
" Advice, as for him who is able to be his own
" Counsellor: I acknowledge both these Qua-
" lities to be in you, O King, but cor-
" rupted by the Suggestions of ill Men; like
" the Sea, which of all these things is the most
" useful to Mankind, yet when agitated by the
" Violence of impetuous Winds, is sometimes
" constrain'd to act contrary to its own Nature.
" As for me, when I heard your Reproaches,
" I was not so much concern'd for myself,
" as griev'd to find that of two Opinions, one
" of which tended no less to propagate Inso-
" lence, than the other to suppress it, and to
" shew the Vanity of inuring the Mind in-
" cessantly

" cessantly to covet new Acquisitions, you had
" chosen the worst and most dangerous to your
" self and the Persians. Yet now, after you
" have taken a better Resolution, and quitted
" the Design of invading *Greece*, you say you
" have seen a Vision, sent by some God to com-
" mand you not to abandon your Enterprize.
" But know, my Son, that this Dream is no-
" thing less than divine: Men are frequently
" misled by these Phantoms; and I, who have
" liv'd many Years more than you, shall in-
" struct you in the Nature of such Visions.
" The things which have employ'd our Thoughts
" by Day, present themselves to us for the
" most part in our Dreams. And you know
" the warm Debate we have had for several
" Days concerning the Expedition to *Greece.*
" Now, if this be indeed a divine Message,
" and not such a Dream as I conjecture, you
" have said all in a Word; and the Vision will
" doubtless appear to me no less than to you
" and command me the same things. But I
" can never imagine that this will rather come
" to pass, if I should be cloth'd in your Robes,
" and lie in your Bed; than if I wear my own
" Garments, and sleep in my own Bed. For
" that which you have seen in your Sleep,
" whatever it be, can never arrive to such a
" Degree of Stupidity, to mistake me for you
" upon exchanging our Apparel only. But if
" the Spectre despise me, and think me un-
" worthy of the same Vision, it will never ap-
" pear to me, whether I be cloth'd in your
" Robes, or in my own; but will certainly visit
" you again; and then such an Event will de-
" serve Consideration. For if you have the
" same Dream frequently repeated, I myself

" will

" will confefs it to be Divine. Neverthelefs,
" if you have refolv'd to proceed this way,
" and will not be diffuaded from your Pur-
" pofe, I am contented to fleep in your Bed,
" as you have order'd ; and then let the Phan-
" tom appear to me alfo. But to that time
" I fhall perfift in my prefent Opinion." After
thefe Words, *Artabanus*, not doubting to fhew
the Vanity of all that *Xerxes* had faid, complied with his Defires ; cloth'd himfelf in
the Royal Robes, and fat in the Throne. But
as he flept in the King's Bed, the fame Phantom appear'd to him in a Dream, and faid :
" Art thou then the Man, who affuming the
" Authority of a Governour, haft diffuaded
" *Xerxes* from invading *Greece* ? But know,
" that thou fhalt not with Impunity contemn
" the Decrees of Fate, either now or in time
" to come : And as for *Xerxes*, he is fuffici-
" ently admonifh'd of the Calamities he fhall
" fuffer upon his Difobedience." *Artabanus*
terrified with thefe Menaces, and obferving in
his Dream that the Apparition advanc'd to burn
out his Eyes with a hot Iron, leap'd out of
Bed with loud Exclamations, and went immediately to *Xerxes* ; where, after he had related
all the Particulars of the Vifion he had feen, he
fpoke to him in this manner : " Having learnt
" by Experience that the greateft Powers have
" been frequently overthrown by fmall Forces,
" I deliver'd my Opinion as a Man ; and
" was unwilling to fee you tranfported by
" the violent Paffions incident to your Age ;
" well underftanding the Dangers that at-
" tend a boundlefs Ambition. I call'd to
" mind the Fortune of that Army which *Cyrus*
" led

" led against the Messagetes; the Expedition
" of *Cambyses* against the Æthiopians; and
" the Invasion of *Scythia*, in which I accom-
" pained your Father *Darius*. From the Con-
" sideration of these Misfortunes, I concluded
" you to be the most happy of all Men, if
" you would live in Peace. But since you are
" mov'd by a divine Impulse, and some great
" Disaster decreed by Heaven, seems ready to
" fall upon the Grecians, I change my Opinion
" and shall contend no longer: Your Part
" therefore will be, to inform the Persians of
" this divine Message, and to command them
" to go on with their Preparations for War,
" according to your former Orders; that no-
" thing of human Assistance may be wanting
" to second the Favour of the Gods." When
he had said these Words, and both had determin'd to place an entire Confidence in the Vision: *Xerxes* early the next Morning acquainted
the Persians with what had happen'd, and *Artabanus*, the only Man who had openly disap-
prov'd the Expedition, now appear'd most zealous to promote it.

IN the mean time *Xerxes* having resolv'd to
put himself at the Head of his Army, had another Dream; which the Magi interpreted to
relate to the whole World, and to signify that
all Mankind should be reduc'd under his Power.
For the King dreamt he saw himself crown'd
with Twigs taken from an Olive-tree, which
extended its Branches over all the Earth; and
that afterwards this Crown disappear'd from
about his Head. Upon this Interpretation of
the Magi, the Persians who were then assembled in Council, departed immediately to their

L 4 several

several Governments, and with the utmost Diligence applied themselves to execute the King's Orders; every Man hoping to obtain the Recompence he had promis'd. All the Regions of the Continent were search'd, in order to compose this Army. For from the time of the Reduction of *Ægypt*, four whole Years were spent in assembling these Forces, and providing all things necessary for this Expedition. In the fifth Year *Xerxes* began his March with an incredible Number of Men. For this Army was so much greater than all others we ever heard of; that neither the Forces led by *Darius* against the Scythians; nor the Scythian Army, which entring *Media* in Pursuit of the Cimmerians, subdued almost all the upper *Asia*, and occasion'd the succeeding Attempt of *Darius*; nor that which under the Conduct of the Atrides march'd, as we are told, to the Siege of *Troy*; nor the joint Forces of the Mysians and Teucrians, who before the Trojan War, pass'd over the *Bosphorus* into *Europe*, subdu'd all *Thrace*, and advancing to the Ionian Sea, penetrated to the Southward as far as the River *Peneus*: In a word, not all these Armies in Conjunction, even tho' we should add divers others, were to be compar'd with this one of *Xerxes*. For what People of *Asia* did he exempt from sending Men to this Expedition against *Greece*? What Waters, except those of great Rivers, were unexhausted by his numerous Forces? Some Nations he commanded to fit out Ships; others were order'd to furnish Horse, and others Foot: Some were oblig'd to build Vessels for the Transportation of Horse; others to prepare long Barks for Bridges, and
some

some to furnish Corn, with Ships to transport it. Three Years had been spent about Mount *Athos*, in contriving to prevent the like Disaster with that which befel the Persians formerly on that Coast. Their Ships had been order'd to the Port of *Elæus*, in the *Chersonesus*; and all the Forces on board were compell'd by Turns to dig, and open a Passage thro' the Mountain. The adjoining Inhabitants assisted them; and *Bubaris* the Son of *Megabyzus*, with *Artachæus* the Son of *Artæus*, both Persians, were the Directors of this Enterprize. *Athos* is a Mountain of great Fame and Magnitude, leaning upon the Sea, and well inhabited. It terminates to the Landward in the Form of a Peninsula, and makes an Isthmus of about twelve Stades in Length; containing a Plain with some Mixture of little Hills, from the Coast of *Acanthus* to that of *Torone*. On this Isthmus, which lies at the Foot of Mount *Athos*, stands *Sana* a Grecian City: But *Xerxes* determin'd to cut off from the Continent all the other Cities, which being built upon the Mountain, and beyond this Place, were *Dion*, *Olophyxus*, *Acrothoon Thysus* and *Cleone*. The Operation was carried on in this manner. The Barbarians having drawn a Line before the City of *Sana*, divided the Ground among the several Nations: And when the Trench was considerably sunk, those who were in the Bottom continued to dig, and deliver'd the Earth to Men standing upon Ladders, who handed the same again to such as were plac'd in a higher Station, till at last others who waited to receive the Burden at the Edge of the Canal, carried it away to another Place. But

by

by digging in a perpendicular manner, and making the Bottom of equal Breadth with the Top, all the Workmen, except the Phœnicians, drew a double Labour upon themſelves; becauſe the Earth, as is natural, fell down continually in great Quantity from the upper Parts. The Phœnicians alone ſhew'd that Ability on this Occaſion, of which they are ſo much Maſters at all times: For they open'd the Part which was aſſign'd to their Care, twice as large as others had done; and ſloping the Ground gradually till they came to the Bottom, they then found the Meaſure equal with the reſt. In the Meadow adjoining to this Place they had a Court of Juſtice, and a Market furniſh'd with great Abundance of Corn brought even from *Aſia.* My Conjectures lead me to think, that *Xerxes* undertook this Enterprize upon a Motive of Oſtentation, in order to ſhew the Greatneſs of his Power, and to perpetuate the Memory of his Name. For tho' he might have caus'd his Fleet to be convey'd over the Land without much Difficulty; yet he would rather command the Iſthmus to be cut, and a Canal to be made to receive the Sea, of ſuch a Breadth as might be ſufficient to carry two Ships ſailing in front. He likewiſe order'd the ſame Men, who had been employ'd in this Work, to lay a Bridge over the River *Strymon;* and commanded all manner of Cordage, and Stores neceſſary for Bridges, to be prepar'd with expedition. He iſſued Orders to the Phœnicians and Ægyptians to take in Proviſions for the Army, that nothing might be wanting either for the Men or the Cattle, which were to be tranſported into *Greece*:

And

And having fully enquir'd into the Nature of each Country, he order'd every thing to be brought from the moſt proper places of *Aſia*, in Ships of great Burden, contriv'd on purpoſe for Tranſportation. Of theſe Proviſions the greater Quantity was carried to that Part of *Thrace*, which goes by the Name of the *White Coaſt*. The reſt was order'd to *Tyrodiza* of the Perinthians; to *Doriſcus*; to *Eion* upon the *Strymon*, and to *Macedonia*. While theſe Men were employ'd in executing the Injunctions they had receiv'd, *Xerxes* having aſſembled his Army, parted from *Critale* in *Cappadocia*, and march'd to *Sardis*; which was the Place appointed for the Rendezvous of all the Forces that were to accompany him from the Continent. But I cannot affirm who was the General that receiv'd the Rewards promis'd by the King, for bringing the beſt Troops into the Field; being altogether uninform'd whether this Queſtion were ever brought into Diſpute. When the Army had paſs'd the River *Halys*, they march'd thro' *Phrygia*, and arriv'd at *Celæne* where riſe the Springs of the *Meander*, and of another River no leſs conſiderable, call'd the *Cataracts*; which, beginning in the midſt of the Place, flows afterwards into the *Meander*: And where, if we may believe the Phrygians, the Skin of *Marſias* the Satyr is ſeen, pull'd off and hung up there by *Apollo*. *Pythius* the Son of *Atys*, a Lydian, then reſiding in *Celæne*, entertain'd the King and all his Army with great Magnificence, and offer'd him his Treaſures towards the Expence of the War: Which Liberality *Xerxes* communicating to the Perſians about him, and aſking, Who this *Pythius* was,

and

and what Riches he might have to enable
him to make such an Offer, receiv'd this Answer: " *Pythius*, said they, is the Person, who
" presented your Father *Darius* with a Plane-
" tree and Vine of Gold: And, after you, is
" the richest Man we know in the World"
Xerxes, surpriz'd with these last Words, ask'd
him, to what sum his Treasures might amount.
" I shall conceal nothing from you, said *Py-*
" *thius*, nor pretend to be ignorant of my own
" Wealth ; but being perfectly inform'd of the
" State of my Accounts, shall tell you the
" Truth with Sincerity. When I heard you
" were ready to begin your March towards
" the Grecian Sea, I resolv'd to present you
" with a sum of Money towards the Charge
" of the War ; and to that end having taken
" an Account of my Riches, I found by Com-
" putation that I had two thousand Talents
" of Silver, and three millions nine hundred
" ninety three thousand Pieces of Gold, bear-
" ing the Stamp of *Darius*. These Treasures
" I freely give you, because I shall be suffi-
" ciently furnish'd with whatever is necessary
" to Life by the Labour of my Servants and
" Husbandmen." *Xerxes* heard these Words
with pleasure, and in answer to *Pythius*, said ;
" My Lydian Host, since I parted from *Susa*,
" I have not found a Man besides yourself, who
" has offer'd to entertain my Army, or volun-
" tarily to contribute his Treasures to promote
" the present Expedition. You alone have
" treated my Army magnificently, and readily
" offer'd me immense Riches: Therefore, in
" return of your Kindness, I make you my
" Host ; and that you may be Master of the
                                    " entire

" entire Sum of four Millions of Gold, I will
" give you seven thousand Darien Pieces out of
" my own Treasure. Keep then all the Riches
" you now possess; and if you know how to
" continue always in the same good Dispo-
" sition, you shall never have Reason to repent
" of your Affection to me, either now or in
" future Time." When *Xerxes* had said this,
and taken care to see his Promise perform'd,
he continued his March; and passing by *Anaua*
a City of *Phrygia*, and a Lake famous for the
making of Salt, he arriv'd at *Colossa*, a considerable City of the same Province; where the
River *Lycus* falling into an Aperture of the
Earth, disappears for the space of about five
Stades in Length; and then rising again runs
afterwards into the *Meander*. From this Place
the Army advanced to the City of *Cydra*, built
on the Borders of *Phrygia* and *Lydia*; where
an Inscription engrav'd on a Pillar, which was
erected by *Cræsus*, declares the Limits of each
Country. After they had enter'd the Territories of *Lydia*, they found the Way divided into two Routs; one on the Left-hand leading
to *Caria*, the other on the Right, to *Sardis*.
Those who take the last of these Ways, are necessitated to pass the *Meander*, and to approach
the City of *Callatebus*, in which Honey is
made by Men, with Wheat and the Shrub
Myrice. *Xerxes* taking his March by this Way,
saw a Plane-tree so beautiful, that he adorn'd
it with Gold; and having committed the
Care of it to one of those Persians who go
under the Name of *Immortal*, arriv'd the next
day at *Sardis*, the Capital of *Lydia*. Upon his
Arrival in that City he sent Heralds to *Greece*,

with

with Orders to demand Earth and Water, and to require all the Cities, except *Athens* and *Lacedemon*, to provide every thing neceſſary for the King's Table; not doubting that the Terror of his Arms would now induce all thoſe to a ready Submiſſion, who had formerly refuſ'd to comply with the like Demand, made on the part of his Father *Darius.* When *Xerxes* had diſpatch'd theſe Heralds, he prepar'd to march towards *Abydus*; and in the mean time commanded a Bridge to be laid over the *Helleſpont*, in order to paſs into *Europe.* The Coaſt of the Helleſpontin *Cherſoneſus*, which Faces the City of *Abydus*, and ſtretches along the Sea between *Seſtus* and *Madytus*, is uneven, and of difficult Acceſs. In that Place, ſome time after this Enterprize, *Zanthippus* the Son of *Ariphron*, an Athenian Commander, took *Artayctes*, the Perſian Governor of *Seſtus*, and empal'd him alive, for conſtraining the Women to enter into the Temple of *Proteſilaus* in *Eleus*, and there committing the moſt execrable Crimes. The Bridge was begun at *Abydus*, by Men appointed to that end, and carried on to the oppoſite Coaſt; which is ſeven Stades diſtant from that City; the Phœnicians making uſe of Cordage of white Hemp, and the Ægyptians of another ſort called *Byblus.* But no ſooner had they finiſh'd the Bridge, than a violent Storm ariſing, broke in pieces, and diſpers'd the whole Work: Which when *Xerxes* heard he fell into ſuch a Tranſport of Anger, that he commanded three hundred Stripes to be inflicted on the Back of the Waters, and a Pair of Fetters to be let down into the *Helleſpont.* I have heard, he likewiſe order'd

that

that Sea to be branded with Marks of Infamy. But nothing is more certain, than that he strictly enjoyn'd those who were entrusted with the Execution of his Orders, to pronounce these barbarous and impertinent Words: " O " thou salt and bitter Water! thy Master has " condemn'd thee to this Punishment, for of- " fending him without Cause, and is resolv'd " to pass over thee in despite of thy Insolence. " With reason all Men neglect to sacrifice to " thee, because thou art both disagreeable and " treacherous." Thus having commanded the *Hellespont* to be chastised, he order'd the Heads of those who had the Direction of the Work- men to be taken off; which was all the Re- compence they had for contriving the Bridge. In their place other Architects were employ'd, who prepar'd two Bridges in the following manner: They brought three hundred and sixty Gallies into a Line, board by board, and facing the *Euxin* Sea. On the other hand they plac'd three hundred and fourteen more, with their Sides turned towards the *Euxin*, and their Heads to the Current of the *Hellespont*, in order to preserve the Cordage en- tire. This done, they drop'd their main An- chors, to secure the Vessels on one side against the Force of those Winds that blow from the *Euxin*, and on the other, from the South and Easterly Winds of the Ægean Sea; leaving three several Passages open to the Eastward, for the Convenience of those who should de- sire to pass from the *Euxin*, or to return thither. After that, they fasten'd Cables to the Shoar, and straining them with Engines of Wood prepar'd for that purpose, bound the Vessels together:

together, allowing only two Ropes of white Hemp for every four made of *Byblus*. For tho' the Thickness and Shape was the same, yet the former were of much greater Strength; every Cubit weighing a full Talent. Having carried on these Lines of Ships from one Shoar to the other, they cover'd the Cordage with Pieces of Timber, cut exactly to the Breadth of the Bridges, and strongly compacted together. Upon these again they laid Planks of Wood rang'd in order; and having thrown a Covering of Earth on the Top, they rais'd a Barrier on each side, that the Horses and other Cattle might not be terrified at the Sight of the Sea. When the Bridges were finish'd, and the Canal at Mount *Athos* secur'd by a Bank of Earth thrown up at each End, to prevent the Floods from choaking the Passage with Sand; the Army being inform'd that all things were ready, departed from *Sardis*, where they had wintered, and directed their March towards *Abydus*. But as they were on the way thither, the Sun quitting his Seat in the Heavens, disappear'd; and tho' the Air was perfectly serene and free from Clouds, a sudden Night ensued in the place of Day: Which *Xerxes* observing with Surprize, and no little Anxiety, enquir'd of the Magi what might be the meaning of the Prodigy. They answer'd, That the Gods by this Presage plainly foretold the Destruction of the Grecian Cities; because the Sun was the Protector of *Greece*, and the Moon of the Persians. *Xerxes* pleas'd with their Interpretation, resolv'd to continue his March: And as the Army was ready to advance, *Pythius* the Lydian, partly terrified by the late Aspect of the

I   Heavens,

Heavens and partly confiding in the Merit of his liberal Offer, went to the King, and spoke to him in these terms : " SIR, Will you " condescend to grant me a thing I desire ? " 'Tis of little Consequence to you, and of " great Importance to me." *Xerxes* suspecting nothing less than what he design'd to ask, assur'd him he would grant his Request, and bid him ask freely. Upon which *Pythius* taking Confidence ; "SIR, said he, I have five Sons, " and they are all in your Army, ready to at- " tend you in this Expedition against *Greece*. " Pity my Age, and exempt my eldest from " the present Service, that he may take care " of me, and of my Estate. Let the rest fol- " low your Fortune ; and when you have ac- " complish'd your Designs, may you return " home in Safety." The King transported with Indignation at these Words, answer'd ; " Unworthy Man ! How dar'st thou mention " thy Son when thou seest me going to hazard " my Person, my Children, my Brothers, and " my Friends ? Thou, I say, who art my Slave, " and bound in duty to follow me with all thy " Family, and even with thy Wife. Know " then, that the Spirit of a Man resides in his " Ears, from whence, as the Pleasure of hear- " ing things grateful is diffus'd thro' the whole " Body, so the contrary is irksome and grie- " vous to every Part. When you did well, " and promis'd to continue in the same good " Disposition, you had nevertheless no rea- " son to boast of having surpass'd the King " in Liberality. Neither shall you now, up- " on this change of your Manners, suffer " that Punishment which your Impudence de-

" ferves. Thy firft Merit has fav'd four of
" thy Sons; and thy Folly has deftroy'd the
" other, who is fo dear to thee." Having finifh'd thefe Words, *Xerxes* commanded the proper Officers to find out the eldeft Son of *Pythius*, and to cut his Body into two Parts; one
of which they were order'd to lay on the Right-
hand, and the other on the Left of the Way,
that the Army might pafs between both. When
they had put the King's Command in execution, the Forces began to move in the following Order. The Baggage, with the Servants,
firft appear'd in the Front, and were follow'd
by Men of all Nations, form'd into a Body
without Diftinction, and amounting to more
than one half of the Army. Behind thefe an
Interval was left, that they might not mix with
that Part where the King was. Before him
march'd a thoufand Horfemen, chofen among
all the Perfians; and next to them, a thoufand
more of the fame Nation, Men equally well
chofen, and bearing Javelins pointing down-
wards. After thefe came ten great Horfes,
bred in the fpacious Plain of the Median *Nifæa*,
adorn'd with the richeft Furniture, and confecrated to *Jupiter*. The Chariot of the God
immediately follow'd, drawn by eight white
Horfes, the Driver on foot holding the Reins,
becaufe no Mortal is permitted to mount the
Seat. Then *Xerxes* himfelf appear'd on a
Chariot drawn by Nifæan Horfes, and driven by *Patiramphes* the Son of *Otanes*, a Perfian.
He departed from *Sardis* in this Equipage, and
chang'd his Chariot for a lighter as often as he
faw convenient. A thoufand Spearmen of the
braveft and moft noble among the Perfians,

march'd

march'd next to the King carrying their Arms
after the manner of that Country; and were
follow'd by another Body of Horse confifting of a thoufand more, all chofen Men of
the fame Nation. After the Horfe ten thoufand Perfian Foot advanc'd; and of thefe one
thoufand arm'd with Javelins, which were
adorn'd on the uppermoft Joint with Pomegranates of Gold inftead of the common Ornaments, border'd the other nine thoufand;
whofe Javelins carried a Pomegranate of Silver
on the fame Joint. All thofe who march'd
neareft to the Perfon of the King, and turn'd
the Points of their Arms towards the Ground
had Pomegranates of Gold in the like manner on
their Javelins. The ten thoufand Foot were
follow'd by ten thoufand Perfian Horfe; and
after an Interval of two Stades, all the reft
of the Forces came on promifcuoufly. Thus
the Army marching from *Lydia*, arriv'd at the
River *Caicus* in *Myfia*; and leaving the Mountain *Cana* on the Left, pafs'd thro' *Atarneus* to
the City *Carina*. From thence they advanc'd
into the Plains of *Thebes*; and paffing by the
Cities of *Adramyttium* and the Pelafgian *Antandrus*, enter'd the Country of *Ilium*, having
Mount *Ida* on the Left-hand. But as they
pafs'd the Night at the Foot of that Mountain,
many of their Men were deftroy'd by Thunder and Lightning. When they arriv'd on the
Banks of *Scamander*, the Waters were not
found fufficient for the Men and for the Cattle, tho' that River was the greateft they
had yet feen in their March. Here *Xerxes*
being defirous to take a View of the adjacent
Places, went up to the Tower of *Priamus*; and

when

when he had satisfied his Curiosity, and enquir'd into divers Particulars, he sacrific'd a
thousand Oxen to the Ilian *Minerva*, and the
Magi pour'd out a Liberation in honour of the
Heroes. But notwithstanding this, a panick
Terrour seizing upon the Army in the following Night, caus'd them to break up early the
next Morning. So passing by the Cities of *Rœ-
tium*, *Ophrynium* and *Dardanus*, which were on
the Left, and leaving the Gergithians and Teucrians at a greater distance on the Right, they
advanc'd to *Abydus*. When *Xerxes* was arriv'd
in that City, he desir'd to see all his Forces together: And to that end, ascending a stately
Edifice of white Stone, which the Abydenians,
in obedience to a former Command, had built
to receive him in a manner suitable to his
Greatness, he had a free Prospect of the Coast
and from his Seat saw at one View both his
Fleet and his Land-Army. Having given himself this Satisfaction, and desiring to be Spectator of a Sea-fight, he commanded all things to
be made ready for that purpose; in which he
was presently obey'd: And having adjudg'd the
Victory to the Sidonian Phœnicians, he shew'd
himself exceedingly pleas'd as well with this
Spectacle, as with the View of his Forces.
Then turning his Eyes upon the *Hellespont*, and
seeing that Sea cover'd with his Ships, and
all the Plain of *Abydus* down to the Sea full
of Men, he seem'd at first to be much
delighted; but afterwards wept. Which
when his Uncle *Artabanus* perceiv'd, he
said to him with the same Liberty he had
us'd in dissuading him from invading *Greece*:
" SIR, your Actions are not uniform:

" In

" In a few Moments you have pafs'd from
" an Excefs of Joy to fhedding Tears." The
King anfwer'd : " When I confider'd the
" fhortnefs of human Life, I could not re-
" ftrain the Effects of my Compaffion : For of
" all thefe Numbers of Men, not one fhall fur-
" vive a hundred Years. But, reply'd *Arta-*
" *banus*, are we not expos'd, during our Lives,
" to other things much more to be lamented ?
" Is any Man fo happy, either among thefe,
" or other Men, who even in this fhort
" Courfe of Life, would not often chufe ra-
" ther to die than to live ? The frequent Ca-
" lamities and Difeafes incident to all, fo
" difturb the beft of our Days, that Life, tho'
" really fhort, yet feems of a tedious Length ;
" and Death remains the only defirable Refuge
" of unhappy Mortals. But the Gods, from
" a Motive of Envy, have infus'd a certain
" Sweetnefs into Life, in order to delude
" Mankind. *Artabanus*, faid the King, fince
" the Condition of human Life is fuch as you
" have defcrib'd, let us fay no more on that
" Subject ; but rejecting all fad Reflections, en-
" tertain ourfelves with the promifing Hopes
" we have now in View. Be plain with me ;
" if you had not feen the Vifion you faw fo
" evidently in your Dream, would you ftill
" perfift in your firft Opinion, and continue
" to diffuade me from making War againft
" *Greece ?* Tell me the Truth with Freedom
" and Sincerity." To this Queftion *Artabanus*
anfwer'd : " May the Event of my Dream be
" fuch as we both defire ; neverthelefs my Fears
" are ftill fo prevalent with me, that I am not Ma-
" fter of myfelf. Upon Reflection I have found

M 3 " divers

" divers things very contrary to your Designs,
" and especially two, which are of the greatest
" Consequence." " Poor Man, said *Xerxes*; and
" what may those two things be, that are so
" contrary to my Designs? Is our Land-
" Army deficient in Numbers? Will the Gre-
" cians bring greater Forces into the Field?
" Or is our Fleet inferior to that of *Greece?*
" Or, in a word, are our Enemies superi-
" or in both? If you think so, we can easi-
" ly add to the Strength of our Forces."
" SIR, answer'd *Artabanus*, no Man of com-
" mon Understanding can think contemptibly,
" either of your Land-Forces, or of the Num-
" ber of your Ships. And if these should
" be augmented, the two things I intended
" would become more contrary to your Af-
" fairs than they are at present. By these
" two things I mean the Sea and the Land.
" For, as I conjecture, no Harbour can be
" found in any Part, sufficient to receive and
" protect your whole Fleet, if a Storm should
" arise: And yet one is not enough: your
" Affairs require many on every Coast of
" the Continent, to which this Expedition
" will lead you. Since therefore you can have
" no safe Harbour for such a Fleet, you will
" do well to remember, that Men are in the
" Power of Fortune, and not Fortune in the
" Power of Men. Having thus explain'd one
" of the two things I propos'd, I shall pro-
" ceed to the other. The Land will be your
" Enemy many ways; and still the more for-
" midable, the farther you are permitted to
" advance without Resistance, and to carry
" all before you. Men are always unwilling to
" stop

" stop in the Career of Success: And if you
" meet with no Opposition, Famine will pro-
" bably overtake you, after you have spent
" much time in penetrating far into a vast
" Country. He only is truly wise and valiant,
" who with the utmost Caution considers every
" thing that may obstruct his Designs: and
" after the maturest Deliberation, boldly exe-
" cutes the Enterprizes he has form'd." To
this *Xerxes* answer'd: " *Artabanus*, your Dis-
" course concerning these Particulars is ra-
" tional; yet we must not fear all things, nor
" examine every Circumstance with such Strict-
" ness. For if we should enter into so nice
" a Discussion of all our Affairs, we should
" never do any thing. Bold and daring En-
" terprizes, tho' attended with one half of all
" the Evils that can possibly ensue, are pre-
" ferable to Inaction, however safe. After
" all, he who disapproves and opposes every
" thing, without proposing something better,
" is no less worthy of Blame, than one who
" contradicts without reason: And I am of o-
" pinion, that no Mortal can determine with
" certainty concerning the Event of human
" Affairs. Experience shews, that those who
" resolve to push boldly, are for the most part
" successful; whereas those, who act with so
" much Caution, and form so many Difficul-
" ties, very rarely do any thing with Advan-
" tage. You see to how high a Degree of Pow-
" er the Persians have attain'd: Which could
" never have been, if the Kings, my Prede-
" cessors, had entertain'd such Thoughts as you
" have; or had not met with Counsellors of
" another sort, to dissuade them from such Opi-

" nions. By despising the Dangers that
" threatned, they arriv'd to this Height of
" Grandeur. And indeed, great Successes
" are no otherwise to be obtain'd, than by
" adventuring boldly. We will therefore en-
" deavour to imitate our Ancestors ; and en-
" tring upon Action in the most agreeable Sea-
" son of the Year, we intend to subdue all *Eu-*
" *rope*, and afterwards to return home, with-
" out suffering by Famine, or any other Mis-
" fortune. For we not only carry a vast Quan-
" tity of Provisions with us, but shall be Mas-
" ters of all the Corn that grows in the Coun-
" tries we are about to invade, which are in-
" habited by Husbandmen, and not by Gra-
" siers. *Artabanus* having heard this Answer
of *Xerxes*, said : " SIR, since you will not per-
" mit me to fear the Success of your Enter-
" prize, yet hearken to my Counsel in another
" thing, and excuse me, if having many things
" to say, I am necessitated to extend my Dis-
" course to a farther length. *Cyrus* the Son of
" *Cambyses* constrain'd all the Ionians, the A-
" thenians only excepted, to be Tributaries of
" the Persians. I advise you therefore, not to
" lead these Men against their Fathers, upon
" any Motive whatever: Especially since we
" have Forces more than sufficient to subdue our
" Enemies without their Assistance. For if
" they accompany you in this Expedition, one
" of these two things must happen ; either
" they will be so base and wicked, to enslave
" their Mother-City, or so just and honest, to
" contribute all their Endeavours to preserve its
" Liberty. If they should be unfaithful to that
" Country, from which they derive their Ori-
" ginal,

" ginal, what can we expect from such Men!
" And if they should do their Duty, what
" Mischiefs might they not bring upon your
" Army? In conclusion, bear always in your
" mind this antient Saying, which will be
" eternally true, That no Man is able to judge
" with certainty of the Issue of things, what-
" ever the Beginning may be. *Artabanus*, re-
" plied *Xerxes*, you are in nothing so much de-
" ceiv'd, as in the Suspicion you have of the
" Ionians. You, and all those who invaded *Scy-*
" *thia* under my Father *Darius*, must own, that
" they gave the most certain Proof of their Af-
" fection to us, when having in their power
" to save or destroy the whole Army of the
" Persians, they refus'd to violate their Faith,
" or do any thing that might be prejudicial to
" our Nation. Besides, they have left their
" Children, their Wives, and their Possessions,
" in our Territories; which are the surest Pled-
" ges of their Fidelity. Fear nothing therefore
" of that sort; but be easy, and prepare to take
" upon you the Care of my Family, and of my
" Government. For of all Men, you are the
" only Person I resolve to entrust with my Au-
" thority." After this Discourse, *Xerxes* dismiss'd *Artabanus* with Orders to return to *Susa*;
and having again assembled the principal Men
among the Persians, he spoke to this purpose:
" I have called you together at this time, to ex-
" hort you to acquit yourselves like Men of
" Courage, without blemishing the great and
" glorious Actions of your Ancestors. Let
" every one therefore in particular, and all of
" us in conjunction, shew our Alacrity and Re-
" solution in this Enterprize, which is under-
" taken

" taken for the common Good. But I could not
" omit to incite you in a peculiar manner to
" shew your Fortitude in this War ; because
" I am inform'd, that our Enemies are a brave
" and warlike People ; and that if we conquer
" them, no other Army will dare to oppose us.
" Prepare then to pass the Sea, after we have
" recommended ourselves to the Care of those
" Gods who are the Protectors of *Persia.*

THE rest of the Day was spent in disposing
all things, in order to their Passage : And waiting the rising of the next Sun, they in the
mean time burnt all sort of Perfumes upon
the Bridges, and strow'd the Way with Myr-
tles. When the Sun was risen, *Xerxes* pouring a Libation into the Sea out of a golden
Cup, addrefs'd a Prayer to the Sun, " That
" he might not meet with any Impediment so
" great, as to hinder him from carrying his
" conquering Arms to the utmost Limits of
" *Europe.*" After which he threw the Cup
into the *Hellespont,* with a Bowl of Gold, and
a Persian Scymetar. But I cannot determine
whether his Intention was to confecrate these
things to the Sun, or whether he made this
Donation to the *Hellespont,* by way of Satif-
faction for the Stripes he had inflicted on that
Sea. After this Ceremony, all the Foot and
Horse of the Army pafs'd over that Bridge,
which was next to the *Euxin* ; while the Servants and Draught-horses, with the Baggage,
pafs'd over the other, which was plac'd nearer
to the Ægean Sea. The ten thousand Persians
I mention'd before, led the Van, with Crowns
on their Heads, and were followed by Troops
promiscuously compos'd of all Nations. These

3   pafs'd

pass'd the first Day. On the second, those Horse, who carried their Javelins pointed to the Ground, pass'd over first, wearing Crowns likewise. Then came the sacred Horses, the sacred Chariot; and *Xerxes* himself, followed by the Spearmen and one thousand Horse. All the rest of the Army clos'd the March; and at the same time the Ships made to the Coast of *Europe*. I have heard that *Xerxes* march'd in the Rear of all. But however that be, he saw his Forces compell'd by Blows to pass over the Bridge; which yet was not effected in less than seven Days and seven Nights, tho' they continued to pass without Intermission during all that time. After his Landing, a certain Man of that Country, as is said, cried out; " O *Jupiter*, why art thou come to destroy " *Greece*, in the Shape of a Persian, and un- " der the Name of *Xerxes*, with all Mankind " following thee; whereas thy own Power is " sufficient to do this without their Assis- " tance?" When the Army began to march, a prodigious thing happen'd, yet not difficult to be understood, tho' altogether neglected by *Xerxes*. A Mare cast a Hare instead of a Colt: From which one might easily conjecture, that after *Xerxes* had transported a mighty Army into *Greece* with great Vanity and Ostentation, he should be afraid for his own Life, and run away to the Place from whence he came. Another Prodigy had been seen before, during the time he staid at *Sardis*, where a Mule brought forth a Colt, with the Parts both of a Male and a Female, tho' the former appear'd more perfect. But *Xerxes* slighting both these Events, continued to advance with his

Land-

Land-Forces; while the Fleet at the same time sailing out of the *Hellespont*, coasted along by the Shoar, and kept on a quite different Course. For they stood to the Westward for the Promontory of *Sarpedon*; where they were commanded to attend farther Orders: But the Land-Forces march'd by the way of *Chersonesus*, facing the East and the rising Sun. Then leaving the Sepulchre of *Hella*, the Daughter of *Athamas*, on the Right-hand, and the City of *Cardia* on the Left, they pass'd through a Place call'd *Agora*; and from thence bending their March towards the Gulph *Melana*, they exhausted the Waters of a River bearing the same Name, and left the Channel dry. After they had pass'd this River, they march'd Westward; and passing by *Ænus*, an Æolian City, and the Lake *Stentoris*, they arriv'd at *Doriscus*. The Shoar of this Part of *Thrace* is of easy access, and opens into a large Plain, divided by the Streams of the great River *Hebrus*. In that Plain stands the City of *Doriscus*, encompass'd by a Royal Wall, and kept by a Persian Garrison plac'd there by *Darius* when he made War against the Scythians. *Xerxes* judging this Place convenient for reviewing and numbring his Forces, commanded the Sea-Captains to bring all their Ships to the Shoar that lay nearest to *Doriscus*, where the Cities of *Sala*, *Samothracia* and *Zona*, are situate, with another called *Serrium*, built upon a famous Promontory, formerly belonging to the Ciconians. When they had brought the Ships to Land, those who were employ'd in that Work, were permitted to rest; and in the mean time *Xerxes* viewed his Army in the Plain of *Doriscus*. What Proportion of

Men

Men each Nation furnifh'd to this Expedition,
I cannot affirm, becaufe they are not enumera-
ted by any Writer: But nothing is more certain, than that the Land-Forces amounted to
the full Number of feventeen hundred thoufand. For they were computed in this manner:
Ten thoufand Men being firft drawn out into one Place, and crouded as clofe together
as might poffibly be, were encompafs'd with
a Circle trac'd upon the Ground: After which
they were order'd to retire, and a fort of
Hedge was planted upon the Circle, to the
Height of a Man's Middle. When this was
done, they caus'd another Ten thoufand to enter the Ground; and continued to proceed in
the fame manner, till they had computed the
whole Army. Then they divided all the Troops
nationally into diftinct Bodies, which I fhall
here defcribe, with their Arms and Clothing.
In the firft place, the Perfians wearing a Tiara
on the Head, fo thick as to be accounted im-
penetrable; and on the Body a Coat of Mail,
wrought with Iron to the likenefs of the Scales
of a Fifh, and adorn'd with Sleeves of various
Colours. Their Thighs were not undefend-
ed; and inftead of a Shield, they carried a
Target of Cane ftrongly compacted; which
ferv'd alfo to cover their Quiver. Their Javelins were fhort, their Bows long, their Arrows
were made of Cane, and their Swords hung
down from a Belt on the Right-fide. They were
commanded by *Otanes*, the Father of *Ameftris*,
the Wife of *Xerxes*. In antient times the Perfians were by the Grecians called Cephenes, and
by themfelves and neareft Neighbours, Artæ-
ans: But *Perfeus*, the Son of *Jupiter* and *Danae*,

3   coming

coming to *Cepheus* the Son of *Belus*, married his Daughter *Andromeda*, and by her had a Son, whom he named *Perseus*, and afterwards left with *Cepheus*, because he had no Male Child; and from him they took the Name of Persians. The Medes were arm'd and cloth'd in the same manner: For the Furniture I have describ'd, belongs properly to the Medes, and not to the Persians. They march'd under the Conduct of *Tigranes*, who was of the Achæmenian Family. The Medes were antiently called Arians by all Nations; but chang'd their Name, as they say themselves, when *Medea* of *Colchis* arriv'd from *Athens* in their Country. The Cissians appearing in every thing like the Persians, except only that they wore Mitres on their Heads, were led by *Anephes* the Son of *Otanes*. The Hyrcanians were also arm'd after the Persian manner, and commanded by *Megapanus*, who was afterwards Governour of *Babylon*. The Assyrians had Helmets of Brass to cover their Heads, contriv'd in so strange a Fashion, as is not easy to be describ'd: Every one had a Buckler, a Javelin, and a short Sword after the manner of the Ægyptians, with a Pectoral made of Flax, and a Truncheon of Wood pointed with Iron. By the Grecians they are call'd Syrians; and by the Barbarians, Assyrians. Among these the Chaldæans were accounted, and *Otaspes* the Son of *Artachæus* was their Leader. The Bactrians had Turbans on their Heads, not unlike those of the Medes; and carried Bows made of Cane after the manner of their Country, with a kind of Javelin very short. The Saces, or rather Scythians, wore a Cap rising to a Point in the Form of of a Pyramid: They had also Thigh-pieces; and for Arms, carried a sort of Bow peculiar to their Nation, with a Dagger, a Bill, and a Scymetar. They came from *Amyrgium* in *Scythia:* but the Persians call them Saces, which is the common Name they give to all the Scythians. The Bactrians and Saces were led by *Hystaspes,* Son of *Darius* by *Atossa* the Daughter of *Cyrus.* The Indians cover'd with a Casaque of Wood, and carrying a Bow, and Arrows of Cane pointed with Iron, were commanded by *Pharnazathres* the Son of *Artabates.* The Arians had Bows made like those of the Medes; and in all other things resembling the Bactrians, march'd under the Conduct of *Sisamnes* the Son of *Hydarnes.* The Parthians, Chorasmians, Sogdians, Gandarians and Dadicians, appear'd in the same Arms and Clothing as the Bactrians, under the following Leaders: *Artabazus,* the Son of *Pharnaces,* commanded the Parthians and the Chorasmians: *Azanes* the Son of *Artæus,* the Sogdians; and *Artyphius* the Son of *Artabanus,* the Gandarians and Dadicians. The Caspians cloth'd in Goat-skins, and arm'd with a Scymetar, and with a Bow made of Cane, after the manner of their Country, had for their Captain *Ariomardus* the Brother of *Artyphius.* The Saranges magnificently dress'd in Garments of the richest Colours, and Buskins drawn up to the Knee, carried a Bow and Javelins, like those of the Medes; and were led by *Pherendates* the Son of *Megabyzus:* The Pactyans clothed likewise in Goat-skins, had a Bow and a short Sword peculiar to that Country, and were commanded by *Atrayntes* the Son of *Itramites.* The Utians, Mycians and Pari-

Paricanians, arm'd and cloth'd like the Pactyans, march'd under the following Captains:
Arsamenes the Son of *Darius* led the Utians and
Mycians; and *Siromitres* the Son of *Oebazus*,
the Paricanians. The Arabians wore a Girdle
over a Surcoat call'd Zeira; and in the Right-
hand carried a crooked Bow of great Length.
The Æthiopians were cover'd with the Skins
of Lions and Leopards, and arm'd with Bows
full four Cubits long, made of the Branches of
the Palm-tree, with Arrows of Cane proportionable, and pointed, instead of Iron, with a
sharp Stone, of that sort they use for Seals.
They had also Javelins pointed with Goats-
horns sharpen'd like the End of a Lance, and
Truncheons arm'd with Iron. When they are
about to engage in Battle, they paint one half
of their Bodies with white Plaster, and the other
half with Vermilion. The Arabians, and
those Æthiopians, who inhabit above *Ægypt*,
were commanded by *Arsames* the Son of *Darius* by *Artystona* the Daughter of *Cyrus*, whose
Image *Darius* caus'd to be made of solid Gold,
because he lov'd her more than all his other
Wives. But the Æthiopians, who inhabit more
Easterly (for *Xerxes* had of both sorts in his
Army) march'd with the Indians, no way unlike the others, except only in the Sound of
their Voice, and in their Hair. For the O-
riental Æthiopians have long streight Hair:
But the Hair of the Lybian Æthiopians is
more curl'd than that of any other People. The
Arms and Habit of the Asiatick Æthiopians
were almost the same with those of the Indians:
But instead of a Helmet, they wore the Skin of
a Horse's Head, stript off with the Ears and
Mane;

Mane; and contrived in such a manner, that the Mane might serve for a Crest; while the Ears appear'd erected on the Head of the Man. They were also defended by a Buckler, which they cover'd with the Skins of Cranes. The Libyans had Coats made of Leather, carried a pointed Lance harden'd at one end by the Fire, and were under the Conduct of *Masanges* the Son of *Aorizus.* The Paphlagonians wore Helmets compos'd of divers Pieces quilted together; they had a Buckler and Javelins of a moderate Size, with Darts and a short Sword: On their Feet they wore Shoes after the manner of their Country, reaching up to the middle of the Leg. The Ligyans, the Matienians and the Mariandynians, with those Syrians, who by the Persians are call'd Cappadocians, were arm'd and cloth'd as the Paphlagonians. The Matienians and the Paphlagonians, were led by *Dotus* the Son of *Megasides*, and the Mariandynians, with the Ligyans and Syrians, by *Gobryas* the Son of *Darius* and *Artystona.* The Phrygians carried Arms little differing from those of the Paphlagonians: This People, if we may believe the Macedonians, went under the Name of Brygians, during all the time they inhabited in *Europe,* within the Territories of *Macedonia;* but upon their Arrival in *Asia,* chang'd their Name with their Country, and have ever since been call'd Phrygians. The Armenians, being a Colony of the Phrygians, appear'd in the same Accoutrements; and both these Nations were commanded by *Artochmes,* who had married a Daughter of *Darius.* The Lydians were arm'd more like to the Grecians than any other People of the Army: They had been

formerly known by the Name of Meonians ;
but were afterwards call'd Lydians from *Ly-
dus* the Son of *Atys*. The Myfians had a fort
of Helmet peculiar to their Country, with a
little Buckler, and pointed Javelins harden'd
at the End by Fire. They are a Colony of the
Lydians, and are call'd Olympians from the
Mountain *Olympus*. Both thefe Nations were
led by *Artaphernes*, the Son of that *Artaphernes* who, with *Datis*, commanded the Perfian
Forces at the Battle of *Marathon*. The Thracians cover'd their Heads with a Cap made
of the Skins of Foxes, and their Bodies with
a Veft, and Surcoat of various Colours : They
had Bufkins tied with Thongs above the Ancle,
and a fmall Buckler made in the form of a
Half-moon, with Javelins and a fhort Dagger.
They have gone under the Name of Bithyni-
ans ever fince they arriv'd in *Afia* ; and if we
may believe their own Report, were formerly
call'd Strymonians, from the River *Strymon*
where they inhabited, and from whence they
were expell'd by the Myfians and by the Teucrians. Thofe Thrafians, who in *Afia* retain'd
their original Name, were commanded by *Bar-
gafaces* the Son of *Artabanus*. They carried a
fmall Buckler compos'd of untann'd Hides, with
two Lycian Javelins, and a Helmet of Brafs,
having the Ears and Horns of an Ox of the
fame Metal. They wore a Creft at the Top of
their Helmet, and their Legs were cover'd with
Phœnician Cloth. They have an Oracle of
Mars in their Country. The Meonian Cabeli-
ans, who are alfo call'd Lafinians, had the fame
Arms and Clothing with the Cilicians, which
I fhall defcribe when I come to fpeak of that
Nation.

Nation. The Mylians carried short Lances, and were cloth'd in a Garment buckled together. Some of them had Lycian Bows, and a Cap compos'd of Skins. All these were commanded by *Badres* the Son of *Hystanes.* The Moschians had a Helmet of Wood, with a little Buckler, and Javelins of a like propotion but deeply pointed. The Tiberenians, Macronians and Mosynœcians were arm'd as the Moschians, who with the Tiberenians march'd under the conduct of *Ariomardus,* the Son of *Darius* by *Parmys* the Daughter of *Smerdis* the Son of *Cyrus.* But the Macronians and Mosynœcians were led by *Artaictes,* the Son of *Cherasmis* and Governour of *Sestus* on the *Hellespont.* The Marians wore a Cap strongly quilted, after the manner of their Country, and carried Javelins, with a little Shield cover'd with Skins. The Colchians had a Helmet of wood, with a Buckler made of untann'd Hides, a short Lance, and a cutting Sword. The Forces of these two Nations had for their Leader *Pherendates* the Son of *Theaspes.* The Allarodians and the Saspirians, arm'd like the Colchians, march'd under the Command of *Masistius* the Son of *Siromitres.* The People that inhabit the Islands of the *Red-Sea,* to which the King usually sends the Persons he resolves to banish, were cloth'd and arm'd like the Medes, and led by *Mardontes,* the Son of *Bagæus,* who was kill'd two Years after at the Battle of *Mycale.* These were the Nations that compos'd the Army, which was to be employ'd on the Continent; and these were the Names of their Leaders, who divided and numbred all the Forces, and had the Power of appointing the Comman-

ders

ders of a Thousand, and of ten Thousand:
But those who had the Command of ten Thousand, were permitted to nominate the Centu-
rions and Decurions. Thus these national
Forces had their inferior Officers; and those
I have mention'd were their Commanders in
chief. But the superior Generals of the Land-
Army, were, *Mardonius* the Son of *Gobryas*;
Trintatæchmes, the Son of *Artabanus* who gave
his Opinion against the War; *Smerdones* the Son
of *Otanes* (both Sons to the Brothers of *Darius*,
and Cousins to *Xerxes*;) *Masistes* the Son of *Darius* by *Atossa*; *Gergys* the Son of *Ariazus*; and
Megabyzus the Son of *Zopyrus*. These were
Captain-Generals of all the Army, except the
ten Thousand Persians, who obey'd no other
Commander than *Hydarnes*, the Son of *Hydarnes*,
and were sirnam'd *Immortal*; because upon the
Death of any one of their Number, whether
by War or Sickness, another is presently substi-
tuted in his Place: So that they never amount
to more or less than ten Thousand. They were
accounted the most valiant among the Persians;
and tho' in their Arms and Habit they were
like the rest of their Countrymen, yet they
were more magnificent, and adorn'd with Gold
in abundance. Besides they had Chariots for
their Women with their Attendants, who were
richly cloth'd; and their Provisions were
brought upon Camels and other Beasts of Burden, appropriated to their own Use. All the
Nations I have mention'd, are accustom'd to
mount on Horseback; but none were furnish'd
with Horses, except those which I shall enumerate. First, the Persians; who were no otherwise arm'd than their Foot; except only that
some

some of them wore a Helmet of Brass or Iron. The Sagartians; who are Breeders of Cattle, of Persian Extraction and Language; but arm'd and cloth'd in a manner participating both of the Persian and Pactyan Fashion; furnish'd eight thousand Horsemen to this Expedition. They had no Weapon either of Iron or Brass, except a short Sword; carrying only a kind of Net made of Cord, instead of all other Arms; and exposing their Persons in War, without any other Defence. When they approach the Enemy, they throw their Net, and having taken either a Man or a Horse, they easily dispatch whatever is so intangled. In this manner they behave themselves in Fight: and being accounted Persians, were drawn up in the same Body. The Median and Cissian Horse were no otherwise equip'd than the Foot of those Nations. The Indians were also arm'd like their Foot; had led Horses, and Chariots drawn by Horses and wild Asses. The Bactrian and Caspian Cavalry were furnish'd in all Points as their Infantry. The Libyans were arm'd and cloth'd like their Foot, and every one of them had a Chariot. The Paricanians imitating the Caspians, carried the same Arms with their Foot. And the Arabians, not at all differing from their Infantry in Arms or Clothing were mounted upon Camels no less swift than Horses. These were the only Nations that compos'd the Cavalry; which amounted to the Number of fourscore Thousand, besides the Camels and the Chariots. All the Horse were dispos'd in proper Order: But the Arabians were plac'd in the Rear, lest the Horses should be affrighted at the Sight of the Camels,

which

which they cannot bear. *Armamithres* and *Tithæus*, the Sons of *Datis*, were Generals of the Cavalry. For *Pharnuches*, who had been appointed the other General, was sick at *Sardis*, by an unfortunate Accident which happen'd to him as he march'd out of the City. His Horse frighted at a Dog that ran between his Legs, rose upright, and threw him to the Ground ; upon which he vomited Blood, and fell into a languishing Distemper. But the Servants of *Pharnuches*, by his Order, punish'd the Horse upon the spot: For leading him to the Ground where he had thrown his Master, they cut off his Legs by the Knee. And thus *Pharnuches* was disabled from performing the Office of a General.

AFTER the Land-Forces had been view'd, the Ships of War were also numbred, and found to be twelve hundred and seven, fitted out by the following Nations, in such Proportions as I shall set down. The Phœnicians and Syrians who inhabit *Palestine*, furnish'd three hundred Ships. with Men arm'd in this manner. On their Heads they wore Helmets, nearly resembling those of the Grecians ; and on their Breast a Pectoral of quilted Flax. They carried Javelins and a round Shield, without any Boss on the Center. These Phœnicians, as they say of themselves, were antiently seated on the *Red Sea* ; and afterwards leaving their Habitations, went and settled in the maritim Parts of *Syria* ; which, with all the Country extending down to *Ægypt*, go under the Name of *Palestine*. The Ægyptians sent two hundred Ships for their part. Their Men had a Cap strongly quilted, a convex Buckler with a great Boss ; Javelins proper

for

for a Sea-fight, and Bills of the largest Size.
The more ordinary sort wore a Corslet, and
were arm'd with a great cutting Sword. The
Cyprians brought a hundred and fifty Ships,
and appear'd in this manner: Their Kings
wore Mitres on their Heads, and the rest were
cloth'd in Vests, and arm'd like the Grecians.
The People of *Cyprus*, if we may believe their
own Report, are descended of divers Nations; some deriving themselves from *Salamis*
and the Athenians; and others from *Arcadia*,
from *Cythnus*, from *Phœnicia*; and some from
the Æthiopians. The Cilicians furnish'd a
hundred Ships. They wore a Cap made after
the manner of their Country; and instead of a
Shield, had a Buckler of the smallest Size, cover'd with untann'd Hides. They were cloth'd
in a woollen Vest, and every one carried
two Javelins, with a Sword not unlike
that of the Ægyptians. The Cilicians were
antiently call'd Hypachæans, and took the
Name they now have, from *Cilix* the Son of
Agenor a Phœnician. The Pamphylians, who are
descended from those that return'd from *Troy*
with *Amphilochus* and *Calchas*, furnish'd thirty
Ships, and were arm'd after the manner of the
Grecians. The Lycians appear'd in fifty Ships:
Their Shoulders were covered with the Skins of
Goats, their Legs with Boots and upon their
Heads they wore a Cap adorn'd with a Crest of
Feathers. They were arm'd with a Corslet,
and carried a Bow of Cornil, with Arrows of
Cane; they had also a Falchion, with Darts
and a short Sword. They derive their Original
from *Crete*, and were formerly call'd Termilians:
But receiv'd the Name of Lycians from *Lycus* the

Son

Son of *Pandion*, an Athenian. The Dorians of *Asia* furnish'd thirty Ships; and as they were Peloponesians by Descent, appear'd, in all Points, arm'd like the Grecians. The Carians contributed Seventy Ships; and, except their Daggers and Faulchions, were arm'd after the manner of *Greece.* What Name they had in antient time, I have mention'd in the former Part of this Work. The Ionians brought a hundred Sail, and were arm'd and cloth'd as the Grecians. Whilst they liv'd in *Peloponesus* and inhabited those Parts which are now call'd *Achaia*, before the Arrival of *Danaus* and *Xuthus*, the Grecians say, they went under the Name of Ægialian Pelasgians; and that they had the Name of Ionians from *Ion*, the Son of *Xuthus.* The Islanders appear'd with no more than seventeen Ships, and were arm'd like the Grecians. These also being of Pelasgian Original were afterwards call'd Ionians for the same Reason; and the twelve Cities in like manner have been so nam'd from the Athenians. The Æolians, who, as the Grecians say, were antiently call'd Pelasgians, brought sixty Ships, and were arm'd after the manner of *Greece.* All the Hellespontins (except the Abydenians, who were order'd by the King to stay at home for the Guard of the Bridges) furnish'd one hundred Sail; and being Colonies of the Ionians and Dorians, appeared in Grecian Arms. Every one of these Ships had Soldiers on board; who were either Persians, or Medes, or Saces. But the Phœnician Ships, and especially those of *Sidonia*, were the best Sailors. All the Divisions of this Fleet, as well as of the Land-Forces, had their own national Officers; but I

shall

shall forbear to mention their Names, as not
necessary to the Design of my History; partly,
because those Commanders were of little Authority; and partly, because they were no less
numerous than the Cities contain'd within the
several Nations, from which they came. For
indeed they were properly Servants, and not
Generals; slavishly obeying their Masters, like
the rest of the Multitude. For the supreme
Command was lodg'd in the Hands of Persians;
whose Names I have already mention'd, as far
as relates to the Land-Army. The Naval Forces were commanded in chief by *Ariabignes* the
Son of *Darius*; by *Prexaspes* the Son of *Aspa-
thines*; by *Megabazus* the Son of *Megabates*; and
by *Achæmenes* the Son of *Darius*. The Ionians
and Barians were under the Conduct of *Ariabignes* the Son of *Darius* by the Daughter of *Go-
brias*; the Ægyptians under that of *Achæmenes*,
Brother to *Xerxes*: and all the rest of the Fleet
was commanded by the two other Generals be-
fore-nam'd. Besides these Ships of War, the
Gallies of fifty and thirty Oars, with the Vessels
of Transportation for Horse and other Necessa-
ries, amounted to the Number of three Thousand. Next to the Generals I have mention'd,
the Commanders of greatest Fame, were, *Te-
tramnestus* the Son of *Allesus*, of *Sidonia*; *Mapen*
the Son of *Sironus*, of *Tyre*; *Narbal* the Son of
Arbalus of *Aridela*; *Syennesis* the Son of *Oromedon*
of *Cicilia*; *Ciberniscus* the Son of *Sica* of *Lycia*;
Gortus the Son of *Cherses*, and *Timonax* the Son of
Timogarus, both Cyprians: And of the Carians,
Histiæus the Son of *Tymnes*; *Pygres* the Son of
Seldomus; and *Damasitbymus* the Son of *Candaules.*
I shall mention no more of the Commanders, be-
cause

caufe I judge it unneceffary. But above all I admire *Artemifia*, who being left a Widow, and having taken upon her the Adminiftration of her Son's Kingdom during his Minority, expos'd her Perfon in this Expedition againft *Greece*; not conftrain'd by any Neceffity, but only to fhew her Generofity and Valour. She was the Daughter of *Lygdamis*, and deriv'd her Original by the Father's Side from *Halicarnaffus*, and from *Crete* by the Mother. The Halicarnaffians, the Coans, the Nifyrians, and the Calydnians were under her Dominion; and fhe join'd the Fleet of *Xerxes* with five Ships of War, better than any of the reft, except thofe of the Sidonians. In a word, her Forefight was fo great, that of all the Confederates fhe gave the moft prudent Counfel to the King. As for the People, which, as I faid before, were under her Government, they are originally Dorians: For the Halicarnaffians are a Colony of the Trœzenians, and the reft are defcended from the Epidaurians.

WHEN *Xerxes* had caus'd all his Forces to be number'd, and drawn into diftinct Bodies, he refolv'd to take a particular View of every Nation. And to that end, ftepping into a Chariot, was carried to the Head of each Divifion; and having ask'd fuch Queftions as he thought neceffary, commanded his Secretaries to put in writing the Anfwers he receiv'd: continuing to proceed in this manner, till he had intirely view'd all the Land-Army, both Horfe and Foot. That done, he left his Chariot, and going on board a Sidonian Ship, plac'd himfelf under a Canopy of Gold: And failing by the Fleet, which was rang'd on a Line he made the like Enquiry, as before in
relation

relation to the Land-Forces, and order'd an Account of all the Particulars to be written down by the same Persons. In order to this Review, the Commanders had put to Sea in due time; and having drawn their Ships into one Line, at the distance of about four hundred Foot from the Shoar, with their Heads fronting that way, they arm'd their Men as for a Battle; and *Xerxes* sailing between the Land and the Ships, saw them all distinctly. When he had made an end of viewing the Fleet, and was return'd to shoar, he sent for *Demaratus* the Son of *Ariston*, and spoke to him in these Terms: " *Demaratus*, said he, I desire to ask
" you a Question: You are a Grecian; and
" moreover, born in a City of *Greece*, which,
" as I am inform'd by you, and other Per-
" sons of that Nation, whom I have seen, is
" neither the least nor the weakest. Tell
" me therefore, whether you think the Grecians
" will dare to resist my Forces? For I am per-
" suaded, that if not only all the Grecians,
" but all the rest of the Western World were
" collected into one Body, they would not
" have the Courage to oppose me. However,
" I am desirous to know your Opinion on
" this Subject." "SIR, said *Demaratus*, shall
" I frame my Answer according to the Truth,
" or must I endeavour to please?" The King bid him speak the Truth with Freedom, and be assur'd he should not lose any part of his Favour on that account. Which when *Demaratus* heard, he began thus: " Since you
" require me to inform you of the Truth with-
" out reserve, I will take care that no Man shall
" hereafter justly accuse me of having de-
" ceived

" ceiv'd you by a Falſhood. Know then, that
" *Greece* was ever inur'd to Poverty, which
" has been her Mother and Nurſe; that ſhe
" accquir'd Virtue by her Wiſdom, and by a
" ſteady Diſcipline, with which ſhe has de-
" fended her Poverty and her Power. Theſe
" Praiſes are juſtly due to all thoſe Grecians,
" who inhabit the Country of the Dorians.
" But I ſhall not now ſpeak of any other People
" than of the Lacedemonians alone. In the
" firſt Place, they never will hearken to your
" Terms, becauſe they are deſtructive to the
" Grecian Liberty: Nay more, they will not
" fail to meet you in the Field, tho' all the reſt
" of the Grecians ſhould ſide with you. To
" ask how many they are in Number, is un-
" neceſſary; for whether they amount to a
" thouſand Men, or more, or even leſs, they
" will moſt certainly appear and give you Bat-
" tle." At theſe Words of *Demaratus*, *Xerxes*
laughing ſaid; " Are you not aſhamed to ſpeak
" in this manner? What! Shall a thouſand
" Men venture to engage ſo great an Army?
" Would you, who have been their King, un-
" dertake to fight ſingly againſt ten Men? If
" your Countrymen are ſo valiant as you pre-
" tend, you, who are their King, ought by
" your own Inſtitutions, to be capable of do-
" ing as much as any two of ordinary Rank;
" and therefore, if one of theſe is able to fight
" ten of my Men, I may juſtly require you to
" fight twenty; and by that Experiment to
" confirm your Diſcourſe. But if they are
" neither of greater Strength, nor of a high-
" er Stature, than you, and the reſt of the
" Grecians I have ſeen, conſider, whether the
" things

" things you have faid of them, may not be
" the Effect of Pride and Vanity. I defire to
" know, how a thoufand Men, or even ten
" thoufand, or, if you will, fifty thoufand; all
" equally free, and not fubject to the Command
" of a fingle Perfon, can poffibly refift fuch
" an Army as mine? And unlefs they are
" more than five thoufand, we have a thoufand
" Men againft one. Were they indeed, like
" our Forces, under the abfolute Command of
" one General, they would doubtlefs be pufh'd
" on to bolder Attempts by their Apprehenfi-
" ons of his Power, than by their own natu-
" ral Courage; and might be conftrain'd by
" Force, to attack a far greater Number than
" themfelves: But now, being under no Com-
" pulfion, they are not likely to do either the
" one or the other. And I am of opinion,
" that the Grecians, upon Tryal, will not be
" a Match for an equal Number of Perfians.
" Thofe Qualities of which you boaft, are
" really in us only, tho' I muft own they are
" rare and uncommon. Yet I have Perfians in
" my Guards, who will not refufe to encoun-
" ter thrice their Number of Grecians, fo
" much magnified with you without Caufe."
To this *Demaratus* replied; " SIR, I knew
" from the Beginning, that the Truth I fhould
" fpeak would be difpleafing to you; but be-
" caufe you encourag'd me to deliver my Opini-
" on with Sincerity, I thought myfelf oblig'd
" to give you a juft Character of the Lacedemo-
" nians. You know how little Caufe I have to
" retain any Affection for thofe, who, after they
" had depriv'd me of the Honours and Digni-
" ty of my Anceftors, conftrain'd me to to aban-

" don

"don my Country. On the other hand, you
"know how generously your Father receiv'd
"me, and made ample Provision for my Sup-
"port; and therefore cannot possibly enter-
"tain the least shadow of Suspicion, that
"a Man in his right Senses will ever cease to
"acknowledge such eminent Benefits with all
"imaginable Gratitude. For my own part,
"I am so far from presuming to enter the
"Lists against ten Men, that I would not wil-
"lingly fight against two, nor even against
"one, without a just Cause; yet in a Case of
"Necessity, or at a time solemnly appointed
"for the Exercise of Valour, I would chuse
"to engage one of those who pretend to be
"singly equal to the three Grecians. The
"Lacedemonians perhaps are not better than
"other Men in single Combat, but in a col-
"lected Body they surpass all Mankind. And
"tho' they are a free People, yet in some
"things they are willing to be restrain'd. For
"the Law is their Sovereign, which they obey
"with a more awful Reverence, than your Sub-
"jects pay to you. They do whatever she en-
"joyns, and her Injunctions are always uniform.
"She forbids them to fly from any Enemy, tho'
"his Forces are ever so numerous; and com-
"mands them to keep their Ranks, and to
"conquer, or die in the Battle. If you think
"I entertain you with impertinent Discourse,
"I shall say no more on this Subject: Nor in-
"deed should have said so much, had I not been
"constrain'd by the Command you laid upon
"me. Nevertheless I wish you all the Prof-
"perity you can desire." When *Demaratus* had
thus spoken, *Xerxes* laughing at his Simplicity,
dismiss'd

difmifs'd him without the leaft fhew of Difcontent: And after he had appointed *Mafcames* the Son of *Megadoftes* to be Governour of *Dorifcus*, in the room of another Perfon who had been plac'd in that Government by *Darius*, he advanc'd with his Army into *Thrace*. To this *Mafcames Xerxes* us'd to fend a Prefent every Year; becaufe he efteem'd him the moft valiant of all the Governours that either he or *Darius* had chofen; and his Son *Artaxerxes* continued the fame Bounty to his Pofterity. For of all thofe who had been appointed to command in *Thrace*, and in all the Cities of the *Hellefpont*, none were able to preferve the Places they held, from falling into the Hands of the Grecians, except only *Mafcames*, who kept himfelf in poffeffion of *Dorifcus*, notwithftanding the many Attempts they made againft him; And on this account he annually receiv'd a Prefent from the King of *Perfia*. But among all the Governours of thofe Cities, which were retaken by the Grecians, *Xerxes* thought no Man had behav'd himfelf with Courage, except *Boges*, who commanded in *Eion*. He took every Occafion to mention him with Praife, and conferr'd the higheft Honours upon the Children he left in *Perfia*. The Truth is, *Boges* deferv'd the greateft Commendation. For when he was befieg'd by the Athenians under the Conduct of *Cimon* the Son of *Miltiades*, and might have march'd out, with leave to return to *Afia* upon his Honour, he refus'd to accept any Conditions, left the King fhould fufpect him of Cowardice: And perfifting conftantly in that Refolution, after his Provifions were quite fpent, he caus'd a great Fire to be kindled; and having kill'd his Wife

4 and

and Children, with his Concubines and Servants, threw their Bodies into the Flames: Then mounting the Walls of the City, he cast all the Silver and Gold, that was to be found, into the River *Strymon*; and after he had so done threw himself into the Fire: Deserving by this Action to be ever remembred with Honour among the Persians.

XERXES marching towards *Greece*, compell'd all the Nations he found in his Way to join his Army with their Forces. For, as I said before, all those Countries, even to *Thessaly*, had been subdued and made tributary to him, by *Megabazus*, and *Mardonius*. In his March from *Doriscus*, he pass'd by the Samothracian Cities; the last and most westwardly of which, is call'd *Mesambria*, situated at a small Distance from *Stryma*, a City of the Thasians. Between these two Places runs the River *Lissus*; which not having Water enough for *Xerxes* and his Army, was intirely exhausted. This Country was antiently known by the Name of *Galaica*, and is now call'd *Briantica*; but of right belongs to the Ciconians. When *Xerxes* had pass'd the dry Channel of the *Lissus*, he march'd by the Grecian Cities of *Maronea*, *Dicæa*, and *Abdera*; with the memorable Lakes of *Ismaris* and *Bistonis*, which lie in their Neighbourhood. For the former of these is situate between *Maronea* and *Stryma*; and the latter is contiguous to *Dicæa*, and receives the Waters of the two Rivers *Travus* and *Compsatus*. *Xerxes* observing no remarkable Lake about *Abdera*, pass'd the River *Nestus*, which runs into the Sea; and after he had travers'd all these Regions, turn'd his March to the midland Cities. In one

2   of

of these, call'd *Pyfirus*, is a Lake about thirty
Stades in Circumference; of a brackish Water,
abounding in Fish; which was drunk up by the
draught Horses, and other Cattle belonging
to the Baggage of his Army. Thus leaving
the Grecian Cities of that Coaft on the Left
Hand, he march'd thro' the Countries of *Thrace*
that belong to the Pætians, the Ciconians, the
Biftonians, the Sapæans, the Derfæans, the
Hedonians, and to the Satrians. As many of
thefe as are fituate near the Sea, attended him
with their Ships; and thofe who inhabited
the inland Parts, were all oblig'd to follow
the Army by Land, except the Satrians. This
People, if we are rightly inform'd, never had
a Mafter; and among all the Thracians, have
fingly continued free to this Day. They inhabit a mountainous Country, cover'd with
Woods and Snow. They are valiant in War;
and have an oracle of *Bacchus* in the higheft
Part of their Hills. The Priefts of this Temple are of *Beffa*; and an Archprieftefs delivers
the Anfwers of the Oracle, which are not more
ambiguous than thofe of *Delphi*. Having pafs'd
thefe Countries, he advanc'd to *Niphagra* and
Pergamus, Cities of the Pierians, leaving *Pangæus* on the Right Hand, which is a great and
high Mountain, abounding in Mines of Gold
and Silver poffefs'd by the Pierians Odoman-
tians; and efpecially by the Satrians. Then
paffing thro' the Territories of the Pæonians,
the Doberes, and the Pæoplians, who inhabit to the North, beyond Mount *Pangæus,*
he bent his March Weftward, till he arriv'd
at *Eion* on the River *Strymon*; of which City,
Boges, whom I have fo lately mention'd,

O   was

was at that time Governour. The Country that lies about the Mountain *Pangæus* is call'd *Phillis*; on the West Side, extending to the River *Argites*, which falls into the *Strymon*; and on the South, to the *Strymon* itself. At their Arrival, the Magi offer'd a Sacrifice of white Horses to this River; and after they had thrown them into the Stream, with a Composition of various Drugs, the Army broke up, and march'd to the *Nine Ways* of the Edonians, where they found Bridges prepar'd for their Passage over the *Strymon*. But being inform'd that this Place was call'd by the Name of the *Nine Ways*, they took nine of the Sons and Daughters of the Inhabitants, and buried them alive, as the Manner of the Persians is. And I have heard that *Amestris*, the Wife of *Xerxes*, having attain'd to a considerable Age, caus'd fourteen Children of the best Families in *Persia* to be interr'd alive, for a Sacrifice of Thanks to that God, who, they say, is beneath the Earth. The Army having left the River *Strymon*, pass'd by a Grecian City call'd *Argilus*; which is situate to the Westward, on the Sea Coast, and, with the Country that lies above it, goes under the Name of *Bisaltia*. Then leaving the Bay, where the Temple of *Neptune* is built, on the Left Hand, they march'd thro' the Plain of *Syleus*; and passing by *Stagyrus* a Grecian City, arriv'd at *Acanthus*; accompanied by the Forces of the Pangæans, and of all the other Nations I have nam'd, which they found in their Way; the Inhabitants of the maritim Places putting to Sea in their Ships, and those of the inland Parts following the Army on Foot. From the time of this March, the Thra-

cians

cians have always shewn so great a Veneration for the Way, by which *Xerxes* led his Forces, that they have totally abstain'd from breaking up or sowing any part of that Ground to this Day.

WHEN the Army was arriv'd at *Acanthus Xerxes* declar'd he would be entertain'd by the Inhabitants; and having presented them with Suits of Apparel made after the manner of the Medes he commended their Readiness to attend him in this War, and express'd great Satisfaction when he heard that the Canal of Mount *Athos* was finish'd. But whilst he continued at *Acanthus*, *Artachæus*, who had been the Director of that Work, fell sick and died. He was highly esteem'd by *Xerxes*, and derived his Blood from *Achæmenes:* His Voice was stronger than that of any other Man; he was in Stature the tallest of all the Persians, and wanted only the Breadth of four Fingers to compleat the full Height of five Royal Cubits. *Xerxes* much lamenting the Loss of this Person, caus'd him to be accompanied to the Grave, and interr'd with great Pomp. All the Army was employed in erecting a Monument to his Memory; and the Acanthians admonish'd by an Oracle, honour him as a Hero, with Sacrifices and Invocations. Such were the Demonstrations, which *Xerxes* gave of his Concern for the Loss of *Artachæus.*

THE Grecians, who were constrain'd to furnish Provisions for the Table of *Xerxes*, and for all his Army, found themselves so oppress'd, that they chose to abandon their Houses But when the Thasians receiv'd him with his Forces, in the Name of those Cities which they possess in the midland Country, *Antipater* the Son of *Oryges*,

an

an eminent and wealthy Citizen, expending four
hundred Talents of Silver in one Supper.   The
Magistrates of the neighbouring Cities having
been inform'd of the Preparations that were
made for this Feast, which was appointed long
before, they propos'd the Example to their
own People, and proclaim'd their Intentions
by proper Officers.   Upon which Notice,
the Inhabitants of those Places, distributed
all the Wheat and Barley they had, in convenient Portions, among themselves; and
ground it into Meal, in such Quantities as
might have been sufficient for many Months.
They bought, and fatted the best of Cattle;
furnish'd their Ponds and Yards with all manner of Land and Water Fowl, and did whatever they could to make Provision for *Xerxes*
and his Army.   Besides, they provided Cups
and Basons of Gold and Silver, with all things
necessary for the Service of a Table.   But these
Preparations were made for the King, and for
those who were admitted to eat with him:
The rest of the Army had only the common
Allowance.   In all Places where *Xerxes* arriv'd
he found a spacious Tent erected for his Reception: But the Forces had no other Covering
than the Air.   At the time of eating, those
who furnish'd the Provisions, had the Labour of
serving their Guests; who after they had been
plentifully treated, and pass'd the Night, carried away the Tent, with all the Furniture,
and Utensils; leaving nothing behind them
at their Departure in the Morning.   On which
Occasion *Megacreon* of *Abdera* said pleasantly,
that he would advise the Abderites to go
in a general Procession, with their Wives and
all

all the People, to the Temples of that City and to befeech the Gods, to avert one half of the Evils to come, as well as to acknowledge their Favour in not inclining *Xerxes* to eat twice every Day: For if the Abderites were commanded to provide a Dinner for him, equal to his Supper, they would be neceſſitated either to abandon their Dwellings, or, if they ſhould ſtay, to become the moſt wretched of all Men. Yet they obeyed the Injunctions they had receiv'd, tho' not without Difficulty. At *Acanthus*, *Xerxes* ſent away the Generals of the Naval Forces, to bring the Fleet to the Bay of *Therma*, which lies below a Place of the ſame Name, and there to attend his Arrival; becauſe he had heard that was the ſhorteſt Way he could take. The Order of his March between the Cities of *Doriſcus* and *Acanthus*, was thus: He divided the Army into three Bodies; one of which, commanded by *Mardonius* and *Maſiſtes*, march'd along the Coaſt, and, as it were, kept company with the Fleet. A ſecond advanc'd by the way of the Inland Countries, under the Conduct of *Trintatæchmes* and *Sergis*: Whilſt the third Body, in which was the King himſelf, march'd between the other two, with *Smerdones* and *Megabyzus* at their Head. But the Fleet having Orders from *Xerxes* to depart, paſs'd thro' the Canal of Mount *Athos*, into the Bay, where the Cities of *Aſſa*, *Pidorus*, *Singus*, and *Sarga* are ſituate; and after they had oblig'd thoſe Places to join them with their Forces, they made the Promontory of *Ampelus* in *Torone*; and, in their way to *Therma*, were furniſh'd with Ships and Men by the Grecian Cities of *Torone*, *Galepſus*, *Sermylia*, *Mecyberna*,

O 3   **and**

and *Olynthus*, all belonging to the Country which is now call'd *Sithonia*. From the Cape of *Ampelus*, crossing over to the Promontory of *Canastrum*, which advances farther into the Sea than any other upon all the Coast of *Pallene*, they had an additional Force of Ships and Men out of the Cities of *Potidæa*, *Alphytis*, *Neapolis*, *Æga*, *Therambus*, *Scione*, *Mende* and *Sane*, Cities of *Pallene*, which was antiently known by the Name of *Phlegra*. Continuing their Voyage along that Coast, they assembled more auxiliary Forces, out of the Cities of *Lipaxus*, *Combrea*, *Lissa*, *Gigonus*, *Campsa*, *Smila*, and *Ænea*; which are situate in the Neighbourhood of *Pallene*, and near the Bay of *Therma*. From *Ænea*, the last of the Places I mention'd, the Fleet stood for the Gulph of *Therma*, and the Mygdonian Coast; till, according to their Instructions, they arriv'd at *Therma*, and at the Cities of *Sindus* and *Chalestra*, both situate on the River *Axius*, which divides the Territories of *Mygdonia* from those of *Bottiæis*; where the Cities of *Ichne* and *Pella* stand in a narrow Region near the Sea. All the Fleet took their Stations, either in the River *Axius*, or near the City of *Therma*, or else in the Places that lie between both; and there waited the Arrival of the King.

IN the mean time *Xerxes* departed from *Acanthus* in his way to *Therma*; and advancing with his Army by the midland Countries, march'd thro' the Territories of the *Pæonians* and *Crestonians*, above the River *Chidorus*; which beginning among the *Crestonians*, passes thro' *Mygdonia*, and falls into a Lake, near the River *Axius*. In this March the Camels that carried
Provisions

Provisions for the Army, were affaulted by Lions; which coming down in the Night from their Haunts, fell upon those Animals only; leaving the Men, and all other Cattle untouch'd; A thing in my Opinion not a little strange: that the Lions should abstain from all the rest, and attack the Camels alone, which were never seen in that Country before. But Lions are very numerous in those Parts; and wild Bulls with large Horns frequently brought into *Greece.* Nevertheless these Lions never pass beyond the River *Neslus* of *Abdera* on one side; nor beyond the Arcarnanian *Achelous* on the other: And no Man ever saw a Lion in *Europe,* Eastward of the River *Neslus*; nor in any Part of the Continent, that lies to the Westward of the *Achelous:* But they breed between these two Rivers. Being arriv'd at *Therma, Xerxes* disposed his Army into a Camp, extended along the maritim Parts, from the Cites of *Therma,* and from *Mygdonia,* to the Rivers *Lydius* and *Haliacmon*; which joining their Streams together, pass between the Territories of *Bottiæis* and *Macedonia.* Here the Barbarians incamp'd; after they had exhausted the Waters of the *Chidorus*; which was the only River they found in this March, that afforded not a sufficient Quantity for the Use of the Army. From *Therma, Xerxes* had a Prospect of the Thessalian Mountains, *Olympus* and *Ossa,* remarkable for their Height and Bigness; and being inform'd that the River *Peneus* runs into the Sea thro' a narrow a Passage, lying between the Ridges of those Hills, and accommodated with a Way leading to the Plains of *Thessaly,* he much desir'd to see the Mouth

O 4

of

of that River; becaufe he defign'd to march
with his Army by the upper Parts of *Macedonia*, and by the City of *Gennus* into the Country of the Peræbians; which he underftood to
be the fafeft Way. Accordingly, leaving his
Forces in their Camp, he went on board a Sidonian Ship, which he always us'd upon fuch Oc-
cafions, and made a Signal for all the reft of the
Fleet to follow. When he arriv'd at the Mouth
of the River *Peneus*, he view'd the Place ; and
being furpriz'd with the Situation, ask'd his
Guides, if any Means could de contriv'd to
divert the Courfe of the Sream, and to carry it
by another Channel into the Sea. *Theffaly* is
reported to have been antiently a Lake, and is
encompaſs'd by vaft Mountains on all fides. For
Pelion and *Offa* joining together at the Foot of
each fhut up that Part which faces the Eaft :
On the North fide ftands Mount *Olympus* ;
Pindus on the Weft ; and *Othrys* clofes that fide
which lies to the Southward. *Theffaly*, is fituate
in the Midft of thefe Mountains, and water'd
by divers Rivers ; of which the principal are,
the *Peneus*, the *Apidanus*, the *Onochonus*, the
Enipeus, and the *Pamifus*. All thefe Rivers defcending fron the Mountains that encompaſs
Theffaly, enter into the Plain ; and joining
their Streams together, paſs thro' the Chops of
a narrow Channel into the Sea ; retaining no
other Name than that of *Peneus*, after their
Conjunction. They fay alfo, that, before this
Channel was laid open, neither thefe Rivers,
nor the Lake *Bœbeis* were known by the Names
they now bear, tho' the Waters then fell down
from the Mountains in the fame Quantity as
at this Day ; but that all *Theffaly* was one entire

tire Lake. The Theffalians tell us, that the Channel, by which the River *Peneus* paffes into the Sea, is the Work of *Neptune*; and perhaps not improperly. For thofe who think that God to be the Author of Earthquakes, and fuch Divulfions of Countries to be the Effect of his Power, will not fail, upon Sight, to attribute this to *Neptune*. And in my Opinion, the Separation of thefe Mountains was effected by an Earthquake. But the Guides of *Xerxes*, in anfwer to his Queftion, whether the River *Peneus* might be convey'd into the Sea by another Channel, faid with Reafon; " O " King, this River has no other way to dif- " charge its Waters, except this alone; be- " caufe all *Theffaly* is furrounded with Hills." " If fo, replied *Xerxes*, the Theffalians have " fhewn themfelves wife Men, in making early " Provifion for their own Safety; becaufe they " knew their Country might be eafily fubdued " in a fhort time. For nothing more is requir'd " to effect this, than to ftop the Mouth of " the River by a Dike; which would cer- " tainly lay all *Theffaly* under Water, except the " Mountains only." *Xerxes* exprefs'd himfelf in this manner, out of a particular Regard to the Aleuadians; who being Theffalians, had put themfelves under his Protection, before any other People of *Greece*: And he hop'd they would not be wanting to perfuade the reft to imitate their Example. Having thus fpoken, and fatisfied his Curiofity, he return'd by Sea to *Therma*, and pafs'd feveral Days about *Pieria*, while one third part of his Forces was employ'd in preparing a Way for all his Army to pafs over a Mountain of *Ma-*

cedonia

cedonia into the Territories of the Peræbians.

IN the mean time the Heralds, who had been sent to *Greece*, return'd to *Xerxes*; some with Earth and Water, and others without. The Nations that presented those Elements, in Compliance with his Demands, were, the Thessalians, the Dolopians, the Enienians, the Peræbians, the Locrians, the Magnetians, the Melians, the Achaians, the Pthiotians, and the Thebans, with all the rest of the Bœotians, except the Thespians and the Platæans. But those Grecians, who resolv'd to defend themselves against the Barbarians by War, took a solemn Oath, " That so soon as " the Affairs of *Greece* should be restor'd to a " good Condition, they would compel every " Grecian Community, which should be con- " victed of having put themselves into the " Hands of the Persians without manifest Ne- " cessity, to the pay the tenth Part of all their " Possessions to the Delphian God."

XERXES sent no Heralds either to *Athens* or *Sparta* to demand Earth and Water ; because they had formerly so ill receiv'd those who had been employ'd thither on the same Message by *Darius* ; having thrown some into Wells and others into deep Pits, bidding them carry Earth and Water to the King from those Places. For that Reason no Heralds were dispatch'd to either of these Nations. What Disaster fell upon the Athenians, in consequence of the Severity they us'd to those Messengers, I cannot affirm. Their City indeed and all their Territories suffer'd great Damage ; but not, as I believe, on that account. As for the Lacedemonians,

nians, they felt the cruel Effects of the Anger of
Talthybius, who had been Herald to *Agamemnon.*
He has a Temple in *Sparta*; and his Posterity,
who go by the Name of Talthybiads, have the
Honour of performing all their Embassies. But
after the bad Reception they gave to the Heralds of *Darius,* they could not sacrifice happily for a long time; and being much disturb'd at
this Calamity, they met together often, and by
publick Proclamation, made Inquiry, " If any
" Lacedemonian would die for *Sparta.*" Upon which Notification, *Sperthies* the Son of *Ane-*
riſtus, and *Bulis* the Son of *Nicolaus,* both Spartans, of eminent Dignity and Interest, voluntarily offer'd their Lives, to make Satisfaction
to *Xerxes* the Son of *Darius,* for the Death of
his Heralds. And accordingly, the Lacedemonians sent these Persons to the Medes, as to certain Death. But as their Courage deserv'd Admiration, so their Words were no less memorable. For when, in their Way to *Suſa,* they
came to *Hydarnes,* the Persian General of the
maritim Parts of *Aſia,* he receiv'd and treated
them with great Magnificence; and among o-
ther Discourse ask'd them this Question; " Men
" of *Lacedæmon,* Why have you such an Aver-
" sion for the King's Friendship? You may see
" by my Example, and the Dignities I pos-
" sess, how well the King understands the Va-
" lue of a brave Man. He has already a high
" Opinion of your Courage; and if you will
" comply with his Desires, he will certainly
" confer the Government of some Part of
" *Greece* upon every one of your Nation." They
answer'd; " *Hydarnes,* you are not a proper
" Person to give us Counsel in this Affair: For
" you

" you determine concerning two things not
" equally underſtood by you. How to be a
" Servant, you know perfectly well ; but you
" have neither tried whether Liberty be valu-
" able, or not. If you had ever experienc'd
" the Worth of Liberty, you would counſel
" us to defend it, not only with Lances, but
" even with Hatchets."

WHEN they arriv'd at *Suſa*, and appear'd before the King, his Guards firſt commanded, and then went about to conſtrain them
by force to proſtrate themſelves, and to adore
him. But they ſaid, they would not comply
with that Uſage, whatever Violence they
might ſuffer : That they had never been accuſtom'd to adore a Man, and came not thither
to that end. Having thus defended themſelves
from this Impoſition, they ſpoke to *Xerxes* in
theſe Words : " King of the Medes, we are
" ſent by the Lacedemonians, to make you
" Satisfaction for the Death of thoſe Heralds
" who were kill'd in *Sparta.*" *Xerxes* having
heard their Meſſage, generouſly anſwered ,
" That he would not be like the Lacedemo-
" nians, who had violated the Rights of Man-
" kind by the Murder of his Heralds ; nor do
" the ſame thing which he blam'd in them ; and
" by the Death of two Men acquit the Spar-
" tans from the Guilt they had contracted."
However, after the Lacedemonians had offer'd
this Satisfaction, the Anger of *Talthybius* ceas'd
for that time, tho' *Sperthies* and *Bulis* return'd
ſafe to *Sparta*. But after many Years, and
during the War between the Peloponeſians and
the Athenians, the Lacedemonians ſay, that
the Wrath of *Talthybius* broke out again, in a
manner

manner which to me appears wonderful. For tho' the Suspension of his Displeasure, when the two Spartans were sent away to *Xerxes* by way of Reparation, was no more than might be justly expected; yet that his Vengeance should overtake the Sons of those very Men, who had been devoted to that End, persuades me to think they were punish'd by a divine Power. For *Nicolaus* the Son of *Bulis*, and *Aneristus* the Son of *Sperthies*, (who had before taken and pillag'd some Tyrinthian Fishermen,) being sent on a Message to *Asia* by the Lacedemonians, were betray'd in their Passage by *Sitalces*, the Son of *Tyreus*, King of *Thrace*; and falling into the Hands of *Nymphodorus* the Son of *Pytheus* of *Abdera*, were carried Prisoners to *Athens*, and put to death by the Athenians, with *Aristeas* the Son of *Adimantus*, a Corinthian. But these things happen'd many Years after the Expedition of *Xerxes*.

TO return now to my Narration: This War was colour'd over with the Pretence of attacking *Athens*; but was really design'd against all *Greece*. Yet the Grecians, who had long heard of the Preparations made by *Xerxes* were not all affected in the same manner. For those who had presented him with Earth and Water, flatter'd themselves, that they should not suffer any kind of Damage from the Barbarians; but those who had refus'd to pay that Acknowledgment, were under terrible Apprehensions; because all *Greece*, was not able to furnish a sufficient Number of Ships to fight the Enemy; and many inclining to favour the *Medes*, were not willing to engage in the war. On this Occasion, I must declare my Opinion, with a Plainness which

perhaps

perhaps may be difpleafing to the greater Number ; and yet I cannot perfuade myfelf to conceal what I think to be true. If the Athenians, terrified with the impending Danger, had abandon'd their Country ; or continuing at Home, had furrender'd to *Xerxes*, no other People would have ventur'd to refift his Fleet. And if he had found no Oppofition by Sea, he would foon have been Mafter of the Land. For tho' the Peloponefians had fortified the Wall of the Ifthmus with many Works ; yet the Lacedemonians, after they had feen their Allies difpoffefs'd of their Cities by the Enemy's Fleet, and conftrain'd by Neceffity to abandon the Confederacy, would inevitably have been left alone to fuftain the Weight of the War : And being thus deferted, they muft have chofen, either to die with immortal Glory in the Field ; or to make their Peace with *Xerxes*, after all the Grecians had taken part with him. In both Cafes *Greece* muft have been reduc'd under the Perfian Power : For I cannot yet learn, of what Advantage the Wall upon the Ifthmus would have prov'd, if the King had been Mafter of the Sea. To fay, therefore, that the Athenians were the Deliverers of *Greece*, is no Deviation from the Truth. They could have caft the Balance, which fide foever they had taken. But having refolv'd to defend the Liberty of *Greece*, they awaken'd the Courage of all thofe Grecians, who had not been corrupted by the Medes ; and with the Affiftance of the Gods, repuls'd the King. They would not be perfuaded to abandon *Greece*, by the terrible Menaces of the Delphian Oracle ; but perfifting in their Refolution, determin'd to fuftain
all

all the Efforts of the Invader. For when the Deputies of the Athenians went to confult the Oracle on their Part, and had perform'd the ufual Ceremonies, they fat down in the Sanctuary and receiv'd this Anfwer from the Pythian, whofe Name was *Ariftonica.*

> *FLY to the fartheft Regions of the Earth,*
> *Unhappy Men, and fhun the impending Ill.*
> *Fly from your Houfes, and defert your Walls;*
> *For total Ruin fhall fubvert that Place.*
> *An angry* Mars, *in* Afia *born, fhall come,*
> *And all your ftately Piles, and Temples burn.*
> *I fee the facred Walls trembling for Fear,*
> *The lofty Roofs cover'd with Sweat and Blood.*
> *Depart; and be prepar'd to bear your Fate.*

Thefe menacing Words put the Athenians, who came to confult the Oracle, into a great Confternation: And while they were difcourfing together concerning this difmal Anfwer, *Timon* the Son of *Androbulus,* a Man of principal Authority in *Delphi,* counfel'd them to return and confult the Oracle again in the humbleft manner, with Olive-Branches in their Hands. The Athenians were eafily perfuaded to follow his Advice; and returning accordingly, addrefs'd the God in thefe Words " O King, vouchfafe to give us an Anfwer " more favourable to our Country; and fhew " fome Regard to thefe Branches, which we " hold in our Hands: Otherwife we will ne- " ver depart from this Place, but will remain " here till we die." After which Prayer the Prieftefs gave a fecond Anfwer in thefe Terms

PALLAS

PALLAS *in vain has us'd her utmost Art,*
To pacify the Wrath of angry Jove.
So that my present Answer must again,
Of almost Adamantin Hardness be.
Yet for Minerva's *sake the God will give*
A safe Protection under Walls of Wood,
To all that lies contain'd within the Bounds
Of Cecrops, *or* Citheron's *sacred Hills.*
These, these alone impregnable shall prove.
But never stay to fight the dreadful Troops
Of Horse and Foot, advancing thro' the Plains:
If e'er you see them, save yourselves by Flight.
The divine Salamis *shall lose her Sons ;*
Tho' Ceres *be brought Home, or left Abroad.*

The Athenians rightly judging this Answer to
be more moderate than the former, wrote down
the Words, and departed for *Athens:* Where
when they were arriv'd, and had acquainted
the People with all that had pass'd, many different Opinions arose about the Meaning of the
Oracle: But I shall mention only such as obtain'd the greatest Credit. Some of the old
Men thought the God had declar'd, that the
Acropolis should remain safe ; because that
Fortress had been formerly encompass'd with
a Circumvallation ; which they suppos'd to
be meant by the wooden Wall. Others said,
that nothing but Ships could possibly be understood by that Expression ; and therefore advis'd, that omitting all other Designs, they
would apply themselves to prepare a Fleet:
Nevertheless this Opinion seem'd to be overthrown by the two last Verses pronounc'd by
the Pythian.

The Divine Salamis *shall lose her Sons,*
Tho' Ceres be brought home, or left abroad.

These Lines, I say, confounded the Sentiment of those, who said, that Ships only could be meant by Walls of Wood: And the Interpreters of Oracles declared themselves of opinion, that their Fleet should be defeated in a Sea-fight, upon the Coast of *Salamis.*

THERE had lately appear'd among the most eminent Athenians, a certain Person, whose Name was *Themistocles*; but commonly call'd the Son of *Neocles.* He maintain'd, that the Interpreters had not rightly understood the Sense of the Oracle; because, if the Prediction had contain'd such a Meaning, the God would certainly have used a harder Expression; and in his Answer have inserted, the *Unhappy Salamis*, instead of the *Divine Salamis*, had the Inhabitants of that Place been destin'd to Destruction: And therefore, that all those, who would judge rightly, ought to conclude, that the Oracle was not intended against the Athenians, but against their Enemies. For this reason he advis'd them to prepare their Naval Forces; which he said, were really *the Walls of Wood.* The Athenians, convinced by these Reasons, preferred the Opinion of *Themistocles* before that of the Interpreters, who dissuaded them from making any Preparations for the Sea, and exhorted them not to resist the Enemy at all; but to abandon *Attica*, and depart to another Country. In this Conjuncture, the Counsel which *Themistocles* had formerly given, prov'd highly advantageous: For when

the Athenians, finding their Treasury enrich'd by the Profits they receiv'd from the
Mines of *Laureus*, had resolv'd to make a
Dividend of ten Drachmas to every Citizen,
not under Age, they were diverted from that
Resolution by the Remonstrances of *Themistocles*, and persuaded to lay out the Money
in building two hundred Ships, to be employ'd against the Æginetes. One may justly
say, that War sav'd *Greece*, by necessitating the
Athenians to apply themselves to maritime Affairs. And though the Ships I mention'd
were not used at that time, yet now they were
of singular advantage : For they were ready to
put to sea on this Occasion, and only needed a
farther Reinforcement. Which having well considered, the Athenians, by common consent, and
in obedience to the Oracle, resolv'd, That all
who were able to bear Arms, should go on
board their Ships, and, with such of the Grecians as would join them, wait the Approach of
the Enemy. In pursuance of this Resolution,
those Grecians, who had the Safety of *Greece* at
heart, met together ; and entering into mutual Engagements of Fidelity to one another, agreed,
before all other things, to forget all former En-
mities and Differences ; for even among these
divers Wars were then actually on Foot, though
none so considerable as that of the Athenians
against the Æginetes. After this Consultation,
being inform'd of the King's Arrival at *Sardis*
with his Army, they determin'd to send some
Persons into *Asia*, in order to discover the true
State of his Affairs ; and to dispatch others to
Argos, to engage the Argians in an Alliance
against the Persians. They also resolv'd to send
an

an Embassy to *Gelon* the Son of *Dinomenes*, the Sicilian; because they had heard, that his Power was great, and his Forces little inferiour to any of the Grecians. With the same Intention, they agreed to send Messengers to the Corcyræans and Cretans, that, as far as might be, the whole Body of the Grecians might be united, and unanimously concur in the defence of the common Cause. Having taken these Resolutions, and promised to lay down their mutual Animosities, they sent three Men for Spies into *Asia*; who arriving at *Sardis*, and endeavouring to get intelligence of the King's Forces, were seiz'd by the Generals of his Army; and, after they had suffer'd the Torture, condemn'd to die. But when *Xerxes* heard of this Proceeding, he disapproved the Action, and immediatly sent some of his Guards with Orders to bring them to him, if they were not already put to death. The Guards obey'd; and finding the Men yet living, brought them before the King: where, after they had acquainted him with the Cause of their coming, he commanded the same Persons to shew them all his Forces, both of Horse and Foot, and afterwards to permit them to go away quietly to whatever Country they should chuse. This he did from an Opinion, that if the Spies were put to death, the Grecians would neither be inform'd, that his Preparations were yet greater than Fame had published, nor suffer any considerable Damage by the Loss of three Men: whereas, if they were allow'd to return to *Greece*, he doubted not that the Grecians, hearing of his numerous Forces, would surrender themselves and their Liberty to his Mercy, before he

should

ſhould invade their Country; and by that means, ſave him the trouble of Compulſion. This Opinion of *Xerxes* was not unlike another Thought he had at *Abydus*; where he ſaw certain Ships laden with Corn, coming from the *Euxine* Sea, and ſailing through the *Helleſpont* to *Ægina*, and to *Peloponneſus.* For when thoſe about him were inform'd that the Veſſels belong'd to the Enemy, and fix'd their Eyes upon the King, in expectation to receive his Orders for ſeizing them, *Xerxes* ask'd to what part they were bound; and underſtanding they had Corn on board for his Enemies, he ſaid, "Are not "we alſo going to the ſame Place, where theſe "Men are bound? And are we not oblig'd, a- "mong other things, to carry Corn with us? "What hurt then can they do us, by carrying "Corn thither, which muſt be ours?

WHEN the Spies had ſeen all the King's Forces, they were diſmiſſed: And after their Return to *Europe,* the Grecians, who had engag'd in a Confederacy againſt the Perſian, ſent a ſecond Embaſſy to *Argos*; of which the Argians gave the following account: That having receiv'd early notice of the Barbarians Deſign againſt *Greece,* and not doubting that the Grecians would ask their Aſſiſtance among the reſt, tho' they had lately loſt ſix thouſand Men, kill'd by the Lacedemonians, under the Conduct of *Cleomenes* the Son of *Anaxandrides,* they ſent to inquire of the Oracle of *Delphi,* what meaſures they ſhould take in this Conjuncture; and that the Anſwer they had from the Pythian, was in theſe Terms:

By

By Neighbours hated, by the Gods belov'd,
Reſt quiet, and from all Engagements free:
Preſerve the Head, for that ſhall ſave the reſt.

That after they had receiv'd this Anſwer, the
Ambaſſadors arriving at *Argos*, were introduc'd into the Senate; and when they had
delivered their Meſſage, the Argians anſwer'd, That they were ready to comply on
their part, and to that end would be willing
to make a Truce with the Lacedemonians for
thirty Years, provided they might have an e-
qual ſhare with them in the command, though
they might juſtly pretend to the whole. This,
they ſay, was the Anſwer of their Senate,
notwithſtanding the Pythian had forbidden
them to enter into any Confederacy with the
Grecians: And therefore they took care to
inſiſt upon a truce of thirty Years, out of a
juſt Apprehenſion of the conſequences of the
Oracle; that their Children might become
Men, before the Expiration of that time, and,
if they ſhould receive another Blow in the
Perſian War, be able to preſerve their Country from falling into the hands of the Lacedemonians. To theſe Propoſitions of the Senate, the Spartans anſwer'd, That the Queſtion
about a Truce ſhould be referr'd to the People:
but as to the leading of the Forces, they were
inſtructed to put them in mind, that they had
two Kings; whereas the Argians had only one;
and that they could not conſent to deprive
either of their Kings of his Power; yet would
not hinder the Argian King from having a Voice
in all Deliberations. Upon which, the Argians

ſaid,

said, They could no longer bear the Arrogance of the Spartans, but would rather chuſe to be ſubject to the Barbarians, than to yield the Superiority to them ; adding that the Ambaſſadors ſhould depart out of the Territories of *Argos* before the ſetting of the Sun, under the Penalty of being treated as Enemies. Thus the Argians relate the Succeſs of this Embaſſy : but a quite different Report is current in other Parts of *Greece;* For they ſay, That before *Xerxes* began to advance with his Army againſt the Grecians, he ſent a Herald to *Argos* with a Meſſage conceiv'd in theſe Terms : " Men of *Argos,* we are well in-
" form'd, that *Perſes,* one of our Progenitors,
" was Son to *Perſeus* the Son of *Danaæ,* by *An-*
" *dromeda,* the Daughter of *Cepheus* ; and there-
" fore as we derive our Original from you,
" we ought not to lead an Army againſt the
" Country of our Fathers : nor ſhould you ap-
" pear in Arms againſt us, to gratify other Men ;
" but rather chuſing to enjoy the Benefit of
" Peace, continue quiet in your own Habita-
" tions : Which if you do, and I ſucceed ac-
" cording to my Expectation, no People ſhall
" have a greater part in my Eſteem, than you."
The Argians not a little pleas'd with this Meſ-
ſage, kept the thing private, and ſaid nothing of the Competition at that time : But when the Grecians would have taken them into the Confederacy, they demanded an equal ſhare of the Supreme Command, which they knew the Lacedemonians would never grant; that they might have a Pretext for refuſing to enter into the War, Which Conduct of the Argians, is not unlike what happened many Years after, if we may

beieve

believe some of the Grecians: For while *Callias* the Son of *Hipponicus*, with other Ambassadors of the Athenians, were treating certain Affairs at *Susa*, the Argians sent an Embassy likewise to the same Place, with Orders to demand of *Artaxerxes*, the Son of *Xerxes*, whether he would observe the Alliance they had with his Father; or whether he accounted them his Enemies. *Artaxerxes* answer'd, That he understood their antient Alliance to be still in force, and that he had no better Friends than the Argians. But I cannot affirm with certainty, either that *Xerxes* sent such a Message to *Argos*, or that the Ambassadors of the Argians went to *Susa* to continue their Alliance with *Artaxerxes*: And am inclin'd rather to believe the Report of the Argians themselves. Only this I know, That if all Men were to bring together their domestic Disgraces into one place, in order to make an Exchange with their Neighbours, they would no sooner have inspected those of others, than they would be most willing to return home with their own. And therefore I cannot think that the Argians behav'd themselves so ill, as some are ready to imagine. However, I am oblig'd to relate what is said, though I am not oblig'd to believe every thing without Distinction; which I desire may be consider'd in all the Course of this History: For the Argians are likewise charg'd with having invited the Persian into *Greece*, thinking any Change more tolerable than the miserable Condition, to which they had been reduc'd, by their ill Success in the War against the Lacedemonians.

IN

I N the mean time, the Ambassadors of the associated Grecians arriv'd in *Sicily*, to confer with *Gelon*; and among them, *Syagrus* on the part of the Lacedemonians. *Oecetor*, one of *Gelon*'s Ancestors, born in the Island *Telus*, which lies over against *Triopium*, left his Country, and came to inhabit in *Gela*. But when *Antiophemes* and the Lyndians of *Rhodes*, possessed themselves of that City, they would not permit him to continue among them: Yet, in succeeding time, his Posterity became Priests of the infernal Gods; which Dignity was first acquired by *Telines*, one of his Descendants. For when some of the Inhabitants of *Gela* were expelled in a Sedition, and had retir'd to the City of *Mactorius*, above *Gela*, *Telines* conducted them back again by the Power of his Function, without any human Assistance; though, where he had these sacred things, or whether he really had them or not, is altogether unknown to me. However, in confidence of his Authority, he brought them home to *Gela*, on condition, that the Priesthood of the infernal Gods should continue in his Descendants. Nevertheless, I admire among other things, how *Telines* could succeed in so great an Enterprize; since such Attempts being above the reach of ordinary Men, seem only reserv'd for sagacious and daring Spirits: Whereas on the contrary, the Inhabitants of *Sicily* say, he was an effeminate Person, without any Virtue or Courage; and yet attain'd to this Dignity by these means. Upon the Death of *Cleander* the Patarean, who was kill'd by *Sabyllus* of *Gela*, after he had reign'd seven Years, his Brother *Hippocrates* took upon him the Government of *Gela*; During whose Reign, this *Gelon*,

who

who was defcended from *Telines* the Prieft, became famous; together with many others, efpecially *Ænefidemus*, the Son of *Pataicus*, one of the Guards of *Hippocrates*, and afterwards made General of the Horfe, on account of his Valour: For in all the Wars made by *Hippocrates* againft the Callipolitans, the Naxians, the Zanclæans, the Leontins, and the Syracufians, befides divers Barbarian Nations, *Gelon* fignaliz'd himfelf by the Glory of his Actions; and was fo fuccefsful, that all thofe People, except the Syracufians, fell into the power of *Hippocrates*. But the Corinthians and Corcyræans fav'd the Syracufians, after they had been defeated upon the River *Florus*; yet with this Condition, That they fhould furrender *Camarina* to *Hippocrates*, which they had always poffeffed to that time. When *Hippocrates* had reigned as many Years as his Brother *Cleander*, he died at the Siege of *Hybla*, carrying on the War againft the Sicilians. Upon which, *Gelon*, under colour of defending the Rights of *Euclides* and *Cleander*, the Sons of *Hippocrates*, againft their Subjects, who would no longer obey, defeated the Geleans; and having excluded the young Men, poffeffed himfelf of the Tyranny. After this Succefs, undertaking to reftore fome Syracufians, who were call'd Gamorians, and had been expell'd by the Populace, and by their own Servants, call'd Cyllirians; he conducted them from *Cafmene* to *Syracufe*, where the Populace, upon his Arrival, put him into poffeffion of that City. When he faw himfelf Mafter of *Syracufe*, he had little regard to *Gela*, and therefore gave that Government to his Brother *Hiero*, retaining *Syracufe* for himfelf, which

which he esteem'd more than all other Places.
By this means that City in a short time attain-
ed to a high degree of Power and Prosperity ;
for he destroyed *Camarina*, and transferring
the Inhabitants to *Syracuse*, gave them the Privilege of Citizens ; as he did likewise to more
than one half of the Geleans. He besieg'd
the Megareans, who had settled in *Sicily*, and
having oblig'd them to surrender their City,
he contented himself to remove the most wealthy of the Inhabitants to *Syracuse*, and conferr'd the same Privileges on them also, though
they expected nothing less than Death, because they had been the Authors of the War
against him. But he dealt otherwise with
the Megarean Plebeians ; and albeit they had
no part in promoting the War against him,
nor expected to suffer any Detriment on that
account, he sold them in *Syracuse* ; with express Condition, that they should be transf-
ported out of *Sicily*. He treated the Euboeans of that Island in the same manner, and
made the same Distinction among the Inhabitants of both Places, out of an opinion, that
a Populace is not easily govern'd. And by
these means the Power of *Gelon* was grown formidable.

WHEN therefore the Ambassadors of the
Grecians were arriv'd in *Syracuse*, and introduc'd
into the Presence of *Gelon*, they deliver'd their
Message in these Terms : " The Lacedemonians
" and their Allies have sent us hither, to desire
" you to enter into their Confederacy against a
" Barbarian King : For doubtless you have heard
" that a Persian is come to invade *Greece:* that
" he has laid a Bridge over the *Hellespont*, and

1   " brings

" brings with him all the Eastern Nations of
" *Asia,* under colour indeed of making war
" against the Athenians, but really designing
" to subdue all the Grecians. You therefore,
" who have so great power, and possess so
" considerable a part of *Greece,* by being the
" principal Potentate of *Sicily,* assist those, who
" would preserve *Greece* from Servitude, and
" concur with them in maintaining the com-
" mon Liberty. If the Grecians will be una-
" nimous on this Occasion, we shall make up
" a formidable Force, sufficient to resist the
" Invader: But if some of us should betray
" the publick Cause, and others refuse to give
" their assistance, the sound and honest part of
" *Greece* must of necessity be reduc'd to so
" small a number, that the Whole would be
" in danger of utter Ruin. Flatter not your-
" self, as if the Persian will spare you, after
" he shall have conquer'd us; think rather by
" proper means how to prevent the Mischief,
" and to preserve your own, by assisting us:
" For Enterprizes founded upon prudent
" Counsels, are generally attended with pros-
" perous Success." After the Ambassadors
had thus spoken, *Gelon,* with some Emotion,
roughly answered: " Men of *Greece,* your
" Presumption is greater than ordinary, to
" desire me to take part with you, against
" the Barbarian, because you denied me your
" assistance in former Occasions. When I im-
" plored your Succour against the Barbarian
" Army of the Carthaginians, and requested
" you to avenge the Death of *Dorieus,* the Son
" of *Anaxandrides,* upon the Ægestans, you re-
" fus'd both; and would neither help me in
" my

" my Neceffity, nor revenge the Death of
" *Dorieus*, though at the fame time I offered
" you my Affiftance to reftore the Liberty of
" thofe Ports, to which you trade with great
" advantage. So that I am no way oblig'd
" to you, if all I poffefs be not now in the
" power of Barbarians. But becaufe my Af-
" fairs have fucceeded better, and the War
" is at laft brought home to your own Coun-
" try, you will now condefcend to remember
" *Gelon.* Neverthelefs, though you treated
" me with Contempt, I fhall not imitate your
" Example: On the contrary, I am ready to
" fupply you with two hundred Gallies, twen-
" ty-thoufand Men compleatly armed, two
" thoufand Horfe, two thoufand Bow-men,
" two thoufand Slingers, and two thoufand
" Light-horfe. I will likewife undertake to
" furnifh the whole Grecian Army with Corn
" during all the time of the War. But I can-
" not engage to perform thefe things, unlefs
" I may be General of the Grecians : Neither
" will I appear in the Field, nor fend any
" Succour to *Greece*, except only on that Con-
" dition." *Syagrus* hearing thefe Words with
impatience, cry'd out ; " How would *Aga-*
" *memnon*, the Son of *Pelops*, grieve, to hear that
" the Spartans had yielded the Supreme Com-
" mand to *Gelon*, and to the Syracufians? For-
" bear to mention this Propofition again ; and if
" you are willing to fuccour *Greece*, refolve to
" march under the Conduct of the Lacedemo-
" nians ; or, if you difdain to obey their Orders,
" we will not accept your Affiftance." *Gelon*
finding *Syagrus* averfe to his Defign, made another Propofition in thefe Terms ; " Spartan
" Friend,

" Friend, *said he*, though injurious Language
" has a natural Tendency to raise the Indig-
" nation of Men, yet I shall not retaliate that
" which I have receiv'd from you, in the same
" kind. Nevertheless, since you so passionately
" affect the Supreme Command, I cannot for-
" bear to tell you, that I might with more
" Justice pretend to that Honour, because I
" have a far greater number than you, both
" of Ships and Land-Forces. However, see-
" ing you are so averse to the Proposition I
" made, I shall abate something of my first
" Pretensions. If then you chuse to command
" the Army by Land, I will have the Conduct
" of the Fleet : or, if you had rather command
" at Sea, I will be General of the Land-For-
" ces. One of these Conditions you must be
" contented to accept, or resolve to return
" home without obtaining any Assistance from
" me." When *Gelon* had made this Offer,
the Ambassador of the Athenians, preventing
the Lacedemonian, reply'd in these Words ;
" King of *Syracuse*, the Grecians have sent
" us to you, not to desire a General, but an
" Army. On the other hand, you tell us, you
" will send none of your Forces, unless you
" may be General of *Greece* ; which you seem
" to affect extremely. We said nothing to
" the Demand you made, of commanding all
" the Forces of *Greece*, because we resolv'd to
" content ourselves with the Answer of the
" Spartan Ambassador, which we knew would
" in that Particular be sufficient for us both.
" But because, since your Exclusion from the
" whole Command you have thought fit to
" require the Generalship of the Sea, we must
" inform

" inform you, that though the Lacedemonians
" should be willing to comply with your De-
" mand, the Athenians will never consent to
" give you such a Power: For the Honour of
" that Command belongs to us, unless the
" Lacedemonians themselves will take it. If
" they have that intention, we shall not oppose
" their Design, but we will never yield the
" Preeminence to any other. In vain should
" we possess the greatest Naval Forces of all
" the Grecians, if we should suffer ourselves
" to be commanded by the Syracusians: we,
" who are Athenians, the most antient People
" of *Greece*, and the only Nation of those Parts
" which has never been compell'd to abandon
" their Country; we, I say, who are of a
" City, which, according to the Testimony of
" *Homer*, the Epick Poet, sent to the Siege of
" *Troy*, the most experienced Men of all others
" in the Art of disposing and drawing up an
" Army to the best advantage. And there-
" fore, we think, we may justly take the great-
" er liberty to speak honourably of the A-
" thenians." To this Speech *Gelon* answered;
" Athenian Stranger, since you seem to abound
" as much in Men who would command, as
" destitute of those who should obey; and since
" you resolve to retain the whole Power in your
" hands without any Competition; depart out
" of my Territories, and carry this News to
" *Greece*, That their Year shall have no Spring."
Intimating by these Words, that his Army was
by so much more considerable than that of
the Grecians, as the Spring is more delicious
than any other Season; and that *Greece*, depriv'd of his Assistance, would be reduc'd to
the

the Condition of a Year which should have no Spring. With this Answer the Ambassadors return'd home from *Sicily*.

IN the mean time, *Gelon*, apprehending that the Grecians would not be able to resist the Barbarian, and yet determining not to go to *Peloponnesus*, because he must there have obey'd the Spartans, which he accounted an intolerable Condition to be impos'd upon a Sicilian Tyrant, took another Resolution: For he was no sooner inform'd that the Persian had passed the *Hellespont*, than he dispatch'd *Cadmus*, the Son of *Scythes*, a Coan, to *Delphi*, with a friendly Message, and three Ships laden with great Riches, enjoining him to wait the Event of a Battle; and if the Barbarian should conquer, to make him a Present of that Treasure, with Earth and Water for all the Places in his possession: but if the Grecians should be victorious, to bring back the Money to *Sicily*. This *Cadmus* had been formerly possess'd of the Dominion of *Coos*, which he receiv'd from his Father: And though his Power was firmly establish'd, and his Affairs in a prosperous Condition, his Love to Justice was so great, that he freely surrendred the Government into the hands of the Coans, and retired into *Sicily*; where he liv'd with the Samians, in the City of *Zanole*, afterwards known by the Name of *Messana*. *Gelon*, who was not unacquainted with these things, nor ignorant of many other Proofs of his Integrity, sent him to *Delphi* on this Occasion: in which he gave no less Testimony of his Probity, than he had done by his preceding Actions. For albeit he might easily have converted the Treasure

with

with which *Gelon* had entrufted him, to his own Profit, he was fo far from taking the advantage, that fo foon as the Grecians had obtain'd the Victory by Sea, and *Xerxes* was retiring with his Forces, he carried back the Money to *Sicily*. But the Sicilians varying from fome Particulars of this Relation, fay, that *Gelon* having at laft prevail'd with himfelf to obey the Lacedemonians, would have affifted the Grecians in that Conjuncture, if at the fame time, *Terillus*, the Son of *Crinippus*, who was Tyrant of *Hymera*, and difpoffeffed of his Government by *Theron*, Son to *Ænefidemus*, and King of the Acragantins, had not brought in an Army of three hundred thoufand Men; confifting of Phœnicians, Libyans, Iberians, Ligyans, Elifycians, Sardinians, and Cyrnians, under the Conduct of *Amilcar*, the Son of *Hanno*, King of *Carthage*. To this Expedition, *Terillus* follicited the Carthaginians, partly on account of their mutual Amity, but principally at the Inftigation of *Anaxilaus*, the Son of *Critineus*, Tyrant of *Rhegium*; who put his Children for Hoftages into the hands of *Amilcar*, to oblige him to pafs into *Sicily*, in order to revenge the Injury done to his Father-in-law: For *Anaxilaus* had married *Cydippe*, the Daughter of *Terillus*. And thus *Gelon* being made uncapable of fuccouring the Grecians in any other manner, refolv'd to fend Money to *Delphi*. They add, that *Gelon* and *Theron* defeated *Amilcar*, the Carthaginian, in *Sicily*, on the fame day in which the Grecians obtain'd the Victory at *Salamis*, againft the Perfian. I am alfo inform'd, that *Amilcar*, who was a Carthaginian by his Father, and of *Syracufe* by his

his Mother, and chosen King of *Carthage* for his Virtue, was never seen, either living or dead, after the Battle in which his Army was defeated, though *Gelon* sought him in all Places with the utmost Care and Diligence. The Carthaginians, who have a great Veneration for his Image, say, That whilst the Barbarians were engag'd with the Grecians of *Sicily*, in that Battle, which began early in the Morning, and lasted to the Twilight of the Evening, *Amilcar* continuing in the Camp, sacrificed entire Victims upon a great Fire, and when he saw his Army flying, poured out a Libation which he held in his hand, threw himself into the Flames, and so disappear'd : But whether he disappear'd in the manner related by the Phœnicians, or as the Fact is reported by the Carthaginians, they not only honour him with Sacrifices, but have erected Monuments to his Memory, in all the Cities they have founded ; though the most memorable are in *Carthage*. These things I have thought fit to say concerning *Sicily*.

THE Corcyræans, in this Conjuncture, acted in a manner very different from the Professions they made : For when the Ambassadors of *Greece* arriv'd at *Corcyra*, and had acquainted the Corcyræans with the Cause of their coming, in such Terms as they had already used to *Gelon* in *Sicily*, they readily promis'd to send Succours ; and took upon them to say, " That " they would by no means neglect the Safety " of *Greece* in this time of imminent Danger, " but would exert their utmost Efforts in the " Defence of the common Cause ; well under- " standing, that if the Enemy prevail'd they

" should soon be reduc'd to the Condition of
" Slaves." This indeed was a specious Answer : but when they ought to have given real
Succours, they discover'd their bad Intentions :
and having after many Delays, fitted out sixty
Ships, they sail'd to the Coast of *Peloponnesus*:
where they anchor'd about *Pylus* and *Tænarus*,
which belongs to the Lacedemonians. In that
Station they waited to see the Event of the War,
not imagining that the Grecians were in any
possibility of prevailing; but that the Persian,
by the Superiority of his Numbers, must inevitably be Master of all *Greece*. By this artful
Conduct, they thought they might have some
colour to say afterwards to the King ; " Sir,
" when the Grecians sollicited us to take part
" in the War, we who have a considerable Force
" by Land, and more Ships than any other Peo-
" ple of *Greece*, except the Athenians, would
" not be persuaded to oppose you, nor to give
" you the least Cause of Discontent." By
which Protestation they hoped to obtain more
Favour than the rest : And if *Xerxes* had conquer'd, I am of opinion, they would not have
been disappointed of their Expectation. On
the other hand, they had prepar'd an Excuse to
the Grecians, which they afterwards alledg'd in
their defence. For when they were accus'd of
neglecting to succour *Greece*, they urg'd that
having arm'd and fitted out sixty Ships, they
were hindred by the Etesian Winds, from
passing the Cape of *Malea*, and consequently
onght not to lie under any Imputation of Ma-
lice, for not being present at the Battle of *Salamis*. In this manner they eluded the Accusation
exhibited against them by the Grecians.

WHEN

WHEN the Cretans were follicited by the fame Ambaſſadors, in purſuance of their Inſtructions, to join in the Defence of *Greece*, they diſpatched certain Perſons, by common Conſent, to enquire of the Oracle of *Delphi*, whether they ſhould beſt conſult their own Advantage, by giving or refuſing, the Aſſiſtance demanded. The Pythian anſwer'd; " Fools " impute to yourſelves all the Calamities which " angry *Minos* brought upon you, for aiding " *Menelaus*. They would not revenge the " Death of *Minos*, who was murdered at *Ca-* " *micus*, and yet you aſſiſted them, to revenge " the Rape of a Woman carried off from *Spar-* " *ta*, by a Barbarian." When the Cretans had receiv'd this Anſwer, they laid aſide the Thoughts of ſuccouring *Greece*. Touching the Fate of *Minos*, the Report is, That having purſued *Dædalus* into *Sicania*, which is now call'd *Sicily*, he there met with a violent Death; That after ſome time, by divine Admonition, all the People of *Crete*, except the Polichnitans and the Ptæſians, undertook an expedition to *Sicania* with a numerous Fleet, and during five Years, beſieg'd the City of *Camicus*, which is now in the poſſeſſion of the Acragantins: That finding themſelves unable to take the Place, or to continue the Siege, becauſe their Numbers were much diminiſhed by Famine, they reimbark'd their Men, and paſſing by the Coaſt of *Japygia*, were forced aſhore by a violent Storm; that ſeeing their Ships daſhed in pieces, and all Hope of returning to *Crete* cut off, they ſettled in that Place; and having built the City of *Hyria*, took the Name of Meſſapian Japygians; and of Iſlanders, became Inhabitants

Q 2

of

of the Continent. After this Eſtabliſhment, they built other Cities in the Neigbourhood of *Hyria*, which, in ſucceeding time, were ruined by the Tarentins, though not without a heavy Loſs on their part, and with the greateſt Slaughter on both ſides that we have ever heard of among the Grecians. For of the Rhegians only, who were conſtrain'd by *Micythus*, the Son of *Chœrus*, to aſſiſt the Tarentins, three thouſand Men died in that Expedition; but the Number of Tarentins, who periſhed on that Occaſion, was never known. This *Micythus* was a Favourite of *Anaxilaus*, and by him made Governour of *Rhegium*; but being diſpoſſeſſed of that Government, he retir'd to *Tegea*, a City of *Arcadia*, and afterwards dedicated a great number of Statues in *Oylmpia*. Theſe things concerning the Rhegians and Tarentins, I thought fit to inſert in this Place by way of Digreſſion. As for *Crete*, the Præſians ſay, that Men of other Nations, and eſpecially the Grecians, went and inhabited that deſolate Country: That *Minos* died about three Generations before the *Trojan* War; in which the Cretans were not the moſt backward to avenge the Injury done to *Menelaus*: That on this account they were afflicted at their Return with Famine and Peſtilence, which deſtroyed both Men and Cattle; and that *Crete* being thus diſpeopled again, was afterwards inhaited by the preſent Poſſeſſors, in conjunction with ſuch as ſurviv'd thoſe great Calamities. The Pythian therefore putting the Cretans in mind of theſe things, quite altered the Diſpoſition they had to aſſiſt the Grecians.

THE

THE Theſſalians were compelled by neceſſity to take part with the Medes; after they
had by their Conduct given ſufficient Evidence,
that they diſapprov'd the Treachery of the
Aleuadians. For they were no ſooner inform'd
that the Perſian was ready to paſs into *Europe*,
than they ſent Ambaſſadors to the Iſthmus;
where the Deputies of the Grecian Cities were
then aſſembled, to conſult about the moſt effectual means to preſerve *Greece:* and when
their Ambaſſadors were arrived, they went into the Aſſembly, and deliver'd their Meſſage in
theſe words: " Men of *Greece,* the Paſs of
" *Olympus* ought to be guarded with the utmoſt
" Care; to the end that not only *Theſſaly,* but
" that all *Greece* may be ſecur'd againſt the
" Efforts of the Enemy. For our own part,
" we are ready with all our Forces to concur
" in defending that important Poſt; but we
" expect at the ſame time, that you ſhould
" ſend a conſiderable Army to act in Conjunc-
" tion with us: and if you refuſe to comply
" with our Demand, be aſſur'd we will make
" our Peace with the Perſian, and not ſuffer our
" ſelves to be deſtroy'd ſingly, becauſe we
" happen to be plac'd on the Frontier of *Greece.*
" If you will not ſuccour us, you cannot con-
" ſtrain us to reſiſt him; for Neceſſity can ne-
" ver be urg'd againſt thoſe who are deſtitute
" of Power. In a word, we muſt endeavour
" to take ſuch meaſures, as may be moſt con-
" ducing to our own Safety."

UPON this Repreſentation of the Theſſalians, the Grecians reſolv'd to ſend an Army to
ſecure that Paſſage into *Theſſaly,* which is near
the Sea; and when they had aſſembled their

Q 3

Forces

Forces to that end, they failed thro' the *Eury-pus*; and landing at *Alus* a City of *Achaia*, they left their Ships, and marching into *Theffaly* by Land, arriv'd at *Tempe*, in the way that leads from the lower *Macedonia* to that Country, by the River *Peneus*, and between the Mountains of *Olympus* and *Offa*. There the Grecians encamped to the number of ten thousand Men well arm'd, and were join'd by the Theffalian Cavalry. The Lacedemonians were led by *Euænetus*, the Son of *Carenus*, chosen from among the Pole-marchs, tho' not of the Royal Blood ; and the Athenians marched under the Conduct of *The-miftocles*, the Son of *Neocles*. But they conti-nued not many days in that Poft, before Mef-fengers arriv'd from *Alexander* of *Macedonia*, the Son of *Amyntas*, and in his Name advis'd them to retire, unlefs they would be trampled under foot by the Forces of the Invader : which they reprefented in the moft formidable manner, both as to the Numbers of his Men and Ships. The Grecians imagining the Macedonian to be their Friend, and his Counfel fafe, determin'd to fol-low his Advice ; tho' I am of opinion, that their own Fear was the moft prevalent Motive to in-duce them to do as they did: For they had heard there was another Paffage leading to *Thef-faly*, thro' the Country of the Peræbians, in the *Upper Macedonia*, by the City of *Gonnus* ; and indeed the Army of *Xerxes* afterwards entred by that way. Thus the Grecians returning to their Ships, fail'd back again to the Ifthmus : And fuch was the Event of the Expedition they made into *Theffaly*, whilft the King ftaid at *Aby-dus*, preparing to pafs from *Afia* into *Europe* with his Army. After which, the Theffalians

finding

finding themfelves abandoned by their Allies, made no farther Scruple to take part with the Medes; and were fo ready to promote the King's Affairs, that they became highly ufeful to him.

THE Grecians being thus return'd to the Ifthmus by the Counfel of *Alexander*; and confulting together by what Means, and in what Places they fhould adventure to' make a Stand with their Forces, came to a fix'd Refolution, that they would defend the pafs of *Thermopyle*, as more narrow than that of *Theffaly*, and nearer to their own Territories. For they knew nothing of the other way, by which thofe Grecians, who undertook to guard the Paffage, were afterwards furprized, till they were informed of it by the Trachinians after their Arrival in thofe Streights. Having refolv'd to defend this Poft, and not to fuffer the Barbarian to enter *Greece* without oppofition, they alfo determin'd to fend their Fleet to *Artemifium*, on the Coaft of *Hiftiæotis*; which being not far diftant from *Thermopyle*, might facilitate a conftant Communication between both. Thefe two Places are thus fituate: *Artemifium* is fpacious at firft, and afterwards ftreighten'd by the Thracian Sea into a narrow Paffage, which lies between the Ifland of *Scyathus* and the Continent of *Magnefia*. The Coaft of *Artemifium* begins at the Mouth of the Eubœan Streight, and has a Temple dedicated to *Diana*. But the way that leads into *Greece* by *Trachis*, is, in the narroweft part, no more than fifty foot in breadth: And yet this Paffage is wider than thofe that lie before and behind *Thermopyle*. For the way is fo narrow near *Alpeni*, which is fituate on the far-

ther

ther fide of *Thermopyle*, that a Chariot can hardly pafs: Nor is the other wider, which lies on
this fide, near the City of *Anthela*, and the River *Phœnix*. *Thermopyle* is bounded on the Weft
by a high and inacceffible Mountain, furrounded
with Precipices, and extends to Mount *Oeta*;
and on the Eaft by the Sea, and by an impracticable Morafs. Within this Paffage are Baths
of hot Water to which the Inhabitants give
the Name of *Cauldrons*; and above thefe there is
an Altar confecrated to *Hercules*. The Phocæans formerly built a Wall with Gates, to fe-
cure the Pafs againft the Theffalians; who having abandon'd *Thefprotia*, came to fettle in that
part of *Æolia* which they now poffefs. By this
means, and by letting in the hot Waters, to
render the way impaffable, they defended themfelves againft the Attempts of the Theffalians,
and omitted nothing that might prevent them
from making Incurfions into their Country. But
becaufe, thro' Length of Time, the greater part
of this Wall was fallen down, the Grecians
thought fit to rebuild it, and refolved to defend
the Pafs againft the Irruption of the Barbarian:
reckoning to be fupply'd with Provifions from
Alpeni, which was nearer than any other Place.
Thus the Grecians having diligently weigh'd all
Circumftances, and maturely confider'd what
means might be more effectual to render ufelefs
the great numbers of the Barbarian Forces, both
of Horfe and Foot, determin'd to expect the
coming of the Enemy in this Poft; and were no
fooner informed that the Perfian Army was advanced to *Pieria*, than breaking up from the
Ifthmus, the Land-Forces march'd away to
Thermopyle, and the Fleet made towards *Artemifium*.

sium. But whilst the Grecians assembled from all Parts to defend the common Cause, according to the Measures they had concerted, the Delphians, terrified by the Dangers impending over themselves and the rest of *Greece,* consulted the Oracle, and receiv'd for Answer, " That " they should address their Prayers to the " Winds, which would be the most strenuous " Defenders of *Greece.*" This Admonition they presently communicated to the confederated Grecians, who being desirous to preserve their Liberty, receiv'd the good News with great Joy, because they were under terrible Apprehensions of the Barbarian Army. After that the Delphians erected an Altar, and offer'd Sacrifices to the Winds in *Thya:* which Place was so called from *Thya,* the Daughter of *Cephyssus,* who has a Temple there. And these Sacrifices to the Winds are to this day celebrated by the Delphians, in obedience to that Oracle.

IN the mean time the naval Forces of *Xerxes* departing from *Therma,* detach'd ten of the nimblest Vessels of the Fleet to the Island of *Scyathus,* where three Grecian Ships lay for a Guard: one of which was of *Træzene,* another of *Ægina,* and a third of *Attica.* The Grecians seeing the Barbarian Ships advancing, betook themselves to flight; but the Enemy chacing, soon became Masters of the Træzenian Ship, which was commanded by *Praxinus*; and bringing out the stoutest Man of her Company, killed him upon the Deck: in this manner sacrificing the most valiant of those they first conquered, for a Pledge of their future Successes. The name of the Man was *Leon*; but his Fortune was not answerable to his Name. They met

4   with

with more difficulty in taking the Ship of *Ægina*, which was commanded by *Afonides.* For *Pytheas*, the Son of *Ifchenous*, diftinguifhing himfelf on that occafion, continued to make refiftance after the Ship was taken; till covered with the number of his Wounds, he fainted and fell. But the Perfians, who took the Ship, perceiving him ftill to breathe, and admiring his Valour, took all poffible care to preferve his Life, by applying Balfams to his Wounds, and binding them with Bandages of the fineft Linen. At their return they fhew'd him with aftonifhment to the whole Army, and gave him all manner of good Ufage, tho' they treated the reft of the Prifoners as Slaves. Thus thefe two Ships were taken: whilft the other, which was commanded by *Phirmus* an Athenian, made away to the Mouth of the River *Peneus*, where fhe fell into the hands of the Barbarians, after the Men had fav'd themfelves afhore. For they had no fooner run the Ship aground, than they abandon'd her; and taking their way thro' *Theffaly*, arrived fafely in *Athens.*

WHEN the Grecians, who had their Station at *Artemifium*, receiv'd the News of this Lofs, they fell into fo great a Confternation, that they retir'd to *Chalcis*, in order to defend the Paffage of the *Euripus*, and plac'd Guards by day on the principal Eminences of *Eubœa.* On the other hand the Barbarians, with three of the ten Ships, advancing to the Rocks which lie between *Scyathus* aad *Magnefia*, went up, and erected a Pillar of Stone for a Monument of their Succefs. In the mean time the Enemy's Fleet having fpent eleven days in

I   their

their Voyage from *Therma*, after the time of
the King's Departure, arriv'd on this Coast,
conducted through the Dangers of the Rocks
by *Pammon* of *Scyrus*. From thence, in one day
they failed along the Coast of *Magnesia*; and
having doubled the Cape of *Sepias*, came to an
Anchor in the Road between that Promontory
and the City of *Casthanæa*. To this Place, and
to *Thermopyle*, the Armies of *Xerxes* advanc'd
without lofs, and, as I am informed, their
Numbers were thus computed. The Ships
that came from *Afia* amounted to one thousand
two hundred and seven; which, at the time
of their Departure, had on board two hundred forty one thousand four hundred Men
of various Nations, allowing two hundred to
each Ship, besides thirty Persians, Medes, or
Saces, who, computed together, made up thirty six thousand two hundred and ten Men
more. To these Numbers I must add those
that were on board the lesser Vessels, which,
as I have already said, amounted to three
thousand: and accounting eighty Men to each,
they will be found to have been two hundred and forty thousand: So that the whole
Naval Force, that arrived from *Afia*, was com-
pofed of five hundred and seventeen thousand,
six hundred and ten Men. The Land-Army
confifted of seventeen hundred thousand Foot,
and fourfcore thousand Horse; besides the
Arabians mounted on Camels, and the Libyans in Chariots; who, as I conjecture, might
amount to about twenty thousand more. In
a word, the number of these Forces, that
were levied in *Afia*, and employ'd either in
the Fleet, or by Land, was two Millions
three

three hundred and seventeen thousand six hundred and ten Men; not including their Train of Servants, nor those who were on board the Ships that carried Provisions. To these must be added, the Forces that were rais'd in *Europe*; which I shall do according to the best Information I have been able to procure. The Grecians of *Thrace*, and the Islands adjacent furnished one hundred and twenty Ships, which had on board twenty four thousand Men. The Thracians, Pæonians, Eordians, Bottiæans, Chalcidians, Brygians, Pierians, Macedonians, Peræbians, Enians, Dolopians, Magnesians, and Achaians, together with those who inhabit the maritime Parts of *Thrace*, sent such a number of Land-Forces, as, in my opinion, were not less than three hundred thousand. So that if we add these Myriads, to those that were levied in *Asia*, we shall find in all, two Millions six hundred forty one thousand six hundred and ten fighting Men. Nevertheless, though these Numbers are so prodigiously great, I am persuaded that the Servants, with those on board the Store-Ships and Tenders, were yet more numerous. But supposing them only equal in number, and not more nor less than the military Part, the total Sum will amount to five Millions two hundred fourscore and three thousand, two hundred and twenty Men, brought by *Xerxes*, the Son of *Darius*, to *Sepias*, and to *Thermopyle.* Such was the number of this Army! But the Women that serv'd for Concubines, and Makers of Bread, the Eunuchs, Draught-Horses, and other Beasts of Burden, with the Indian Dogs that follow'd the Forces, were so many, that no Man can affirm any thing with

certainty

certainty touching their Numbers. Therefore
I am not aſtoniſhed, if the Streams of ſome Rivers prov'd inſufficient for this Multitude; but
rather, how ſo many Myriads were ſupplied
with Proviſions: For allowing only a Chœnix
of Wheat by day to each Man, the Total will
amount to one hundred and ten thouſand,
three hundred and forty Mines, conſumed every day; without including the Food of the
Women, the Eunuchs, the Cattel, and the
Dogs. But of all this prodigious Number,
no Man, either for Stature or Beauty, ſeem'd
more worthy to command, than *Xerxes* himſelf.

WHEN the Fleet arriv'd in the Road that
lies between the City of *Caſthanæa* and the Promontory of *Sepias*, on the Coaſt of *Magneſia*, the
foremoſt Ships were rang'd cloſe by the Land.
But becauſe the Shoar was not ſufficiently capa-
cious to contain their Numbers, all the reſt were
oblig'd to ride at Anchor; and to that end,
having turn'd the Heads of their Ships to the
Sea, they form'd eight ſeveral Lines, one behind
another; and in that Poſture paſs'd the Night.
The next Morning at day-break, after a ſerene
Sky and ſtill Weather, the Sea began to riſe, and
a terrible Storm enſued, with a violent North-
Eaſt-Wind, which, by the Inhabitants of that
Coaſt, is called Helleſpontin. Thoſe who perceiv'd the Wind increaſing, and were not hin-
dered by their Station, prevented the Miſchiefs
of the Tempeſt; and haling under the Shore, ſav'd
themſelves and their Ships: But of thoſe who
were ſurpriz'd out at Sea, ſome were driven
into the Gulphs of *Pelion*, others were forc'd
aground; ſome ſpilt upon the Promontory of
Sepias;

Sepias; some bulg'd upon the Shallows of *Me-libæa*, and others near the City of *Casthanæa*: So intolerable was the Violence of the Storm. The Report is, that the Athenians having been admonished by another Oracle, to implore the Assistance of their Son-in-law, addressed themselves to *Boreas:* who, according to the Tradition of the *Grecians*, marry'd *Orithya*, a Woman of *Attica*, and Daughter to *Erechtheus.* On that account, they say, the Athenians were persuaded of their Relation to *Boreas*; and therefore, while they lay at *Chalcis* in *Eubœa* with their Fleet, both before and after they perceiv'd the Storm, they offer'd Sacrifices to *Boreas* and *Orithya*, invoking their Aid, and praying that they would destroy the Barbarian Ships, as they had done before at Mount *Athos.* For my own part, I shall not undertake to say, that their Prayers prevailed with *Boreas* to fall upon the Barbarians in this Station: But the Athenians say, that this and the former Aid they receiv'd, were both owing to *Boreas*; and therefore, at their Return, they built him a Temple upon the River *Ilissus.* In this Disaster the Barbarians, according to the most moderate Computation, lost four hundred Ships, besides great numbers of Men, and infinite Riches; which prov'd afterwards of great advantage to *Aminocles*, the Son of *Cretinus.* For afterwards breaking up some Ground about *Sepias*, he found many Cups, and other Vessels both of Gold and Silver, with so great a Treasure belonging to the Persians, that he presently became extremely opulent; though in other things he was unfortunate, and much afflicted for the untimely Death of his Children. The Store-Ships

Ships and other Veſſels caſt away in the Storm, were ſo many, that the Commanders, fearing to be attack'd by the Theſſalians after thiſ Diſaſter, fortified themſelves with a Rampart of a conſiderable height, compoſed of the broken Pieces of the Wreck. Three whole Days the Tempeſt continued; but on the fourth after the Mages had immolated the Victims appropriated to the infernal Powers, and endeavoured to charm the Winds by Enchantments, they ſacrificed to *Thetis*, and to the Nereides, and laid the Storm : or perhaps the Wind fell of courſe, as at other times. They ſacrificed to theſe Deities, becauſe they had learnt from the Ionians, that *Thetis* was taken away by *Peleus* out of this Country, and that all the Coaſt of *Sepias* is dedicated to her, and to the reſt of the Nereides. Thus the Tempeſt ceaſed on the fourth day.

BUT thoſe who had been left to obſerve from the Eminences of *Eubæa*, what ſhould paſs within their View, came running on the ſecond Day after the riſing of the Storm, and acquainted the Grecians with this Shipwreck : Which when they had heard, they pour'd out a Libation with Thankſgiving, to *Neptune* the Deliverer, and immediately ſet ſail for *Artemiſium*, hoping they ſhould not find many of the Enemies Ships on that Coaſt. Thus arriving a ſecond time at *Artemiſium*, they came to an anchor : And ever ſince, even to this day, have given to *Neptune* the Sirname of the *Deliverer*. On the other hand, the Barbarians ſeeing the Storm blown over, and the Sea quiet, weigh'd their Anchors; and coaſting along the Shore of the Continent, paſſed the Promontory of
Magneſia,

Magnesia, and stood into the Bay of *Pegasæa*. 'Tis reported, that in one part of the Country, adjacent to this Bay, *Hercules* was abandon'd by *Jason* and his Companions, whilst he went to take in fresh Water for the Voyage they design'd to *Aia* in *Colchis*, for the Golden Fleece; and that the Place goes by the Name of *Aphete*, on account of this Action. Into that Station the Persian Fleet retir'd: But fifteen of their Ships, which put to Sea some time after the rest, seeing the Grecians about *Artemisium*, and thinking they were Friends, fell in among their Enemies. The Barbarians were commanded by *Sandoces*, the Son of *Thaumasius*, Governour of *Cyme*, an Æolian City. He had been formerly condemned by *Darius* to be crucified, for taking a Bribe to pronounce an unjust Sentence, when he was one of the Royal Judges. But whilst he was actually hanging on the Cross, the King considering with himself, that the Services he had done to his Family, were greater than his Crime, and that his Condemnation was rather the Effect of Passion than of Prudence, ordered him to be set at liberty. In this manner he escaped the Punishment, to which he had been condemned by *Darius*: But now falling in among the Grecians, he found no way to escape. For when they saw him making towards them, they presently perceiv'd the Mistake, and advancing to meet him, soon made themselves Masters of all the Ships. In one of these, *Aridolis*, the Carian Tyrant of *Alabanda*, was taken; and in another, *Penthylus*, the Son of *Demonous*, Commander of the Paphians: He had twelve Ships when he sail'd from *Paphos*; but having lost eleven in the Storm, he was taken at *Artemisium*,

sium, with only one remaining of that number. When the Grecians had examin'd the Prisoners, and made inquiry into such things as they desir'd to know, concerning the Forces of *Xerxes*, they sent them away under a Guard to the Isthmus of *Corinth:* The rest of the Barbarian Fleet, except these fifteen Ships, which were under the Conduct of *Sandoces* arriv'd safe at *Aphetæ.*

IN the mean time *Xerxes*, with the Land-Forces, marched from *Thessaly*, and advancing by the way of *Achaia*, arriv'd on the third day in the Territories of the Melians. In *Thessaly* he made tryal of the Swiftness of his Mares, against those of that Country, which he had heard were the fleetest of all *Greece*; and the Grecian Mares were left far behind in the Race. Of all the Rivers of *Thessaly*, only the *Onochonus* had not a sufficient Quantity of water for the Use of the Army: whereas the *Apidanus*, which is the greatest River of *Achaia*, could hardly afford enough to supply their Necessities. When *Xerxes* arriv'd at *Alus* in *Achaia*, his Guides, who were always ready to inform him of every thing remarkable, gave him an account of the Tradition of the Country, concerning the Temple of the Aphlystian *Jupiter*, and how *Athamas*, the Son of *Æolus*, conspir'd with *Inus* to take away the Life of *Phryxus*. They told him, that the Achaians, to punish his Descendants, decreed, by the Counsel of an Oracle, that the eldest Person of his Race should never be permitted to enter into the Senate, which they call *Leitum*; and that, if ever he should presume to go in, he should not go out again, except in order to be sacrific'd: So that many, for fear of

this

this Punifhment, chofe rather to abandon the
Country: That in fucceeding time, when any
one of thefe return'd, and happen'd to be taken
in the *Prytaneum*, they cover'd his Body with
facred Fillets, and led him out in great Ceremony to be facrificed: That the Pofterity of
Cytifforus, the Son of *Phryxus*, became liable to
the fame Punifhment; becaufe, when the
Achaians, by the Advice of an Oracle, were
ready to expiate this Guilt with the Sacrifice
of *Athamas*, the Son of *Æolus*, *Cytifforus* arriving in that inftant from *Aia* in *Colchis*, forced
him out of their hands, and by that Action
drew the Anger of the Gods upon his Defcendants.   When *Xerxes* had heard this Relation,
and was come to the facred Grove, he not only
left the Place untouched, but commanded all
the Army to follow his Example; fhewing great
Regard to the Temple of *Athamas*, and even
to the Houfes of his Pofterity. Having done
thefe things in *Theffaly* and *Achaia*, he arriv'd
at the City of *Melis*, fituate in a Bay near the
Sea, where the Tides ebb and flow every day.
About this Shore lies a Plain of a confiderable
Breadth in one Part, and very narrow in the
other; inclos'd by high and inacceffible Mountains, which, furrounding the whole Country of the Melians, are known by the Name
of the Trachinean Rocks. The firft City
that appears in this Bay, to thofe who come
from *Achaia*, is *Anticyra*, by which the River
Sperchius defcending from *Eniene*, falls into
the Sea: And about twenty Stades from thence
another River is feen call'd the *Dyras*; which,
they fay, rofe up to fuccour *Hercules* when he
was ftruggling with the Flames. At a like Diftance

stance from this, we meet with the River
Melas ; and five Stades farther, the City of
Trachis is built in the moſt ſpacious Part of all
the Plain ; which in that Place contains two
and twenty thouſand Plethrons in breadth. In
theſe Mountains that ſurround the Plain, a
Paſſage is open on the South ſide of *Trachis*,
through which the River *Aſopus* runs, at the
foot of the Hills. Another River, not very
large, called the *Phœnix*, deſcending Northward
from the ſame Mountains, falls into the *Aſopus*.
The way is ſo narrow by the River *Phœnix*,
that no more than one Chariot can paſs. *Thermopyle* is fifteen Stades beyond that River ; and
between both lies the Town of *Anthela*. The
Aſopus paſſes by this Place, and afterwards falls
into the Sea. The Country about *Anthela* is
open, and has a Temple dedicated to the Am-
phictyonian *Ceres* ; in which are the Seats of
the Amphictyons, and the Chapel of *Amphictyon*
himſelf.

T H E Perſian King encamp'd with his Army in the Plain of *Trachis*, belonging to the
Melians ; and the Grecians at the Paſs, which,
by the Inhabitants of the Place, and their
Neighbours, is c ll'd *Pyle*, and by the greater
part of *Greece*, *Thermopyle*. *Xerxes* was in poſſeſſion of all the Countries that lie to the
Northward, down to *Trachis* ; and the Grecians of thoſe Parts of that Continent, which
lean to the South, and South-Weſt. The
Grecians drawn together in this place to ſuſtain the Aſſault of the Perſian Army, were
theſe : Three hundred Spartans in heavy Armour ; one thouſand Tageans, and a like number from *Mantiene*: One hundred and twenty

Arcadians of *Orchomenus*, and one thousand more from the other Parts of *Arcadia*. Four hundred Corinthians; two hundred Men from *Philius*, and fourscore from *Mycene*. All these were Peloponnesians. Of the Bœotians, seven hundred Thespians, and four hundred Thebans. These Grecians invited the Locrians of *Opus* to join them with all their Forces, and the Phocæans with a thousand Men; representing by a Message, that they were already arriv'd, and daily expected the rest of their Confederates: That the Sea was sufficiently guarded by the Athenians, the Æginetes, and others, who were entrusted with the Conduct of the Naval Forces; and that they had nothing to fear: That the Invader was not a God, but a Man; and that no Mortal ever was, or ever should be born, exempted from the Calamities of Life, which attend the greatest in the greatest proportion; and therefore, the Enemy being no more than a Man, might find himself mistaken in the Opinion he had entertain'd. Persuaded by this Exhortation, these People also march'd to assist their Allies in the Country of *Trachis*. The Nations that compos'd these Forces had their own particular Leaders; but the General, who was in most esteem, and had the command of all, was *Leonidas*, a Lacedemonian, the Son of *Anaxandrides*, descended from *Leon*, *Eurycratides*, *Anaxander*, *Eurycrates*, *Polydorus*, *Alcamenes*, *Teleclus*, *Archelaus*, *Agesilaus*, *Doryagus*, *Leolotes*, *Echestratus*, *Hegesis*, *Eurysthenes*, *Aristodemus*, *Aristomachus*, *Cleodæus*, *Hyllus*, and *Hercules*. He became King of *Sparta*, contrary to his own Expectation: For during the Lives of *Cleomenes* and *Dorieus*, his elder Brothers, he was far from thinking to obtain

the

the Kingdom. But after the Death of *Cleomenes,* who left no Son to fucceed him, the Kingdom defcended to *Leonidas*; becaufe *Dorieus* was dead before in *Sicily*, and he himfelf was elder than *Cleombrotus*, the youngeft of all the Sons of *Anaxandrides*, and had married the Daughter of *Cleomenes*. He march'd to *Thermopyle* at the head of three hundred Spartans, all chofen by himfelf; Men of mature Years, and Fathers of Sons. In his March he took the Thebans with him, amounting to the Numbers I mention'd before, and led by *Leontiades* the Son of *Eurymachus*. This he did induftrioufly and with Defign, becaufe they of all the Grecians were the People he moft fufpected to favour the Medes; by that means refolving to fee whether they would accompany him in this Expedition, or openly renounce their Alliance with the Grecians. But the Thebans, tho' they had no good Intentions, yet would not omit to furnifh their Part. The Spartans fent thefe Men with *Leonidas* before the reft of their Troops, to the end that the Confederates feeing their Diligence, might be encourag'd to take the Field, and not think of fiding with the Medes, tho' thefe fhould be defeated: determining after the Carnian Feftival, which they were then celebrating, to leave fome Forces for the Guard of the City, and to march immediately with their whole Strength to the Defence of *Greece*. The reft of their Confederates taking like Meafures, becaufe the new Olympiad began at that time, and not imagining the Difpute at *Thermopyle* could fo foon be decided; difpatch'd fome of their Men before to the Rendezvous. In the mean while thofe Gre-

cians

cians, who were already arrived at *Thermopyle*, seeing the Persian advance so near the Pass, and apprehending the Event, began to think of retiring. All the Peloponnesians, except the Spartans, were of opinion they should march away to *Peloponnesus*, and defend the Isthmus of *Corinth*. But *Leonidas* perceiving the Phocæans and Locrians offended with the Indignity of that Proposition, determin'd them all to stay, and to dispatch Messengers to the Confederates, with Instructions to desire Succour, because they were not sufficient to resist the Army of the Medes.

DURING the time of these Deliberations, *Xerxes* sent a Scout on horseback to View their Numbers, and to discover how they were employ'd. For whilst he staid in *Thessaly* he was inform'd that the Grecians had assembled a small Army, in which the Lacedemonians had the principal Authority; and that *Leonidas*, of the Race of *Hercules*, was their General. The Scout approaching the Grecian Camp, could not see their whole Force, because the Wall, which they had rebuilt, covered all those who were upon the Guard within; so that he discovered no more of their Men, than those who were on the other side, with their Arms lying before the Wall. On that day the Lacedemonians happened to be without, as their Turn was; and by that means he saw some of them performing their Exercises, and others putting their Hair in order. When he had seen these things with Astonishment, and inform'd himself of their Number, he retired at his Leisure; no Man pursuing nor seeming to take any notice of him. At his Return he gave an account to

Xerxes of every thing he had difcovered : But when the King had heard his Report, he could not imagine that the Grecians were come thither only as Men prepared to die, and to deftroy as many of their Enemies as they could ; tho' nothing was more true. And therefore deriding the Vanity of their Enterprize, he fent for *Demaràtus* the Son of *Arifton*, who was then in the Army ; and when he was come into his Prefence, examined him touching each Particular, fhewing himfelf defirous to know what the Lacedemonians might mean by the Meafures they had taken. " S I R, faid *Demaratus*, You have already heard my Opinion
" concerning thefe Men, when we were about
" to invade *Greece*: And tho' I told you no
" more than I forefaw would come to pafs,
" you entertain'd my Difcourfe with Derifion.
" I know the Danger of defending Truth
" againft the King : yet I defire you would
" hear me once more. Thefe Spartans are
" advanced to this Place with a Refolution to
" fight, and are now preparing themfelves to
" difpute our Paffage ; for their Cuftom is to
" put their Hair in order when they are going
" to expofe their Lives to the greateft Dangers.
" But if you conquer thefe Lacedemonians,
" and thofe they left behind in *Sparta*, be af-
" fur'd no other Nation will dare to lift up a
" Hand againft your Power. For you are
" now to attack the moft valiant Men, and the
" beft govern'd State of all *Greece.*" Thefe things feeming incredible to *Xerxes*, he afk'd him again how fo fmall a Number could poffibly refift his Army. " O King, replied *Demaratus*,
" deal with me as with a Lyar, if every thing

" I

" I have faid come not to pafs." Nevertheless
his Words made no impreſſion upon *Xerxes* ;
who being ſtill in hope they would retire, un-
de took nothing during four Days after this
Diſcourſe. But on the fifth Day, perceiving
they were not yet withdrawn, and imputing
their Stay to Arrogance and Raſhneſs ; tranſported with Indignation , he ſent out the
Medes and the Ciſſians, with Orders to take
them alive, and bring them Priſoners to him.
They attacked the Grecians furiouſly, but
were repulſed with conſiderable Slaughter ;
and tho' the Places of thoſe that fell were in-
ceſſantly ſupplied by others, yet they could
not ſucceed in their Attempt : the great Loſs
they ſuſtained, plainly demonſtrating to all, no
leſs than to the King, that they were indeed
many Men, but few Soldiers. This Action
happen'd by day. When the Medes ſaw they
could maintain the Fight no longer, they retir'd ; and in their room *Hydarnes* advanc'd with
that Body of Perſians who by the King were
call'd *immortal*, nor doubting to put an end to
the Diſpute. But when they came to cloſe with
the Grecians they ſucceeded no better than the
Medes. For they fought in a narrow Paſs, and
their pointed Arms being ſhorter than thoſe of
the Grecians, render'd their Numbers uſeleſs.
The Lacedemonians deſerve ever to be remember'd with Honour for the Actions they perform'd that day ; in which, among other things,
they ſhew'd how much they were ſuperior to
the Enemy in military Knowledge. For whenever they retired, they made their Retreat
in cloſe order. And when they found they
were purſued by the Barbarians with noiſe
and

and shouting, then facing about on a sudden, they kill'd an inconceivable Number of the Persians, with little Loss on their side. So that after the Enemy had in vain attempted to force the Pass, both in separate Bodies, and all together, they were at last obliged to retire. The Report is, that the King, who was Spectator of this Fight, rose thrice from his Seat during the Action, being under great Apprehensions of losing his Army. The next day the Barbarians, considering how few the Grecians were in number, and supposing so many of them to be already wounded, that they would not be able to maintain a second Fight, resolved to make another Attempt; in which they had no better Success than before. For the Grecians having drawn up their Forces in good order, and in national Bodies, excepting only the Phocæans, who were sent to guard the Passage of the Mountain, gave them so warm a Reception, that the Persians finding no Probability of succeeding better than they had done the preceding day, abandon'd their Enterprize.

BUT whilst the King was doubtful what Measures he should take in this Sate of Affairs, *Epialtes* the Son of *Eurydemus* a Melian, coming to him in expectation of a great Reward, inform'd him of the Passage which leads to *Thermopyle* by the way of the Mountain; and by that means caused the Dispersion of those who were left there for a Guard. Afterwards, fearing the Indignation of the Lacedemonians, he fled to *Thessaly*: And during his Flight the Assembly of Amphictyons held at *Pyle* proscrib'd him, and set a Price upon his Head. But after

some

some time he was kill'd at *Anticyra* by *Athenades* a Trachinian ; who, though he kill'd him for another reason, which I shall mention hereafter, was yet rewarded by the Lacedemonians. Some indeed relate this Story in a different manner, and pretend, that *Onates* the Son of *Phanagoras*, a Caryftian, and *Corydalus* of *Anticyra*, were the Men who discovered the Passage to the King, and conducted the Persians by the way of the Mountain. But to me this seems altogether incredible ; partly because we ought to believe, that when the Amphictyons set a Price upon the Head of *Epialtes* the Trachinian, and not upon *Onates* and *Corydalus*, they were perfectly well inform'd of his Guilt. In the second place, we are certain *Epialtes* ran away on this Occasion. And lastly, *Onates* not being a Melian, could not well be acquainted with this way, unless he had been much conversant in that Country. From all which I conclude, that *Epialtes* was the Enemy's Guide and guilty of betraying the Passage to the Persians.

XERXES having heard with Satisfaction what *Epialtes* took upon him to perform, shew'd himself extremely pleas'd, and order'd *Hydarnes* to march away immediately with the Forces he commanded. In the Evening *Hydarnes* began to advance towards the way, by which formerly the Inhabitants of *Melis*, who were the first Discoverers, conducted the Thessalians against the Phocæans ; when, having built a Wall to defend the other Pass , they thought themselves secure from any such Attempt. This Passage is not at all fortified, because not useful to the Melians ; and beginning at the River *Asopus* (which

(which passes thro' an Aperture of the Mountain *Anopæa*) goes under the same Name with the Mountain; and extending along the back of the Hills, leads down to *Alpeni*, a Locrian City near the Frontier of *Melis*, by the Stone of *Melampygus*, and the Seats of the Cercopians: where the Way is more narrow than in any other part. In this Passage, thus situate, the Persians march'd all night, after they had pass'd the River *Asopus*, having the Mountains of *Oeta* on their Right, and those of *Trachis* on their Left-hand; and at Day-break arrived at the Top of the Hills: where, as I have already said, a thousand Phocæans were posted, as well to secure their own Country, as to prevent an Irruption on that side. For the lower Pass was guarded by those I mention'd before: And the Phocæans had voluntarily undertaken to *Leonidas* to defend that of the Mountain. The Persians were not discover'd by the Phocæans till they had reach'd the top of the Hills, having been all that time conceal'd by the great number of Oaks which grew in the way. But then, the noise of the Leaves they trod upon, gave notice of their Approach; the rather, because the Air was perfectly serene and quiet. Upon this Alarm the Phocæans ran to their Arms, and had no sooner put themselves in order, than the Barbarians appear'd; but were not a little surpriz'd to find such a Body of Men, in a place where they expected not to meet with any Resistance. *Hydarnes* fearing the Phocæans might be Lacedemonians, demanded of *Epialtes*, of what Nation the Enemy was; and being inform'd who they were, he drew up the Persians in order of Battel. The

Phocæans

Phocæans finding themselves gall'd by the great numbers of Darts, which the Persians threw inceffantly among them, retir'd with Precipitation to the highest part of the Mountain; and being perfuaded that this Enterprize was form'd againft them, prepar'd to die gallantly. But *Epialtes* and *Hydarnes*, with the Persians, neglecting to follow the Phocæans, as a thing of little Importance, march'd down from the Mountain with all poffible expedition. The Augur *Megistias* having infpected the Sacrifices, was the firft who acquainted the Grecians at *Thermopyle*, that they were all threaten'd with Death. After which, certain Deferters arriving in the night, gave notice, that the Persians were paffing over the Mountain: And at day-break the ordinary Guard came running from the Hills with the fame Advice. Upon this the Grecians call'd a Council of War, and divided in their Opinions. For fome would not hear of abandoning their Station, and others were of a contrary Sentiment. In this confufion they feparated, and one part of their Forces return'd home, whilft the reft with *Leonidas* prepar'd themfelves to receive the Enemy. Some fay, that *Leonidas*, out of an earneft defire to preferve their Lives, difmiff'd all thofe who march'd away ; but that he and the Spartans with him, thought themfelves obliged in honour to maintain the Poft they came to defend. For my own part, I incline to think, that *Leonidas* obferving his Allies averfe and unwilling to run the fame hazard with him, gave them leave to retire ; and that he himfelf refolv'd to ftay, in order to preferve his own Reputation, to leave a glorious Name behind him,

and

and to secure the Felicity of *Sparta.* For the Spartans having already consulted the Pythian touching the Event of this War, had receiv'd for Answer, That *Sparta* should be destroyed by the Barbarians, or their King should lose his Life. The Oracle was deliver'd in the following Hexameters:

The Spartan Plains shall feel the Persian Rage,
Their City under Servitude shall groan;
Unless a King, born of Herculean Race,
Oppress'd in War, shall die to save the rest.

My Opinion therefore is, that *Leonidas* resolving these things in his mind, and being desirous that the Spartans alone should have the Glory of this Action, sent away the Confederates; and not, that those who marched away, separated themselves from the rest in an indecent manner, on account of their mutual Animosities. The Conduct of *Leonidas* himself is no small Argument to confirm what I say: For since, among others, he would have dismiss'd *Megistias* the Acarnian, who was reported to be descended from *Melampus,* and had predicted the Event of this Enterprize by inspecting the Sacrifices, nothing is more manifest than that he gave him leave to depart, lest he should perish with the Spartans; tho' *Megistias* would not make use of that Permission, but contented himself to send home his only Son, who had attended him on this occasion. So that in truth the Allies, that went away, retired by the Persuasion of *Leonidas:* Only the Thespians and the Thebans remain'd with the Lacedemonians; the Thebans indeed unwilling-
ly,

ly, and against their Inclination, detain'd as Hostages by *Leonidas*; but the Thespians voluntarily, and with their Leader *Demophilus*, the Son of *Diadromeus*, constantly refusing to abandon *Leonidas* and his Spartans, died with them in the Field.

XERXES, after he had pour'd out a Libation at the time of the Rising of the Sun, and staid till the hour Men usually meet in the publick Places, began to move on with his Army, as *Epialtes* had advis'd; because the Descent of the Mountain is much shorter and more free from Windings than the Ascent. Upon their Approach, *Leonidas*, with the Grecians, leaving the Wall guarded, advanced to the broadest part of the Passage, in far greater Expectation of Death than at any time before. They fought the preceding Days in the narrowest way of the Pass; but now engaging in the widest, great numbers of the Barbarians fell: for their Officers standing behind the Divisions they commanded, forced them to advance with Blows and Menaces: so that many falling into the Sea were drowned, and many more were trampled under foot, without any regard had to those that perished. The Grecians, on their part, knowing they could not avoid Death upon the Arrival of those who were coming by the way of the Mountain, push'd on desperately, and exerted their utmost Efforts against the Barbarians. And because most of their Javelins were already broken, they drew their Swords, and made a great Slaughter among the Persians. In this Action fell *Leonidas*, after he had done all that a brave Man could do; and with him other eminent Spartans, whose

Names

Names I have heard repeated with Honour, as well as the rest of the three hundred. The Loss of the Persians was great, and many illustrious Men were killed on their side. Among these *Abrocomes* and *Hyperanthes,* Sons of *Darius,* by *Phrataguna,* the Daughter of his Brother *Atarnes,* who was Son to *Hystaspes,* and Grandson to *Arsames.* When *Atarnes* married his Daughter to *Darius,* he gave him all his Possessions, because he had no other Offspring. These two Brothers of *Xerxes* were killed fighting for the Body of *Leonidas,* which the Lacedemonians and Persians obstinately disputed, till at last the Grecians rescued it by their Valour, and four times repuls'd the Enemy. This was the State of things, when the Army with *Epialtes* arriv'd ; of which the Grecians were no sooner inform'd, than Victory shifted to the other side: For returning into the narrow way, and passing within the Wall, they all drew together, except the Thebans, and posted themselves in close Order on a rising Ground, where a Lion of Stone is now seen, erected for a Monument to *Leonidas.* In this place they defended themselves, with the Swords they had left, against the Barbarians, who pour'd in from every part with a horrible Noise ; some beating down the Wall, and entering by the Breaches, whilst Multitudes of others came in, and surrounded them on all sides. The general Opinion is, that tho' the Lacedemonians and Thespians shew'd such invincible Courage, yet *Dieneces* the Spartan distinguish'd himself beyond all others: And when a Trachinian told him, before the Fight began, that the Multitude of the Barbarians was so great, that they

would

would let fly such a number of Arrows at once, as should hide the Light of the Sun; he was so far from being astonish'd, that, in Contempt of their Numbers, he said, The News was good; and that if the Sun was intercepted by the Medes, they should then fight in the Shade. This, and other memorable Sayings, are attributed to *Dieneces* the Lacedemonian. After him those who signalized themselves most among the Lacedemonians, were two Brothers, *Alpheus* and *Maron*, Sons of *Orisiphantus*; and of the Thespians, *Dithyrambus*, the Son of *Harmatideus*. They were all buried in the Place where they fought, as well those who fell in this Action, as those who were killed before *Leonidas* dismissed the Confederates; and a Monument was erected to their Memory, with this Inscription:

> *Four thousand Men, from antient* Pelops *nam'd,*
> *Upon this Ground against three Millions fought.*

This Epitaph was made for all; that which follows only for the Lacedemonians:

> *Go,* Friend, *acquaint the Spartans how we fell*
> *With Glory, and their just Commands obey'd.*

Besides these, there was another Inscription for the Prophet *Megistias*, conceiv'd in these words:

> *Slain by the Medes, divine* Megistias *lies*
> *Under this Stone; he saw approaching Fate*
> *With Heart undaunted, and refus'd to live*
> *When the brave Spartans had resolv'd to die.*

The

The two former Inscriptions were order'd by
the Amphictyons; but this of *Megistias* was
erected by *Simonides*, the Son of *Leoprepes*, in
Testimony of their mutual Friendship. Some
say, that *Eurytus* and *Aristodemus*, two of the
three hundred Lacedemonians, being desperately afflicted with a Disease of the Eyes, retir'd to *Alpheni* by the Permission of *Leonidas*;
and though they might have preserved their
Lives by returning to *Sparta*, or, refusing to
return, might have died with the rest, they
could not agree in either; but continu'd to differ in their Opinions, till at last *Eurytus* hearing the Persians were arrived by the way of the
Mountain, call'd for his Arms; and when he
had them on, order'd his Servant to lead him
into the Field of Battle; where falling in a-
mong the thickest of the Enemy, he lost his
Life: whilst *Aristodemus*, wanting Courage, staid
behind at *Alpheni*. As for the Servant of *Eurytus*
he had no sooner conducted his Master to the
Place where the Fight was, than he left him,
and ran away. Now if *Aristodemus* alone had
been disabled by his Distemper, and in that
Condition had return'd to *Sparta*; or if both
had gone home together, I cannot think the Lacedemonians would have been displeased. But
one of these dying in the Field, put them under
a Necessity of shewing their Resentment against
the Survivor; who refus'd to die, albeit he
was in the same Circumstance with the other.
Thus, some Men say, *Aristodemus* return'd safe
to *Sparta*, under colour of his Disease; but o-
thers pretend, that being sent with Orders from
the Army, he might have been present at the
Fight, and would not, tho' his Companion ar-

riv'd in due time, and died in the Field. However, at his Return, he was punish'd with Ignominy and Contempt: with Contempt, in
that no Lacedemonian would converse with
him, or suffer him to make use of his Fire;
with Ignominy, in that they gave him the name
of *Aristodemus* the Fugitive. But he afterwards
wiped off all the Guilt of this Action, by his
Behaviour at the Battel of *Platæa*. They say
also, that another of the three hundred, whose
Name was *Panites*, having been sent on a Message to *Thessaly*, surviv'd this Action, and return'd to *Sparta*; but being unable to bear the
Reproaches of the Spartans, he strangled himself. As for the Thebans, and their General
Leontiades, they were necessitated for some
time to fight against the King's Army, in conjunction with the Grecians: but they no sooner saw the Persians victorious, than they abandon'd the rest of their Allies, as they were
hastening to the Hill; and with extended
Hands approaching the Barbarians, most truly
said, That they had always been Partizans of
the Medes; that they were among the first
who presented the King with Earth and Water; that they came to *Thermopyle* by force, and
were no way guilty of the Loss he had sustain'd.
By these words, which the Thessalians confirm'd with their Testimony, the Thebans
saved their Lives, but had no great reason to
boast: For the Barbarians kill'd many of their
Men, as they advanc'd to surrender themselves;
and, by the Command of *Xerxes*, branded a
much greater number with the Royal Mark,
beginning at their General *Leontiades*; whose
Son *Eurymachus* having afterwards surpriz'd the

City

City of *Platæa*, at the head of four hundred Thebans, was killed by the Platæans. Thus the Grecians fought at *Thermopyle.*

UPON this Event, *Xerxes* having sent for *Demaratus,* began his Discourse in this manner; " *Demaratus, said he,* I find by the certain " Evidence of Truth, that you are a Man of " Probity ; for all things have happen'd as you " foretold. Tell me now how many the rest " of the Lacedemonians may be? What Num- " ber of such Men as these they can bring in- " to the Field? And whether they have all the " same Courage?" " SIR, *said,* Demaratus, " the Lacedemonians are numerous, and have " many Cities ; but I shall inform you of that " which you desire to know. The City of " *Sparta* has about eight thousand Men, all " equal in Valour to those who have fought on " this Occasion ; and the rest of the Lacede- " monians are valiant, tho' not altogether like " these." " Let me know then; *said* Xerxes, " the readiest way to conquer these Men, for " you have been their King, and consequently " are well acquainted with the Tendency of " their Counsels." " SIR, *reply'd* Demaratus, " since you condescend to ask my Advice, I " am bound to give you the best I can : The " most probable way to effect our Design, is " to send a Fleet of three hundred Ships to " the Lacedemonian Coast. For there is an " Island, call'd *Cythera,* lying off that Shore ; " which *Chilon,* one of the wisest Men of our " Nation, said would be more advantageous to " the Spartans, if drown'd in the bottom of " the Sea, than in the present Situation : al- " ways apprehending such an Enterprize as I

" am

" am about to propose : Not that he foresaw
" the Arrival of your Fleet, but fearing such
" an Attempt might be made at one time or
" other. From this Island you may continual-
" ly alarm the Lacedemonians; who finding
" themselves involved in a defensive War at
" home, will be no longer formidable to you,
" nor in a condition to succour the rest of the
" Grecians, when they shall be attack'd by
" your Land-Forces." In a word, when by
" this means you have subdued the other Parts
" of *Greece*, the Lacedemonians alone will not
" be able to resist. But if you act otherwise,
" expect another kind of Event: For the Pe-
" loponnesians have in their Country a narrow
" Isthmus, to which they will not fail to draw
" all their Forces, and constrain you to engage
" in Actions more bloody than you have yet
" seen; whereas if you put my Advice in exe-
" cution, not only the Isthmus, but their Ci-
" ties also will be yours without hazard."
When he had finish'd these words, *Achæmenes*,
Brother to *Xerxes*, and Commander in chief at
Sea, being present at this Discourse, and fearing the King might be induc'd to follow the
Counsel of *Demaratus*; " SIR, *said he*, I per-
" ceive you hearken to the Suggestions of a
" Man, who either envies your Prosperity, or
" perhaps would betray your Affairs. For the
" constant manner of the Grecians is to envy
" the Fortunate, and to hate the Powerful :
" If therefore, after you have lost four hun-
" dred Ships by the Storm, you shall send
" three hundred more to hover about the Coast
" of Peloponnesus, our Enemies might fight us
" upon equal Terms; but will never dare to

I

" engage

" engage us, if our Fleet be kept in a Body,
" becaufe we fhall be much fuperior in num-
" ber. Befides, if the whole Fleet be order'd
" to attend the Motions of the Land-Army,
" they will be able mutually to affift each o-
" ther ; whereas if you feparate your Naval
" Forces, they can be no way ufeful to you,
" nor you to them. Would you then have all
" to go well, refolve not to enter into a parti-
" cular Difcuffion of your Enemy's Affairs,
" nor inquire what they will do, where they
" will make a Stand, or what Numbers they
" are ? They beft know how to take care of
" themfelves, and we, on our part, no lefs. If
" the Lacedemonians dare venture a Battel a-
" gainft the Perfians, they will find no Cure for
" fuch a Blow as they muft of Neceffity re-
" ceive." " *Achemænes, reply'd* Xerxes, I ap-
" prove your Reafons, and will do as you ad-
" vife ; but I am perfuaded *Demaratus* gave me
" that Counfel which he thought moft advan-
" tageous to me, tho' at the fame time I think
" your Opinion more rational ; for I can by
" no means fufpect him of Difaffection to my
" Affairs, when I duly confider his former
" Difcourfes all confirm'd by the Event. A
" Citizen indeed generally envies his Fellow-
" Citizen, if he fees him profper ; he hates him
" privately, and unlefs he hath attain'd to an
" uncommon Degree of Virtue, will not give
" him Counfel with Sincerity. But a Friend
" loves to fee his Friend in Profperity, and, if
" he ask his Advice, always gives him the beft
" he can. For the future therefore I enjoin all
" Men to abftain from fuch indecent Expref-
" fions concerning *Demaratus*, who is my Hoft

" and

" and Friend." When *Xerxes* had said these words, he went out among the Dead; and having heard that *Leonidas* was King and General of the Lacedemonians, he commanded his Head to be taken ʃoff, and fixed upon a Pole. By which Action, and many other Proofs, I am persuaded that *Xerxes* was highly incensed against *Leonidas* during his Life, else he would not have violated the Laws of Humanity upon his dead Body; because the Persians are accustom'd to pay a greater Reverence to Men eminent in military Virtue, than any other Nation we know. However, the King's Command was executed in the manner he had order'd. But to return to my Narration.

T H E Lacedemonians were the first who had notice of the King's Expedition against *Greece*; and on that occasion sending to the Oracle at *Delphi*, receiv'd the Answer I lately mention'd. But the way, by which they had their Information, deserves to be remember'd. *Demaratus*, the Son of *Ariʃton*, being at that time an Exile among the Medes, had as I conjecture, and Appearances confirm, no great Kindness for the Lacedemonians: But whether he acted in this Affair by a Motive of Affection, or in order to insult his Country, I shall leave to the Judgment of others; yet when *Xerxes* had resolv'd to make war against *Greece*, and *Demaratus*, who was then in *Suʃa*, had heard of his Intention, he determin'd to acquaint the Lacedemonians with the Design. But because he could contrive no other means, and apprehended the Danger of a Discovery, he fell upon this Invention: He took a double Table-Book, and having shav'd off the Wax, he en-

grav'd

grav'd the King's Refolution on the Wood; which when he had done, he laid another Covering of Wax upon the Letters, that his Meffenger might meet with no Impediment from the Guards of the Way.   In this manner the Table-Book was brought to *Sparta*; but the Lacedemonians could not comprehend the Secret, till *Gorgo*, the Daughter of *Cleomenes*, and Wife to *Leonidas*, making a right Conjecture, bid them break up the Wax, and they fhould find Letters written underneath.   The Lacedemonians did as fhe order'd, and after they had read the Contents, fent the Letters to the reft of the Grecians.

THE

THE
Hiſtory of *Herodotus*.

BOOK VIII.

URANIA.

THESE things are thus reported ; and as for the Naval Forces of the Grecians, they were compos'd of the following numbers : The Athenians furniſhed one hundred and twenty ſeven Ships, mounted by themſelves, and the Platæans ; who with great Alacrity and Courage, tho' unexperienced in Sea-Affairs, went on board with them. The Corinthians brought in forty Sail, the Megareans twenty ; the Chalcidæans mann'd twenty Ships, borrow'd of the Athenians ; the People of *Ægina* furniſhed eighteen Sail, the Sicyonians twelve, the Lacedemonians ten, the Epidaurians eight, the Eretrians ſeven, the Trœzenians five, the Styreans two. The Chians contributed two Ships of War, with two Gallies of fifty Oars each ; and the Locrians of *Opus* brought in ſeven Gallies of like force. All theſe Ships, being two hundred and ſeventy one in number, befides the Gallies, had their Station at *Artemi-fium*; and the principal Command was in the hands of *Eurybiades*, the Son of *Euryclides*, nominated to that Dignity by the Spartans, becaufe the Confederates had declar'd, that they would not follow the Athenians, but would break the Fleet, and return home, unlefs they might have a Lacedemonian for their Leader. For before they fent Ambaffadors to make an Alliance in *Sicily*, they had debated about the Expediency of giving the Conduct of the Naval Forces to the Athenians. But the Athenians finding the Confederates averfe to that Propofal, and being extremely defirous to preferve *Greece*, which they knew muft inevitably be deftroyed, if they fhould fplit into Factions for the Precedency, defifted voluntarily, and gave a great Proof of their Wifdom in fo doing : For inteftine Diffenfions are by fo much more pernicious than a War carried on with Unanimity, as War in general is more prejudicial than Peace. This they well underftood, and therefore chofe rather to recede from their Pretenfions, than to contend in that Exigency of Affairs, as the Event demonftrated. For when they had driven out the Perfian, and carried the War into his own Territories, they took occafion from the Arrogance of *Paufanias*, to deprive the Lacedemonians of the chief Command; but thefe things were done afterwards.

IN the mean time the Grecians at *Artemifium* feeing a prodigious number of the Enemies Ships at *Aphete*, all Places fill'd with their Forces, and the Barbarians fuccefsful beyond their Expectation and Opinion; in a great Confternation deliberated to retire to the remoteft Parts of *Greece.*

Greece. The Euboeans hearing of this Consultation, earnestly begg'd of *Eurybiades* to defer the Departure of the Fleet, till they could carry off their Children and Families: But finding him inflexible, they addressed themselves to *Themistocles*, the Athenian General, and by a Present of thirty Talents prevail'd with him to promise, that they would stay and fight the Enemy on that Coast; which he effected in this manner: He gave five Talents of this Money to *Eurybiades*, as from himself; and having gain'd his Consent by that means, he went to the Corinthian Commander, *Adimantus*, the Son of *Ocytus*; because he was now the only Person, who refusing to stay, had peremptorily declar'd he would leave *Artemisium*, and with an Oath said to him, " *Adimantus*, you shall not abandon " us; for I will make you a greater Present " than the King of the Medes would send you " for deserting the Allies." When he had spoken these Words, he presently sent him three Talents of Silver on board his Ship; and by this Bribery, having prevail'd with the Commanders to stay, he at once gratify'd the Euboeans, and secur'd all the rest to himself; whilst those who took part of the Money, knew nothing of the Remainder, but thought the Athenians had entrusted him with that Sum, to be employed in such an Occasion. Thus the Grecians continued on the Coast of *Euboea*, till they came to an Engagement; which happen'd in this manner: The Barbarians arriving in the Road of *Aphete* about Day-break, and observing that the Grecians were at *Artemisium* with a small number of Ships, as they had been already inform'd, shew'd a general Disposition to try if

they

they could furprize them in that Station; but they were not of opinion to attack them in Front, left the Grecians, feeing them approaching, fhould betake themfelves to flight; and favour'd by the enfuing Night, fhould make their efcape: Whereas, in their account, every Ship was already condemn'd to fall into their hands, without excepting even that which carried the Light. In this Defign they detach'd two hundred Ships, chofen out of all their Fleet, with Orders to fail behind *Sciathus*, and fhape their Courfe to the *Euripus*, by *Caphareus* and *Gereftus*, that the Enemy might thus be circumvented, and not difcover them paffing along the Coaft of *Eubœa:* Not doubting, by this Force, to prevent their Efcape on that fide, whilft all the reft of the Fleet fhould attack them in Front. When they had taken this Refolution, they fent away the two hundred Ships; and determining to attempt nothing againft the Grecians that Day, nor before they fhould fee the Signal agreed upon, to notify the Arrival of their Detachment, they applied themfelves to take a view of their Numbers remaining at *Aphete.* In this Fleet was *Scyllias*, a Native of *Scyone*, who being the beft Diver of his time, had fav'd for the Ufe of the Perfians a great part of the Treafure funk in the Shipwreck at *Pelion*, and diverted a confiderable Sum to his own Profit. He had been long defirous to go over to the Grecians, but not finding a proper Opportunity, had deferr'd his Defign to the time of this Review. By what means he made his efcape to the Grecians, I cannot certainly affirm, and am aftonifhed at the account given of him: For the Report is, that he plung'd under water at *Aphete*, and rofe

no more till he arriv'd at *Artemisium*; which Places are about fourscore Stades distant from each other. Many other things are related of this Man, that have the Air of Falshood; and some that are true. Yet after all, my Opinion is, that he made his Passage to *Artemisium* in a Boat. At his Arrival he inform'd the Commanders of the Particulars of the Shipwreck, and of the Ships that were ordered to sail round *Eubœa:* Which when the Grecians heard, they call'd a Council of War, and after divers Opinions had been propos'd, came to a Resolution, That they would continue in their Station all that day, and at midnight weigh anchor to advance to meet the Fleet, which was sent out to prevent their Escape: But not discovering any Ships making towards them, they lay by till Sun-set; and then advancing against the Barbarians, resolv'd to make a tryal of their Courage in Fight, and of their Skill in maritime Affairs. When the Enemy, both Officers and Soldiers, saw them approaching with so few Ships, they attributed their Enterprize to extreme Folly; and advancing likewise on their part, doubted not of an easy Victory: The truth is, they had great reason to expect Success. And therefore, seeing the Grecian Ships were few, and their own not only far more in number, but much better Sailors, they with Scorn encompassed them on all sides. Some of the Ionians retaining an Affection for the Grecians, were with regret among the Enemies Forces, and extremely concern'd to see them surrounded in such a manner; thinking their Condition so desperate, that not a Man could possibly escape. But others, pleas'd with their Distress, labour'd with all
their

their might, who should take the first Athenian
Ship, and merit a Recompence from the King:
For the Athenians were in greater esteem among
the Enemy than any of the other Confederates.
At the first Signal the Grecians drew into a
Circle, and turn'd the Heads of all their Ships
against the Barbarians. At the second Signal
they began the Fight, crouded into a narrow
Compass, and having the Enemy in front on e-
very part: yet in a short time they took thirty
Ships from the Barbarians, with *Philaon*, the Son
of *Cherfis*, Brother to *Gorges*, King of the Salaminians; a Man highly esteem'd in their Army. *Ly-*
comedes, the Son of *Æschreus*, an Athenian, was
the first who took a Ship from the Enemy, and
was honour'd in the usual manner for that Action.
But Night coming on, put an end to the Dispute,
after they had fought with various Success on
both sides; the Grecians returning to *Artemisium*,
and the Barbarians to *Aphete*, with less Good fortune than they expected. In this Engagement,
Antidorus the Lemnian was the only Grecian that
revolted from the King; and on that account,
the Athenians rewarded him with Lands in *Sa-*
lamis. This Battle was fought in the midst of
Summer; and during all the Night, so prodigious a Storm of Rain fell, accompanied with
hard Thunder, breaking out from about *Pelion*,
that the dead Bodies, and Pieces of Wreck driven
to *Aphete*, rolling to the Heads of their Ships,
disturb'd the Order of their Oars: Which the
Barbarians observing, were struck with Consternation, and expected nothing but Death,
when they saw so many Calamities succeeding
one another. For before they had recover'd
Breath after the former Tempest and Shipwreck

at Mount *Pelion*, they were forced to fight a dangerous Battle at Sea ; and before that Engagement was well over, were surpriz'd by impetuous Rains, and horrid Thunder with Torrents of Water driving through the Sea. In this Terror they passed that Night : But those who had been ordered to sail round *Eubœa*, met with a much greater Disaster, and being out at Sea the same Night, they all perished miserably. For as they approached the Gulphs of *Eubœa*, the Storm and Rain fell upon them with such Violence, that they were driven they knew not where, by the Force of the Winds, and dashed in Pieces upon the Rocks. This the Gods did, to reduce the Persian Fleet to an Equality with that of the Grecians ; or at least, not to leave them so much superior in Number. And thus these Ships perished on the Coast of *Eubœa*.

THE Light of the next Day was welcome to the Barbarians at *Aphete* ; who keeping themselves quiet in their Station, were contented after their ill Success, to attempt nothing more for the present : On the other hand, the Grecians receiv'd a Reinforcement of fifty three Athenian Ships ; which, with the News they brought, that all the Barbarians that were sailing by *Eubœa*, had perished in the Storms, so heighten'd their Courage, that having waited to the same Hour they chose the day before, they attacked and ruin'd the Squadrons of the Cilicians, and return'd at night to *Artemisium*. On the third Day, the Commanders of the Barbarians, mov'd with Indignation to be thus insulted by a few Ships, and fearing the Displeasure of Xerxes, would not stay to be again attacked by the Grecians ; but encouraging their Men to acquit themselves valiantly,

liantly, unmoor'd about Noon, and prepar'd to fight. These Actions by Sea happen'd on the same Days with those by Land at *Thermopyle*; and the Contest in both Places was of the same nature: For as *Leonidas*, and those who were with him, endeavour'd to defend the Pass of *Thermopyle*, so the naval Forces fought to prevent the Enemy from entring the *Euripus*; the Grecians, on their part, encouraging one another not to suffer the Barbarians to break into *Greece*; and these, on the other hand, animating their Men to force the Grecians, and make themselves Masters of the Passages.

IN this View, the Barbarians having drawn out their Fleet, advanc'd towards the Grecians; who lying quiet at *Artemisium*, no sooner saw the Enemy approaching in the Form of a Half-moon, and endeavouring to make sure of them, by surrounding their whole number, than they came out likewise, and fell on immediately. The Battle was fought with almost equal Success on both sides: For though the Enemies Ships, being large, and in great number, fell foul on each other, and confounded their Order, yet they continued to fight, and would not retire, because they were ashamed to be beaten by so few. So that many of the Grecian Ships perish'd in the Action, and many Men; but the Loss of the Barbarians was much greater in both. Thus they fought with equal Resolution, and after an obstinate Fight, retir'd to their former Stations. In this Battle the Egyptians signaliz'd their Courage above the rest of the Enemies Forces; and, besides other memorable Actions, took five Grecian Ships, with all the Men on board. On the part of the Grecians, the Athenians behav'd
them-

themselves with the greatest Valour; and among the Athenians, *Clinias* the Son of *Alcibiades*, who fought in his own Ship, which he had mann'd with two hundred Men, maintain'd at his own Expence. But after both the Fleets had voluntarily separated, the Grecians, tho' they were in possession of the Dead, and of all the Wreck; yet being in a shatter'd condition, and especially the Athenians, whose Ships were for the most part disabled, took into their consideration, whether they should retire to the remoter Parts of *Greece.* At the same time *Themistocles* persuaded himself, that if they could prevail with the Ionians and Carians to abandon the Barbarians, they might be able to overcome the rest; and therefore as the Euboeans were driving their Cattle down to the Shore, he assembled the Grecian Commanders together, and told them he had contriv'd a Stratagem, by which he hoped to deprive the King of the best of his Allies. He discover'd no more for the present; only adding, that in order to forward his Design, they should kill as many of the Cattle belonging to the Euboeans as they thought fit, because their own Army ought rather to have them than the Enemy. He also exhorted them to direct their Men to kindle Fires, and promised he would chuse so convenient a time for their Departure, that they should all arrive safe in *Greece.* The Captains resolv'd to do as he advis'd; and after they had order'd Fires to be lighted, they began to seize the Cattle. For the Euboeans slighting the Answer they receiv'd from the Oracle of *Bacis*, as frivolous, had sent nothing away, nor brought in any thing; as Men would do, who expect a

War: and by that means had put themselves into ill Circumstances. The Oracle was conceiv'd in these Words:

When a Barbarian with a Yoke of Hemp
Shall curb the Sea, then drive your Flocks and Herds
Far from Eubœan Shores.

But the Eubœans shewing no regard to this Admonition, tho' they were in a bad condition at present, and in expectation of farther Misfortunes, fell into the greatest Distress.

IN the mean time a Messenger arriv'd express from *Trachis.* For as *Polyas* of *Anticyra* was appointed to stay at *Artemisium,* and had a Vessel ready to attend him, in order to inform the Grecians at *Thermopyle,* if the Fleet should come to an Action; so *Abronychus* the Son of *Lisicles* an Athenian, was with *Leonidas,* and had Instructions to come away to *Artemisium* in a Galley of thirty Oars, if any thing considerable should happen to the Land-Forces. This *Abronychus* arriving, gave an account of what had befallen *Leonidas,* and those who were with him: Which when the Grecians heard, they resolv'd not to defer their Departure, but stood away immediately in the order they were; the Corinthians in the Van, and the Athenians in the Rear. *Themistocles,* at the same time, having chosen the nimblest of the Athenian Ships, sail'd to the place where they us'd to take in fresh Water, and engrav'd these Words upon the Stones; which were read the next day by the Ionians when they arrived at *Artemisium:* " Men of " *Ionia,* you are guilty of a heinous Crime,

I   " in

" in fighting againſt your Fathers, and help-
" ing to enſlave *Greece.* Reſolve therefore to
" come over to us: Or if you cannot do
" that, withdraw your Forces from the Ene-
" my, and perſuade the Carians to imitate
" your Example. But if both theſe ways are
" impracticable, and you find yourſelves un-
" der an abſolute neceſſity of continuing in
" the Perſian Fleet, favour us at leaſt when
" we come to an Engagement; and remem-
" ber that you are not only deſcended from
" us, but are the original Cauſe of the Bar-
" barians Enmity againſt us." I ſuppoſe
Themiſtocles did this with a double View;
hoping that if theſe Words were not diſcover'd
to the King, he ſhould induce the Ionians to
come over to the Grecians; or if they were reported to him, and imputed to the Ionians for a
Crime, he ſhould bring them into ſuch a Suſpicion, that *Xerxes* would for the future refuſe
to accept their Aſſiſtance.

SOON after the Departure of the Grecians,
a certain Man of *Hiſtiæa* arriving by Sea, gave
the Barbarians an account of their Fleet from
Artemiſium. But they ſuſpecting the Meſſenger,
ſecur'd him under a Guard, and ſent out ſome
light Veſſels to diſcover the ſtate of things. At
their return, being inform'd of the Truth, all
the Fleet weigh'd Anchor upon the riſing of the
Sun, and ſailed directly to *Artemiſium*; where
they continued till about Noon, and then proceeding to *Hiſtiæa*, poſſeſſed themſelves of that
City, and ravag'd all the Maritime Territories
which are in the Diſtrict of *Ellopia.* Whilſt
they were on this Coaſt, they receiv'd a Meſſage
from *Xerxes*, after he had diſpoſed of the dead

Bodies

Bodies of his Men as he thought most convenient. For of twenty thousand of his Army, who were kill'd at *Thermopyle*, leaving only one thousand unburied, he caused all the rest to be interred, with Leaves strew'd over their Bodies, and then to be cover'd with Earth, that they might not be seen by those who should come from the Fleet. When his Messenger arriv'd at *Histiæa*, he summon'd a general meeting of all the Naval Forces, and said, " Friends and Allies, all those among you
" that are desirous to see how the King's Forces
" have fought against inconsiderate Men, who
" vainly imagin'd they could conquer his Army,
" may leave this Station, and go to *Thermopyle*
" with his Permission." Upon which Notification the Number of those who went thither was so great, that the remaining Ships were very few. When they arriv'd, they view'd the Field of Battel, supposing all the Dead to be Lacedemonians and Thespians, tho' indeed many Helots were among them : But the method *Xerxes* had taken to dispose of the Bodies of his own Men, could not be conceal'd from those who came from the Fleet. And indeed the thing was ridiculous, to shew only a thousand Barbarians kill'd, when all the four thousand Grecians lay dead in Heaps upon the spot. In this view they spent that day, and on the next return'd with their Ships to *Histiæa*, whilst *Xerxes* advanc'd with his Army. In his March a small number of Arcadians, indigent, and desirous of Employment, deserted to him ; and being brought into the King's Presence, were examin'd touching the Grecians. Among others, one of the Persians, in the name of all the rest, ask'd what the
Grecians

Grecians were then doing: The Arcadians answer'd, they were employ'd in celebrating the
Olympian Exercises, and in viewing the Horse-
Races and Gymnick Combats. The Persian
ask'd farther, what Reward the Victorious
were to have; they replied, a Crown of Olive.
Upon which, *Tigranes* the Son of *Artabanus*
delivered his Opinion with a noble Generosity;
which yet the King thought to be the Effect
of Fear. For when he heard that the Recompence of the Conquerors was a Crown, and not
Riches, he could not forbear breaking out into
this Expression, " O *Mardonius*, said he, against
" what kind of Men have you persuaded us to
" make War? Men who fight not for Gold or
" Silver, but for Virtue only."

IN the mean time the Thessalians, incessantly mindful of their former Enmity to the
Phoceans, and now more exasperated since
the Slaughter at *Thermopyle*, sent a Herald
to them. For not many Years before the
Expedition of *Xerxes*, the Thessalians, in conjunction with their Allies, having invaded
the Territories of the Phoceans with all their
Forces, had been repulsed with great Loss,
in this manner: The Phoceans being compelled to retire to Mount *Parnassus*, made use
of this Stratagem by the Advice of the Prophet
Tellias of *Elis*, who was then in their Camp;
they cover'd the Armour and Faces of six hundred of their best Men with white Plaster, and
sent them out by night against the Thessalians,
with Orders to kill every Man they should not
find painted like themselves. They were first
seen by the Thessalian Guards, and soon after by their whole Army; who taking them

for

for some prodigious Apparition, were struck with such a Terror, that the Phoceans killed three thousand upon the place; and being Masters of the Dead, sent one half of their Shields to *Abe*, and the rest to *Delphi*. The tenth Part of the Booty they took in this Fight, was employ'd to purchase those great Statues which stand about the Tripos in the Temple of *Delphi*, and others of equal Dimensions erected in *Abe*. Thus the Phoceans dealt with the Foot of the Thessalians, by which they had been in a manner besieged; and by another Stratagem ruin'd their Horse, when they made an Irruption into their Territories. For having open'd a vast Trench in the way near the City of *Hyampolis*, and filled the Vacuity with empty Pots, which they cover'd with Earth, and brought to a level with the rest of the Ground, they waited the coming of the Thessalians: Who advancing hastily to attack the Phoceans, fell in among the Earthen Vessels, and spoiled the Legs of their Horses. Both these Actions so irritated the Thessalians, that they sent this Message by their Herald to the Phoceans: " Be convinc'd now more than ever,
" O Phoceans, that you are inferior to us. For
" during all the time we chose to take part with
" the Grecians, we were justly esteemed your
" Superiors; and now we have so great Power
" with the Barbarian, that we can without
" difficulty dispossess you of your Country, and
" enslave your Persons: Nevertheless, tho' you
" are entirely at our mercy, we forget the In-
" juries you have done us, and ask no more than
" fifty Talents of Silver by way of Reparation;
" engaging, upon your compliance, to prevent
" the

" the Dangers impending over you." The
Theſſalians ſent to make this Demand, principally becauſe the Phoceans were the only
People of thoſe Parts, who had not fallen in
with the Intereſt of the Medes : From which,
as I conjecture, they were reſtrain'd by no
other reaſon, than their Enmity to the Theſſalians ; and I am of opinion that the Phoceans would have join'd with the Medes,
if the Theſſalians had taken part with the
Grecians. However, in anſwer to this Meſſage, the Phoceans peremptorily refuſed to
give the Money, and ſaid, if they were diſpoſed to revolt to the Medes, the way was
open to them as well as to the Theſſalians ;
but that they would not be Traytors to *Greece*
without neceſſity. When their Anſwer was reported to the Theſſalians, they were ſo incens'd
againſt the Phoceans, that ſerving for Guides to
the Barbarians, and marching in the Van of their
Army from *Trachis*, they enter'd the narrow Plain
of *Doris* ; which being about thirty Stades in
breadth, and ſituated between *Melis* and the Territories of the Phoceans, (antiently known by
the Name of *Dryopis*) is the Mother Country of
all the Dorians in *Peloponneſus*. The Barbarians
made no Depredations in their Paſſage thro' the
Territories of *Doris*, becauſe the Inhabitants were
Partizans of the Medes ; which yet was not
known to the Theſſalians. From thence advancing into *Phocis*, and not meeting with the
Phoceans, they were conducted over all Parts
of the Country by the Theſſalians, and carrying Fire and Sword wherever they came, deſtroy'd both their Cities and their Temples. For
ſome of the Phoceans were retired to the top

of

of Mount *Parnaſſus*, on that ſide which deſcends to the City of *Neon*, and goes by the Name of *Tithorea*; where the Ground is ſpacious enough to contain conſiderable Numbers of Men: but the greater part had betaken themſelves to *Amphiſſa*, a City belonging to the Locrians of *Ozole*, and built in the Plain of *Criſæus*. In their March the Barbarians ravaged all the Country along the River *Cephiſſus*, and burnt the Cities of *Drymus*, *Charadra*, *Erochus*, *Amphicæa*, *Neon*, *Pedica*, *Tritea*, *Elatea*, and *Hyampolis*; with all the Places in the Neighbourhood of the River, and particularly the City of *Abe*, in which was a Temple of *Apollo* enrich'd with many Treaſures and conſecrated Donations, where Oracles were deliver'd in thoſe Days, as they are at preſent. This Temple they plunder'd and burnt; and purſuing the Phoceans into the Mountains, took ſeveral Priſoners: ſuch Numbers of Men forcing the Women who fell into their hands, that divers died in the place. After the Barbarians had thus paſs'd the Countries bordering on the River, they divided their Army into two Bodies. The moſt numerous and beſt part of their Forces march'd towards *Athens* with *Xerxes*, and enter'd *Bœotia* by the way of *Orchomenus*. But becauſe all the Bœotians were in the Intereſt of the Medes, their Cities were preſerved by Macedonian Forces, which *Alexander* had ſent, to ſatisfy *Xerxes* that they were entirely at his Devotion.

WHILST theſe Barbarians march'd this way, the reſt, with their Leaders, ſtretching their Right to the foot of Mount Parnaſſus, advanced towards the Temple of Delphi; and deſtroying all

they

they found in their way belonging to *Phocis*, set fire to the Cities of *Panopea*, *Daulis*, and *Æolium*. These Forces were detach'd from the other Part of the Army, and sent this way, in order to plunder the Temple of *Delphi*, and to put the Booty into the hands of *Xerxes* ; who, as I have heard, was better inform'd of all the valuable things there, than of those he left behind him at home : so many Persons continually entertain'd him with Discourses concerning these Treasures, and more especially of the Donations made by *Cræsus* the Son of *Alyattes.* When the Delphians heard of their Design, they fell into a great Consternation, and with dreadful Apprehensions consulted the Oracle, whether they should hide their Treasures under ground, or transport them to another Country: But the God would not suffer the Treasures to be remov'd, saying, he was sufficiently able to defend his own. The Delphians having receiv'd this Answer, began to think of themselves ; and after they had sent their Wives and Children by Sea to *Achaia*, the greater part of the Men went either to the top of *Parnassus*, or into the Cave of *Corycium* ; whilst others retir'd to *Amphissa*, belonging to the Locrians: In a word, all the Inhabitants of *Delphi* abandon'd the City, except only sixty Men, and the Prophet. When the Barbarians were advanc'd within sight of the Temple, the Prophet, whose Name was *Aceratus*, seeing the Arms, which no Mortal may touch, brought out and laid before the sacred Place, went and told the Prodigy to the Delphians who were left in the City. But when the Barbarians arriv'd at the Temple of *Minerva* the Provident,

much

much greater Prodigies than the former were
feen. And indeed though the fight of thofe In-
ftruments of War, which had mov'd out of the
Temple of themfelves, was very wonderful ;
yet the fecond Prodigies were far more afto-
nifhing than all others : For immediately after
the Arrival of the Barbarians at *Minerva*'s Temple, Thunder fell from Heaven upon their
Troops ; the two Heads of *Parnaffus* breaking
from the Mountain with a horrible Noife, and,
rolling down killed many of their Men, and a
Voice, accompany'd with Shouts of Joy, was
heard iffuing from the Temple of the Goddefs.
All thefe things, in conjunction, fo terrified
the Barbarians, that they betook themfelves to
flight ; which when the Delphians heard, they
came down from the Mountain, and made a
great Slaughter among them. The reft fled
into *Bœotia*, and, as I am inform'd, declar'd,
that befides other miraculous things, they faw
two Perfons of more than human Stature, compleatly armed, purfuing and killing them in
their Flight. The Delphians fay thefe two were
Phylacus and *Autonous*, Heroes of the Country,
whofe Altars are not far from the Temple ; that
of *Phylacus* ftanding by the Highway beyond
the Temple of *Minerva*, and the other near the
Caftalian Spring, under the Brow of *Hyampea*.
The Stones that broke from *Parnaffus*, are feen
to this day lying in the Grove of *Minerva*, on
the Place where they fell among the Barbarians :
And fuch was the Succefs of this Enterprize
againft the Temple.

T H E Grecian Fleet, in their Return from
Artemifium, put in at *Salamis*, at the Sollicitation of the Athenians ; who made this Requeft,
in

in order to carry off their Wives and Children out of *Attica*, and to consult of measures to be taken in that Conjuncture, the present Condition of Affairs requiring new Counsels, because they had been disappointed in their Expectation: For whereas they thought to find the Peloponnesians, with all their Forces, waiting in *Bœotia* to receive the Barbarians, they found nothing less than what they expected: but, on the contrary, were inform'd that they were employ'd in fortifying the Isthmus with a Wall, taking great care to preserve themselves, and to secure the *Peloponnesus*, without any regard to others; and for these Reasons the Athenians desir'd the Allies to stay at *Salamis.* But while the rest continu'd in that Station, the Athenians return'd home: and at their Arrival caus'd Proclamation to be made, that every one should endeavour to save his Wife and Children by the best means he could contrive. Accordingly they sent the greater part to *Trœzene*, some to *Ægina*, and others to *Salamis*, using all possible Diligence in transporting their Families, not only in obedience to the Oracle, but out of a desire of Victory, and for another reason of no less Efficacy: For the Athenians say, that the *Acropolis* was guarded by a great Serpent kept in the Temple; and, as if the thing had been true, they every month brought thither a certain quantity of Paste mix'd with Honey; which, in former time having always been consum'd, now remain'd intire and untouch'd: So that when the Priestess had given publick notice of this Event, the Athenians were willing to leave the City, because they concluded the God had abandon'd

the

the Fortress; and therefore after they had embark'd whatever they thought convenient, they made the best of their way to join the Fleet.

WHEN the rest of the Naval Forces of the Grecians understood, that those who had lain at *Artemisium* were arriv'd at *Salamis*, they hasten'd thither from *Trœzene*, where their Rendezvous had been appointed in the Harbour of *Pogon*. This Fleet, much more numerous than that which fought at *Artemisium*, as being furnish'd by a greater number of Cities, was still commanded by *Eurybiades* the Lacedemonian, though he was not of the Royal Family. The Athenians brought in more Ships and better Sailors than any other People, and the whole Fleet consisted of these particular Proportions: The Lacedemonians furnish'd eleven Ships, the Corinthians the same number they had at *Artemisium*, the Sicyonians fifteen, the Epidaurians ten, the Trœzenians five, and the Hermionians three. All these, except the last, were of Dorian or Macedonian Original, antiently transplanted from *Erineus*, *Pindus*, and *Dryopis*. The Hermionians indeed are of Dryopian Extraction; but they were ejected by *Hercules* and the Melians out of that Country which is now called *Doris*. These were the Forces of the Peloponnesians. From the Continent beyond the Isthmus, the Athenians alone furnished one hundred and eighty Ships; for the Platæans were not with them at the Battle of *Salamis*, by this Accident. When the Grecians had abandon'd *Artemisium*, and were arriv'd on the Coast of *Chalcis*, the Platæans landed in a Place adjoining to the farther part of *Bœotia*, in order to

I   carry

carry off their Wives and Children; and whilst
they took care to preserve their Families, were
themselves left behind. When the Pelasgians
possess'd those Countries, which now go by
the name of *Greece*, the Athenians were called
Cranian Pelasgians. Under the Reign of *Cecrops*, they had the name of Cecropians; which
in the time of their King *Erechtheus*, they
changed for that of Athenians: and lastly were
nam'd Ionians from *Ion* the Son of *Xuthus*, who
was their General. The Megareans appear'd
with the same number of Ships they had at
Artemisium; the Ambracians furnish'd seven,
and the Leucadians, who are Dorians, of Corinthian Extraction, three. From the Islands
the Æginetes brought in thirty Ships, and
having left divers others at home for the Guard
of their Country, fought at *Salamis* in these
thirty, which were the best Sailors they had.
The Æginetes are Dorians, descended from
Epidaurus, and their Island was formerly known
by the name of *Oenone*. Next to these the
Chalcideans appear'd with twenty Sail, being
the same they had at *Artemisium*; and the Eretrians with seven: both these Nations are Ionians. The Chians, who are likewise Ionians,
and descended from the Athenians, came with
the same number they had before. The Naxians brought in four Ships, though they had
been sent by their Principals to join the Medes
with the rest of the Islanders; but slighting
their Orders, they chose to side with the
Grecians, chiefly by the Persuasion of *Democri-
tus*, an eminent Citizen of *Naxus*, and their
Commander in chief. The Naxians also are
Ionians, and derive their Blood from the Athenians.

nians. The Styreans came in with the same
Ships they had at *Artemifium*, and the Cyn-
thians with one Ship of War, and a Galley of
fifty Oars: Both these People are Dryopians.
The Seriphians, the Siphnians, and the Melians took part with the Grecians likewise, having already diftinguifh'd themfelves from all the
reft of the Iflanders, by refufing Earth and
Water to the Barbarian. All thefe Nations are
fituate between the River *Acheron* and the
Thefprotians, who inhabiting beyond *Ambracia*
and *Leucadia*, came to this Expedition from a
greater diftance than the reft. But of all the
People that inhabit the Countries above the
Thefprotians, the Crotonians, originally of
Achaia, came fingly to fuccour *Greece* in this
time of Danger, and brought in one Ship of
War, commanded by *Phyallus*, who had thrice
been victorious in the Pythian Exercifes. The
Melians, the Siphnians, and the Seriphians arriv'd in Gallies of fifty Oars, but the reft of the
Fleet confifted of Ships built with three Ranks.
The Melians, who are defcended from the Lacedemonians, furnifh'd two; and the Siphnians, with the Seriphians, both Ionians, of A-
thenian Original, two more. So that the whole
number of thefe Ships, without accounting the
Gallies, amounted to three hundred and feventy eight.

WHEN they were all affembled at *Salamis*
from the feveral Cities I have mention'd, they
held a Council of War; in which *Eurybiades* propos'd to the reft of the Captains, that every
Man would freely deliver his Opinion, where
he thought they might fight with moft advantage, inthofe Parts which were yet in their Poffeffion.

seffion. For having already laid afide all thoughts
of *Attica* as of a loft Country, and now only
confulting in what other Place they fhould engage, the greater number agreed in opinion,
that they fhould fail to the Ifthmus, and fight
upon the Coafts of *Peloponnefus:* alledging for
their Reafons, that if they fhould lofe a Battle
at *Salamis,* they fhould be befieg'd in the Ifland,
without the leaft hope of Succour; whereas if
the like Misfortune fhould happen at the Ifthmus, they might retire to their own Cities.
When the Peloponnefians were come to this Conclufion, a certain Athenian arriv'd with Advice, that the Barbarian had enter'd *Attica,*
and fet fire to all the Places he found in his
way: For *Xerxes,* with his Army, having paffed thro' *Bæotia,* where he burnt the City of the
Thefpians, who were retir'd to *Peloponnefus,*
and the City of the Platæans, marched to *A-
thens,* and deftroyed every thing. He fet fire
to *Thefpia* and *Platæa,* upon the information he
had from the Thebans, that thofe Cities were
not in the Intereft of the Medes. The Barbarians had fpent a month in paffing the *Hellefpont,*
and bringing their Forces into *Europe:* In three
months more they arriv'd in *Attica,* when *Callia-
des* was Archon of the Athenians, and took the
City, abandon'd by all the Inhabitants, except
a few Men they found in the Temple, with the
Officers of that Place, and fome indigent Perfons, who having fortified the *Acropolis* with
Gates, and Palifadoes of Wood, defended themfelves againft the Enemy. Thefe Men did not
go to *Salamis;* partly by reafon of their Poverty, and partly becaufe they thought they had
found the Senfe of the Oracle deliver'd by the

Pythian,

Pythian, " That the Wall of Wood should be
" impregnable : " imagining that this was the
Defence predicted by the Priestess, and not the
Navy. The Persians, on their part, posted
themselves over against the Fort upon a Hill,
which the Athenians call *Areopagus*, and began
their Attack in this manner. Having wrapped
their Arrows in Tow, and set fire to them,
they shot into the Works of the Besieged,
who, though they were in the utmost extremity, and saw their Palisadoes all in flames, yet
resolving to defend themselves to the last, refused to accept the Terms that were offer'd by
the Pisistratides, if they would surrender : and,
among other things they contriv'd for their Defence, threw down Mill-stones upon the Barbarians, as they made their Approaches to the
Gates. So that *Xerxes* was in no little perplexity, for a considerable time, to find he could
not reduce the Place. At last the Barbarians
surmounted these Difficulties, by discovering
another way to enter the Fort, according to the
Prediction of the Oracle : " That all the Ter-
" ritories of *Attica*, which are situate on the
" Continent, should be subdued by the Per-
" sians." Having therefore found out a certain
Passage behind the Gates, and the Ascent that
leads to the Front of the *Acropolis*, where the
Athenians had plac'd no Guard, because they
had no suspicion that any Man could pass
that way, some of the Barbarians mounted the
Precipice, by the Temple of *Aglaura*, the
Daughter of *Cecrops*. When the Athenians saw
the Enemy within the *Acropolis*, some threw
themselves down from the Walls, and were killed, and others retir'd into the Temple. But the
Persians

Perfians, who had enter'd, went immediately
to the Gates; and having forced them open,
kill'd all thofe that had taken Sanctuary there:
after which Slaughter, they pillag'd the Temple, and fet fire to every part of the *Acropolis.*

XERXES being thus entirely Mafter of *A-
thens,* difpatch'd a Meffenger to *Sufa* on horfeback, to acquaint *Artabanus* with the profperous
Condition of his Affairs: And the next day
after the Departure of this Courier, he call'd
together the Athenian Exiles, who were in his
Army, and order'd them to go up to the *Acropolis,* and to facrifice according to the Cuftom
of their own Country. But whether he commanded this by the impulfe of a Dream, or
from a Motive of Remorfe for burning the
Temple, is uncertain. However that be, the
Exiles perform'd his Command; and I fhall now
give the Reafon that mov'd me to mention the
thing. In the *Acropolis* ftands a Temple dedicated to *Erechtheus,* who is reported to have
been born of the Earth; and within that Build-
ding an Olive-tree, with a Reprefentation of a
Sea, ferving for a Monument, as the Athenians
fay, of the Contention between *Neptune* and *Minerva,* about that Country. The Olive-tree
was burnt with the Temple by the Fire of the
Barbarians; and yet the next day after, when
the Athenians went thither to facrifice, by the
King's Command, they faw a Shoot rifen from
the Trunk, of a full Cubit in height: at leaft
the Exiles faid fo.

WHEN the Grecians at *Salamis* were inform'd of what had happen'd to the Fortrefs of
Athens, they fell into fo great a Confternation,
that fome of the Commanders went out of the

Council without staying to hear the Result of
the Deliberation, and hastening to their Ships,
hoisted sail in order to depart; whilst those
who continued to sit, came to a Resolution,
to return and fight at the Isthmus. The Af-
sembly broke up at night, and every one departed to his own Ship. But when *Themistocles*
was come on board, *Mnesiphilus*, an Athenian,
asked him what they had determined to do ;
and being told they had resolv'd to return to
the Isthmus, and fight to defend *Peloponnesus*,
" Then, *said he*, if these Men carry off their
" Ships from *Salamis*, you will fight for no
" Country at all ; because they will certainly
" return home to their several Cities : and nei-
" ther *Eurybiades*, nor any other Man living,
" will be able to prevent the Dispersion of
" the Fleet; and *Greece* must perish by bad
" Counsel. Therefore, without delay, endea-
" vour to contrive some means to break these
" Measures ; and try by all possible Ways, to
" persuade *Eurybiades* to alter his Opinion, and
" to continue in this Station." *Themistocles*
heard his Advice with great Joy, and, without returning any Answer, went immediately
on board the Ship of *Eurybiades*; and after
he had acquainted him that he had something to communicate to him, which concern'd
the common Safety, the Lacedemonian desir'd
him to speak with freedom. Then *Themistocles*
sat down, and appropriating to himself the
Counsel of *Mnesiphilus*, spoke to him in the same
Terms, and prevail'd with him to go ashore, and
to summon the Commanders together. When
they were all assembled, before Eurybiades had
acquainted then with the Cause of their meet-

ing,

ing, *Themiſtocles*, as he had too great reaſon,
enter'd into an ample Deduction of the State of
their Affairs: But whilſt he was ſpeaking, *Adimantus*, the Son of *Ocytus*, Commander of the
Corinthians, interrupting him, ſaid, " *Themi-
" ſtocles*, thoſe who ſtand up before others
" are corrected with a Switch." True, reply'd
" Themiſtocles: But thoſe who falter in the
" Race, never win the Crown." Having
thus calmly anſwer'd the Corinthian, he turn'd
to *Eurybiades* ; and, omitting that part of his
former Diſcourſe, which foretold their Separation, in caſe they ſhould leave *Salamis*, becauſe
he thought himſelf oblig'd by Decency, not to
accuſe any of the Confederates in the pre-
ſence of the reſt, took a different Method and
ſaid, " The Safety of *Greece*, O *Eurybiades*, is
" now entirely in your Power, if, approving my
" Opinion, you will ſtay and fight in this Place;
" and not hearken to thoſe who would per-
" ſuade you to retire with the Fleet to the
" Iſthmus. You will ſee this plainly, when I
" ſhall have ſhewn you the Conſequences of
" each Propoſition. If you fight before the
" Iſthmus, you muſt fight in an open Sea ;
" which will be a Diſadvantage to us, becauſe
" our Ships are not only more ſlow, but fewer
" in number than thoſe of the Enemy ; and
" beſies, you will inevitably ſacrifice *Salamis*,
" *Megara*, and *Ægina*, though we ſhould hap-
" pen to meet with better Fortune in other
" Places: And as the Land-Army of the Bar-
" barians will certainly follow their Fleet, you
" will by this mean, draw all their Forces
" into Peloponneſus, and bring all Greece into
" the utmoſt danger. But on the other hand,

" if

" if you will do as I advise you will reap the
" following Advantages: In the first place,
" being oblig'd with few Ships to fight against
" a great number, we shall gain much in
" point of Strength, if we come to an Engage-
" ment in a narrow Channel, unless things vary
" from their usual Course; for our Interest
" obliges us to fight in such Place, as much
" as the Enemy should endeavour to engage
" in the wide Sea. Besides we shall preserve
" *Salamis*, where we have left our Wives and
" Children. But that which ought principally
" to prevail with you, is, that if you stay and
" fight here, you will defend *Peloponnesus* no
" less effectually, than by fighting at the Isth-
" mus; and, if you consult your prudence, you
" will never lead the Enemy thither. In a
" word, if we beat the Barbarians at Sea, as
" I hope we shall, they will neither proceed
" to the Isthmus, nor penetrate farther than
" *Attica*, but must return home with Disgrace;
" and we shall have this additional Advantage,
" that we shall preserve *Megara*, *Ægina*, and
" *Salamis*; where we may reasonably expect to
" be superior to the Enemy. Men generally
" meet with Success, when their Enterprizes
" are founded upon prudent Counsels; but
" God himself will not indulge their ill-con-
" ceiv'd Opinions, if they determine to take
" such Measures as carry no Probability of a
" prosperous Event." When *Themistocles* had
said these Words, *Adimantus* the Corinthian,
breaking out a second time into Invectives a-
gainst him, said, He ought now to be silent
because he had no Country to speak for; and
not bearing with patience, that *Eurybiades*
should

should permit him to deliver his Opinion, told
him, he might then have a Voice in the Council,
when he should be able to say he had a Home:
Upbraiding him in this manner, because *Athens*
was taken, and in the hands of the Persian.
Themistocles, thus provoked, said many things to
the disadvantage of the Corinthians, and of
Adimantus in particular; telling them, that he
had yet a Country of greater power than *Corinth*, since the Athenians had still two hundred
Ships of War, arm'd and mann'd by themselves,
which no Nation of *Greece* was able to resist.
And after he had vindicated himself, addressing
his Discourse again to *Eurybiades*, he said, with
some Emotion; " If you stay, you will do the
" part of an honest Man; if you go, you will
" ruin *Greece*; for the Fate of the War rests
" wholly in our Fleet. Be persuaded then by
" my Reasons; or, if you are resolv'd not to
" do as I desire, we will immediately take our
" Families on board, and depart to *Siris*, a Ci-
" ty of *Italy*, belonging to us from antient time,
" which we are told by an oracle, is to be
" built and peopled by the Athenians: Per-
" haps you will remember my Words, when
" you shall find yourself abandon'd by so con-
" siderable a Part of your Allies." When
Themistocles had thus spoken, *Eurybiades* alter'd
his Opinion; or rather, as I conjecture, the
Apprehensions he had, that the Athenians
would leave him, if he should sail with the Fleet
to the Isthmus, prevail'd upon him to change
his Resolution: For, without the Assistance of
the Athenians, the rest were no way able to
resist the Enemy. So, adhering to the Opinion
of *Themistocles*, he determin'd to stay and come

to

to a Battel at *Salamis*. Which Refolution was no fooner taken, than thofe, who before had difputed with fuch Warmth, prepar'd themfelves unanimoufly for an Engagement. But after day-break, upon the rifing of the Sun, a Shog was felt both by Land and Sea : Upon which, they refolv'd to invoke the Gods, and to implore the Help of the *Æacides.* Accordingly, having addreffed their Prayers to all the Gods, and invoked *Ajax* and *Telamon,* in the Place where they were, they fent a Ship to *Ægina,* with like Inftructions, in reference to *Æacus,* and the *Æacides. Dicæus,* the Son of *Theocydes,* an Atnenian Exile, in great reputation with the Medes, reported, That after the Territories of *Attica* had been ravag'd by the Land-Forces of *Xerxes,* and abandon'd by the Athenians, he happen'd to be at that time with *Demaratus,* in the Plain of *Thriafium* ; where he faw fo great a Duft rifing from *Eleufis,* as might probably be rais'd by thirty thoufand Men ; That wondring at the Sight, and who fhould be the Caufe, they heard a Voice, which to him feem'd like that of *Myftical Iachus :* That *Demaratus* being unacquainted with the Eleufinian Myfteries, ask'd him the meaning of the Noife, and that he made the following Anfwer ;
" *Demaratus, faid he,* fome fignal Difafter will
" certainly befall the King's Army ; for fince
" *Attica* is utterly abandon'd, this can be no o-
" ther than the Voice of God, coming from
" *Eleufis,* to fuccour the Athenians and their
" Allies. If he goes to *Peloponnefus,* the King
" and his Land-Forces will be in danger on the
" Continent ; and if he takes his way to *Salamis,* the King will run the hazard of lofing
" his

" his Fleet.   The Athenians annually celebrate
" this Festival to *Ceres* and *Proserpina* ; admit-
" ting all other Grecians, who desire it, to be
" initiated in these Mysteries : and the Cries
" you hear, are such as they make at the Ce-
" lebration of this Solemnity."   To these
Words, *Demaratus* replied ; " Be silent, and say
" nothing to any Man of this Matter ; for if the
" King should be inform'd of your Discourse,
" he would take off your Head ; and neither I
" nor any other could possibly save you :
" Therefore keep the thing secret ; and as for
" the Army, let the Care of that rest with the
" Gods."   After *Demaratus* had given him this
Counsel, and both together had seen the Dust
and heard the Voice, they perceiv'd a Cloud ascending in the same Place, rolling thro' the Air
to *Salamis*, and there hovering over the Grecian
Fleet :   By which they understood, that the
Navy of *Xerxes* should be destroy'd.   These
things were affirm'd by *Dicæus*, the Son of *Theocydes*, appealing to the Testimony of *Demaratus*, and other Witnesses.

WHEN the naval Forces of *Xerxes* had
view'd the dead Bodies of the Lacedemonians,
they passed over from *Trachis* to *Histiæa*, and after three days stay, sail'd through the *Euripus*,
and in three days more, arriv'd at *Phaleron*.
Their Numbers, in my opinion, were no less,
both by Land and by Sea, when they came to
Athens, than when they arriv'd at *Sepias* and at
Thermopyle.   For I balance the Loss of those
that perished in the Storm, and at *Thermopyle*,
as well as of those that were kill'd in the Sea-
fight at *Artemisium*, with the additional Forces
they receiv'd from the Melians, the Dorians,

U 4   the

the Locrians, and generally from all the Bœotians, except the Thespians and the Platæans;
none of these People having before join'd the
King's Army. To this Number I must also
add the Caryſtians, the Andrians, and the Tenians, with all the reſt of the Iſlanders, except
the five Cities I mentioned before: For the
farther the Perſian penetrated into *Greece,* the
more was his Army increaſed, by the Nations
that follow'd his Fortune. When they were all
arriv'd at *Phaleron,* and at *Athens,* except only
the Parians, who ſtaid at *Cythnus,* in expectation of the Event, *Xerxes* himſelf went on board
the Fleet to confer with the Commanders, and
to know their Opinions: Where, after he had
taken his ſeat, and the Kings of the ſeveral Nations, with the other Generals of his Marine
Forces, were aſſembled, by his Direction, they
ſat down likewiſe in the Order appointed by
him; the King of *Sidon* firſt; next to him, the
King of *Tyre;* then the reſt in their reſpective
Ranks; and when they were all placed, *Xerxes*
ſent *Mardonius* to put the queſtion to every one
in particular, whether they ſhould venture an
Engagement by Sea, or not. Accordingly, *Mardonius* beginning at the King of *Sidon,* collected
the Opinions of the whole Aſſembly; which
were unanimous for fighting, except only that
of *Artemiſia,* who ſaid; " *Mardonius,* tell the
" King I give my opinion in theſe Words:
" Sir, ſince I have not behav'd myſelf worſe
" nor done leſs than others, in the Actions up-
" on the Coaſt of *Eubœa,* I may with reaſon
" ſpeak my Thoughts freely; and let you know
" what I think moſt advantageous to your Affairs
" I adviſe you then to ſave your Ships, and not
" to

" to come to an Engagement againſt thoſe,
" who, by Sea, are as much ſuperior to your
" Forces as Men are to Women. Beſides, what
" need have you to hazard another Battel at
" Sea? Is not *Athens* in your poſſeſſion, for
" which you undertook the War? And you
" are Maſter of the reſt of *Greece*; for no
" Man now oppoſes you, ſince thoſe who
" ventur'd to reſiſt, met with the Fate they
" deſerv'd. But, to tell you what I think
" will be the Fortune of the Enemy: If you
" abſtain from hazarding a Sea-fight, and or-
" der the Fleet to continue here, you will
" eaſily compaſs the Deſign you came a-
" bout; whether you ſtay aſhore in this
" place, or advance to *Peloponneſus* in perſon.
" For the Grecians cannot be long in a
" condition to reſiſt, but muſt ſeparate, and
" fly to their own Cities; becauſe, as I am
" inform'd, they have no Proviſions in this
" Iſland. Neither can we with any reaſon
" believe, that, when you have march'd your
" Land-Forces into *Peloponneſus*, thoſe who came
" hither from thence, will continue here, and
" fight a Battel by Sea, in order to defend the
" Territories of the Athenians. But if you
" determine to engage the Enemy at this time,
" I fear the Defeat of your Naval Forces will
" cauſe the Deſtruction of your Land-Army.
" Conſider, S I R, that good Men have ſome-
" times bad Servants, and bad Men good. You
" are the beſt of Men, but you have bad Ser-
" vants, who yet go under the name of your
" Confederates; and ſuch are the Ægyptians,
" the Cyprians, the Cilicians, and the Pamphy-
" lians, all utterly inſignificant." When *Artemiſia*
had

had said these words to *Mardonius*, her Friends were not a little disturb'd, fearing she might fall under the King's Displeasure, for dissuading him from a Battel at Sea. But those who envied her, because she was no less honour'd than the most considerable among the Confederates, were glad she had delivered such an Opinion, as they thought must certainly ruin her. Yet when the Report was made to *Xerxes*, he shew'd himself extremely pleas'd with the Opinion of *Artemisia* ; and having always esteem'd her zealous for his Interests, he now honour'd her with greater Praises than before. Nevertheless he determin'd to comply with the Majority ; and thinking his Forces had not done their best at *Eubœa*, because he was not present, he resolv'd to be Spectator of the Engagement. To that end Orders were given out for sailing, and the whole Fleet stood towards *Salamis*, drawing up into national Squadrons at leisure. But because Night was coming on, and the remaining Light not sufficient for a Battle, they prepar'd themselves to fight the next Day. In the mean time the Grecians were under much Fear and Apprehensions, of which the Peloponnesians had the greatest share ; reflecting with Astonishment, that they were then at *Salamis*, ready to fight for a Place belonging to the Athenians ; and that if they were beaten, they should be besieg'd, and prevented from retiring to their own Country, which they had left without defence.

IN that same Night the Land-Army of the Barbarians march'd towards *Peloponnesus*, where the Grecians had done all they could to prevent an Irruption by the way of the Continent. For so

soon

foon as they had heard of the Slaughter of the Peloponnefians with *Leonidas*, they drew together from their Cities to the Ifthmus, and put themfelves under the Conduct of *Cleombrotus*, the Son of *Anaxandrides*, and Brother to *Leonidas*. Being encamped there, they firft fortified the Paffage of *Sciron* ; and afterwards having refolv'd to erect a Wall upon the Ifthmus, they brought that Work to perfection, every Man, of fo many thoufands that were in the Army, performing his part, without exception. For they were all employ'd in carrying Stones, Bricks, Timber, or Hodds of Sand, working without intermiffion both by night and by day. The Grecians who came to fuccour the common Caufe at the Ifthmus, were, the Lacedemonians, the Arcadians, the Eleans, the Corinthians, the Sicyonians, the Epidaurians, the Phliafians, the Tœzenians, and the Hermionians ; all highly concern'd for the Danger of *Greece*. But the reft of the Peloponnefians took no care of any thing, tho' the Olympian and Carnian Solemnities were paft.

PELOPONNESUS is inhabited by feven Nations, two of which are the Arcadians and the Cynurians, who being originally of that Country, have always dwelt in the fame Places they now poffefs. After thefe the Achaians, who, tho' they never abandoned *Peloponnefus*, yet left their antient Seat, and fettled themfelves in another. The remaining four are Strangers, and confift of Dorians, Ætolians, Dryopians, and Lemnians. The Cities of the Dorians are many, and of great Fame : The Ætolians have only *Elis* : The Dryopians, *Hermione* and *Afina*, fituate near *Cardamyla*, a City of *Laconia* ; and the Lemnians

are

are Masters of all the Places that lie at the
foot of the Mountains. Among these, the
Cynurians alone appear to have been Ionians;
but were accounted Dorians after they fell
under the Power of the Argians, as were
also the Orneates and their Neighbours. Now
except those Nations I mention'd before, the
rest of the seven sat still; or rather, if I may
speak with freedom, absented themselves, because they favour'd the Medes. Nevertheless
the Grecians at the Isthmus concurr'd with
all possible Diligence to finish the Work they
had undertaken, expecting no Success from
their Navy. On the other hand, those at
Salamis were much disturb'd when they heard
these things, as being more concern'd for *Peloponnesus* than for themselves. They first began to whisper to one another, and to wonder at the Imprudence of *Eurybiades*; till at
last breaking out into open Murmurings, a
Council of War was called, and a long Debate
arose. Some said they ought to sail for *Peloponnesus*, and hazard a Battel for that Country, rather than to stay and fight for a Place already
in the power of the Enemy. But the Athenians,
the Æginetes, and the Megareans, voted to stay
and fight at *Salamis*. Then *Themistocles* seeing his
Opinion set aside by the Peloponnesians, went
privately out of the Council, and sent away a
Man to the Enemy's Fleet, in a small Vessel,
with such Orders as he thought necessary. The
Name of the Man was *Sicinus*, he lived in his
Family, had the care of instructing his Sons; and
in succeeding time, when the Thespians augmented the Number of their Citizens, *Themistocles* pro-
cur'd him to be made a Citizen of *Thespia*, and
gave

gave him confiderable Riches. This Perfon
arriving in the Fleet, delivered his Meffage
to the Barbarian Generals in thefe Words:
" The Captain of the Athenians, who is in
" the Intereft of the King, and defires your
" Affairs may profper, rather than thofe of
" *Greece*, has fent me privately away, with
" Orders to let you know, that the Greci-
" ans in great confternation have determin'd
" to betake themfelves to flight; and that
" you have now an Opportunity of atchiev-
" ing the moft glorious of all Enterprizes,
" unlefs your Negligence opens a Way to
" their Efcape. For being divided in their
" Opinions, they will not oppofe your For-
" ces; but you will fee thofe who are your
" Friends, fighting againft thofe who are not
" of your Party." *Sicinus* having thus deliver'd
his Meffage, departed immediately; and the
Enemy believing what he faid, landed a confiderable Number of Perfians in *Pfyttalea*, an
Ifland lying between *Salamis* and the Continent:
And about midnight ftretching the weftwardly
Point of their Fleet towards *Salamis*, whilft thofe
who were about *Ceos* and *Cynofura* extended the
other to *Munychia*, they fhut up the whole Coaft
with their Ships. In this manner they difpos'd
their Fleet, that the Grecians nnding no way to
efcape, might be all taken at *Salamis*, to com-
penfate the Lofs of the Barbarians in the Action
of *Artemifium*; and landed the Perfians in *Pfyttalea*, to the end that, as they expected the moft
part of the difabled Ships and diftreffed Men
would be driven thither, becaufe that Ifland is
fituate near the place where the Battle was like
to be fought, they might be ready to fave what-

I ever

ever they thought fit, and to deſtoy the reſt.
But theſe things they endeavour'd to conceal
from the Grecians, and paſs'd the whole Night
without Sleep in making all neceſſary Preparations. Conſidering the Event of this War, I
have nothing to ſay againſt the Truth of Oracles, reſolving not to attempt to invalidate ſo
manifeſt a Prediction.

*When circling Ships ſhall join the ſacred Shore
Of* Artemis *to* Cynoſura's *Coaſt,
Juſt Vengeance then ſhall reach the furious Youth,
True Son of Violence, who vainly proud
Of ravag'd* Athens, *inſolently thought
That all muſt ſtoop to his audacious Rage:
For claſhing Swords ſhall meet, and* Mars *ſhall ſtain
The foaming Billows with a purple Gore.
Then Saturn's Son and Victory ſhall bring
A glorious Day of Liberty to* Greece.

Theſe Words of *Bacis* are ſo clear, that I dare
not diſpute the Veracity of Oracles, nor ſhall
admit the Objections of others.

IN the mean time the Generals at *Salamis*
continued their Debates with great Animoſity,
not knowing that they were ſurrounded by the
Ships of the Barbarians. But when Day was
come, they ſaw the Enemy ſo diſpoſ'd, as if they
deſign'd to make towards the Shore. And whilſt
they were ſtill in Council *Ariſtides* the Son of
Lyſimachus arrived from *Ægina.* He was an
Athenian, but voted into Exile by the People:
And yet, for as much as I have learnt of his
Manners, he was the beſt and juſteſt Man in
Athens. This Perſon coming to the place where
the Council ſat, ſent for *Themiſtocles* out, who
was

was not his Friend, but rather the fierceſt of
his Enemies: yet the Greatneſs of the impending Danger made him forget their former
Enmity, and reſolve to confer with him; becauſe he had heard that the Peloponneſians were
determined to retire with the Fleet to the Iſthmus. When *Themiſtocles* came out, *Ariſtides* ſaid,
" We ought at this time, and on all occaſions,
" to contend who ſhall do the greateſt Ser-
" vice to our Country. I aſſure you, that to
" ſay little or much to the Peloponneſians, about
" their Departure, is the ſame thing: For I
" tell you as an Eye-witneſs, that neither *Eu-*
" *rybiades* himſelf, nor the Corinthians, can now
" retire, if they would, becauſe we are on all
" ſides incloſed by the Enemies Fleet. Go in
" again therefore, and acquaint the Council
" with our Condition." *Themiſtocles* anſwer'd,
" Your Admonition is exceeding grateful, and
" the News you bring moſt acceptable: For
" you tell me you have ſeen that, which I
" deſir'd ſhould come to paſs above all things.
" Know then, that what the Medes have done,
" proceeds from me: for neceſſity requir'd,
" that thoſe Grecians, who would not fight
" voluntarily, ſhould be compelled to an Engagement againſt their will. But ſince you
" have brought ſo good News, let the Council hear it from yourſelf; becauſe if I ſhould
" be the Reporter, they would think it a Fiction, and I ſhall not perſuade them that the
" Barbarians are doing ſuch a thing. Go in
" therefore and inform them of the Fact: If
" they believe you, nothing better can happen; if not, we are ſtill in the ſame Condition: for they have no way open to
" eſcape

" escape by Flight, if, as you say, we are al-
" ready encompassed on all sides." Accordingly *Aristides* going in, gave the same Account
to the Council, acquainting them that he
came from *Ægina*, after he had with great
difficulty made his Passage, and eluded the
Vigilance of the Enemy, who with the whole
Navy of *Xerxes* had entirely encompassed the
Grecian Ships. He counselled them therefore
to prepare themselves with all Diligence for
their Defence; and when he had said this, he
retired. But yet the Dissension continued a-
mong the Generals, and the greater part gave
no credit to the Report, till a Tenian Ship,
commanded by *Panætius*, the Son of *Socime-
nes*, arriving from the Enemy to join the Grecians, discover'd the whole Truth; and for
that Action the name of the Tenians was engrav'd upon the Tripos consecrated at *Delphi*,
among those who defeated the Barbarian. By
the addition of this Ship, and that of *Lemnos*,
which came over at *Artemisium*, the Grecian
Fleet now amounted to three hundred and
eighty Sail; for before, they wanted two of
that number.

THE Grecians believing the Account they
receiv'd from the Tenians, prepar'd for an Engagement; and at day-break called a general
Assembly of the Men at Arms: in which *Themistocles* having first declar'd the hopes he had of
a prosperous Event, framed all his Discourse to
shew the Difference between Actions of the
greatest Glory, and those of less importance;
animating them to chuse the most noble, as far
as the Nature and Condition of Man permit.
When he had finish'd his Speech, he encourag'd

them

them to return on board; which they had no
sooner done, than the Ship they had sent to
Ægina, with Orders touching the *Æacides*,
return'd to *Salamis*, and at the same time the
Grecians weigh'd all their Anchors.   The Barbarians seeing them coming out, advanc'd
with diligence; but the Grecians continu'd
luffing, and bearing upon the Stern: when
Aminias, an Athenian of the Pallenian Tribe,
breaking out of the Line, fell in among the
Enemy, and fasten'd the Grappling-Iron to one
of their Ships; which the rest perceiving, and
that there was no other way to bring him off,
they made up to his Assistance: and thus the
Athenians say the Fight began.   But the Æginetes affirm, that the Ship which went to *Ægina*, with the Instructions about the *Æacides*,
was the first engag'd.   There is also a Report
that a Phantom appear'd in the shape of a Woman, incouraging the Grecians with so loud a
Voice, that she was heard by all the Fleet, after she had first reproach'd them in these
words: " Infatuated Men! how long will you
" rest upon your Oars, and forbear to ad-
" vance?" In the Order of Battel, the Phœnicians were placed on that Wing which fronted
the Athenians, and extended Westward towards *Eleusis*.   The Ionians were rang'd on the
other Point, facing the Lacedemonians, and
stretching towards the East and the *Piræus*. Of
these some few, persuaded by the Admonition
of *Themistocles*, voluntarily omitted to perform
their part; yet the greatest number did their
best: And I could give the Names of many
Captains who took Ships from the Grecians,
though I shall mention no more than *Theomestor*

the

the Son of *Androdamas* ,and *Phylacus* the Son of
Hiſtiæus, both Samians. I name theſe two, becauſe *Theomeſtor* was afterwards made Tyrant
of *Samos* by the Perſians, for his Service on
this occaſion, and *Phylacus* was not only admitted into the number of thoſe, who by deſerving well of the King, are call'd among
the Perſians *Oroſanges*, but rewarded with large
Poſſeſſions in Land: and ſuch were the Recom-
pences of theſe two Commanders. Nevertheleſs this numerous Fleet was defeated at *Salamis*, and receiv'd a terrible Blow, principally
from the Athenians and the Æginetes : For the
Grecians obſerved ſo good Order, and ſuch a
ſteddy Conduct in the Fight, whilſt the Barbarians fought in a diſorderly manner, and without judgment, that no other Event could be
expected ; yet the Enemy ſhew'd far more
Courage that day, than they had done before on
the Coaſt of *Eubœa*, or at any other time ; every
one exerting himſelf vigorouſly, in fear of the
King's Diſpleaſure, becauſe they all imagin'd
that their Actions were obſerv'd by him. I cannot exactly relate how each particular Perſon,
either of the Grecians or Barbarians, behav'd
himſelf in this Engagement ; but an Adventure
happen'd to *Artemiſia*, which ſerved to augment
her Credit with *Xerxes*. For when the King's
Fleet was in the utmoſt Confuſion, *Artemiſia*
finding ſhe was chas'd by an Athenian Ship, and
not knowing whither to fly, becauſe ſhe had
thoſe of her own Party in Front, and the Enemy in the Rear, contriv'd to do a thing which
turn'd to her great advantage: As ſhe fled
from the Athenian, ſhe drove directly upon a
Ship of her own ſide, belonging to the Calyn-

dians,

dians, and having their King *Damaſithymus* on
board: But whether on account of a Conteſta-
tion they had together at the *Helleſpont*, ſhe pur-
poſely run down his Ship; or whether the Ca-
lyndians were in her way by accident, I cannot
affirm. However, the Ship went down to rights,
and *Artemiſia* had the good fortune to reap a
double advantage by that Blow: For the Captain of the Athenian Ship, when he ſaw the
Barbarian ſunk, concluding *Artemiſia*'s Ship to
be a Grecian, or at leaſt one that had abandon'd the Enemy to join with the Grecians,
gave over the Chace, and left her. By which
means *Artemiſia* not only eſcap'd the Danger,
but advanc'd her Reputation with *Xerxes* by a
bad Action: For they ſay, that when the King,
who was Spectator of the Exploit, had taken
notice of the Ship which gave the ſhock, one of
thoſe about him ſaid, "SIR, You ſee with
"what Courage *Artemiſia* fights, and has ſunk
"one of the Enemy's Ships." Then the King
asking, if indeed *Artemiſia* had done that Action? they anſwer'd, that they knew the Flag
perfectly well, ſtill imagining the loſt Ship to
be an Enemy. For to the reſt of her good Fortune, which I mention'd before, this alſo was
added, that none of the Company belonging to
the Calyndian Ship ſurviv'd to accuſe her. So
that when *Xerxes* heard their Anſwer, he is reported to have ſaid, "My Men have fought
"like Women, and my Women like Men." In
this Battle *Ariabignes*, the Son of *Darius*, and
Brother of *Xerxes*, was killed, with great numbers of illuſtrious Men, as well Perſians and
Medes as their Confederates. On the part of
the Grecians the Slaughter was not great; be-

cauſe

cause those who lost their Ships, and surviv'd
the Fate of War, saved themselves by their Skill
in swimming, and got ashore at *Salamis*; whereas most of the Barbarians being ignorant of that
Art, perish'd in the Sea. The greatest loss the
Enemy sustained, began after their headmost
Ships were put to flight; for those who lay a-
stern, endeavouring to come up into the Van,
that they might shew the King some proof of
their Courage, fell foul upon their own flying
Ships. In this Confusion some Phœnicians,
whose Ships were destroyed, going to the King,
told him, the Ionians had betray'd all, and been
the Cause of their Disaster: But contrary to
their Expectation, the Punishment they design'd to bring upon the Ionian Commanders,
fell upon the Accusers themselves: For whilst
they were yet speaking, a Samothracian Ship
attacking one of *Attica*, sunk the Athenian; and
a Ship of *Ægina* coming up in that instant, sunk
the Samothracian. But the Samothracians being armed with Javelins, poured in such a
shower from the sinking Vessel upon the Æginetes, that venturing to board the conquering
Ship, they carry'd her. This Success sav'd the
Ionians: For *Xerxes* having seen them perform
so great an Action, turn'd about to the Phœnicians; and being above measure troubled, and
ready to fling the blame every where, commanded their Heads to be struck off, that they
might no more accuse those who had fought
better than themselves. He sat upon the Descent of a Hill, called *Ægaleos*, over against
Salamis; and whenever he saw a remarkable
Action done in the Fight by any one of his Officers, he made Inquiry touching the Man, and
caus'd

caus'd his Secretaries to write down his Name,
his Family, and his Country. But not satisfy'd
with the Slaughter of the Phœnicians, he added that of *Ariaramnes*, a Persian, and his Favourite, who had been present at their Death.
In the end the Barbarians betaking themselves
to open flight, made the best of their way towards *Phaleron*; but the Æginetes waiting for
them in their Passage through the Streights, gave
memorable proof of their Valour: And as the
Athenians destroy'd those flying Ships, which
ventur'd to resist in the Confusion ; the Æginetes did no less execution upon those which
escap'd out of the Battel: So that, for the most
part, when any Ship happen'd to avoid the A-
thenians, they fell into the hands of the Æginetes. In this Rout the Ship of *Themistocles* giving chase to one of the Enemy, came up with
another commanded by *Polycritus* of *Ægina*, the
Son of *Crius*, as he was ready to attack a Sidonian Ship, which prov'd to be the same that
took the Guardship of the Æginetes near *Scyathus*, with *Pytheas* the Son of *Ischenous* on board ;
who being cover'd with Wounds, was exempted
from Death by the Persians, in admiration of
his Valour, and kept Prisoner in the Ship. In
this Action the Sidonian Ship was taken with all
the Men on board, and by that means *Pytheas*
return'd safe to *Ægina*. But when *Polycritus*
saw the Athenian Ship, which he knew to be
the Admiral by the Flag she carry'd, he call'd
aloud to *Themistocles*, and in a jesting manner
bid him take notice how the Æginetes favour'd
the Medes. In the mean time the Barbarians,
with the Ships they had left, fled in great disorder towards their Land Forces, and arriv'd

at

at *Phaleron.* Among the Grecians, that fought this Battel, the Æginetes were most commended; and next to these the Athenians. Among the Captains, *Polycritus* of *Ægina*; and among the Athenians, *Eumeneus* of the Anagyrasian, with *Aminias* of the Pallenian Tribe, who gave chase to *Artemisia*; and if he had known she had been in the Ship, would not have given over the Pursuit, till either he had taken her, or she him. For the Athenians had given Orders to that purpose to all their Captains, and promis'd a Reward of ten thousand Drachmas to the Person who should take her alive; resenting, with great Indignation, that a Woman should make war against *Athens.* But, as I said before, she made her Escape, and with divers other Ships arriv'd at *Phaleron.* The Athenians say, that *Adimantus,* the Corinthian General, struck with a panick Fear in the beginning of the Fight, put up all his Sails, and betook himself to flight: That the Corinthians seeing their Leader run, bore away after him; and when they had reach'd the Temple of *Minerva* at *Sciras* in *Salamis,* a Frigate magnificently adorn'd fell in with their Squadron: That when they found she made no Discovery whence she came, nor had brought any Message to the Corinthians from the Army, they concluded the thing to be divine; for as soon as the Frigate came up with their Ships, those on board cry'd out, " *Adimantus,* thou hast by thy flight " depriv'd the Grecians of the Assistance of " these Ships, and art a Traytor to *Greece*; yet " know, they shall conquer their Enemies as " compleatly as they desire." That finding *Adimantus* gave no credit to their words, they

added,

added, that they would be contented to remain as Hoftages, and be put to death, if the Grecians were not victorious. Upon which *Adimantus*, with the reft of the Corinthians, return'd to the Fleet, but came not in till the Work was done. This Report is current among the Athenians; yet the Corinthians deny the Fact, and affirm they fought no lefs valiantly than the beft; all the reft of *Greece* concurring to confirm their Affertion. Whilft things were in this Confufion on the Coaft of *Salamis*, *Ariftides*, the Son of *Lyfimachus* the Athenian, mention'd by me a little before as a moft excellent Perfon, taking with him a confiderable number of Men, all of Athenian Blood, who were drawn up along that Shore in their Arms, paffed over to *Pfyttalea*, and put to the fword all the Perfians he found in the Ifland. The Grecians, after the Engagement by Sea was over, brought to *Salamis* all the Wreck that continu'd floating about that Coaft, and prepar'd for another Battel, expecting the King would make ufe of his remaining Ships to that end. But the greater part of the broken Veffels were carried by a South-Wind to the Shore of *Colias* in *Attica*; that not only chofe Predictions of *Bacis* and *Mufæus*, touching the Succefs of the Seafight, might be verified; but that alfo relating to the fhatter'd Remains rolling to that Coaft, which many years before had been deliver'd in thefe Terms to *Lyfiftratus* an Athenian Augur, and concealed from all the Grecians:

The Colian *Dames fhall fhake to fee the Oars.*

This

This was to happen in the time of the King's Expedition.

WHEN *Xerxes* was inform'd of the Loss he had sustain'd, he began to apprehend that some of the Ionians, either upon the Suggestion of the Grecians, or from their own Inclination, might go and break the bridge at the *Hellespont*, and by that means, cutting off his Retreat out of *Europe*, might bring his Person into danger. Under these Apprehensions he resolv'd upon his Departure; but being willing to conceal his Intentions both from the Grecians, and from his own Forces, he attempted to form a Digue extending down to *Salamis*; and having fasten'd together the Phœnician Tenders, to serve for a Bridge and a Rampart, he prepar'd all things, as if he design'd to fight another Battel at Sea. Every one that saw him thus employ'd, firmly believ'd he had determin'd to stay, and to carry on the War in Person; except only *Mardonius*, who, by the knowledge he had of the King's Genius, was not ignorant of his Intentions. Whilst *Xerxes* was making these Preparations he dispatch'd a Message to the Persians, with an account of the Misfortune which had befallen him. Nothing is found among Men more expeditious than these Messengers, invented by the Persians, and regulated in this manner. For every Day's Journey they appoint a Man with a Horse, to be always ready to ride out that day, obliging him to perform his Course with the utmost diligence, and not to be prevented either by Snow, Rain, Heat, or the Darkness of Night. The first of these Couriers delivers his Orders to the second, the second to the third, and so
forward

forward to the laſt; as the Torch conſecrated
to *Vulcan* paſſes from hand to hand among the
Grecians. And this Expedition by laid Horſes, the Perſians call *Angarion*. The firſt Meſſage which was brought to *Suſa* from *Xerxes*,
with the News that he had taken *Athens*,
cans'd ſo great Joy among the Perſians there,
that they ſtrew'd the Streets with Myrtle,
burnt Perfumes, ſacrific'd, and abandon'd themſelves to Pleaſure. But the ſecond Meſſenger
arriving, put them all into ſuch a Conſternation
that they tore their Clothes, and with inceſſant
Howlings and Lamentations threw all the
blame upon *Mardonius :* Not that the Perſians
were ſo much troubled for the Diſaſter of the
Fleet, but they dreaded the Danger of the
King's Perſon; and continued in their Fears
during all the time that paſſed between this
Meſſage, and the Return of *Xerxes.* In the
mean time, *Mardonius* ſeeing *Xerxes* much diſturb'd at the unhappy Event of the Sea-fight,
and conjecturing he had meditated his Eſcape
from *Attica*, began to think, he ſhould ſuffer the
Penalty of having perſuaded the King to make
war againſt the Grecians; and therefore, that
nothing could be more advantageous to him
than to put all to the hazard, either to conquer *Greece*, or die with Glory in ſo great an
Attempt. Reflecting upon theſe things, and inclining to believe he might ſubdue *Greece*, he
addreſſed himſelf to the King in theſe Words :
" Sir, be not diſturb'd, nor think you have
" receiv'd ſo great a Loſs by the late Action ;
" for we are not to determine this Diſpute with
" Timber, but with Men and Horſes. None
" of thoſe, who imagine they have given us
" a

" a finishing Blow, will quit their Ships to
" appear aginst you in Arms by Land; nei-
" ther have we any thing to fear from those
" of the Continent, because they have paid
" so dear already for their Resistance. If then
" you think fit, we will make an attempt
" upon *Peloponnesus*; or, if you had rather take
" time to consider of that Enterprize, you
" may do so without hazard: only be not
" discourag'd; for the Grecians have no way
" to exempt themselves from rendering a se-
" vere Account of their past and present Ac-
" tions; and must submit to be your Servants.
" In this manner I woud advise you to act; but
" if you have determin'd to return, and to
" withdraw the Army, I have other Counsel
" to offer on that Subject. Above all things,
" Sir, let not the Persians be expos'd to the
" Derision of the Grecians; for they have
" brought no Disaster upon your Affairs, nor
" can you charge us with want of Courage
" on any Occasion. If the Phœnicians, Ægyp-
" tians, Cyprians, and Cilicians, have behav'd
" themselves ill, their Faults are not to be
" attributed to the Persians. Since therefore
" the Persians cannot be justly blam'd, let me
" persuade you, if you have resolv'd your Re-
" turn, to take with you the greatest part of
" the Army, and to leave me three hundred
" thousand chosen Men; with which I take up-
" on me to reduce all *Greece* to your Obedi-
" ence." *Xerxes* having heard these Words
with as much Joy and Satisfaction, as his De-
spondency had been great, told *Mardonius*, he
would consider his Propositions, and let him
know which of the two he should approve. To
that

that end, after he had call'd together a Council of Persians, he determin'd to send for *Artemisia*, in order to consult with her also, because she alone seem'd to have understood the Measures that ought to have been taken before. When *Artemisia* came, *Xerxes* order'd the Council and Guards to withdraw, and spoke to her in these Terms: " *Mardonius* encourages me
" to stay here, and to attack *Peloponnesus* ; telling
" me that the Persians are not at all guilty of
" the Defeat I have receiv'd, but wish for an
" Occasion to give me Demonstration of their
" Valour. This Enterprize he counsels me to
" attempt; or else, with three hundred thou-
" sand Men chosen out of my Forces, he him-
" self proposes to conquer *Greece* for me, and
" desires I would return home with the rest of
" the Army. You therefore, who gave me
" such prudent Counsel, in dissuading me from
" hazarding a Battle at Sea, advise me now, which
" of these two Propositions you think most ad-
" vantageous to my Affairs." To this Demand, *Artemisia* answer'd ; " Sir, I am under
" no little Difficulty how to give you the good
" Counsel you desire; yet, considering the pre-
" sent State of things, I am of opinion, you
" should return home, and leave *Mardonius*
" here with the Troops he requires, if he will
" take this Enterprize upon him : For if he
" conquers these Countries, as he promises,
" and all things succeed to his mind, the Ho-
" nour, Sir, will redound to you, because your
" Servants were the Instruments of the Success :
" But if, contrary to the Expectation of *Mar-
" donius*, the Event should prove unprosperous,
" the Misfortune cannot be great, so long as
" you

" you furvive, and your own Affairs are fafe
" at home: For whilſt you and your Houſe
" are in being, the Grecians will be often dri-
" ven to run the utmoſt hazards to preſerve
" themſelves; ſo that whatever Diſaſter may
" fall upon *Mardonius*, is of no importance:
" Neither could the Grecians call themſelves
" Conquerors, though they ſhould happen to
" deſtroy your Slave. In a word, having burnt
" *Athens*, which was the thing you propos'd
" to do in this War, you may with reaſon re-
" turn home." This Counſel being ſo agreeable to the Inclination of *Xerxes*, pleas'd him
exceedingly; for his Fears were ſo great, that
if all the Men and Women of the World had
advis'd him to ſtay, I believe he would never
have conſented. He applauded the Wiſdom
of *Artemiſia*; and when ſhe had taken leave, ſhe
departed from *Epheſus* with ſome of his natural Sons, who had accompanied him in his Expedition. With theſe Children he ſent *Hermotimus* their Governour, by Deſcent a Pedaſean,
and among the Eunuchs, inferiour to none in
the King's Favour. The Pedaſeans inhabit a-
bove *Halicarnaſſus*; and 'tis ſaid, that when any
Calamity is, within a certain time, to fall upon
themſelves, and all thoſe who live about their
City, a great Beard ſhoots from the Chin of
Minerva's Prieſteſs; which Prodigy has been
ſeen twice in that Place. *Hermotimus* was born
among theſe Pedaſeans; and of all the Men we
know, reveng'd himſelf in the ſevereſt manner
for an Injury he had receiv'd. He was taken
by an Enemy, and ſold to one *Panionius*, a Chi-
an, who liv'd by a moſt infamous Practice; for
whenever he purchas'd Boys of excellent Beau-

ty,

ty, he caſtrated them, and ſold them at *Sardis*
and *Epheſus* for immenſe Sums; becauſe the
Barbarians ſet a greater Value upon Eunuchs
than upon others, on account of their Fidelity
in all reſpects.   Among the many *Panionius* had
caſtrated, *Hermotimus* was one; yet, not being
unfortunate in every thing, he was ſent from
Sardis, with other Preſents to the King; and
in time became the greateſt Favourite of all
his Eunuchs.   Whilſt *Xerxes* was at *Sardis*,
preparing to lead his Army againſt *Athens*, *Hermotimus* went on ſome occaſion to *Atarneus*, a
Town of *Myſia*, poſſeſs'd by the Chians, and
found *Panionius* there: He knew him, and
entertaining him with much Diſcourſe in a
friendly manner, acquainted him firſt with the
many Felicities he had acquir'd by his means,
and promiſed him great things in requital, if
he would come to his Houſe, and bring his
Sons with him. *Panionius* heard all this with
ſatisfaction, and accordingly came with his
Wife and Children.   But when *Hermotimus* ſaw
the whole Family in his power, he ſaid, " O
" thou, who haſt to this time ſuſtain'd thy moſt
" wicked Life, by tranſcending all others in a
" deteſtable Commerce, what had I, or any of
" my Anceſtors done to thee or thine, that of
" a Man, thou haſt made me nothing?   Thy
" Opinion ſurely was, that the Gods would
" not ſee that Action: But they, for thy
" Crimes, have now deliver'd thee into my
" hands with ſo much Juſtice, that thou canſt
" have no colour to complain of the Puniſh-
" ment I ſhall inflict upon thee." When he
had thus upbraided him, he order'd his four
Sons to be brought in, and compell'd the Fa-

2   ther

ther to caftrate them in his prefence. *Panionius,*
conftrain'd by inevitable Neceffity, did as he
commanded; and after he had done, his Sons
were forced to do the fame to him. In this
manner *Hermotimus* was reveng'd, and *Panionius*
punifh'd in the way he deferv'd. *Xerxes* having committed his Sons to *Artemifia*'s Care, in
order to be conducted to *Ephefus*, fent for *Mardonius*, and bid him chufe what Forces he would
out of the Army, that he might be able to perform the things he had promis'd. Nothing
more was done that day; but in the night, the
Generals, by the King's Order, fail'd with the
Fleet from *Phaleron*, making towards the *Hellefpont* with all poffible diligence, to preferve the
Bridges, over which he was to pafs in his Return. The Barbarians, as they fail'd by *Zofter*,
imagining the little Promontories they faw on
that Coaft, to be Ships of War, difperfed and
fled for a confiderable time; but afterwards, perceiving they were Promontories, and not Ships,
they rallied again, and purfued their Voyage.
The next Morning, the Grecians feeing the E-
nemies Land-Forces ftill encamped in the fame
Place, fuppos'd their Fleet to be at *Phaleron*;
and therefore, in expectation of another Engagement, prepar'd to defend themfelves; when being inform'd of their Departure, they prefently
determin'd to fail in queft of them. But coming
up to *Andros* without having difcover'd any of
the Enemies Ships, they called a Council of
War; in which *Themiftocles* mov'd, that fhaping
their Purfuit by the way of the Iflands, they
would make directly to the *Hellefpont*, and deftroy the Bridges. But *Eurybiades* was of a
contrary Opinion, and faid, that nothing could
be

be more destructive to *Greece*, than to break
those Bridges; for if the *Persian*, intercepted
by that means, should be constrain'd to continue
in *Europe*, he would certainly make some Attempt; because by Inaction, he could neither
advance his Affairs, nor open a Way to his Return, but his Army must inevitably perish by
Want: That if he should be the Aggressor, and
enter upon Action, all the Cities and Nations
of *Europe* must probably become an Accession to
his Empire, either by Force, or by a preceding
Agreement; and for Provisions, the annual
Produce of *Greece* would furnish him sufficiently: That being of opinion, *Xerxes* would not
willingly continue in *Europe* after the Defeat
he had receiv'd at Sea, he was for favouring his
Flight, till he should arrive in *Asia*; after which
he advis'd them to carry the War thither, and
compel him to fight for his own Territories.
To this Opinion the other Captains of the *Peloponnesians* unanimously adher'd; and *Themistocles*, finding he could not persuade the greater
number to sail for the *Hellespont*, addressed himself to the Athenians; who, of all the Allies,
being most averse from suffering the Enemy to
escape, were dispos'd to proceed thither with
their own Ships, if the rest should refuse to concur in that Design. " I have often seen, *said*
" *he*, and much more often heard, that Men,
" constrain'd by unavoidable Necessity, have
" fought again, and repair'd their former Los-
" ses. Since therefore we have found means
" to repel that Cloud of Men, which threaten'd
" us and all *Greece*, let us no longer pursue
" those that fly; for this Success is not owing
" to our own Force, but to the Gods, and to the
" He-

4.

" Heroes, who were too jealous to permit one
" Man to be King both of *Asia* and *Europe*;
" a Man of such Impiety and Insolence, that
" he burnt all Places, sacred and profane, with-
" out distinction, overthrew the Images of the
" Gods, and attempted to chastise the Sea with
" Stripes and Fetters. Since then, our Af-
" fairs are in so good a Condition, that we have
" quite driven out the Barbarian, let us conti-
" nue in *Greece*, and taking care for ourselves
" and our Families, rebuild our Houses, and
" sow our Lands with diligence; deferring our
" Expedition to the *Hellespont* and to *Ionia*, till
" the Beginning of the next Spring." This
turn *Themistocles* gave to his Discourse, in order
to insinuate himself into the Favour of the Persian, that he might have a Place of Refuge, if
any Misfortune should overtake him at *Athens*,
as afterwards fell out: And tho' his Words were
counterfeit, yet he persuaded the Athenians;
who having always thought him a wise Man, and
now seeing such manifest Proofs of his consummate Prudence, and excellent Counsels, were
entirely dispos'd to believe him in every thing.
But after they had assented to his Opinion, he
presently sent off certain Persons in a Sloop, and
among them that *Sicinus* I mention'd before,
with Orders to carry a Message to the King, and
not to discover it to any other Person, whatever
Torture they might endure. When they arriv'd
in *Attica*, the rest continu'd on board, and *Sicinus* going alone to the King, said, " *Themistocles*,
" the Son of *Neocles*, General of the Athenians,
" the most wise and valiant of all the Confede-
" rates, sent me to tell you, that being desirous
" to do you a good Office, he has prevail'd with
" the

" the Grecians to defift from the Refolution
" they had taken to purfue your Ships, and to
" deftroy your Bridges on the *Hellefpont:* So
" that you may now retire at your leifure."
And after he had deliver'd his Meffage, they all
return'd to *Themiftocles.*

THE Grecians having thus determin'd,
neither to continue their Purfuit, nor to fail
for the *Hellefpont,* to break the Enemies Bridges,
befieg'd *Andros,* with intention to deftroy that
City; becaufe the Andrians were the firft of
all the Iflanders, who refufed to give Money
to *Themiftocles:* For when he told them, that
the Athenians were come thither accompanied
by two great Deities, Perfuafion and Force,
and that therefore they muft part with their
Money; the Andrians anfwer'd, that the A-
thenians, having fuch ufeful Goddeffes, were
great and profperous of courfe; but that the
Andrians being confin'd to a narrow Slip of
Land, and having two unprofitable Goddeffes,
Poverty and Impoffibility, always refiding in
their Ifland, and fond of living among them,
fhould give no Money fo long as they had
fuch Deities: adding that the Power of *Athens*
was not greater than their Inability. Thus
they anfwer'd; and for refufing to give Money, were befieg'd: During which time, *Themiftocles,* inceffantly coveting more Wealth,
fent threatning Meffages to the other Iflands,
by the fame Perfons he had employ'd before
to the Andrians, with Orders to demand
Money in the fame Terms; and to let the
Iflanders know, that if they refus'd to fend
him the Sum he requir'd, he would bring the
Grecian Forces againft them, and deftroy their

Countries. By thefe Menaces he extorted great Riches from the Caryftians, and from the Parians; who being inform'd that the Andrians were befieg'd, for corresponding with the Medes, and that *Themiftocles* was in the greateft Reputation of all the Generals, terrify'd with Apprehenfions of his Indignation, fent him the Money he demanded. Whether any more of the Iflanders gave him Money or not, I cannot affirm; but I am of opinion that fome others did, and that thefe were not the only People that comply'd. Yet for all this, the Caryftians could not avoid their ill Fortune, though the Parians efcaped the Vifit of the Army, by pacifying *Themiftocles* with Money. Thus in a clandeftine manner, and without the Participation of the other Generals, *Themiftocles* demanded Money of the Iflanders, beginning with the Andrians.

THE Army of *Xerxes* having continued a few Days in their Camp, after the Sea-fight, march'd back into *Bœotia* by the fame way they came; becaufe *Mardonius* defigning to attend the King in his way, and feeing the Seafon of the Year improper for military Action, inclin'd to winter in *Theffaly*, and to attack *Peloponnefus* early the next Spring. Upon his Arrival in *Theffaly*, he in the firft place made choice of the ten thoufand Perfians, who are call'd *Immortal*; but their General *Hydarnes* refus'd to ftay with them, declaring he would not leave the King. After thefe, he chofe out of the Perfians, all the Cuiraffiers, and that Body of a thoufand Horfe, which I mention'd before. Of the Medes, Saces, Bactrians, and Indians, he omitted none

either

either Foot or Horse: But of the other Nations he took few, only chuſing ſuch as were of a promiſing Aſpect, or known to him by ſome remarkable Action. Among the Forces he choſe, thoſe of the Perſian Nation were moſt conſiderable, and wore Bracelets and Chains for ornament. Next to them, the Medes, not leſs numerous than the Perſians, but inferiour in Valour. And thus, including the Horſe, he made up the Number of three hundred thouſand. But whilſt *Mardonius* ſelected his Army, and *Xerxes* ſtaid in *Theſſaly*, an Oracle was brought to *Sparta* from *Delphi*, admoniſhing the Lacedemonians to demand Satisfaction of the King for the Death of *Leonidas*; and to hear the Anſwer he would give. Accordingly, they immediately ſent away a Herald, who finding all the Army of *Xerxes* in *Theſſaly*, went to him, and ſaid; " King of " the Medes, the Lacedemonians and Hera- " clides of *Sparta*, require you to make repa- " ration for killing their King, whilſt he en- " deavour'd to defend the Liberty of *Greece*." At theſe Words the King laugh'd; and after he had long forborn to anſwer, pointing at laſt to *Mardonius*, " There, ſaid he, is the Man " who ſhall give them the Satisfaction they " deſerve." When the Herald had receiv'd this Anſwer, he went away; and *Xerxes*, leaving *Mardonius* in *Theſſaly*, marched with precipitation to the *Helleſpont*. His haſte was ſo great, that he arriv'd at the Paſſage in forty five Days, follow'd only by an inconſiderable Part of the Army: For among all People without diſtinction, and in all Places that lay in their way, they plucked the Corn and Fruit they

met

met with, for their Nourishment; but where they found no kind of Fruit, press'd by extreme Want, they fed upon the Herbage, that grew spontaneously on the Ground, and eat even the Bark and Leaves, which they stripped from the Trees, both wild and cultivated, leaving nothing behind. This brought a Plague into the Army, with frequent Dysenteries, and destroyed great Numbers in their March. The Sick *Xerxes* left in the Cities, through which he passed, commanding the Inhabitants to take care of them, and to furnish them with Provisions. Some he left in *Thessaly*, others at *Siris*, a Pæonian City, and some in *Macedonia:* But he could not recover the sacred Chariot of *Jupiter*, which he deposited there, as he was marching to invade *Greece*; for the Pæonians having given it before to the Thracians, told *Xerxes*, when he demanded the Chariot, that those who inhabit the upper Parts of *Thrace*, about the Springs of the River *Strymon*, had taken it away, and the Mares out of the Pasture at the same time. In that Country, a Thracian, King of the Bysaltians and Chrestonians, did an Action of an extraordinary nature: For after he had declar'd he would not willingly be a Slave to *Xerxes*, and commanded his six Sons not to join in the Expedition against *Greece*, he retir'd to the top of Mount *Rhodope*. Nevertheless, either in contempt of his Command, or from a desire to see the War, they enter'd into the Army of *Xerxes*; but at their Return, the Father, to punish their Disobedience, caus'd all their Eyes to be put out

THE

THE Perſians arriving at the *Boſphorus*, by precipitate Marches through *Thrace*, paſſed over the *Helleſpont* to *Abydus* in their Ships: becauſe they found their Bridges broken and diſſipated by a Storm. But being now more plentifully furniſhed with Proviſions than before they fill'd themſelves ſo immoderately, that this Exceſs, together with the Change of Water, deſtroy'd a great part of the remaining Army; and *Xerxes*, with the reſt, arriv'd at *Sardis*. Some relating this Retreat in another manner, ſay, that *Xerxes* went from *Athens* to *Eion*, upon the *Strymon*, and made no more Marches by Land; but leaving *Hydarnes* to take care of conducting the Army to the *Helleſpont*, he went on board a Phœnician Ship, and paſſed over to *Aſia*: That in his Voyage, a violent Wind ariſing, made ſo high a Sea, that his Ship being over-charged with Numbers of Perſians, who were above Deck, was in imminent Danger from the Storm: That *Xerxes* fearing the Event, called aloud to the Pilot, asking him if he had any hope to ſave the Ship, and that the Pilot anſwered, " Sir, l have none, unleſs ſome way " might be found to remove theſe Paſſengers:" That the King having heard his Anſwer, ſaid to the Perſians, " Who among you will ſhew " his Love to the King, and ſave my Life, " which now ſeems to be in your power?" That when he had pronounc'd theſe Words, all the Perſians ador'd the King, leaping into the Sea, lighten'd the Ship; by which means he arriv'd ſafe in *Aſia*: That ſoon after his landing he rewarded the Pilot with a Crown of Gold, for ſaving the King's Life; but commanded his Head to be ſtruck off, for deſtroying ſo many

Y 3

Per-

Perfians. Neverthelefs, this Manner of relating the Retreat of *Xerxes* is of no credit with me, for divers Reafons, and efpecially on account of the Cataftrophe of the Perfians: For granting that the Pilot faid thofe Words to *Xerxes*, yet hardly one Man of a thoufand will deny, that the King would have done thus: He would have fent down into the Body of the Ship, the Perfians above Deck, who were principal Men of that Nation, and would as certainly have thrown into the Sea an equal number of Phœnicians, who were at the Oar. But indeed he return'd to *Afia* by Land, with the reft of the Army, as I faid before: And to confirm this, we are affur'd, that *Xerxes* in his Return, was at *Abdera*; that he made an Alliance with the Abderites, and prefented them with a Scymeter of Gold, and a gilded Ship; to which the Abderites add, tho' I can by no means believe the thing, that he took off his Girdle in their Country, for the firft time, after his Flight from *Athens*, not thinking himfelf fafe before. Befides *Abdera* is nearer to the *Hellefpont*, than the River *Strymon*, or the City of *Eion*, where they fay he imbarked.

IN the mean time, the Grecians finding themfelves unable to reduce *Andros*, departed to *Caryftus*, and after they had ravag'd the Country, return'd to *Salamis*. There, in the firft place, they fet apart the Spoil they intended to confecrate to the Gods, and, among other things, three Phœnician Ships; one to be depofited at the Ifthmus, which continued there to my time; a fecond at *Sunium*, and the third they dedicated to *Ajax*, at *Salamis*. After that, they parted the Booty among themfelves, and fent Offerings to *Delphi*,

Delphi, of which a Statue was made, twelve
Cubits high, holding the Prow of a Ship in
one hand; and erected in that Place, where
Alexander the Macedonian stands in Gold.
When the Grecians had made their Present to
Delphi, they inquir'd of the God, in the Name
of all, if he had receiv'd a grateful and satis-
factory Offering: To which he answer'd, That
from the rest of the Grecians he had, but not
from the Æginetes; of whom he expected a
due Acknowledgement, for having behav'd
themselves with the greatest Valour in the Sea-
fight. The Æginetes being inform'd of this
Answer, sent three Stars of Gold, which were
affixed to a Mast of solid Brass, and are seen
in a Corner of the Temple, next to the Bowl
of *Crœsus*. After the Grecians had thus dispos'd of the Booty, they set sail for the Isthmus,
with a Resolution to confer the accustomed
Honours upon the Person, who should be found
to have behaved himself best in this War; and
accordingly, at their Arrival, the Captains
brought in, and laid upon the Altar of *Neptune*,
the Names of those they judg'd to deserve the
first and second Place. But every one thinking
he had perform'd his part best, every one wrote
down his own Name first; and for the most
part gave his second Vote for *Themistocles:* So
that each General adjudging the first Place to
himself, in which they were single, left the second to *Themistocles* uncontested. And tho' the
Grecians, out of mutual Jealousy, would not
determine this Dispute, but return'd to their
several Countries, without coming to a Decision, yet *Themistocles* was universally applauded
and obtain'd the Reputation of the most pru-

dent

dent Man in *Greece*. Nevertheless, because those
who fought the Battle at *Salamis*, had not honour'd him as he expected, he went presently
away to *Lacedemon*, that he might there receive
the Honours he desir'd. The Lacedemonians
receiv'd him splendidly, and paid him the greatest Respects. They decreed the Prize of Valour to *Eurybiades*; of Dexterity and Prudence
to *Themistocles*; and therefore presented each
with a Crown of Olive. They also gave *Themi-*
stocles the most magnificent Chariot in *Sparta*;
and after they had said much in his praise, three
hundred eminent Spartans of the Equestrian Order, attended him in his Return, to the Borders
of *Tegea*; which is the single Example we know
of a Man accompanied by the Lacedemonians
at his Departure. But upon his Return to *A-*
thens, from *Sparta*, *Timodemus*, of *Aphidna*, one
of his Enemies, tho' otherwise of no great figure,
invidiously snatching the Occasion, reproached
Themistocles with his Journey to *Lacedemon*, and
objected, that the Honours he receiv'd from the
Spartans, were not conferred on him for his
own Merit, but on account of the Athenians.
And because he continued to repeat the same
things with importunity, *Themistocles* at last answered him; " The truth is, *said he*, were I
" of *Belbina*, I should not have receiv'd so much
" Honour in *Sparta*, nor you, tho' you are an
" Athenian."

ARTABAZUS, the Son of *Pharnaces*, a Man
of great Reputation among the Persians before,
and of much greater after the Battel of *Plataea*,
having with him sixty thousand Men, drawn
out of that Army which *Mardonius* had chosen,
conducted *Xerxes* to the Passage; and after the

King's Arrival in *Aſia*, return'd back, and encamp'd about *Pallene*. But becauſe *Mardonius*,
wintering in *Theſſaly* and in *Macedonia*, was not
willing to augment his Camp with theſe Men,
Artabazus thought to take that opportunity, to
puniſh the Defection of the Potidæans with the
utmoſt Rigour. For as ſoon as the King had
paſſed by, and the Perſian Fleet, flying from
Salamis, was out of ſight, they openly revolted
from the Barbarians, and the Inhabitants of *Pallene* did the ſame: For that cauſe *Artabazus* laid
ſiege to *Potidæa*; and ſuſpecting the Olynthi-
ans would follow their Example, beſieg'd *Olynthus* alſo, which was then in the poſſeſſion of
thoſe Bottiæans, who had been driven out of
the Bay of *Therma* by the Macedonians. Theſe,
when he had taken the City, he brought down
into a Moraſs, and put them all to death; after
which he gave the Government to *Critobulus* of
Torone, by Deſcent a Chalcidian, and by that
means the Chalcidians became Maſters of *Olynthus*. After the Reduction of this Place, *Artabazus* apply'd himſelf with more attention to
the Siege of *Potidæa*; and as he was earneſtly
deſirous to ſucceed in his Attempt, *Timoxenus*,
Captain of the Scionæans, agreed to betray the
City to him. Touching the beginning of their
Correſpondence I can ſay nothing, becauſe nothing is reported; but the Event was thus:
When *Timoxenus* had any thing to impart to *Artabazus*, or *Artabazus* to *Timoxenus*, they put a
Letter into the Head of an Arrow; and afterwards affixing the Feathers, ſhot the Arrow
into the Place they had agreed upon. But the
Traytor *Timoxenus* was at laſt detected: For an
Arrow of *Artabazus* happening to fall in a
wrong

wrong Place, wounded one of the Potidæans in the Shoulder; upon which the Multitude running together about the wounded Man, as is ufual in time of War, drew out the Arrow, and having found the Letter, carried it to the principal Officers of the Potidæans, and of the other Pallenians their Confederates, who were then in the City. When they had read the Letter, and difcover'd the Author of the Treachery, they determin'd, in favour of *Scione*, not to punifh *Timoxenus* with death, left the Scionæans fhould ever after be accounted Traitors. Thus the Treafon of *Timoxenus* was detected: And as for *Artabazus*, after he had continu'd the Siege during three Months, the Tides rofe fo high, and lafted fo long, that the Barbarians feeing all the Shore full of Water and Mire, retired towards *Pallene*; and when they had paffed two parts in five, of the March they had to make through that way, before they could arrive there, fo great an Inundation came pouring in from the Sea, that the Inhabitants fay the like never happen'd before, though more moderate Floods are frequent on that Coaft. Thofe that could not fwim, perifh'd by the Waters; and thofe that could, were killed by the Potidæans, who purfued them in Boats. The Caufe of this Inundation and Difafter of the Perfians, is, by the Potidæans, attributed to the Indignities done by thofe who were drown'd, to the Image and Temple of *Neptune*, which ftands in the Suburbs; and to me they feem to have made a right Judgment. The reft return'd with *Artabazus* to the Camp of *Mardonius* in *Theffaly*; and fuch was the Fortune of thofe Troops that were fent to conduct the King.

THE

THE Remains of the Fleet of *Xerxes*, which fled from *Salamis*, arriving on the Coast of *Afia*, landed the King with his Army at *Abydus*, paffed the Winter at *Cyme*, and in the Beginning of the next enfuing Spring affembled at *Samos*, where fome of their Ships had been laid up. The fighting Men they had on board, being for the moft part Perfians and Medes, were under the Conduct of *Mardontes*, the Son of *Bagæus*, and *Artayntes*, the Son of *Artachæus*, in conjunction with *Amitres*, Uncle to the latter. And as they were extremely difpirited, and not compelled by neceffity, they would not adventure to the Weftward, but continu'd at *Samos* with three hundred Ships, including thofe of *Ionia*, to prevent the Ionians from revolting: not imagining that the Grecians would come thither, but be well contented to preferve their own Country; becaufe they had fo readily retir'd, without purfuing the Perfians, when they fled from *Salamis*. Thus defpairing of Victory by Sea, and yet believing *Mardonius*, with his Land-Forces, would be more fuccefsful, they confulted together at *Samos* what damage they might be able to do the Enemy, and at the fame time were attentive to the Event of his Enterprize: But the Spring coming on, and *Mardonius* in *Theffaly*, awaken'd the Grecians; and though their Land-Army was not yet affembled, they arrived at *Ægina* with one hundred and ten Ships, putting themfelves under the Conduct of *Leutychides*, defcended from *Menares*, *Agefilaus*, *Hippocratides*, *Leutychides*, *Anaxilaus*, *Archidanus*, *Anaxandrides*, *Theopompus*, *Nicander*, *Charilus*, *Eunomus*, *Polydectes*, *Prytanis*, *Euryphon*, *Procles*,

Procles, Aristodemus, Aristomachus, Cleodæus, Hyllus, and *Hercules.* He was of the other Branch of the Royal Family, and his Progenitors were all Kings of *Sparta,* except the four last, and the seven I mention'd immediately after *Leutychides. Xanthippus,* the Son of *Ariphron,* was General of the Athenians; and when all these Ships were assembled at *Ægina,* certain Ionians arrived in the Grecian Fleet, being the same Persons who a little before had been at *Sparta,* to desire the Lacedemonians to deliver *Ionia* from Servitude; and of these *Herodotus,* the Son of *Basilides,* was one. They had been at the beginning seven, and having determin'd to kill *Strattes,* Tyrant of the Chians, were discover'd by one of their Accomplices; so that the other six withdrawing privately from *Chio,* went first to *Sparta,* and then to *Ægina,* beseeching the Grecians to sail to *Ionia,* but could hardly prevail with them to advance to *Delos:* for all beyond that Place seem'd terrible to the Grecians; who being ignorant of the Countries, thought every part to be full of Enemies, and that *Samos* was as far distant from them, as the Columns of *Hercules.* Thus because the Barbarians durst not venture to sail beyond *Samos* Westward, nor the Grecians Eastward beyond *Delos,* though earnestly pressed by the Chians, their mutual Fears preserved the Nations that lay between both.

DURING the time of this Voyage to *Delos, Mardonius* having passed the Winter in *Thessaly,* and being ready to march out of that Country, sent away a certain Person of Europæan Extraction, named *Mus,* with order to contrive some means to get access to the Oracles,

cles, and to confult for him. What Queftions he commanded him to propofe to the Oracles, I cannot determine, becaufe Fame is filent in that particulur; but I am of opinion, that he fent to enquire about the Affairs then depending, and not of other things. However, we are certain that this *Mus* arriv'd in *Lebadia*, and having corrupted a Native of the Place, defcended into the Cave of *Trophonius*; that he procured Accefs to the Oracle of *Abe* in *Phocis*, and that he had been before at *Thebes*, where he confulted the Ifmenian *Apollo*, offering fuch Sacrifices as are ufed in *Olympia*, and bribed a Stranger, not a Theban, to fleep in the Temple of *Amphiaraus*: For none of the Thebans are permitted to confult there, becaufe when *Amphiaraus* left to their choice, whether they would have him for their Prophet, or their Ally, the Thebans rather chofe to take him for their Ally; and for this caufe no Theban may fleep in his Temple. In that time a furprizing thing happened, as I was informed by the Thebans; they told me, that this *Mus* of *Europus*, as he went round to all the Oracles, arrived at the Temple of the Ptoan *Apollo*; which, tho' called by that Name, belongs to the Thebans, and ftands beyond the Lake *Copais*, at the foot of the Mountain, near the City of *Acræphia*: That he had no fooner entered the Temple, accompanied by three Citizens, chofen by the Publick to write down the words of the Oracle, than the Archprieftefs immediately fpoke in a barbarous Tongue: That when thofe Thebans, who follow'd him, ftood amazed to hear a Barbarian Language inftead of Greek, and knew not what to do on that occafion, *Mus*

fuddenly

ſuddenly ſnatching the Table book they brought
with them, wrote down the words of the
Prieſteſs, which, they ſay, were in a Carian
Tongue ; and after he had done, departed for
Theſſaly.

WHEN *Mardonius* had read the Anſwers
of the Oracles, he ſent *Alexander*, the Son
of *Amyntas*, a Macedonian, to *Athens* ; as well on
account of his Relation to the Perſians, by the
Marriage of his Siſter *Gygea* to *Bubares* a Perſian, who had by her a Son named after his
Grandfather *Amyntas*, to whom the King of
Phrygia had given the Revenues of *Alabanda* ;
as becauſe he was informed of the mutual
Friendſhip and Hoſpitality that paſſed between him and the Athenians. This way he
thought moſt effectual to gain the Athenians ;
and having not only heard that they were a
numerous and valiant People, but believing
they had been the principal Cauſe of the late
Diſaſter of the Perſians in the Sea-fight, he
hoped, with reaſon, that if he could bring
them over, he ſhould eaſily become Maſter at
Sea ; and being perſuaded of the Superiority
of his Land-Forces, concluded, that he ſhould
be able to conquer *Greece.* Perhaps alſo the
Oracles counſelled him to procure the Alliance of the Athenians. However, for the Rea-
ſons above-mentioned, he ſent away *Alexander*,
Succeſſor, in the ſeventh Generation, of that
Perdiccas, who obtained the Monarchy of *Macedonia*, in the following manner: *Gauanes*, *Æ-
ropus*, and *Perdiccas*, three Brothers, Deſcendants of *Temenus*, fled from *Argos* to *Illyria*, and
from thence paſſing into the *Upper Macedonia*,
arrived in the City of *Lebæa*, where they entered

tered into the King's Service for Wages. One
of them had the care of his Horses, another of
his Oxen, and *Perdiccas*, who was the youngest, kept the lesser Cattle ; for in antient
time, not only the People, but Monarchs too,
had little Wealth. And as the Wife of this
King made their Bread, she constantly perceived
that of *Perdiccas* increased to double the Quantity of the rest ; which when she had long ob-
served, she acquainted her Husband with what
she had seen. The King having heard her,
and taking the thing for a Prodigy portending
some considerable Event, sent for the Brothers,
and commanded them to depart out of his Territories. They answered, That in justice they
ought to receive their Salaries, and then they
would readily go. But the King hearing them
mention their Salary, and at the same time
seeing the Sun shining through the Chimney
into the House, blasphemously said, " This I
" give you as a sufficient Reward of your Ser-
" vice :" pointing to the Sun, as he pronounc'd those words. *Gauanes* and *Æropus*,
the elder Brothers, stood amazed at his Discourse ; but the youngest answering, " We
" accept thy Offer, O King," took out a
Sword, which he happened to have about him ;
and having drawn a Circle upon the Floor
round the Brightness, made three several Motions to put up the Light of the Sun into his
Bosom, and then departed with his Brothers.
After their Departure, one of those who were
present, told the King what the Youth had
done, and that being the youngest, he must
have had some Design in accepting his Offer :
Which when the King heard, he fell into a
                                        great

great Rage, and fent away Men on horfeback,
with Orders to purfue and kill the Brothers.
In this Country is a River, to which the Defcendants of thefe Argians facrifice in comme-
moration of their Deliverance; becaufe they
had no fooner paffed, than the Streams ran fo
high, and with fuch Violence, that the Horfemen could not poffibly get over. The Teme-
nides thus efcaping, went to inhabit in another
Country of *Macedonia*, near the Gardens that
are faid to have belonged to *Midas*, the Son of
Gordias; where Rofes of fixty Leaves each, and
of a more fragrant Scent than any other, grow
naturally without Cultivation. If we may believe the Macedonians, *Silenus* was taken in thefe
Gardens; which are fhelter'd by a Mountain
called *Bermion*, inacceffible in Winter. Here
they began their firft Enterprizes; and after they
had reduced thefe Parts, they fubdued the reft
of *Macedonia*. From this *Perdiccas*, *Alexander*
derived his Blood, in the following manner:
Alexander was the Son of *Amyntas*, *Amyntas* of
Alectes, *Alectes* of *Æropus*, *Æropus* of *Philip*,
Philip of *Aræus*, and *Aræus* of *Perdiccas*, who
acquired the Kingdom.

ALEXANDER, the Son of *Amyntas*, arriv-
ing at *Athens* on the part of *Mardonius*, fpoke thus
to the Athenians: " Men of *Athens*, *Mardonius*
" has fent me to tell you, that he has re-
" ceived a Meffage from the King, containing
" thefe words: I forgive the Athenians all the
" Injuries they have done me; and therefore,
" *Mardonius*, obferve the following Orders: Re-
" inftate them in the Poffeffion of their own
" Territories; give them moreover whatever
                                            " other

" other Country they shall chuse; let them
" govern by their own Laws, and rebuild all
" their Temples which I have burnt, if they
" will come to an Agreement with me. Hav-
" ing received these Orders, I am obliged to
" put them in execution, unless you prevent
" me: And now I myself would ask you, what
" Madness pushes you on to make war against
" a King you will never conquer, nor always
" be able to resist? You are not ignorant of the
" numerous Forces and great Actions of *Xerxes*;
" you have heard of the Army I have, and if
" you should happen to be victorious, and to
" defeat us, which you can never hope so long
" as you have the use of Reason, another much
" more powerful will come against you. Suf-
" fer not yourselves then to be dispossessed of
" your Country, and continually alarmed for
" your own Lives, by measuring your Strength
" with the King; but be reconciled to him,
" since you have now so favourable an Opportu-
" nity in your hands, from the present Dispo-
" sition of *Xerxes*. Enter therefore into an
" Alliance with us, sincerely and without
" fraud, and continue to be a free People.
" These, O *Athenians*, are the words which
" *Mardonius* ordered me to say to you: For
" my own part, I shall not mention my con-
" stant Affection to your State, because you
" have had sufficient proof of that in the former
" time. I beseech you then, hearken to the
" Counsel of *Mardonius*; for I see you will not
" be always able to make war against *Xerxes*.
" Had I not known this, I should never have
" undertaken to bring you such a Message; but
" the King's Power is incomparably greater

" than that of all other Mortals, and his Reach
" so extensive, that, unless you immediately
" accept the favourable Conditions he offers, I
" dread the Consequence to you, who lying in
" the way of Danger more than any other of
" the Confederates, and possessing a Country,
" placed as a Prize between the contending
" Parties, must be always most exposed to
" Ruin. Let these Reasons prevail with you,
" and consider the important Advantages you
" will receive, if the great King forgives you
" alone among all the Grecians, and becomes
" your Friend." Thus spoke *Alexander*. But
the Lacedemonians having been informed that
he was gone to *Athens*, in order to persuade the
Athenians to an Agreement with the Barbarian;
and remembring the Oracles had predicted, that
they, together with the rest of the Dorians,
should be ejected out of *Peloponnesus* by the
Medes and the Athenians, were not a little
afraid that the Athenians would make Peace
with the Persian; and therefore resolved forthwith to send Ambassadors to *Athens*, who happened to be present in this Assembly. For the
Athenians had purposely protracted the time of
their meeting, that, as a point of Decency, they
might openly shew their Intentions to the Lacedemonians; not doubting, that when they
should hear of a Messenger coming to *Athens*
from the Barbarian to treat of Peace, they would
immediately send to them. By this means *A-
lexander* had no sooner finished his Discourse,
than the Spartan Ambassadors speaking next,
said, " The Lacedemonians have sent us hither,
" to desire you not to introduce Innovations in-
" to *Greece*, nor to hearken to the Propositions
" of

" of the Barbarians; becaufe fuch Actions are
" altogether unjuft, and difhonourable in any
" of the Grecians, and leaft of all becoming
" you, for many Reafons. In the firft place,
" you were the Authors of the War againft our
" Inclination; the Difpute was about your
" Territories, which is now fpread through all
" *Greece*; and what can be more intolerable,
" than that the Grecians fhould be brought in-
" to Servitude by means of the Athenians, who,
" in all preceding Times, have been famous
" for delivering many Nations from Oppref-
" fion? We affectionately take part in your
" Sufferings, we are grieved to fee you twice
" lofe the Produce of your Lands, and be fo
" long deprived of your Families and Habita-
" tions. But in compenfation, the Lacedemo-
" nians, with the other Allies, promife to pro-
" vide Subfiftence for your Wives, and all o-
" ther Perfons unfit to bear Arms, and belong-
" ing to you, as long as the War fhall conti-
" nue. Be not therefore feduced by the delu-
" five Colours which *Alexander* the Macedo-
" nian has put upon the words of *Mardonius.*
" He acts in conformity to his Condition; he
" helps the Tyrant, becaufe he is a Tyrant
" himfelf. But you ought to act in another
" manner, if you judge rightly, becaufe you
" know the Barbarians have no regard either to
" Truth or Juftice." When the Spartan Ambaffadors had thus fpoken, the Athenians gave
the following Anfwer to *Alexander:* " We know
" the Forces of the Medes are far greater than
" ours, and therefore that Infult was unnecef-
" fary; yet, in order to preferve our Liberty,
" we will defend ourfelves as long as we can.

" But

" But we would have you forbear attempting
" to perfuade us to treat with the Barbarian,
" becaufe you fhall never prevail. Go then,
" and tell *Mardonius*, that the Athenians de-
" clare, they will never make Peace with
" *Xerxes*, fo long as the Sun fhall continue to
" perform his Courfe; and that, trufting to
" the Affiftance of the Gods and Heroes, whofe
" Temples and Images he has burnt in con-
" tempt, we refolve to refift him to the laft
" extremity. In conclufion, appear no more
" in the Prefence of the Athenians with fuch
" Meffages, nor exhort us to deteftable Actions,
" under colour of doing us good Offices: For
" we are unwilling to ufe Methods that may
" be uneafy to you, who are our Friend, and
" engaged with us in a reciprocal Hofpitality."
This was their Anfwer to *Alexander*; and to
the Spartan Ambaffadors they faid, " If the
" Lacedemonians have been apprehenfive, left
" we fhould come to an Accommodation with
" the Barbarian, their Thought was very na-
" tural, as they are Men; but fuch Fears feem
" indecent in you, who know the Sentiments
" of the Athenians. Not all the Gold in the
" World, nor the greateft, richeft, and moft
" beautiful Country, fhall ever induce us to
" join with the Medes, and to betray the Li-
" berty of *Greece*. Many and powerful Rea-
" fons forbid us to do this, even though we
" had the Inclination. The firft and greateft
" is, that the Temples and Images of the Gods
" have been burnt, and laid in Heaps of Ruin.
" This we are under a neceffity of avenging
" with the utmoft Rigour, rather than to make
" Peace with the Man who has perpetrated the
" Crime.

" Crime.   Besides, as the Grecians are of one
" Blood and Language, have the same Altars
" and Sacrifices, and altogether resemble one
" another in Manners,   the Athenians would
" act an unbecoming Part, should they be the
" Betrayers of *Greece:* In a word, be now in-
" formed, if you knew it not before, that so
" long as one Athenian is left alive, we will ne-
" ver make an Accommodation with *Xerxes.*
" We acknowledge your provident Care of us,
" in the Willingness you express to furnish
" Subsistence for our Families,   now we have
" lost our Houses and Harvests, and return you
" Thanks in as full a manner, as if we had re-
" ceived the Benefit; but shall continue to
" make Provision for ourselves, without being
" a Burden to you.   At present, in regard to
" the Condition of Affairs,   let your Army
" march out with all possible Expedition: For
" we are of opinion, that the Barbarian will
" not delay to invade our Territories, but ad-
" vance immediately, after he shall hear that
" we will do none of the things he demands of
" us.   The best way therefore that we can
" take, is to prevent him, by marching into
" *Bœotia* with our Forces, before he arrives in
" *Attica.*"

THE

History of *Herodotus*.

BOOK IX.

CALLIOPE.

THE Lacedemonians having receiv'd this Answer of the Athenians, departed for *Sparta* ; and when *Mardonius* was inform'd by *Alexander*, at his Return, how things had passed, he set out from *Thessaly*, and led his Army with diligence towards *Athens*, taking with him the Forces of all those Places that lay upon his March. The Thessalians of most Authority, were so far from repenting of their former Actions, that they pressed the Persian more than ever, to go on with his Enterprize; and among them, one *Thorax* of *Larissa*, who had serv'd for a Guide to *Xerxes* in his Flight, now openly conducted *Mardonius* into *Greece.* When the Persian Army arriv'd in *Bœotia*, the Thebans went to *Mardonius*, and told him by way of Advice, that their Country, of all other, was most convenient for his Camp,

and

and that, if he would continue there, and advance no farther, he might be Mafter of *Greece* without hazarding a Battle: That the Grecians, when unanimous, were fo ftrong, as hardly to be conquered by all Mankind, which he had already experienc'd: " But if, *faid they*, you will " do as we advife, you may without difficulty " fruftrate their beft concerted Meafures: Send " Money to the principal Perfons of every Ci- " ty; for by that means you will fplit *Greece* " into Factions, and then you may eafily fub- " due thofe who are not in your Intereft, and " the Factions at the fame time." Such Coun- fel the Thebans gave to *Mardonius*; but he, partly from a vehement Defire he had to take *Athens* a fecond time, and partly out of Vanity, imagining, that by firing the Beacons in the Iflands, he fhould fhew the King at *Sardis*, that he was Mafter of *Athens*, would not be perfua- ded. When he arriv'd in *Attica*, he found no Athenians there; but being inform'd that moft of them were at *Salamis*, and on board the Fleet, he took poffeffion of the abandon'd City in the tenth Month after the King's Entrance. Being poffeffed of *Athens*, he difpatch'd *Muri- chides*, a Hellefpontin, to *Salamis*, with the fame Inftructions, which *Alexander* the Macedonian had already carried to the Athenians; not that he was ignorant of the little Friendfhip they had for him, but hoping they would remit fome- thing of their Haughtinefs, fince *Attica*, reduced by the Fortune of War, was now in his power. Accordingly, *Murichides* arriving at *Salamis*, Went into the Council; and when he had fpoken as he was inftructed by *Mardonius*, *Lycidas*, one of the Senators, delivered for his Opinion, that

the

the beſt Reſolution they could take, would be, to receive the Propoſitions brought by *Muri-chides*, and refer them to the People. This he ſaid, either becauſe he was corrupted by *Mar-donius* with Money, or becauſe he was really of that opinion. But the Athenians, who were in the Council, having heard his Words, and thoſe without being ſoon inform'd of what he had ſaid, they all reſented the thing with the higheſt Indignation; and immediately gathering about *Lycidas*, ſtoned him to Death, diſmiſſing *Murichides* the Helleſpontin without Hurt. The Athenian Women obſerving the Tumult that happen'd at *Salamis* on this Occaſion, and in-quiring into the Cauſe, were no ſooner inform'd of the Fact, than taking one another by the Hand, with mutual Exhortations, they went without other Inducement to the Houſe of *Ly-cidas*, and ſtoned his Wife with his Children. The Reaſon that mov'd the Athenians to go to *Salamis*, was this: They had continued in *At-tica* as long as they had any Hope that the For-ces of the Peloponneſians would come to their aſſiſtance; but when they perceiv'd their Indo-lence, and inſupportable Delays, and were in-form'd that *Mardonius* was already advanced in-to *Bœotia*, they tranſported themſelves with their Goods to *Salamis*. From thence they ſent Ambaſſadors to *Sparta*, to complain of the La-cedemonians, for ſhewing no Concern at the Irruption of the Barbarian into *Attica*, and neg-lecting to join the Athenians with their Forces, in order to oppoſe the common Enemy in *Bœotia*. They were alſo to remind them of the great Advantages the Perſian had offer'd, if the Athe-nians would embrace his Intereſt; and to fore-

warn

warn them, that unless they were succoured,
they would find some Remedy themselves. At
the same time the Lacedemonians were employ'd
in celebrating the Festival of *Hyacinthus*, which
they observe with great Solemnity, and in building a Wall for themselves upon the Isthmus,
which was already cover'd with Battlements.
In this Conjuncture the Athenian Ambassadors,
accompanied by those of *Megara* and *Platæa*, arriving in *Sparta*, went to the Ephori, and said;
" The Athenians have sent us hither, with
" Orders to speak thus to you: The King of
" the Medes is willing to restore our Territo-
" ries ; and not only to make an Alliance with
" us upon a foot of Equality, without Fraud
" or Dissimulation, but to give us any other
" Country we shall chuse: Yet the Reverence
" we bear to the Grecian *Jupiter*, and our Ab-
" horrence of the Crime of betraying *Greece*,
" have prevail'd with us to refuse our Consent,
" and to reject his Offers ; though in requital,
" we are injur'd and betrayed by the Grecians.
" We know we should consult our own Interest
" more, by making Peace with the Persian, than
" by continuing the War; but we will never
" willingly come to an Accommodation with
" him. This is our Way of demonstrating our
" sincere Affection to the Grecians : But you,
" who where then in the utmost Consternation
" lest we should make our Peace with the Per-
" sian, were no sooner assured of our constant
" Resolution never to betray *Greece*, and had
" built a Wall for your own Defence upon the
" Isthmus, than you threw off all Concern for
" the Athenians. For after you had promis'd
" to advance into *Bœotia* with us, in order to
3   " prevent

" prevent the Perſian, you left us to ſhift for
" ourſelves, and looked upon the Irruption of
" the Barbarian into *Attica*, with Indifference.
" Hitherto the Athenians are diſſatisfied with
" you, for neglecting to do that which was be-
" coming: At preſent they exhort you to ſend
" your Forces, to join them with all Expedition;
" that having loſt the Opportunity of meeting
" the Enemy in *Bœotia*, we may find him in
" *Attica*, where the Plain of *Thria* is the moſt
" commodious Place of all our Territories for
" fighting the Battel." When the Ephori had
heard this Meſſage, they put off their Anſwer
to the next Day, and from that to another, ſtill
protracting the time from day to day, till ten
Days were paſſed: During which, all the Peloponneſians wrought with the utmoſt diligence
at the Iſthmus, and finiſh'd the Wall. I can give
no other Reaſon of the great Induſtry they uſed
to prevent the Athenians from taking part with
the Medes, when *Alexander* the Macedonian was
at *Athens*, and of their total Neglect of them afterwards, than that having fenced the Iſthmus
with a Wall, they thought they had no farther
need of the Athenians: Whereas, when *Alexander* went to *Athens*, their Wall was not yet built,
but they were hard at work, and much afraid of
the Perſians. At length, things turn'd in the
following manner, with relation to their Anſwer
and March: The day before the meeting of the
laſt publick Aſſembly, *Chileus*, of *Tegea*, a Man
of the greateſt Credit with the Spartans, of any
Stranger, being told by one of the Ephori
what the Athenians had ſaid, ſpoke to them
in theſe Terms: " The Matter in ſhort, is
" thus: If the Athenians divide from you, and
join

" join with the Barbarian, he will enter *Peloponne-*
" *sus* by Passages large enough, notwithstanding
" the strong Wall you have built upon the Isth-
" mus; therefore hearken to the Athenians,
" before they come to any Resolution that may
" be prejudicial to *Greece*." Such was the
Counsel of *Chileus*; which the Ephori having
considered with Attention, they immediately
the same night, and without speaking to the
Ambassadors, sent out five thousand Spartans,
with seven Helots to attend each, under the
Conduct of *Pausanias*, the Son of *Cleombrotus*.
These Forces should have been led by *Plistar-*
chus, the Son of *Leonidas*; but because he was
under Age, they were committed to the care of
Pausanias, who was his Guardian and Cousin-
German: For *Cleombrotus*, the Father of *Pausa-*
nias and Son to *Anaxandrides*, died in his Return with the Army, after they had built the
Wall upon the Isthmus: from whence he decamp'd with his Forces, because the Sun was
darkened in the Heavens, whilst he sacrificed
for Success against the Persian. *Pausanias* chose
Euryanax, the Son of *Doris*, a Man of his own
Blood, to assist him in the Conduct of this Army.

WHEN these Forces were gone from *Spar-*
ta with *Pausanias*, the Ambassadors knowing nothing of their Departure, and designing to return forthwith to their Principals, went early
the next morning to the Ephori, and said, " You
" are here, O Lacedemonians, at your ease,
" celebrating the Festival of *Hyacinthus*, and di-
" verting yourselves, whilst you betray your
" Allies. But know that the Athenians, in-
" jured by you, and destitute of Succour, will
" make Peace with the Persian on such Terms
" as

" as they can obtain. When we have done fo,
" and are become the King's Allies, we fhall be
" oblig'd to march with him againft whatever
" Country he fhall lead us, and then you will
" fee the Event of thefe Counfels." After the
Ambaffadors had thus fpoken, the Ephori affured them with an Oath, that their Army was
in full March againft the Foreigners, for by
that name they call the Barbarians, and that
they doubted not they were already arrived at
Oreftia. The Ambaffadors not comprehending
this Difcourfe, defired to know their meaning;
and being much furpriz'd when they heard the
whole Truth, departed with all poffible Expedition to follow the Troops. Five thoufand
Men more, drawn out of the Places adjacent to
Lacedemon, marched out at the fame time to
join *Paufanias.*

WHILST thefe Forces advanced in diligence towards the Ifthmus, the Argians, who
had before undertaken to *Mardonius,* that they
would prevent the Spartans from going out,
hearing they were actually upon the March, under the Conduct of *Paufanias,* difpatched the
beft Courier they had to *Attica;* where, at his
Arrival, he fpoke thus to *Mardonius:* " The
" Argians have fent me to inform you, that the
" Youth of *Lacedemon* are marched out, and that
" they could find no way to hinder them: they
" wifh you may take the moft advantageous
" meafures in this Emergency." When he had
faid thefe words, he went away, in order to
return home; but *Mardonius* having received
this Information, would not venture to ftay longer in *Attica,* where he had continued to that
time, to fee what the Athenians would do, and
had

had neither intrenched himself, nor ravag'd the Country, being in daily expectation that the Athenians would make their Peace. But now finding he could not prevail with them, and understanding how things had passed, he withdrew his Army out of *Attica*, before *Pausanias* arrived at the Isthmus, having first set fire to *Athens*, and demolished whatever remained standing of the Walls, Houses, and Temples, laying all in Heaps of Ruin. He quitted *Attica*, because the Country is not proper for Cavalry; and if he should have lost a Battel, he had no way to get off except thro' narrow Passes, in which a small number of Men might have intercepted his Retreat. For these Reasons he determined to retire to *Thebes*, and to fight in a Country commodious for Horse, and Friends to the Persians. In this manner he abandoned *Attica*, and in his Retreat receiv'd a Message, with information, that a Body of a thousand Lacedemonians were gone towards *Megara*: which he no sooner understood, than resolving to make his first Attempt upon these, he turned his March that way, and sent out his Horse before to scour the Country. So far this Persian Army penetrated into *Europe* Westward, and no farther.

AFTER this, *Mardonius* being informed by a second Message, that the Grecian Forces were assembled at the Isthmus, returned back by the way of *Decelia*, having for his Guides certain Persons sent to him by the Bœotians from the Country adjoining to the River *Asopus*. They conducted him first to *Sphendale*, then to *Tanagra*, where he passed the Night, and the next day to *Colon*, a Place belonging to the Thebans. After his Arrival, he ravaged their Territories

for

for Provisions, tho' they were in the Interest of the Medes, not out of Enmity to the Thebans, but compelled by Necessity: For he resolved to intrench himself with his Army, that he might have a Place of Refuge, in case he should not meet with the Success he desired in a Battel. His Camp extended from *Erythræa* to the Country of the Platæans, by the way of *Hysia*, stretching along the River *Asopus*, and was strengthened by a Wall of less Circumference than one might expect, having only about ten Stades on each Front. While the Barbarians were employed in this Work, *Attaginus*, the Son of *Phryno*, a Theban, invited *Mardonius*, with fifty of the most eminent Persians, to a magnificent Feast, which he had prepared at *Thebes*; and they came accordingly. The rest of this Relation I heard from the mouth of *Thersander* of *Orchomenus*, a Man of great Reputation among the Orchomenians. He told me, that he was one of fifty Thebans, invited by *Attaginus* to this Feast, and that each Person had not a Table to himself, but that two Men were placed at each, a Persian and a Theban: That after Supper, in the midst of their Cups, the Persian, who sat by him, asking him, in the Grecian Tongue, of what Country he was; and finding by his Answer that he was of *Orchomenus*, said to him: "Since we are Companions, in eating and "drinking at the same Table, I will leave my "Opinion with you, that you may remember "me; and foreseeing the Event, may prudent- "ly consult your own Safety. You see these "Persians, now feasting here, and you have seen "the Army we left encamped upon the River. "Of all these you will see few Survivors in a "little

" little time." *Therfander* added, That the
Perfian, having thus fpoken, fhed abundance of
Tears, and that he himfelf being much aftonifhed at his words, asked him, if thefe things
fhould not rather be communicated to *Mardonius*, and to thofe Perfons, who, next to him,
were the moft confiderable of the Army? To
which he anfwered, " That which God has
" determined, Men cannot avert; befides, a-
" mong us, the beft Advice prevails with no
" Man. Many of the Perfians are convinced of
" thefe things, but we are neceffitated to follow
" *Mardonius*; and the moft pernicious of all
" the Evils that infeft Mankind, is, when he
" who underftands much, has nothing in his
" power." This Relation I had from *Therfander* the Orchomenian, who told me, at the fame
time, that he had given an account of his Difcourfe with the Perfians to divers others, before
the Battel was fought at *Platæa*.

DURING the time *Mardonius* was incamped
in *Bæotia*, all the Grecians of the adjacent Parts
that were in the Intereft of the Medes, fent in
their Forces, and marched with him to *Athens*;
except only the Phoceans, who had been con-
ftrained by neceffity to take part with them,
much againft their Inclination. But, not many
days after his Arrival at *Thebes*, they alfo joined
him with a thoufand Men well armed, and led
by *Harmocydes*, a Citizen of principal Authority among them. When they were arrived at
Thebes, *Mardonius* fent out fome Horfe, to order
the Phoceans to encamp by themfelves in the
Plain; which they had no fooner done than all
the Cavalry of the Army appeared in fight. By
this means a Rumour was fpread among the

Grecian

Grecian Forces with *Mardonius*, that the Horſe
were ordered to maſſacre all the Phoceans with
their Javelins: and after the ſame had been alſo
divulged among the Phoceans themſelves, their
captain *Harmocydes*, to awaken their Courage,
ſaid, " Theſe Men, O Phoceans, have a mani-
" feſt Deſign to take away our Lives, and I be-
" lieve the Theſſalians are our Accuſers. Eve-
" ry one of you therefore muſt exert himſelf
" to the utmoſt on this occaſion; becauſe we
" ought rather to die reſiſting, and doing
" ſomething in our own defence, than tamely
" to expoſe ourſelves to ſuffer a moſt diſgraceful
" Death. Let us then convince ſome of theſe
" Barbarians, that they are not a Match for theſe
" Grecians, whoſe Murder they deſigned."
Thus *Harmocydes* encouraged the Phoceans; and
at the ſame time the Horſe having ſurrounded
them on all ſides, moved on in a hoſtile Poſture, brandiſhing their Javelins, and ſome actually threw. But when they ſaw the Phoceans
ſtanding firm, drawn into the cloſeſt Order,
and fronting every way, they turned about and
retired to their Army. I cannot certainly tell
whether this Cavalry came to deſtroy the Phoceans at the deſire of the Theſſalians, and ſeeing
them determined to reſiſt, retired for fear of
expoſing their Perſons, covering their Retreat
with the Pretext of Orders from *Mardonius*;
or whether they came only with a deſign to try
the Courage of the Phoceans. But after the
return of the Horſe, *Mardonius* ſent them a Meſſage, in theſe words: " Fear nothing, O Pho-
" ceans! you have given manifeſt proof that
" you are Men of Valour, contrary to the In-
" formation I had received. Bear the Toils of

" this War with Refolution, and be affured
" that you fhall never do more for me, and
" for the King, than we will do for you." Such
was the Event of this Affair concerning the
Phoceans.

WHEN the Lacedemonians were advanced
to the Ifthmus, and encamped with their Army ; the other Peloponnefians, at leaft as many
as had the common Caufe at heart, having heard
of their Arrival, and perceiving the Spartans
difpofed to march on, thought they could not
ftay behind without difgrace. Accordingly,
after they had performed their Sacrifices aufpi-
cioufly, they all marched out from the Ifthmus ; and advancing to *Eleufis,* facrificed again
there with the fame fortunate Prefages, and
continued their March, in conjunction with the
Athenians, who arriving from *Salamis,* had
joined the Peloponnefians at *Eleufis.* When they
were advanced to *Erythra* in *Bœotia,* and perceived the Barbarians encamped by the River
Afopus, they confulted together, and placed
their Camp right againft the Enemy, at the
foot of the Mountain *Cytheron :* But *Mardonius*
finding that the Grecians declined to come out
into the Plain, fent all his Cavalry, commanded
by *Mafiftius,* a Man of great Efteem among the
Perfians, and called by the Grecians *Macifius,* to
infult their Camp. He mounted a Nifean Horfe
that wore a Bridle of Gold, and all other Furniture fuitably magnificent. The Cavalry advancing to the Camp of the Grecians, made
their Attacks by Parties, in which they did
great mifchief, and challenged them under the
name of Women. In thefe Attempts the Megareans, who were accidentally pofted in that

2   part,

part, which was moft acccefible, and lay moft
expofed to the Enemies Horfe, finding themfelves hard preffed, fent a Trumpeter to the
Grecian Generals, with a Meffage, which he
delivered in thefe Terms: " The Megareans
" fay thus, Friends and Allies, we are not able
" alone to fuftain the Efforts of the Perfian
" Horfe, having had the fame Station from the
" beginning, in which we now are, and where
" we have hitherto maintained ourfelves by our
" Conftancy and Fortitude, though not with-
" out great difficulty ; but now, unlefs you
" will fend fome other Forces to relieve us, we
" muft abandon our Poft." When the Meffenger had thus fpoken, *Paufanias* founded the
Grecians, to fee if any of them would voluntarily offer to march into that Quarter to relieve
the Megareans. But after they had all refufed,
the Athenians undertook the Charge with a
Body of three hundred chofen Men, led by
Olympiodorus, the Son of *Lampon.* Thefe were
they who took upon them to defend that Poft,
which the reft of the Grecians at *Erythra* had
declined ; and being accompanied by a Party of
Archers, chofen by themfelves, fought the Enemy for fome time : till at laft, as the Cavalry
continued to attack in Squadrons, the Horfe of
Mafiftius appearing before the reft, was wounded
in the Side with an Arrow ; and rifing upright,
impatient of the Pain, threw his Rider to the
ground. The Athenians feeing *Mafiftius* fall,
immediately furrounded him ; and having firft
feized his Horfe, killed him, as he endeavoured
to defend himfelf. Yet this they could not do
prefently, becaufe he wore a Cuirafs underneath
covered with Mails of Gold and a purple

Cloke

Cloke for his upper Garment. They tried in vain to penetrate his Cuirafs; which an Athenian perceiving, thruft him into the Eye, and by that Wound he fell down and died. His own Troops at firft knew nothing of his Death; for they neither faw him, when he fell from his Horfe, nor when he was killed, nor even, at the time of their Retreat, had they heard of the Accident. But coming to make a halt, they prefently enquired for their General, becaufe they perceived there was no Commander; and as foon as they were informed of his Fate, animating one another, they all together pufhed their Horfes againft the Enemy, in order to carry off the dead Body. When the Athenians faw that they no longer attacked in Parties, but with their whole Force, they called out for Succour to the reft of the Army: Yet before the Infantry could come to their Relief, the Difpute about the Body of *Mafiftius* was fo fharp and unequal, that the three hundred, being unable to keep their Ground, were obliged to retire: But after the Grecian Forces came in to their Affiftance, the Enemies Horfe not daring to continue the Fight, abandoned the dead Body, with many of their Men killed upon the Place; and retiring to the diftance of about two Stades to confult together, refolved to return to *Mardonius*, becaufe they had then no General. When they arrived in the Camp, *Mardonius*, and all the Army, broke out into the loudeft Lamentations for the Death of *Mafiftius*, cutting off not only their own Hair, but that of their Horfes and Cattel of Draught. Their Ejulations were heard all over *Bæotia*, as for the Lofs of a Man, who, next to *Mardonius*,

was

was in moſt Eſteem among the Perſians, and with the King. In this manner the Barbarians lamented the Death of *Maſiſtius,* according to the Cuſtom of their own Country

THE Grecians having thus ſuſtained and repulſed the Enemies Cavalry, were much encouraged ; and becauſe their Men, out of a deſire to view the Body of *Maſiſtius,* left their Stations in great numbers, they placed it on a Chariot, and carried it through every Quarter of the Camp ; a Spectacle deſerving admiration, on account of his Stature and Comelineſs. After this they reſolved to march down into the Territories of the Platæans, judging thoſe Parts much more commodious for their Camp, than the Country about *Erythra,* in divers reſpects, and eſpecially that they might be well ſupplied with Water. For this reaſon having determined to encamp near the Spring of *Gargaphia,* which is in that Country, they marched with their Arms by the foot of Mount *Cytheron,* at a little diſtance from *Hyſia,* into the Territories of *Platæa,* where when they arrived, they encamped in a Plain, intermixed with ſome ſmall Elevations of Ground, near the Gargaphian Spring, and the Temple of the Hero *Androcrates,* aſſigning a ſeparate Quarter to the Troops of every Nation. In the Diſtribution of theſe Stations a long Diſpute aroſe between the Tegeans and the Athenians, both ſides claiming a Right to be placed at the Head of one of the Wings, and alledging their antient and late Actions to juſtify their Pretenſions. " We, ſaid the Tegeans, have always " been honoured with this Poſt among the al- " lies, whenever the Peloponneſians have

" marched out with united Forces, from the
" time in which the Heraclides attempted to re-
" turn into *Peloponnesus*, after the Death of *Eu-*
" *rystheus* ; and we then obtained this Dignity in
" the following manner : When we, in conjunc-
" tion with the Achaians and Ionians of *Pelopon-*
" *nesus*, had marched to the Isthmus, and were
" encamped in sight of the Invaders, *Hyllus* said
" publickly, that they ought not to expose the
" Armies to the danger of a Battel ; but that
" the Peloponnesians ought rather to pick out
" the Man they should think the most valiant of
" all their Camp, to fight singly with him, and
" so put an end to the Dispute. The Pelopon-
" nesians accepted the Condition, and an Agree-
" ment, confirmed by an Oath, was made be-
" tween both Armies, in these Terms : If *Hyllus*
" conquer the Peloponnesian Captain, the Coun-
" tries that were possessed by his Father, shall
" be restored to him ; but if he be conquered,
" the Heraclides shall depart with their Army,
" and not endeavour to return into *Peloponnesus*
" during the space of an hundred years. On
" this occasion *Echemus*, the Son of *Æropus*,
" and Grandson of *Phegeus*, our King and Ge-
" neral, being preferred by the Confederates be-
" fore all others, to his great satisfaction, fought
" the Duel, and killed *Hyllus*. By that Action
" we obtained of the Peloponnesians several great
" Prerogatives, which we enjoy to this day ;
" and particularly that of having the Post of
" Honour in one of the Wings, whensoever we
" should march out upon an Expedition by com-
" mon Consent. We pretend not to contest
" with you, O Lacedemonians, but are ready
" to give you the Preference, and to acquiesce
" in

"in the choice you shall make: Only we
" challenge the leading of the other Wing, ac-
" cording to the Custom of former times. Be-
" sides, though we should set aside the Merit of
" the Action we have mentioned, we are yet
" more worthy of that Station than the Athe-
" nians, on account of the many prosperous
" Successes we have had, in conjunction with
" your Forces, as well as with others. For
" these Reasons we ought to obtain the second
" Post of Honour, and not the Athenians;
" whose Actions, either old or new, are no
" way comparable to ours." To this Speech,
the Athenians answered, "We are not igno-
" rant, that these Forces were assembled, in or-
" der to fight the Barbarian, and not to dispute
" about Precedency: Yet the Tegeans having
" thought fit to mention the great Actions they
" have done, both in antient and latter time,
" have put us under a Necessity of shewing you
" that for our Ancestors Merit and our own,
" we ought always to be preferred before the
" Arcadians: We alone receiv'd the Heracli-
" des, (whose Captain these Men boast to have
" kill'd at the Isthmus) after they had been re-
" jected by all the Grecians, to whom they ap-
" plied themselves for Protection, when they
" fled from the Oppression of the Mycenians;
" and joining with them, we punished the In-
" solence of *Euristheus*, and defeated the Forces
" of those, who were then in possession of *Pelo-*
" *ponnesus*. We made war upon the Cadmæans;
" in which, having recovered the Bodies of the
" Argians, who were kill'd in the Expedition
" of *Polynices* against *Thebes*, and lay unburied,
" we interr'd them at *Eleusis*, in our own
A a 4   "Coun-

" Country: We fought successfully against the
" Amazons, when arriving from the River *Ther-*
" *modon*, they invaded *Attica*; and in the great
" Actions perform'd during the Trojan War,
" we were inferior to none. But to what pur-
" pose should we mention these things? For
" perhaps those who were than valiant, may
" have degenerated; and those who had little
" Courage then, may now be brave. There-
" fore, to say no more of the Actions of our
" Ancestors, let us see who we are at present:
" And certainly, though we could produce no
" other Examples, as we can undoubtedly, as
" many and as illustrious, as any People of *Greece*;
" yet what we did at the Battel of *Marathon*,
" renders us worthy of this, and greater Ho-
" nour. For, without the Assistance of the
" Grecians, we alone undertook that hazardous
" Enterprize, fought the Persian with our own
" Forces, and obtain'd a Victory over the
" Troops of six and forty Nations. This sin-
" gle Action gives us a just Title to the Rank
" we claim. But, because the present Con-
" juncture is altogether improper for such Con-
" testations, we readily refer the Decision to
" you, O Lacedemonians, and will take our
" Station in whatever Order you shall judge most
" convenient: For wheresoever we are placed
" we shall endeavour to do our best. Give Judg-
" ment therefore in this Affair, and be assured
" of our ready Compliance." Thus said the
Athenians; and immediately the whole Army of
the Lacedemonians cried out with one Voice,
that the Athenians were more worthy to be at
the Head of the other Wing, than the Arcadians.
So they obtained the Rank they demanded, and
were

were preferred before the Tegeans. After which, the Grecians, as well those who came at the beginning, as those who arrived afterwards, were drawn up in the following manner: Ten thousand Lacedemonians had the Right, and five thousand of these, being of *Sparta*, were guarded by thirty five thousand Helots, lightly arm'd, every Spartan having seven Helots about his Person: Next to themselves the Lacedemonians placed the Tegeans, consisting of fifteen hundred Men, partly to do them honour, and partly in consideration of their Valour. After these, five thousand Corinthians; who by the Permission of *Pausanias*, had three hundred Potidæans of *Pallene*, join'd with them: Next in order stood six hundred Arcadians, of *Orchomenus*, three thousand Trœzenians, and two hundred Men from *Leprion*: After these, four hundred Mycenians and Tyrinthians; one thousand Phliasians, three hundred Hermionians, six hundred Eretrians and Styrians; four hundred Chalcideans, five hundred Ambracians, eight hundred Leucadians and Anactorians; two hundred Paleans of *Cephalonia*, five hundred from *Ægina*; three thousand Megareans, six hundred Platæans; and last of all, but in a Post of principal Honour, eight thousand Athenians took their Station at the head of the Left, conducted by *Aristides*, the Son of *Lysimachus*. All these, exclusive of the seven Helots attending every Spartan, amounted to thirty eight thousand seven hundred Men; which was the whole number of those who came solidly arm'd to fight the Barbarian. Their Light-arm'd Forces were as follows: Of the Helots belonging to the Spartans, thirty five thousand, all

ex-

exercifed to War; and thirty four thoufand five hundred Men more, in Light-Arms, attending the reft of the Lacedemonians and other Grecians, one to each Man. So that the Numbers of thefe light-arm'd Forces, amounting to fixty nine thoufand five hundred fighting Men; the whole Army of the Grecians, affembled at *Platæa*, including both forts, wanted only one thoufand eight hundred, to compleat the Number of a hundred and ten thoufand: which yet was made up by the Arrival of the furviving Thefpians, tho' they came to the Camp without Arms. And in this Order the Grecians encamp'd on the fide of the River *Afopus*.

On the other part, *Mardonius*, with the Barbarians, having perform'd the Obfequies of *Mafiftius* with great Lamentation, and hearing that the Grecians were in the Territories of the Platæans, marched thither alfo: and arriving at the River *Afopus*, drew up his Army in the following manner: Over againft the Lacedemonians he placed the Perfians; and becaufe they were far more in number, he extended their Ranks to an equal length with thofe of the Tegeans, but chofe the beft Men to face the Lacedemonians, and the worft to oppofe the Tegeans: which he did by the Counfel and Information of the Thebans. Next to the Perfians he placed the Medes, fronting the Corinthians, the Potidæans, the Orchomenians, and the Sicyonians: After thefe, he pofted the Bactrians, oppofite to the Epidaurians, Trœzenians, Lepreates, Tyrinthians, Mycenians, and Phliafians. The Indians had the next Station to the Bactrians, over againft the Hermionians, Eretrians, Styrians, and Chalcideans

cideans: Contiguous to the Indians, *Mardo-nius* placed the Saces, facing towards the Ambracians, Anactorians, Leucadians, Paleans, and Æginetes: But after the Saces, and opposite to the Athenians, Platæans, and Megareans, he rang'd the Bœotians, the Locrians, the Melians, the Thessalians, and the thousand Phoceans I mention'd before; for only some of the Phoceans were in the Party of the Medes, but others among them favouring the Grecians, retir'd to Mount *Parnassus*, and making Excursions from thence, pillag'd and harassed the Troops of *Mardonius*, and of the Grecians who were in his Army. The Macedonians, with the Forces of the Countries adjoining to *Thessaly*, were added to those who faced the Front of the Athenians. And these are the Names of all the most considerable and illustrious Nations, which *Mardonius* drew up, in order of Battel: Yet they were mixed with Men of other Countries, Phrygians, Thracians, Mysians, Pæonians, Ethiopians, and others. They had also among them some Hermotybians and Calasirians of *Ægypt*, distinguished by the Sword they wore, and singly fit for War of all the Ægyptians. These Men he took out of their Ships, whilst he was at *Phaleron*; for no Ægyptians were in the Land-Army, which follow'd *Xerxes* in his Expedition against *Athens*. The Barbarian Forces of *Mardonius*, as I have already said, amounted to three hundred thousand Men; but no one certainly knows how many his Grecian Allies were, because their Number was not taken: Yet, if I may give my Opinion, I guess they might be about fifty thousand. When the Infantry was drawn

into

into the Order before mention'd, the Cavalry
was placed in separate Stations; and the next
day, after the two Armies were thus dispos'd
into national and distinct Bodies, they offer'd
Sacrifices on both sides. Those of the Grecians
were perform'd by *Tisamenus,* the Son of *An-*
tiochus, an Elean of the Clytidean Family, descended from *Iamus,* who accompanied the Army in the Quality of Augur, and had been admitted by the Lacedemonians into the Number
of their Citizens, in this manner: *Tisamenus*
consulting the Oracle of *Delphi* about Children,
and being told by the Pythian, that he should
obtain five great Victories, mistaking the Sense
of her Answer, frequented the Places of publick
Exercise, as if he were to be victorious in the
Gymnic Contentions; and having inured himself to all the five sorts, appear'd at the Olympian Solemnity, and ran for the Prize against
Hieronymus the Andrian. But the Lacedemonians conceiving that the Oracle was to be understood of Victories in War, and no other,
endeavour'd, by Offers of Money, to persuade
Tisamenus to assist their Kings, and the Heraclides, in the Direction of military Affairs.
When he saw the Spartans so extremely desirous
of his Friendship, he set a great Value upon
himself, acquainting them, that unless they
would make him a Citizen of *Sparta,* with all
the Privileges they themselves enjoy'd, he
would never give his consent on any other
Terms: Which Answer being brought to the
Lacedemonians, was at first receiv'd with Scorn,
and the Oracle slighted; yet afterwards, falling
under great Apprehensions of the Persian Army, they complied, and offer'd him all the
Rights

Rights of a Citizen. But *Tisamenus* being inform'd that the Lacedemonians had chang'd their minds, said, he would not now be contented with what he demanded, unless they would also make his Brother *Hegias* a Spartan, with the same Privileges; intimating, as one may guess, the Example of *Melampus*, who asked a Kingdom, as well as the Privilege of a Citizen. For when the Argians would have hired him to come from *Pylon*, to cure their Women of a Frenzy, with which they were infested, he demanded one half of the Kingdom for his Recompence. The Argians rejected his Proposal, and went away: But many more of their Women falling into the same Distemper, they return'd to him, and offer'd to comply with his Demands. *Melampus* seeing this Change, requir'd yet more, and said, that unless they would give a third Part of their Kingdom to his Brother *Bias*, he would not do as they desir'd; so that the Argians, reduced to these Streights, granted him whatever he demanded. In like manner, the Lacedemonians, out of a vehement Desire to gain *Tisamenus*, assented to every thing he ask'd; by which means, of an Elean becoming a Spartan, and accompanying their Forces as Augur, he atchiev'd, in conjunction with them, five great Enterprizes. These were the only Men the Spartans ever admitted into their Community; and the five Actions were as follows: In the first place, this of *Platæa*; the second was against the Tegeans and Argians, in the Territories of *Tegea*; the third at *Dipæa*, against all the Arcadians, except the Mantineans; the fourth against the Messenians at the Isthmus; and the fifth and last, at *Tanagra*, against

gainſt the Athenians and Argians. This *Tiſa-menus* being then conducted to *Platæa* by the Spartans, and officiating as Prophet to the Grecian Army, acquainted them, that their Sacrifices promiſed Succeſs, if they would ſtand upon the defenſive ; and the contrary, if they ſhould paſs the River *Aſopus*, and begin the Battel. On the ſide of *Mardonius* likewiſe, who was very deſirous to attack the Grecians, the Sacrifices were not at all favourable to that purpoſe, but very promiſing, if he would ſtand to receive the Enemy: For he alſo ſacrificed after the manner of the Grecians, and had for his Augur, *Hegeſiſtratus* of *Elis*, the moſt famous of the Telliades. This Man had been formerly taken by the Spartans, and condemned to die, for the many Indignities they had ſuffered from him: When finding his Condition deſperate, his Life in the utmoſt hazard, and being in expectation of various Tortures before Death, he perform'd an Action beyond belief: For after he was made faſt to a Clog plaited with Iron, having by ſome means or other got a Knife into his poſſeſſion, he contriv'd the moſt reſolute thing I ever heard: He took the exact meaſure of as much of his Foot as he could draw out, and then cut off all the reſt. When he had done this, he dug a Hole through the Wall, and eſcaping the Vigilance of his Guards, made towards *Tegea*, travelling by night, and hiding himſelf by day in the Woods: So that he arriv'd in *Tegea* the third Night, notwithſtanding the moſt diligent Search of the Lacedemonians ; who, when they ſaw half his Foot lying on the ground, and yet could not find his Perſon, admired the Reſolution of the Man.

Man. Thus *Hegesistratus* having made his escape, betook himself to the *Tegeans*, who were at that time in discord with the Lacedemonians; and after he was cured of his Wound, put on a wooden Foot, and declared himself their mortal Enemy. Nevertheless, in the end, his Enmity to the Lacedemonians was fatal to him; for they took him at *Zacynthus*, exercising his Profession of Augur, and put him to death: But this happen'd not till after the Battel of *Platæa*. *Hegesistratus* therefore being hired with a considerable Sum, accompanied *Mardonius* to the River *Asopus*, and there sacrificed with great Zeal; partly out of hatred to the Lacedemonians, and partly for his own Profit. But as these Sacrifices were not such as might encourage the Persian to attack, no more than those perform'd on the part of the Grecians in his Camp, who had also an Augur named *Hippomachus*, of *Leucadia*; *Timogenides*, the Son of *Herpys*, a Theban, perceiving the Grecian Army incessantly increasing by the Arrival of other Forces, counsel'd *Mardonius* to guard the Passage of Mount *Cytheron*, assuring him, that he might surprize great Numbers of them, as they came daily. The two Armies had been eight Days encamped, fronting to each other, when *Timogenides* gave this Advice; which *Mardonius* approving, sent some Horse, in the Beginning of the Night, to the Passage of Mount *Cytheron*, that leads to *Platæa*, and is called by the Bœotians, *The three Heads*; but by the Athenians, *The Heads of Oak*. This Cavalry was not sent out in vain; for entring into the Plain, they took five hundred Cattel, carrying Provisions from *Peloponnesus* to the Army, my, with the Men that attended the Convoy; and when they had taken this Booty, killed both Man and Beaft without diftinction: After which Execution, they carried off what they thought fit to preferve, and return'd to the Camp of *Mardonius*. Both Armies pafied two Days more, after this Action, without being willing on either fide to begin the Battle; for though the Barbarians advanced to the Bank of the *Afopus*, to irritate the Grecians, yet neither would venture to pafs the River. In the mean time, the Cavalry of *Mardonius* making continual Excurfions, haraffed the Grecian Camp; and the Thebans being entirely in the Intereft of the Medes, perform'd their part with Vigour, leading their Forces as near as poffible to the Grecians, that a general Battel might enfue. In thefe Actions, they were fupported by the Perfians and Medes, who gave fignal Demonftrations of their Valour. Nothing more was done during ten Days; but on the eleventh Day, after the two Armies had faced each other in the Country of *Plataea*, and the Grecian Forces were confiderably augmented, *Mardonius*, the Son of *Gobryas*, tired with thefe Delays, went to confer with *Artabazus*, the Son of *Pharnaces*, a Perfian of eminent Reputation with *Xerxes*; in which Conference they gave their Opinions to this effect: *Artabazus* advis'd, that they fhould break up with all their Forces, and, without farther delay, march to the Walls of *Thebes*; where they fhould find plenty of Provifions for themfelves, with Forage for their Horfes; and that being encamped there, they might accomplifh their Enterprize at leifure, if his Advice was follow'd: For, having a great

quantity

quantity of Gold, coin'd and uncoin'd, with much Silver and wrought Plate ; if they would not be sparing of these Treasures, but send them to the Grecians, especially to those of principal Authority in each Nation, they should undoubtedly prevail with them to betray the common Liberty, without hazarding the Event of a Battel.   The Thebans were of the same Sentiment with *Artabazus*, as thinking him a Person of greater Foresight than the other. But the Opinion of *Mardonius* was more bold, inconsiderate, and pertinacious : He said, that conceiving his Army to be better than that of the Grecians, he was for fighting immediately, not for looking on idly, till farther Supplies should join their Forces ; and that they ought not to heed the Sacrifices of *Hegesistratus*, but resolve to fight, according to the manner of the Persians.   *Mardonius* having delivered his Opinion in these Terms, was not contradicted ; and his Sentiment prevail'd, because the King had given the Command of his Army to him, and not to *Artabazus*.   Then calling together the Commanders of his Forces, and the Grecian Generals who were in his Camp, he asked if they had heard of any Oracles that threaten'd the Persians with Destruction in *Greece :* but they gave him no Answer ; because as some of the Assembly knew nothing of the Predictions, so others were afraid to speak what they knew : Which *Mardonius* perceiving, said, " Since you either know nothing, or dare " not speak, I shall tell you what I know per- " fectly well.   There is an Oracle importing, " that the Persians arriving in *Greece,* shall " plunder the Temple of *Delphi,* and be all de-

" ftroy'd after that Fact : Therefore being ap-
" pris'd of this Prediction, we will neither
" pillage that Temple, nor go to that Place ;
" and thus we fhall preferve ourfelves from
" being deftroy'd on that account.   Let every
" one then, who wifhes well to the Perfians,
" rejoice, and be affur'd that we fhall con-
" quer the Grecians." Having finifhed thefe
Words, he required them to difpofe all things
in order to a Battel, and prepare to fight
early the next Morning.   Neverthelefs, I certainly know, that the Oracle pretended by
Mardonius to have been pronounced againft the
Perfians, was really delivered to the Illyrians,
and to the Forces of the Enchelians, and no
way concern'd the Perfians. But the Prediction of *Bacis*, relating to the Battel, was in
thefe Terms :

In verdant Plains, which far extended lie
On the Afopus, *and the* Thermodon,
The Grecians fhall againft Barbarians fight,
And Medes in numerous Crouds their Fate fhall meet.

Befides this Oracle of *Bacis*, I have heard of
others of a like Tenour, denounced by *Mufæus*
againft the Perfians : As for the *Thermodon*, that
River runs between the Cities of *Tanagra* and
Glifas.

AFTER *Mardonius* had made inquiry
touching the Oracles, and encourag'd his Men,
Night came on, and the Guards were placed :
But when the Night was fo far fpent, that all
things feem'd quiet in the Camp, and the Army in profound Sleep, *Alexander*, the Son of
Amyntas, King and General of the Macedonians
mounting

mounting on horseback, advanced to the Athenian Guard, and defir'd to fpeak with their
principal Leaders. The greater part of the
Guard continu'd in their Station, while fome
haften'd to the Generals, and acquainted them,
that a certain Perfon on horfeback, arriving
from the Army of the Medes, demanded to
fpeak with them; and having repeated their
Names, difcovered no more of his Bufinefs.
When the Generals had receiv'd this Information, they went immediately to the Guard; and
were no fooner arriv'd, than *Alexander* began
thus: " I come to depofit a Secret with you,
" O Athenians, on condition you will conceal
" it from all Men, except only *Paufanias*, left
" you fhould ruin me. I would not make this
" difcovery to you, if I were not extremely
" concern'd for the Safety of *Greece*, and, be-
" ing myfelf of Grecian Original, were not
" very unwilling to fee the Liberty of *Greece* op-
" preffed. Know then, that *Mardonius* would
" have fought long before this time, if the Sa-
" crifices offer'd for him and his Army had
" been found favourable: but now, he has ta-
" ken a refolution to have no regard to the Sa-
" crifices, and to attack you at break of day;
" fearing, as I conjecture, that more Forces
" may come in to your Succour. Be therefore
" in a readinefs to receive him. But if *Mardo-*
" *nius* fhould defer the Execution of his Pur-
" pofe, and not come to a Battel, continue in
" your camp; for his Provifions are not fuffi-
" cient to laft many Days. And if this War
" terminates happily on your fide, fome of you
" ought to remember me; who, for the fake
" of the Grecians, and out of a defire to preferve

their

" their Liberty, have voluntarily undertaken so
" dangerous an Enterprize, and acquainted you
" with the Intention of *Mardonius*, to the end
" that the Barbarians may not surprize you,
" and fall upon your Forces, before you are
" prepar'd to receive them. I am *Alexander* the
" *Macedonian*." Having finished these Words,
he return'd to his Station in the Camp. And
the Athenian Captains went to the head of the
Right; where, after they had told *Pausanias*
all that they had heard from *Alexander*, he began to be afraid of the Persians, and said,
" Seeing the two Armies are about to engage
" when the Day appears, you, O Athenians,
" ought in reason to be placed opposite to the
" Persians, and we against the Boeotians and
" Grecians, who are now drawn up against
" your Forces; because you know the Medes,
" and their manner of fighting, having fought
" with them already at *Marathon*; whereas, we
" are so utterly unacquainted with those Men,
" that none of us Spartans have ever been en-
" gag'd in any Action against their Troops:
" but the Boeotians and the Thessalians we ex-
" perimentally know. For this reason we
" would have you march with your Arms into
" our Post, and we will take the Left." To
this Proposal, the Athenians answered; " From
" the time we first saw the Persians drawn up
" against you, we were inclin'd to mention the
" Expedient you now propose to us, and only
" refrain'd, out of an apprehension that our Ad-
" vice might not be well receiv'd; but seeing
" you are pleas'd to make the Offer, we are
" ready to do as you desire." Thus having
voluntarily taken this Resolution on both sides,

4

they

they chang'd their Stations; which the Bœotians obferving upon the firft Appearance of Light, gave notice to *Mardonius* of what they had done; and when he had heard their Report, he prefently made a motion to change his Poft, and to place the Perfians againft the Front of the Lacedemonians again. But *Paufanias* perceiving he was difcover'd, return'd with the Spartans to the Right of the Line; and *Mardonius* in like manner to the Left. When both fides had refum'd their former Stations, *Mardonius* fent a Herald to the Spartans with the following Meffage: "You, O Lacedemo-
"nians, are reported to be the beft Soldiers of
"all the People in thefe Parts, and formidable
"to the reft, as Men who never abandon the
"Field of Battel, nor quit your Ranks, but
"continue firm, till either you have deftroy'd
"your Enemies, or die upon the Place. Yet
"none of thefe things are true: For even be-
"fore you come to engage, and to try the
"Fortune of War, we fee you fly, and aban-
"don your Station, obliging the Athenians, at
"their peril, to make the firft Trial of our
"Valour, and placing yourfelves againft the
"Front of our Servants, which is not the part
"of brave Men. We were much deceiv'd,
"when we expected, that to fuftain your Re-
"putation, you would have fent a Herald, to
"bid us defiance, and to let us know, that re-
"lying on the Goodnefs of your Forces, you
"had determin'd to fight fingly againft the Per-
"fians. We find nothing of this fort in you,
"but rather manifeft Signs of Fear. Now
"therefore, feeing you have declin'd to chal-
"lenge us, we fhall begin with you, and ask,

Bb 3 "why

" why you, who are thought the best of the
" Grecian Forces, and we, who have the same
" Esteem among the Barbarians, may not ter-
" minate this Dispute with equal Numbers:
" If you think the rest ought also to fight, let
" them engage afterwards; but if you are of
" another opinion, and judge that unnecessary,
" let us fight alone: and let that side which
" shall obtain the Victory, be accounted victo-
" rious of the whole Army." After the Herald had thus spoken, and staid some time without receiving any Answer, he return'd to *Mardonius*, and gave him an account of his Com-
mission. Upon which, *Mardonius* being above
measure joyful, and proud of an imaginary Victory, gave order to insult the Grecians with his
Horse; who, by the Showers of Arrows and
Darts they pour'd in among them with great dexterity, put all their Camp into disorder, and
choak'd the Fountain of *Gargaphia*, which sup-
plied the Army with Water. This Spring was
in the Quarter of the Lacedemonians, and more
or less distant from the rest of the Grecians, as
their Stations were appointed. The *Asopus* was
near at hand indeed, but they were hindred by
the Enemies Cavalry from approaching that River, and constrain'd to water at the Gargaphian
Spring only. In this Condition of things, destitute of Water for the Army, and put into great
confusion by the Barbarian Horse, the Grecian
Generals went together to the right Wing, in
order to deliberate about these, and other Affairs. For though their Circumstances were bad
in these Particulars, yet they were in much
greater perplexity for want of Provisions; which
they could not receive from *Peloponnesus*, because
the

the Enemies Cavalry being Masters of the Passages, hindred the Servants they had sent thither, from returning with Convoys to the Camp.
In this Assembly the Captains resolv'd, if the
Persian should defer their Attack all that day,
to remove with the Army into an Island, ten
Stades distant from the River *Asopus*, and the
Spring of *Gargaphia*, were they were then
encamped. This Island lies opposite to the
City of *Platæa*, and is in some measure join'd
to the Continent: For the River, descending
from Mount *Cytheron*, and running into the
Plain, divides its Streams for the space of
about three Stades, and then rejoining, forms
an Island, which is call'd by the Name of *Oeroe*;
who, as the Inhabitants say, was the Daughter
of *Asopus*. Into this Place the Grecians determining to remove, that they might have a sufficient Supply of Water, and be no longer infested by the Enemies Horse, agreed to decamp
in the Night, at the time of placing the second
Watch, left, as they quitted their Camp, they
should be discovered, and disturb'd by the Persian Cavalry in their March. They also resolv'd, that when they should arrive where the
Asopian *Oeroe* is encompassed by the Waters
which descend from *Cytheron*, they would detach
one half of their Forces to that Mountain, in
order to bring in a Convoy of Provisions, which
had stopped there for fear of the Enemy. Having taken these Resolutions, they continued all
that day in their Camp, and suffer'd much by
the Horse: But in the Evening the Enemy retir'd; and when the Hour of Night was come,
in which they had agreed to decamp, the greater
part took up their Arms, and marched away

without

without any Intention of going to the Place appointed: Whilst others, upon their breaking up, being desirous to avoid the Enemies Cavalry, made towards *Platæa*; and arriving at the Temple of *Juno*, which stands before the City, twenty Stades distant from the Spring of *Gargaphia*, grounded their Arms, and encamped there. *Pausanias* having seen these Forces file off out of the Camp, and supposing they were marching to the Rendezvous, order'd the Lacedemonians to take up their Arms, and follow. All the rest of the Leaders were ready to obey, when *Amompharetus*, the Son of *Poliades*, Captain of the Pitanean Division, protested he would not fly from the Barbarians, nor willingly bring a Disgrace upon *Sparta*; and was the more astonished at what he saw, because he had not been present in the Council where this Resolution was taken. *Pausanias* and *Euryanax*, not a little disturb'd at his Refusal, and more deeply concern'd to leave the Pitanean Cohort behind them, left by executing the Measures they had concerted with the rest of the Grecians, *Amompharetus*, and all those who were under his Conduct, should be cut in pieces, suspended the Departure of the Spartans, and endeavour'd to dissuade him from his Purpose. But whilst they were exhorting *Amompharetus*, that he alone of all the Lacedemonians and Tegeans would not suffer himself to be left in the Camp, the Athenians well knowing the Genius of the Spartans, and that they are accustom'd to say one thing and mean another, continued in their Station, contenting themselves, when they saw the Army begin to move, to send a Horseman to see, if indeed the Lacedemonians

cedemonians intended to decamp, or had abfo-
lutely refolv'd to ftay; and in that cafe, to enquire of *Paufanias* what was fit to be done.
This Meffenger arriving, found the Lacedemonians drawn up in their Poft, and their principal Leaders engag'd in a warm Debate: For
though *Euryanax* and *Paufanias* had endeavour'd
to perfuade *Amompharetus*, not to bring the
Lacedemonians into the danger of continuing
fingly in the Camp, yet, having not been able
to prevail with him, they were fallen into an
open Conteftation, when the Athenian Meffenger arriv'd. In this Difpute, *Amompharetus*
taking up a Stone with both his Hands, and
laying it down at the Feet of *Paufanias*, faid,
" There is my Vote, to teftify that we ought
" not to fly from the Strangers:" meaning the
Barbarians. But *Paufanias* telling him he was
diftracted, and not in his right Senfes, turn'd
to the Meffenger, and in Anfwer to the Queftions
he was inftructed to ask, bid him report the
prefent Condition of their Affairs to the Athenians, and their earneft Defire, that they would
join in one common Refolution, and act in relation to their Departure, as the Lacedemonians
fhould do. With this Anfwer the Meffenger
return'd to the Athenians, and the Difpute
continued till the Morning; when *Paufanias*
having ftaid to that time, and fuppofing, as indeed happen'd, that *Amompharetus* would not be
left behind, gave the Signal, and marched away
by the Hills, with the reft of the Lacedemonians, and the Tegeans. On the other hand,
the Athenians marched in order of Battel, by
the Way of the Plain; becaufe the Spartans apprehending the Enemies Horfe, kept clofe to
the

the higher Ground, about the Foot of the Mountain *Cytheron.* But when *Amompharetus* saw that *Pausanias*, with the rest, had actually left the Camp, he thought they had deserted him on purpose, and taking up his Arms, led his Men slowly after the main Body: Which nevertheless, after a March of about ten Stades, halted at the River *Molois*, in the Plain of *Argiopis*, (where a Temple stands dedicated to the Elusian *Ceres*) in order to wait his coming up, or else to return to his assistance, if he and his Forces should persist in their Resolution, not to leave their Station. However, at length *Amompharetus* join'd the rest of the Army, and the Barbarian Horse went to attack the Camp, as they were accustom'd to do: But finding no Man in the Place, where the Enemy had encamped, they pursued without delay, and overtaking the Grecians, incommoded them in their March.

WHEN *Mardonius* was inform'd that the Grecians were retir'd by night, he view'd the abandon'd Camp; and having sent for *Throax* of *Larissa*, with his Brother *Eurypilus* and *Thrasydius*, he spoke to them in these Terms: " What will " you say now, O *Aleuadians*, to the things " you see? You, who being Neighbours to the " *Lacedemonians*, affirm, they were the most " warlike of all People, and that they would " never quit the Field of Battel. These Men " you saw, first shifting their Station, and now " we all know, they fled away last night, be " cause they found they were to engage against " those Forces, which are deservedly esteem'd " the most valiant in the World; demonstrating " by these Actions, that having no real Worth
" in

" in themfelves, they made only a vain Often-
" tation of their Bravery among the Grecians,
" who have no more Valour than they. I rea-
" dily forgave you, when you extoll'd the
" Spartans, becaufe you knew fomething of
" their Actions, and were altogether unac-
" quainted with the Perfians ; but I wondered
" more at *Artabazus*, who was in fo great fear
" of the Lacedemonians, that he bafely ad-
" vifed us, as a thing expedient, to break up
" with our Army, and retire to *Thebes*, in ex-
" pectation of a Siege, which the King fhall
" know from me, though of that I fhall fay
" more another time. At prefent, feeing the
" Grecians have fhewn fo little Courage, we
" ought not to fuffer them to efcape out of our
" hands ; but by a fpeedy Purfuit make them
" bear the Penalty of all the Mifchiefs they
" have done to the Perfians. Having finifh'd
thefe Words, he put himfelf at the head of the
Perfians, and paffing the *Afopus* with precipitation, purfued the Grecians, as if they had betaken themfelves to flight ; but overtook only
the Lacedemonians, and the Tegeans, not perceiving the Athenian Forces, who, turning
fhort, had paffed from the Hills into the Plain.
When the other Commanders of the Barbarian
Troops faw the Perfians advancing in purfuit
of the Grecians, they alfo took up their Stan-
dards, and haftened after them, without obferving either Rank or Order, crouding together in Multitudes, and making a hideous Noife,
as if they had been fure of tearing the Grecians
in pieces. *Paufanias,* in the mean time, finding himfelf preffed by the Enemies Cavalry, difpatched a Meffenger on horfeback to the Athenians

nians, with this Meſſage : " Men of *Athens*, in
" the great Queſtion before us, whether *Greece*
" ſhall be enſlaved, or continue free, our Al-
" lies have betrayed both you and the Lacede-
" monians, and fled away during the laſt night.
" What remains now to be done, is to defend
" ourſelves in the beſt manner we can, and to
" ſuccour each other. Had the Enemies Horſe
" attacked you firſt, we and the Tegeans who
" are with us, and have not betray'd the com-
" mon Cauſe, ought to have aſſiſted you : But
" ſeeing all their Cavalry is fallen upon us, you
" are obliged in juſtice to come to the Succour
" of that part which is moſt hardly preſſed. If
" any inſuperable Impediment ſhould hinder
" you from coming to our Relief, we promiſe
" ourſelves, from the great Zeal you have
" ſhewn for carrying on the preſent War, that
" you will not refuſe to ſend us ſome of your
" Men armed with pointed Weapons." The
Athenians no ſooner heard theſe Words, than
they prepared to ſuccour the Lacedemonians to
the utmoſt of their power ; but as they were
actually marching with that Deſign, they were
attacked, and to their great regret prevented,
by thoſe Grecians who ſided with the Perſian,
and had been drawn up oppoſite to the Athenians. The Lacedemonians and the Tegeans
being thus deprived of Aſſiſtance, and neceſſitated to engage alone againſt *Mardonius* and the
Forces with him, began to offer their uſual Sacrifices : The former, including the light-
armed Men, amounted to the number of fifty
thouſand ; and the Tegeans, who had never
parted from the Lacedemonians, to three thouſand. During theſe Sacrifices, which were not

at

at all favourable, they had many Men killed, and more wounded, by the great number of pointed Arms which the Perſians let fly among them, whilſt they themſelves ſtood covered with their Bucklers. When *Pauſanias* ſaw the Spartans ſo terribly galled, and their Sacrifices diſturbed, turning his Eyes towards the Temple of *Juno* in *Platæa*, he prayed the Goddeſs, that his Hopes might not be fruſtrated; and before he had finiſhed theſe words, the Tegeans began to advance againſt the Barbarians. Immediately after the Prayer of *Pauſanias*, the Lacedemonians ſacrificed happily, and in a little time marched out likewiſe againſt the Perſians; who laying aſide their Bows and Darts, ſtood firm, and maintained a long and obſtinate Fight near the Temple of *Ceres*, till both ſides came to cloſe: For the Barbarians venturing to lay hold of the Enemies Lances, broke them in pieces. And indeed in Courage and Strength the Perſians were not inferior to the Grecians; but they were ill-armed, ignorant of military diſcipline, and no way comparable to their Adverſaries in prudent Management: So that whether one, or ten, or more, or leſs, fell in among the Lacedemonians, they were certainly deſtroyed, becauſe they obſerved no manner of Order. Nevertheleſs, in that part where *Mardonius*, mounted on a white Horſe, fought at the head of a thouſand Men, the beſt among the Perſians, there the Grecians were attacked with moſt Vigour: For as long as he continued alive, the Perſians made a ſtrenuous Defence, and killed many of the Spartans; but when *Mardonius* fell, and the choſen Troops about him were defeated, the reſt turned their
backs,

backs, and fled before the Lacedemonians, being much embarraffed with their Garments, and
fighting naked againft armed Men. Here
the Death of *Leonidas* was revenged by the
Spartans upon *Mardonius*, according to the O-
racle ; and here the moft glorious Victory, we
ever heard of, was obtained by *Paufanias*, the
Son of *Cleombrotus*, and Grandfon to *Anaxandrides*, whofe Anceftors I mentioned before in the
Genealogy of *Leonidas*, for they were the fame.
Mardonius died by the hand of *Aimneftus*, a confiderable Spartan, who, fome time after this Perfian War, was killed at *Stenyclerus*, with three
hundred Lacedemonians, fighting againft all
the Forces of the Meffenians. The Perfians
thus put to the Rout by the Spartans in the
Territories of *Platæa*, fled in confufion to their
Camp, which they had fortified with a Wall of
Wood in the Plains of *Thebes*. But I am furpriz'd, that feeing the Battle was fought near
the Grove of *Ceres*, not one of the Barbarians
was feen to enter into the Temple, nor to die
in any part of the facred Ground, tho' great
numbers fell in other Places ; and if a Man
may be permitted to form a Conjecture concerning divine things, I imagined the Goddefs
would not receive them, after they had burnt
her Royal Temple at *Eleufis*. Such was the E-
vent of this Battel.

IN the mean time *Artabazus*, the Son of
Pharnaces, who from the beginning had difap-
proved the King's affenting to leave *Mardonius*
in *Greece*, and who, by all the Reafons he could
alledge, was not able to prevail with him to
forbear fighting, thought fit to act in this manner : Being difpleafed at the Conduct of *Mardonius*,

nius, and rightly judging what the Issue would be, he gave Orders, during the Battel, for all the Forces he commanded, consisting of forty thousand Men, to follow him wheresoever he should lead them, with the same diligence they should see him make: And after he had given these Instructions, advancing with his Men, as if he designed to charge the Enemy, he discovered the Persians flying. Upon which, continuing no longer to lead his Forces in an orderly manner, he presently betook himself to flight not towards the Walls of Wood, nor the City of Thebes, but into the Territories of the Phoceans, with intention to reach the *Hellespont* as soon as he could.

IN this Battel, while the rest of the Grecians in the King's Army behaved themselves ill on purpose, the Bœotians maintained an obstinate Fight against the Athenians. In particular the Thebans, who favoured the Medes, and would not remit of their utmost Efforts, fought with such Ardour, that three hundred of the principal and most valiant were killed by the Athenians upon the Place: And the rest, after they were broken and put to flight, would not follow the Persians, nor the vast multitude of their Associates, who either fought not at all, or performed nothing considerable, but retired to *Thebes.* The Barbarians appear to me to have been totally influenced by the Conduct of the Persians on this occasion: For when they saw the Persians flying, they abandoned the Field, even without striking a Blow, and by their example at length betook themselves all to flight, except some of the Horse, consisting of Bœotians and others. Yet these, in their

3   Retreat,

Retreat, being nearest to the Enemy, were of some advantage to those that fled, by defending their Friends from the Grecians; who vigorously pursuing their Victory, pressed hard upon the broken Forces of *Xerxes*, and made a great Slaughter among them. During this Pursuit, a Message was brought to those Grecians who had absented themselves from the Battel, and retired to the Temple of *Juno*, that the Armies had engaged, and that the Grecians with *Pausanias* were victorious. Upon which News they hastened back, without observing any kind of Order; the Corinthians by the way of the Hills, that leads directly to the Temple of *Ceres*; and the Megareans, with the Phliasians, by the Plain: But the Theban Cavalry, commanded by *Asopodorus*, the Son of *Timander*, seeing the Megareans and Phliasians approaching in so disorderly a manner, pushed on their Horses immediately, and falling upon them, killed six hundred on the spot, and drove the rest to the Mountain *Cytheron*. Thus these Men fell without Honour.

THE Persians and the rest of the Multitude arriving within their Intrenchments; mounted the Towers before the coming of the Lacedemonians, and improved their Works in the best manner they could: So that when the Lacedemonians arrived, they found a vigorous Resistance from the Walls; and indeed so long as the Athenians were absent, the Barbarians not only defended themselves, but were too hard for the Lacedemonians, who knew not how to attack a Fortification: But upon the Arrival of the Athenians, the Action grew hotter on both sides, and continued for a long time;

time; till, in the end, by their Valour and Conftancy, the Athenians mounted the Walls, and opened a Paffage to the reft of the Grecians. The firft that entered by the Breach were the Tegeans, who plundered the Tent of *Mardonius*, and, among other things, took away a Manger for Horfes, all of folid Brafs, and admirably wrought; which they afterwards placed in the Temple of the Alean *Minerva*: But the reft of their Booty they brought to the common Heap, and depofited with that taken by the other Grecians. The Barbarians, after the forcing of their Intrenchment, rallied no more, nor thought of defending themfelves; but terrified to fee their Troops, confifting of fo many Myriads, intercepted within a fmall Compafs of Ground, fell into the utmoft Confternation. By which means they were fo eafily cut in pieces by the Grecians, that of three hundred thoufand Men, not full three thoufand efcaped the Sword, befides thofe forty thoufand who fled away with *Artabazus*. Of the Lacedemonian Spartans, ninety one were killed in the Battel; of the Tegeans fixteen, and of the Athenians fifty two. Thofe among the Barbarians who fought beft, were, of the Foot, the Perfians; of the Horfe, the Saces; and of the Generals, *Mardonius*. Of the Grecians, the Tegeans and Athenians acquired great Glory, but the Lacedemonians greater: For though the former beat all the Forces they engaged, yet the Lacedemonians broke and defeated the firmeft part of the Enemy's Army. But among all the Lacedemonians, no Man, in my Opinion, gave fo great Proofs of Valour as *Ariftodemus*, who was before difgraced and difesteemed,

esteemed, becaufe he alone, of the three hundred, had faved himfelf from the Slaughter of
Thermopyle. After him *Pofidonius, Philocyon,* and
Amompharetus diftinguifhed themfelves among
the Spartans ; yet when the Queftion came to be
debated, who had behaved himfelf beft, thofe
Spartans, that were prefent, gave judgment,
that *Ariftodemus,* refolving to die in the fight of
his Countrymen, to wipe off the Blemifh of his
former Conduct, and to that end breaking his
Rank, and advancing beyond his Companions,
had performed Actions of great Glory ; but
that *Pofidonius* having no occafion to defire
Death, deferved greater Honour for the Valour
he fhewed on this occafion. Perhaps they gave
that Judgment from a Motive of Envy. However, they paid great Honours to all thofe that
died in the Battel, excepting only *Ariftodemus,*
who was deprived of that Glory, becaufe he
had predetermined to lofe his Life for the fore-
going Reafon. Thefe were the Men who acquired the greateft Fame in the Battel of *Platæa.*
For *Callicratides,* the moft valiant, not only of
the Lacedemonians, but of all others in the
Grecian Army, died not in the Action ; but
ftanding in his Rank, after *Paufanias* had facrificed, he received a Wound in the Side by an
Arrow ; and, as they carried him off, regret-
ting his Fate, he turn'd to *Aimneftus* a Platæan,
and told him, that he was not at all difcontented to die for *Greece* ; but to die before he
had fought, or done any thing worthy of himfelf, and of his Zeal to the common Caufe. Of
the Athenians, *Sophanes,* the Son of *Eutychides,*
a Decelian, is reported to have diftinguifhed
himfelf by his Valour. The Inhabitants of

Decelia, as the Athenians say, were the Authors of a thing, which has been ever since of advantage to them: For, in antient time, when the Tyndarides, seeking to recover *Helena,* entered the Territories of *Attica* with a numerous Army, and dispossessed the People of their Habitations, not knowing to what Place she was carried; the Decelians, and, as some say, *Decelus* himself, disturbed at the Injury done to *Theseus,* and fearing that all the Country of the Athenians might be ravaged, discovered the whole Intrigue, and conducted the Tyndarides to *Aphidna;* which *Titacus,* a Native of the Place, delivered into their hands. From the time of that Action, even to this day, the Decelians have been always treated with such Distinction and Preference by the Spartans, that in the War, which happened many years after, between the Athenians and Peloponnesians, the Lacedemonians pillaged the rest of *Attica,* and left *Decelia* untouched. Of that place was *Sophanes,* who distinguished himself above all the Athenians on this occasion; but two different Accounts are given of him: Some say, he carried an Anchor of Iron fastened to the Girdle of his Breast-plate with a Chain of Brass, which he fixed before him when he approached the Enemy, to hinder them from forcing him out of his Rank; and when they were repulsed, taking up his Anchor again, he pursued with the rest. But others, varying from this Account, say, that he had no Anchor of Iron fastened to his Cuirass, but one engraved on his Shield, which was made to turn round incessantly. *Sophanes* did another signal Action, when the Athenians besieged *Ægina:* For in a single

Combat

Combat he killed *Eurybates* of *Argos*, who had been victorious in all the five Olympian Contentions. But some time after the Persian War, commanding the Athenian Forces jointly with *Leagrus* the Son of *Glaucon*, he was killed by the Edonians at *Daton*, fighting for the Mines of Gold, with the same Valour he had shewn on all other Occasions.

WHEN the Barbarians were thus defeated at *Platæa*, a Woman, who had been a Concubine to *Pharandates*, the Son of *Theaspes*, a Persian, hearing of the Disaster of the Persians, and of the Victory obtained by the Grecians, came voluntarily to the Army, magnificently dressed, both she and her Attendants, in Gold and the richest of their Attire ; and alighting from her Chariot, went towards the Lacedemonians, who were still employed in the Slaughter of the Enemy ; when observing that *Pausanias* had the Direction of all things, and having often heard his Name and his Country, she addressed herself to him, and embracing his Knees, said, " King of *Sparta*, deliver me, I beseech you, " from a slavish Captivity. You have already " done me one Favour, in destroying those who " had no regard either to the Demons or to the " Gods. I am of a Coan Family, Daughter " to *Hegetorides*, the Son of *Antagoras*. The " Persian took me away by force at *Coos*, and " kept me to this time." " Woman, *answered* " *Pausanias*, thou hast nothing to fear, partly " because thou art come as a Suppliant to seek " Protection, and much more if thou hast spo- " ken the Truth, and art indeed the Daugh- " ter of *Hegetorides* the Coan, who is the best " Friend I have in that Country." Having

3   thus

thus spoken, he committed her to the care of
the Ephori, who were present, and afterwards
sent her to *Ægina*, where she desired to go.
Presently after her Departure the Mantineans
arrived with their Forces, when all was over ;
and finding they were come too late to fight,
were much disturbed, and said, They were yet
worthy in having some part in punishing the
Barbarians. Upon which being informed of
the flight of *Artabazus* and the Medes, they
pursued them into *Thessaly*, against the Opinion of the Lacedemonians ; but at their Return home, their Leaders were all banished.
After them came the Eleans, and shewing the
same Regret, marched back again ; but arriving in their own Country, they punished
their Captains also with Banishment. Such
was the Conduct of the Mantineans, and of
the Eleans.

LAMPON, the Son of *Pytheus*, one of the
principal Men of *Ægina*, being then at *Platæa*
in the Camp of the *Æginetes*, came in haste to
Pausanias ; and solliciting him to a most detestable Action, said, " Son of *Cleombrotus*, the
" Enterprize you have atchieved, is, beyond
" example, great and illustrious ; God has ena-
" bled you to acquire more Glory, in pre-
" serving *Greece* from Servitude, than any o-
" ther Grecian, we ever heard of, obtained.
" Yet something remains to be done, in order
" to render your Name more famous, and to
" deter all the Barbarians for the future from
" daring to irritate the Grecians by unjust
" Attempts. You know that after *Leonidas*
" was killed at *Thermopyle*, *Mardonius* and *Xerxes*
" took off his Head, and fixed it on a Pole.

" if

" If you will punish that Insolence by a just
" Retaliation, you will be praised, not only
" by all the Spartans, but by the rest of the
" Grecians: In a word, if you order *Mardo-*
" *nius* to be empaled, you revenge the Indig-
" nity done to your Uncle *Leonidas.*" This he
said with a design to please: But *Pausanias* answered, " Friend of *Ægina,* I thankfully ac-
" cept your good Meaning and provident
" Care, but you are far from making a right
" Judgment; for after having highly magnified
" me, my Country, and my Atchievement, you
" throw all down again, by solliciting me to
" insult the Dead, and telling me I shall in-
" crease my Fame, if I do that, which is more
" fit to be done by Barbarians than by Gre-
" cians, and which we blame even in them.
" I cannot therefore assent to the Æginetes,
" nor to any other Men who delight in such
" Actions, contented to please the Spartans,
" and never to do nor to speak an unbecom-
" ing thing. As for *Leonidas,* whose Death
" you exhort me to revenge, I affirm, that, by
" sacrificing the Lives of such an innumerable
" Multitude, we have made a magnificent Re-
" paration to him, and to all those who fell at
" *Thermopyle.* Come no more then to me with
" such Discourses, nor venture to give me such
" Counsel; and take for a Favour, that you
" now escape unpunished." *Lampon* having received this answer, retired; and *Pausanias,* after he had caused Proclamation to be made,
that no Man should meddle with the Booty,
commanded the Helots to bring together all
the Riches they could find. Accordingly dis-
persing themselves through the Camp, they
found

found great quantities of Gold and Silver in the Tents ; Couches plated with Gold and Silver ; Bowls, Phials, and other drinking Vessels of Gold, besides boiling Pots of Gold and Silver, which they found lying in Sacks upon the Waggons. They took the Chains, Bracelets, and Scimetars of Gold from the Dead, but left the rich Apparel of various Colours, as things of no value. The Helots purloined much of the Booty, which they sold to the Æginetes, producing only so much as they could not hide ; and this was the first Foundation of the great Wealth of the Æginetes, who purchased Gold from the Helots at the Price of Brass. With the tenth part of this collected Treasure, the Grecians dedicated to the God at *Delphi*, a Tripos of Gold, supported by a three-headed Serpent of Brass, and placed close to the Altar to the God at *Olympia*, a *Jupiter* of Brass ten Cubits high ; and a *Neptune* of Brass seven Cubits to the God at the Isthmus. When they had taken out this Part, they divided the rest of the Booty, consisting of Gold, Silver, and other Treasure, together with the Concubines of the Persians, and all the Cattel, according to the Merit of each Person. How much was given to those who were reputed to have fought with the greatest Valour in the Battel of *Plataea*, is reported by none ; yet I am of opinion they were considered in a particular manner. But to *Pausanias* they gave the Tenth of all ; Women, Horses, Camels, Talents, and every thing else.

AMONG other things reported to have passed in this Expedition, they say, that when *Xerxes* fled out of *Greece*, he left all his Equipage

to

to *Mardonius*; and that *Paufanias* feeing fuch magnificent Furniture of Gold, Silver, and Tapeftry of various Colours, commanded the Cooks and Bakers to prepare a Supper for him, as they ufed to do for *Mardonius:* That when they had fo done, in obedience to his Command, and *Paufanias* had viewed the Couches of Gold and Silver, covered with the richeft Cufhions, the Tables of the fame Metals, and the expenfive Supper prepared; furprized at the Profufion he faw before him, he ordered his Attendants, with a Smile, to make ready a Lacedemonian Meal: And that after he had obferved the vaft difference between the two Suppers, fending for the Grecian Generals, and fhewing them both the one and the other, he faid; " I have called you together, O Gre- " cians, with a defign to let you fee the Folly " of the King of the Medes; who leading fuch " a Life at home, came hither to pillage us, " who fare fo hardly." Some time after this Defeat, many of the Platæans found Treafures of Gold and Silver, with other Riches buried under ground; and among the dead Bodies, when the Flefh was confumed from the Bones, which lay together at a certain Place, they difcovered a Skull, of one folid Piece, without any Sutures. They found alfo an upper Jaw, with all the Teeth diftinct, but fhooting from one fingle Bone; and the Skeleton of a Man five Cubits high.

THE next day after the Battel, *Mardonius* was not found among the dead, though by what Perfon his Body was taken away, I never could learn with Certainty. But I have heard that many Men, of different Nations, were concerned in

giving

giving him burial, and I know that divers had Presents from *Artontes,* the Son of *Mardonius,* on that account: Yet who, among them all, was the Man that carried off, and took care of the Body, I could never discover; whatever Report has been spread abroad, concerning *Dionysiophanes* the Ephesian, as if he had buried *Mardonius.* And thus that Question remains undetermin'd. But the Grecians, after they had parted the Booty in the Fields of *Plataea,* buried their Dead separately: The Lacedemonians made three Graves; in one of which they interred *Posidonius, Amompharetus, Phylocion* and *Callicrates,* who were of the Priesthood: In another they put the rest of the Spartans; and in the third the Helots. The Tegeans buried all their Dead together in one Grave; the Athenians did the same; and so did the Megareans and Phliasians to those of their Forces, who were killed by the Enemies Cavalry. All these Sepulchres were filled with the Bodies of Men; but the rest, which are seen about *Plataea,* were erected, as I am inform'd, by those, who being asham'd of their Absence from the Battel, threw up those Mounds by common Consent, to deceive Posterity. Among these, there is one, bearing the Name of the *Aeginetes;* which, I have heard, was erected at their Request, ten Years after this War, by *Cleades,* the Son of *Autodicus,* a Plataean, oblig'd to them by the Tyes of Hospitality.

WHEN the Grecians had buried their Dead in the Territories of *Plataea,* they took a resolution in Council, to lead their Army to *Thebes,* and to demand the Partizans of the Medes, especially *Timegenides* and *Attaginus,* the Ring-

leaders

leaders of the Faction; and not to depart, till they had deftroy'd the City, if the Thebans fhould refufe to furrender them. Having all confented to thefe Meafures, they broke up; and on the eleventh Day after the Battel, arriving at *Thebes*, demanded the Men: But receiving a denial from the Thebans, they ravag'd the Country, and made approaches to the Walls. On the twentieth Day after thefe Hoftilities began, which the Grecians inceffantly continu'd, *Timegenides* fpoke thus to the Thebans: "Men of Thebes, feeing the Grecians "are refolv'd not to withdraw their Army till "either they fhall have taken the City, or you "deliver us into their hands, we are far from "defiring that *Bæotia* fhould any longer fuffer "for our fake: If, under the pretext of de-"manding our Perfons, they defign to exact a "Sum of Money, let us give it by a general "Contribution; for we were not the only Par-"tizans of the Medes, but join'd with them "by general Confent: Neverthelefs, if they "really befiege *Thebes* becaufe they would have "us deliver'd up, we are ready to juftify our "Conduct in their prefence." The Thebans approving his Propofition, as juft and feafonable, fent to acquaint *Paufanias*, that they were willing to furrender the Perfons he demanded. After this Agreement was made, *Attaginus* made his efcape from *Thebes*; but, in place of him, his Sons were fent out to *Paufanias*; who difcharged them, faying, they were too young to have any part in the Guilt of joining with the Medes. Of thofe who were deliver'd up by the Thebans, fome thought to clear themfelves by pleading their Innocence, or

elfe

else to come off by Money; but *Pausanias* suspecting their Intention, dismiss'd the Confederate Army, and conducting the Prisoners to *Corinth*, put them all to death. Such was the Event of things in the Territories of *Platæa* and of *Thebes*.

IN the mean time, *Artabazus* the Son of *Pharnaces* continuing his Flight from *Platæa*, arriv'd in the Country of the Thessalians; who receiving him in a friendly manner, and being altogether ignorant of what had past, asked him News of the rest of the Army. But *Artabazus* considering, that if he should discover the whole Truth, both he and his Forces would be in danger of Destruction, (because he thought every one would fall upon him, when they should be inform'd of the Success of things) had conceal'd all from the Phoceans; and to the Thessalians spoke thus: "Men of *Thessaly*, "you see I am hastening to *Thrace* with the ut- "most Expedition, being sent with these For- "ces from the Camp upon a certain Affair. "*Mardonius* with his Army follows me close, "and may be suddenly expected. Receive him "as a Friend, and do him all the good Offices "you can, for you will never have cause to "repent of the Proofs you shall give him of your "Amity." Having said this, he broke up with his Army, and marched through *Thessaly* and *Macedonia*, directly towards *Thrace*, with great Precipitation, and by the shortest Ways of the midland Country, as indeed his Affairs had called him to those Parts. But arriving at *Byzantium*, after he had left many of his Men by the way, who were part killed by the Thracians, and part consumed by Hunger and Fatigue,

tigue, he went on board the Ships, and return'd into *Asia.*

THE same Day on which the Persians were defeated at *Platæa,* they receiv'd another Blow at *Mycale* in *Ionia,* by this means. Whilst the Grecians, under the Conduct of *Leutychides* the Lacedemonian, continued with their Ships at *Delos, Lampon,* the Son of *Thrasycleus, Athenagoras,* the Son of *Archestratides,* and *Hegesistratus,* the Son of *Aristagoras,* arriv'd there from *Samos;* being sent thither privately with a Message by the Samians, who had taken care to conceal their Intentions, both from the Persians, and from the Tyrant *Theomestor,* the Son of *Androdamas,* impos'd upon them by the Barbarians. These Ambassadors, upon their Arrival, went to the Generals; and *Hegesistratus,* among many other things said, that the Ionians would not fail to revolt from the Persians so soon as they should see the Grecian Fleet, and that the Barbarians would never stand an Engagement; or if they should, the Booty would be greater than could be found in any other Place. He adjur'd them by the Gods they worship'd in common, that they would deliver the Grecians from Servitude, and repel the Barbarians; which he affirm'd was easy to be done, because their Ships were sluggish, and no way comparable in fight to those of *Greece.* He added, that if they suspected any Fraud to lie conceal'd under this Invitation, they were ready to go on board with them, and to remain in the Ships, as Hostages of their Sincerity. But as he continued his Sollicitations with much Earnestness, *Leutychides* resolving to ask his Name, either as a thing he accounted ominous, or perhaps by a

divine

divine Impulse, put the Question to him accordingly; and no sooner heard that he was called * *Hegesistratus*, than interrupting the rest of his Discourse, if indeed he intended any; "Sa-
"mian Friend, *said he*, I accept the Presage of
"thy Name; and therefore, in order to sail,
"let us have thy solemn Promise, and the Faith
"of those with thee, that the Samians shall
"readily assist us." When he had said this, he proceeded to finish the Work; and the Samians having on their part given their Promise and Oath, with great Readiness, to be the Confederates of the Grecians, set sail to return home; except only *Hegesistratus*, whose Name *Leutychides* taking for a Presage of Good-Fortune, order'd him to accompany them in the Expedition. The Grecians continued in their Station that day, and on the next sacrificed auspiciously, by the hands of the Augur *Deiphonus*, a Native of *Apollonia*, in the Gulph of *Ionia*, and Son to *Euenus*, of whom the following account is given. In the Territories of *Apollonia*, a Flock of Sheep, sacred to the Sun, feed by day on the Banks of a River, which descending from the Mountain *Lacmon*, runs thro' that Country into the Sea, at the Port of *Oricus*; but by night, they are folded in a Cave, far distant from the City, and guarded by Men chosen annually to that end, out of the most eminent among the Citizens for Birth and Riches; because the People of *Apollonia* set a high Value upon these Sheep, pursuant to the Admonition of an Oracle. *Euenus* being chosen Keeper of this Flock, neglecting his Charge, fell asleep, and in the mean time, Wolves en-

---

* *The Word signifies* Leader of an Army.

tring

tring the Cave, deftroy'd about fixty of the Sheep. When he awak'd and faw what was done, he faid nothing to any Man, thinking to purchafe the like number, and to put them among the reft. But the Apollonians being foon inform'd of the thing, caufed him to appear without delay before the Court of juftice, and fentenced him to lofe his Eyes, for fleeping when he ought to have watched. Neverthelefs, after they had thus punifh'd *Euenus* with Blindnefs, the Sheep brought no more Lambs, nor the Earth her ufual Increafe, as the Oracles of *Dodona* and *Delphi* had predicted: And when they applied themfelves to the Prophets, to know the Caufe of the prefent Calamities, they told them, that they had unjuftly put out the Eyes of *Euenus*, the Keeper of the facred Sheep: That they themfelves had fent in the Wolves, and would not difcontinue their Vengeance, till the Apollonians fhould make him full Satisfaction, and fuch Amends for the Injury he had receiv'd, as he himfelf fhould chufe, and judge fufficient; after which, they would make fo valuable a prefent to *Euenus*, that the greater part of Men fhould think him happy. Thefe Predictions the Apollonians kept fecret, and appointed fome of their Citizens to act in conformity to their Intentions; which they did in this manner: Having found *Euenus* fitting on a Chair, they fat down by him; and, after other Difcourfe, expreffed their Sorrow for his Affliction, taking occafion from thence, to ask him what Reparation he would chufe, if the Apollonians were difpofed to give him Satisfaction. *Euenus*, who had not heard of the Oracle, faid, if they would give him the Lands of Inheritance, belonging to two Citizens he named, and which

4

he

he knew to be the beſt of that Country, and would moreover add to that Gift the moſt magnificent Houſe of the City, he would be reconciled to them, and contented with that Satisfaction. Thoſe who ſat by him immediately taking hold of his Anſwer, *Euenus*, ſaid they, the Apollonians offer you the Reparation you demand for the loſs of your Eyes, in obedience to an Oracle they have received. Which when *Euenus* heard, he was not a little mortified, to find himſelf deceived by this Artifice. However, the Apollonians having firſt ſatisfied the Poſſeſſors, made him a Preſent of the Lands he demanded, and in a ſhort time he obtained the Spirit of Divination, and acquired a conſiderable Name. *Deiphonus* was the Son of this *Euenus*, and officiated as Augur in the Army, being conducted thither by the Corinthians: yet I have formerly heard that he was not really the Son of *Euenus*, but had been under ſome Diſgrace in *Greece* for aſſuming that Quality.

THE Grecians having ſacrificed favourably, departed from *Delos* with their Fleet, ſtanding towards *Samos* ; and arriving before *Calamiſus*, belonging to the Samians, came to an Anchor near the Temple of *Juno*, and made all things ready for an Engagement. But the Perſians being informed of their Approach, and having determined not to hazard a Sea-fight, becauſe they thought themſelves inferiour in force to the Grecians, permitted the Phœnicians to return home, and with all the reſt of their Ships made towards the Shore of the Continent. This they did, that they might betake themſelves to the Protection of their Land-Forces, which were encamped at *Mycale*, to the number
ber

ber of sixty thousand Men, having been left for
a Guard to *Ionia*, by the order of *Xerxes*, under the Conduct of *Tigranes*, a Man surpassing all the Persians in good Mien and Stature. To that Army the Sea-Commanders
resolved to fly for Protection, to draw their
Ships to the Shore, and to throw up an Intrenchment quite round, which might serve for
a Defence to the Fleet and for a place of Refuge to themselves. Having taken this Resolution, they brought off their Ships, and an-
chored near the Temple of the Potnians in
Mycale, at *Geson*, and at *Scolopis*, where a Temple stands dedicated to *Ceres* of *Eleusis*, built by
Philistus, the Son of *Pasicles*, who accompanied
Neleus, the Son of *Codrus*, when he founded *Miletus*. There, having drawn the Ships ashore,
they encompassed them with a Circumvallation
of Timber and Stone, strengthened quite round
with Palisadoes made of Fruit-Trees, which
they cut down in the place, preparing themselves deliberately both to sustain a Siege, and
to come off victorious. When the Grecians understood that the Barbarians were retired to the
Continent, vexed that the Enemy had thus escaped, they began to doubt what course to take,
and whether they should return home, or proceed to the *Hellespont*: But at length laying aside
the Thoughts of both these, they determined to
make to the Continent ; and having prepared
Ladders for boarding, and all other things necessary for fighting at Sea, they sailed to *Mycale*.
When they arrived near the Camp, they saw no
Enemy in a readiness to meet them ; but all
their Ships drawn within the Circumvallation,
and a numerous Army disposed along the Coast.
Upon

Upon which, *Leutychides* advancing before the rest, and standing in to the Shore as near as he could, ordered a Herald to speak thus to the Ionians in his Name: " Men of *Ionia*, all those " among you, who hear me, hearken with " Attention to my words; for the Persians will " understand nothing of the Advice I give " you. When the Battel begins, every one of " you ought, in the first place, to remember " *Liberty*; and next, that the word agreed up- " on, is *Hebe:* If any of you hear me not, let " those who hear inform him." In doing this his meaning was the same as that of *Themistocles* at *Artemisium*; for he expected that if these words were concealed from the Barbarians; the Ionians would be persuaded to revolt, or be brought under suspicion, if they should be reported to them. When *Leutychides* had given the Ionians this Admonition, the Grecians, in the next place, putting to shore, landed their Men, and drew up in Order of Battel: Which when the Persians saw, and were informed of the Exhortation they had made to the Ionians, they disarmed the Samians, fearing they were more particularly disposed to favour the Enemy; because they had already redeemed all the Athenians taken in *Attica* by the Forces of *Xerxes*, brought them to *Samos* in the Barbarian Ships, and sent them back to *Athens*, furnished with provisions for their Voyage; by which means they had set at Liberty five hundred Men of the Enemies of *Xerxes*. Having done this, they committed the care of guarding the Passes, that lead to the Eminencies of *Mycale*, to the Milesians, as knowing they were well acquainted with the Country, and intending, under that

colour to remove them from the Army. When
they had taken thefe Precautions, to make fure
of thofe among the Ionians, who feemed moſt
like to endeavour a Change, if they could come
at the power, they joined their Bucklers together, in order to their Defence. On the other
part the Grecians, after they had prepared all
things for a Battel, advanced towards the Barbarians; when, at the fame time, a Herald's
Staff was feen lying upon the Shore, and a
fudden Rumour fpread through the Army, that
the Grecians had defeated the Forces of *Mardonius* in the Territories of *Bœotia*. In this the
Direction of a Divine Power was manifeſt in
many refpects; for though the Blow already
given at *Platæa*, and that now ready to be given at *Mycale*, happened both on the fame day,
the News thus reaching the Grecians, infpired
their Army with a greater Refolution, and a
more vigorous Boldnefs, to meet the prefent
Danger. Befides, in each of thefe Places, which
is farther remarkable, there ſtood a Temple, dedicated to *Ceres* of *Eleufis*, by the Field of Battel: For at *Platæa*, as I have already faid, they
fought near the Temple of *Ceres*, and were
now about to fight again in *Mycale* near another belonging to the fame Goddefs: So that
the Rumour of the Victory obtained by the
Grecians, under the Conduct of *Paufanias* came
rightly to *Mycale*, becaufe the Battel of *Platæa*
was fought in the Morning, and this of *Mycale* in the Evening: But that both were fought
on the fame Day of the fame Month, they plainly underſtood in a little time by mutual Information. Before they heard the Fame of the
Victory of *Platæa*, they had been in great pain,
not

not so much for themselves, as for the Safety of *Greece*, fearing lest *Mardonius* should defeat the Grecian Army: But after they had that Rumour among them, they advanced towards the Enemy with greater Readiness and Alacrity: And thus both the Grecians and Barbarians hastened to begin the Fight, being equally persuaded that the Islands and the *Hellespont* must be the Recompence of the Victorious. The Athenians, with those who were drawn up in that part of the Army which they led, advanced through the Plains, and along the Shore; but the Lacedemonians, with those who were in the other part with them, marched through the broken Ways among the Hills: So that whilst the Lacedemonians were obliged to take a wider Compass, those of the other Line were already engaged with the Enemy. The Persians, so long as they were covered by their Bucklers, defended themselves strenuously, and maintain'd their Ground. But when the Athenians and the rest, to the end that they, and not the Lacedemonians, might have the honour of the Action, had mutually encouraged one another, they soon changed the face of Affairs, struck down the Shields of the Enemy, and in close order broke in among the Persians. At first they were received with Vigour; but after the Persians had continued to defend themselves, during a considerable time, they fled to their Intrenchments; and the Athenians, with the Forces which were drawn up next to them, consisting of the Corinthians, the Sicyonians, and the Trœzenians, pursued them so close, that they entered their Camp at the same time. When the Barbarians saw their Intrenchments

forced,

forced, they thought no longer of resisting, but betook themselves all to flight, except the Persians; who, though reduced to a small number, still continued to dispute the Entrance of their Camp, against the Grecians pouring in on all sides. Of the Persian Generals, two made their Escape, and two were killed. *Artayntes* and *Ithramites*, Commanders of the Naval Forces, fled; *Mardontes* and *Tigranes*, Generals of the Land-Army, died in the Field. At length, whilst the Persians were yet fighting, the Lacedemonians arrived with the other part of the Forces, and made an end of the Slaughter. On the part of the Grecians many were killed, especially of the Sicyonians, who lost their General *Perilaus*. The Samians, who were in the Camp of the Medes, and had been disarmed before the Action, when they saw the Event doubtful at the beginning of the Fight, did all they could to help the Grecians; and the rest of the Ionians seeing the Samians lead the way, abandoned the Enemy in like manner, and fell upon the Forces of the Barbarians. The Persians to provide for their own Safety, had appointed the Milesians to keep the Passages, to the end that, if such a Misfortune should overtake them, as happened, they might save themselves upon the Mountains of *Mycale* by their Direction. For this reason, and lest they should foment any Alteration by staying in the Army, the Milesians were posted in those Stations: But acting quite contrary to their Orders, they brought back, by other ways, to the Enemy, many of those that fled out of the Battel, and at last shewed greater Fierceness than all others in the Slaughter of the Barbarians.

Thus

Thus *Ionia* revolted a second time from the Persians.

IN this Battel the Athenians fought with the greatest Valour among all the Grecians; and among the Athenians, *Hermolycus*, the Son of *Euthoinus*, a famous Athelete; who being afterwards killed at *Cyrnus*, during the war between the Athenians and the Carystians, was buried at *Gereflus*. After the Athenians, those that had most Applause were the Corinthians, the Trœzenians, and the Sicyonians.

THE Grecians, after they had killed great numbers of the Barbarians, both in the Field and in the Pursuit, set fire to the Ships, burnt the whole Camp, and brought out upon the shore all the Booty, among which were several Chests of Money. Having done this, they sailed to *Samos*; and arriving there, consulted together about transporting the Ionians to some part of *Greece*, which was in their power, and then leaving *Ionia* to the Barbarians, because they judged themselves unable to protect the Ionians at all times, and had no hope, unless they were protected, that they would have cause to be pleased with their Revolt from the Persians. The principal of the Peloponnesians proposed to expel those Nations of *Greece*, which had sided with the Medes, and to give their Territories and Cities of Commerce to the Ionians; but the Athenians were not of opinion, either that the Ionians should be removed; or that the Peloponnesians should intermeddle with the Affairs of their Colonies. In this Contestation the Peloponnesians readily yielded to the Athenians; and after they had obliged the Samians, Chians, Lesbians, and other

ther

ther Iflanders, who were then in their Army,
to fwear, that they would be their conftant
Confederates, and continue in their Alliance
without revolting, they fail'd for the *Helleffont*,
in order to ruin the Bridges, which they imagined ftill to find entire.

IN the mean time the Barbarians, who fled
out of the Field, and were forced to betake
themfelves to the Eminences of *Mycale*, made off
towards *Sardis*, reduced to an inconfiderable
number: But as they were upon their way,
Mafiftes, the Son of *Darius*, having been prefent
in the late unfortunte Action, gave many
hard words to *Artayntes*; and, among other Reproaches, told him, That he had fhewn lefs
Courage than a Woman, in performing the
part of a General fo ill, and deferved the worft
of punifhment, for bringing fo great a Difafter upon the King's Houfe. Now, becaufe
among the Perfians, to tell a Man he has lefs
Courage than a Woman, is accounted the moft
infupportable of all Affronts, *Artayntes*, having
already borne many Reproaches, loft all Patience, and drew his Scymetar to kill *Mafiftes*:
But *Xenagoras*, the Son of *Praxilaus*, a Halicar-
naffean, ftanding behind him, prevented the
Blow; and grafping *Artayntes* round the middle,
lifted him up in his Arms, and threw him
down flat upon the Ground. Upon which the
Guards of *Mafiftes* immediately interpofed. By
this Action *Xenagoras* acquired the favour of
Mafiftes, and of *Xerxes* himfelf, whofe Brother
he had faved, and was rewarded by the King
with the Government of all *Cilicia*. Nothing
more paffed among the Barbarians in their way;
but when they arrived at *Sardis*, they found

Xerxes

Xerxes there, having continued in that Place from the time he fled thither from *Athens*, after his ill Succefs in the Engagement by Sea.

DURING his Stay at *Sardis*, he fell in love with the Wife of *Mafiftes*, who was then in that City: but finding he could not prevail with her by prefents, he abftained from force, out of regard to his Brother; and the fame Confideration was alfo a Reftraint to the Woman, becaufe fhe well knew he would not offer any Violence to her Perfon. *Xerxes* feeing he had no other way left, refolved to marry a Daughter fhe had by *Mafiftes* to his Son *Darius*, thinking by that means to compafs his Defign with greater facility. Accordingly the Contract was made, and when the ufual Ceremonies were performed he departed for *Sufa*, conducting the Bride home to *Darius*. But after his Arrival, he forgot his Paffion for the Wife of *Mafiftes*; and changing his Inclinations, made love to his Daughter *Artaynte*, who was now the Wife of his own Son; which Intrigue was afterwards difcovered in the following manner: *Ameftris*, the Wife of *Xerxes*, having woven a Mantle of various Colours, large and beautiful, made a Prefent of it to her Husband; which he receiving, with great joy, put it on, and went to *Artaynte*: where, after he had taken his Satisfaction, he bid her ask whatever fhe moft defired for her Recompence; adding, that he would deny her nothing. Upon this Invitation (for the misfortune of all his Family was inevitable) fhe faid to *Xerxes*, Will you then give me whatever I fhall ask? He faid he would, and affirmed his Promife by an Oath; not at all imagining her Demand would termi-

nate

nate in the thing she chose: But he had no sooner sworn, than she boldly demanded the Mantle. *Xerxes* being unwilling to comply; and endeavouring to get off by any Contrivance he could invent, lest *Amestris* should make a plain Discovery of an Intrigue she only suspected before, offered her immense Treasures, with Cities, and an Army to be solely at her Disposal, which is one of the greatest Presents that can be made in *Persia*. At last, finding she would not be persuaded, he gave her the Mantle; and she, with a womanish Vanity, put it on, and wore it. When *Amestris* was informed of the thing, and heard that *Artaynte* had the Garment, she was not angry with her; but believing her Mother to be the Author and Contriver of all, determined to destroy the Wife of *Masistes*. To that end she expected till *Xerxes* should make the Royal Feast, by the Persians called *Tycta*, and in the Language of *Greece*, *Telion*, which is celebrated once every year on the King's Birth-day, when he alone wears magnificent Ornaments on his Head, and makes Presents to the Persians. *Amestris* having waited to that day, asked *Xerxes* to give her the Wife of *Masistes* for a Present: And though the King detested the Indignity of giving the Wife of his Brother, and knew her to be innocent of the thing which was the Cause of this Petition; yet, in the end, overcome by continued Sollicitation, and constrained by the Custom of *Persia*, which forbids the Denial of any thing during the Royal Feast, he consented with the utmost Reluctancy, to the Request of *Amestris*; and putting the Woman into her hands, told her, She might do as pleased her best.

beft. But immediately after, having fent for his Brother, he faid to him, "*Mafiftes*, you "are my Brother, the Son of *Darius*, and, "which is yet more, a man of Honour. Be "perfuaded by me to cohabit no longer with "the Wife you have, and I will give you my "own Daughter to fupply her Place. Difmifs "then this Woman; for my opinion is, that "you ought to do fo." *Mafiftes*, aftonifhed to hear thefe words, anfwered, "SIR, What "vain Difcourfe is this? You bid me leave a "Woman I love, and by whom I have three "young Sons, befides Daughters, of which "you have chofen one to be your Son's Wife; "and then, you tell me, I fhall marry your "Daughter. But, SIR, though I fet a due "Value upon the Honour of being thought "worthy of your Daughter, yet I fhall do nei- "ther of thefe things; and therefore let not "your Defire to bring about this Matter, put "you upon offering Violence to my Inclina- "tions. Some other Perfon, not inferior to "me, will be found for your Daughter; in the "mean time permit me to keep my Wife." When he had made this Anfwer, *Xerxes*, in a great Rage, reply'd, "Know, *Mafiftes*, that "your Affairs ftand thus: you fhall not marry "my Daughter, nor cohabit for the time to "come with your own Wife, to the end you "may learn to accept what I give. *Mafiftes* having heard thefe words, retired, and as he went out, faid, "SIR, you have not yet ta- "ken away my Life." Whilft *Xerxes* was in Conference with his Brother, *Ameftris* fent for his Guards, and exercifed her Cruelty upon the Wife of *Mafiftes*. She cut off her Breafts, which

fhe

she threw to the Dogs, her Nose, Ears, Lips, and Tongue, and in that mangled Condition sent her home. *Masistes* had heard nothing of this, but suspecting some Injury was intended him, he returned to his House with all possible Diligence; where finding his Wife so barbarously mutilated, he consulted with his Sons, and accompanied by them, and others, departed for *Bactria*, designing to induce the Bactrians to revolt, and to revenge himself of the King in the severest manner: In which Design, as I conjecture, he must have succeeded, had he been able to arrive among the Bactrians and Saces; for he was Governour of *Bactria*, and much beloved by both those Nations. But *Xerxes* being informed of his Intentions, sent some Troops after him with expedition, who killed him and his Sons upon the way, and cut his Forces in pieces. Thus died *Masistes*, and such Success had *Xerxes* in his Love.

THE Grecians failing, from *Mycale* towards the *Hellespont*, were obliged by tempestuous Weather to put in about *Lecton*; and from thence arriving at *Abydus*, they perceived the Bridges were taken in pieces, which they thought to have found entire, and which were the principal Motive to their Enterprize. Upon this Emergency *Leutychides*, with the Peloponnesians, determined to return to *Greece*; but the Athenians, with their General *Xanthippus*, resolved to stay, and to make an Attempt upon *Chersonesus*. Accordingly, after the Peloponnesians were withdrawn, the Athenians set sail from *Abydus*, and landing in *Chersonesus* besieg'd *Sestus*. To that Place as to the strongest of those Parts, great Numbers came from the adjacent Country, when they heard that the

Grecians

Grecians were arriv'd in the *Hellespont*; and, a-
mong others, *Oibazus*, a Persian from *Cardia*, who
had already caused all the Materials of the Bridges to be brought thither. The Inhabitants were
Æolians, but a great Multitude of Persians and
their Confederates had been drawn together, in order to defend the City. The Government of the
whole Province was in the hands of *Artayctes*, a
Persian of profligate and detestable Manners,
who had been placed in that Station by *Xerxes*;
and by imposing a Fraud upon him, when he
marched to *Athens*, had rifled the Treasures of
Protesilaus, the Son of *Iphicles*, which were at *E-
leus*. For in the City of *Eleus* in *Chersonesus*, the
Sepulcher of *Protesilaus* was erected in the midst
of this Temple; and a great Sum of Money, with
Gold and Silver Plate, Vessels of Brass, and o-
ther Offerings, were taken from thence by *Artayctes*, in vertue of a Grant from the King;
which he obtain'd by this Artifice: " Sir, *said*
" *he*, here is the Habitation of a Certain Gre-
" cian, who having enter'd your Territories with
" an Army, perish'd, as he well deserv'd. Give
" me the House of this Man, that for the future
" none may dare to invade any Part of your Do-
" minions." By this Representation he doubted
not to obtain the House from *Xerxes*, because he
could have no Suspicion of his Project; and
told him *Protesilaus* had invaded the Royal Dominions, because the Persians imagine, that all
Asia is the Property of their Kings. Thus after *Artayctes* had obtain'd his Request he brought
away the Treasure to *Sestus*, converted the sacred Place into Pasture and Arable Land; and
when he was at *Eleus*, lay with divers Women
in the Sanctuary. This Man being now besieg'd

by

by the Athenians, was utterly unprepar'd to defend himself; having never thought of being attacked by the Grecians, who fell upon him unexpected. But while they were engag'd in this Enterprize, Autumn came on, and the Athenians growing uneasy to be so far from home, without any Appearance of taking the City, besought their Leaders to conduct them back to their own Country. This, the Generals said they would not do, till either they should take the Place, or be recalled by the People of *Athens:* So great was their Affection to the State. In the mean time, those who were with *Artayctes* in the City being reduced to the last Extremity, boil'd and eat the Cords of their Beds; and when that Food likewise fail'd, *Artayctes* and *Oibazus,* with the rest of the Persians, made their escape from the Land-side of the Wall, in a Part where the Besiegers had not placed a sufficient Force. In the Morning, the Chersonesians from their Towers, having first given notice to the Athenians of what had passed, open'd their Gates; and some of the Athenian Forces enter'd the City, whilst the greater part went in pursuit of the Enemy. The Thracians of *Apsynthus* seizing upon *Oibazus* as he fled thro' *Thrace,* sacrificed him to *Plestorus* a God of the Country, according to their Custom, and killed all his Companions in another manner. But *Artayctes* and his Company, being few in number, and beginning to shift for themselves later than the rest, were overtaken at the River of *Ægos;* where, after they had defended themselves a considerable time, some were killed upon the Place, and the rest, with *Artayctes* and his Son, were made Prisoners, and carried back to *Sestus.* The Chersonesians say, that one of

4

his

his Guards saw a thing prodigious, as he stood broiling salted Fish ; the pieces which lay upon the Fire moving and leaping like Fishes newly taken out of the Water ; and that, when divers Persons crouded about the Place, and wondred at the Sight, *Artayctes* observing the Miracle, call'd the Man who broil'd the Fish, and said to him, " Athenian Friend, be not afraid ; you " are not at all concern'd in this Prodigy : *Pro-* " *tesilaus*, though dead and embalm'd at *Eleus*, " admonishes me, by this Sign, that the Gods " have given him power to revenge the Injury " he has receiv'd : Resolving therefore to make " him reparation, I will consecrate a hundred " Talents to his Divinity, instead of the Riches " I took out of his Temple ; and I will give " two hundred Talents to the Athenians, if " they will spare my Life, and the Life of my " Son." But their General *Xanthippus* would not be persuaded by these Promises ; partly because he himself was averse to the thing, and partly because the People of *Eleus*, to avenge the Injury done to *Protesilaus*, earnestly sollicited him, that *Artayctes* might be put to death. Having therefore conducted him to that part of the Shore, where the Bridges of *Xerxes* terminated ; or, as others say, to an Eminence standing near the City of *Madytus*, they caus'd him to be impaled on a Stake, fixed in the Ground for that purpose ; and at the same time stoned his Son before his eyes. When the Athenians had done these things, they return'd with their Fleet to *Greece* ; carrying, besides other Riches, all the Materials of the Bridges, in order to be consecrated in their Temples : and nothing more was done that Year.

THIS

THIS *Artayctes*, thus executed by the Grecians, was descended by the Male Line from *Artembares*; who in his time fram'd a Discourse for the Persians, which they approving, repeated to *Cyrus* in these Terms: " Since *Jupiter* " has given the Superiority to the Persians, and " the principal Authority among Men to thee, " O *Cyrus*; give us leave to remove out of our " Country, which is narrow and mountainous, " into a better. Many such are near our Con- " fines, and many at a greater Distance. The " Possession of one of these will render us more " reverenc'd by most Men; and this Conduct " becomes a People, who have the Power in " their hands. In a word, what Opportunity " can ever be more favourable to us, than the " present, when we have the Command of so " many Nations, and the Dominion of all *Asia*? *Cyrus* heard these words without wonder, and bid them do as they desir'd; but withal, admonish'd them to prepare for the future to obey, and not to command, as in time past: Because Nature has so ordered things, that delicious Countries produce an effeminate Race, and Men excellent in War, are not bred in those Regions which yield the most admirable Fruits. The Persians perceiving their Error, receded from their Purpose, and yielded to the Opinion of *Cyrus*; chusing rather to live in a barren Country, and to command, than to cultivate the richest Plains, and be subject to other Men.

F I N I S.

An INDEX to the Second Volume of the *History* of HERODOTUS.

A.

ACh*æmenes*, Brother to *Xerxes*, and Commander of his Fleet, his Speech, 276.

Adimantus, the Corinthian, his Dispute with *Themistocles* at *Salamis*, 307. He run away out of the Fight there, 326.

Æginetes, several Actions of theirs related, 47, 96, 109, 115, 119. They do great Service, and acquire much Honour in the Fight at *Salamis*, 322, 325, 326.

Alcmæon, some Account of him 137.

Alcmæcnides, being banish'd *Athens* by the Pisistratides, build the Temple at *Delphi*, and corrupt the Pythian with Money, to deliver such Oracles as serv'd their Interest, 34. By which means, they brought the Spartans against the Pisistratides, whom they expell'd, and restor'd the Liberty of *Athens*, 35. They are highly prais'd by *Herodotus*, 136.

Alexander of *Macedonia*, Son of *Amyntas*, induces the Grecians to abandon the Defence of *Thessaly*, against the Persians, 246. Is sent by *Mardonius* to make an Alliance between the King and the Athenians, 350. His Speech to the Athenians on that Subject, 352. He personally gives private Intelligence to the Grecian Generals at *Platæa*, 386.

Amestris, see *Artaynte*.

Amompharetus, the Spartan, resolutely refuses to draw off with his Cohort from before the Persians at *Platæa*, 392. He is abandon'd by the rest of the Army, 393. And therefore follows and rejoins them, 394.

Amyntas, of *Macedonia*, treats the Persians sent to require him to acknowledge King *Darius*; but his Son *Alexander* kills them for their Insolence in their Wine, 9.

Andrians, receiving a Message from *Themistocles*, importing, that the Athenians were coming against them with two Deities, Persuasion and Force, and therefore they must part with their Money; return'd answer,

INDEX.

INDEX.

B.

Callicratides

3

INDEX.

C

D.

mines

INDEX.

sians,

INDEX.

serve

INDEX.

serve the Publick, his House is demolished; he escapes to *Tegea*, and dies there, 109.

Leutychides, commanding in chief the Grecian Fleet, resolves to assist the Samians, to recover their Liberty, 412. Sails from *Delos* to *Samos*, and thence to *Mycale*, 415. Where landing, he defeats the Persians. 418.

Lycidas the Athenian, stoned to death, (as was also his Wife) for proposing to his Countrymen to accept the Propositions of *Mardonius* the Persian, 360.

M.

Marathon, the Battel there, 131.

Mardonius, the Persian, deposes all the Ionian Tyrants, and settles a popular Government in every City, 93. Passes over into *Europe*, *ib*. Conquers *Macedonia*, *ib*. Losing half his Fleet by a Storm near Mount *Athos*, and suffering loss by Land, in *Macedonia*, he returns to *Asia*, 94. His Speech and Arguments to induce *Xerxes* to undertake the Expedition against *Greece*. 151. His Speech to the principal Persians, who were called by *Xerxes*, to consult about that Expedition, 155. He is reproach'd by *Tigranes*, on a proper Occasion for persuading the Persians to make war against the Grecians who fought not for Riches, but for Virtue only, 293. He prevails with *Xerxes*, to leave him in *Greece*, with 300,000 Men, 329. He accompanies *Xerxes* back to *Bœotia*, and there chuses out of the whole Army his 300,000 Men, 338. He sends *Alexander* the Macedonian to procure an Alliance with the Athenians, 350. Who rejecting his Propositions, he advances with his Army towards *Athens* : Advice given him by the Thebans, 359. He takes possession of *Athens*, which the Inhabitants had abandon'd, 360. Being inform'd by the Argians, of the March of the Spartans toward him, he burns *Athens*, retires out of *Attica*, and encamps in *Bœotia*, 365. Is treated by *Attaginus* at *Thebes*, 367. His Treatment of the thousand Phoceans who join'd his Army in *Bœotia*, 369. He loses *Masistius*, General of his Cavalry, near Mount *Cytheron*, 351. He follows the Grecians to *Platæa*, and

draws

3

INDEX.

O.

an

INDEX.

INDEX.

F I N I S.